Modern Hungarian Society in the Making

Modern Hungarian Society in the Making
The Unfinished Experience

ANDRÁS GERŐ

TRANSLATED BY JAMES PATTERSON AND ENIKŐ KONCZ

John Lukácsnak

barátsággal

1995. nov. 21.

G—

CEU

CENTRAL EUROPEAN UNIVERSITY PRESS
BUDAPEST · LONDON · NEW YORK

Published by
Central European University Press
1051 Budapest, Nádor utca 9, Hungary

Distributed by
Oxford University Press, Walton Street, Oxford OX2 6DP
Oxford New York Athens Auckland Bangkok Bombay Toronto
Calcutta Cape Town Dar es Salaam Delhi Florence Hong Kong
Istanbul Karachi Kuala Lumpur Madras Madrid Melbourne
Mexico City Nairobi Paris Singapore Taipei Tokyo Toronto
and associated companies in Berlin Ibadan
Distributed in the United States
by Oxford University Press Inc., New York

First published in Hungarian as *Magyar polgárosodás* in 1993 by
Atlantisz Könyvkiadó (Medvetánc), Budapest

First published in English as
Modern Hungarian Society in the Making: The Unfinished Experience in 1995

British Library Cataloguing in Publication Data
A CIP catalogue record for this book is available from the British Library

ISBN 1-85866-023-8 Hardback
ISBN 1-85866-024-6 Paperback

Library of Congress Cataloging in Publication Data
A CIP catalog record for this book is available from the Library of Congress

Designed, typeset and produced by John Saunders Design & Production, Reading, UK
Printed and bound in Great Britain by Biddles of Guildford, UK

Contents

List of illustrations

The publishers are grateful to the Magyar Nemzeti Múzeum Fényképtára (Historical Photo Archive of the Hungarian National Museum) for permission to reproduce the photographs in this book. Special thanks go to Katalin Jalsovszky and Emőke Tomsics, who made the selection.

For my son, Ivan

Preface

Most of Central and Eastern Europe began to emerge from feudalism as early as the 1840s. In some cases this emergence took more radical forms (uprisings and revolutions), while in others it manifested itself in more peaceful processes, for example, change initiated from above.

In my opinion, the modern history of this region – and so of Hungary – is the story of a still ongoing process of transition from a feudal to a civil society. This seems to be supported by the economic, social and intellectual changes that occurred in Central and Eastern Europe in the 1980s.

In these circumstances the issues surrounding the emergence of a civil society must be regarded as crucial for an understanding of our present, as well as of our past.

I am aware that the term itself – the emergence of civil society – is a product of the history of this region, and that it might sound strange and unfamiliar to readers in countries with a different historical background. I cannot do without it, however, because the term commonly used in the West to describe similar processes – modernization – has in a Central and East European context a quite different content and set of connotations. Indeed, an important part of the modern tragedy of the region is an object lesson in how 'modernization' can take place without a civil society emerging alongside it – even under circumstances of blatant suppression of the values of a civil society. The region underwent a number of such 'experiments' in the nineteenth century (1849–67) – Habsburg neo-absolutism was committed to modernization, though by no means adhering to the values of a civil society – while in the twentieth century we might point to a number of right-wing authoritarian attempts aiming, among other things, at the severe curtailment of private ownership. The most clear-cut division between modernization and the emergence of a civil society, however, occurred under socialism, in which 'modernity' was contrasted with 'bourgeois' notions in the most thoroughgoing manner possible. In my opinion, such modernization led only to the emergence of a particular kind of post-feudal society, in which political activity was open only to a privileged few, commerce and manufacture were pursued on the basis of supra-economic considerations, and bourgeois values became the target of ridicule and even persecution.

I am fully aware that the bourgeoisie and the emergence of civil society are topics difficult to encompass in their entirety and broad development, owing to the peculiarities and sheer magnitude of the historical process involved. Nevertheless, some brief remarks might be in order.

The bourgeoisie – like any social category – must be understood in terms of at least three elements: social standing, values, and life-style.

Historically, the bourgeoisie is a social group essentially oriented towards trade, manufacture and freelance intellectual endeavour, so enjoying a degree of comparative independence in relation to the system of feudal dependency; wealth and social standing depend for the bourgeois more on his own performance than on his position in a hierarchy.

What must be emphasized above all, however, is the extent to which the bourgeoisie gave rise almost to a whole new civilization: to be a bourgeois entailed an extraordinarily imposing, colourful and controversial set of values with a life-style to match. The bourgeois way of life rapidly outgrew its original confines and became increasingly available to wider and wider sections of the population, serving as a model for *déclassé* elements, as well as those who had been prevented from establishing themselves partly by the bourgeoisie itself, and those who continued to lead their lives under conditions of feudal privilege. There have been several historical examples of existing civil societies stimulating the emergence of bourgeois private ownership in Central and Eastern Europe, in which sense the achievements of the former served as points of departure for the latter.

With the widening of the scope of the bourgeoisie, social status began to lose its dominant role, while civil values and life-style acquired greater importance, leading to radical political changes within the secluded world of feudalism. All three elements of the notion of the bourgeoisie that I outlined above continued to exist, but a shift of emphasis occurred between them of such magnitude that a large part of nineteenth-century social studies now reads as analyses of purely historical interest instead of general descriptions with a wider relevance.

It seems that not only our terminology is subject to certain limitations but the number of directions from which our topic may be approached. No one can claim to know everything about the emergence of civil society. To obtain even an adequate picture of the process as a whole would take the work of generations of scholars. One can only attempt to outline more or less refined cross-sections from which individual elements or dimensions may emerge with some clarity.

In this volume each study constitutes such a cross-section. I began working on the questions tackled here at the end of the 1970s and have continued to work on them ever since. Over the years my focus and methodology have changed to a certain degree, as the texts presented here will give evidence; and though nineteenth-century developments preponderate, the twentieth century has not been forgotten.

The present volume consists of three parts and comes complete with a biographical index that will allow the non-specialist to become better acquainted with the period in question and its protagonists.

Part One concentrates mostly upon the first half of the nineteenth century, a time when images of a new Hungary and a new society were being shaped in theory rather than in practice. What kind of society did the reformers have in mind? Whom did they regard as their allies and whom their enemies? How did they resolve internal dilemmas? What kinds of role emerged for the reformers? How did they confront failure? These are the questions that the studies included here seek to answer.

Part Two investigates the implementation of the reformers' ideas in practice and does so along two co-ordinates, liberalism and conservatism. I have attempted to analyse first of all the concrete historical aspects and controversies of the modern manner of legitimizing power. In my view legitimation is more than just a legal skeleton, it is a 'living creature' with its own personality: rationally chosen 'forms of life' are capable of serving as models and establishing norms. I have thus focused particularly on the analysis of various *mentalités* embodying particular sets of values. Given that in the region of Central and Eastern Europe the Jews have played an outstanding role in the formation of bourgeois values, I have devoted a separate chapter to this question. The second part of my book concludes with a survey of the course of bourgeois transformation in Hungary up to the present day.

Part Three is devoted to attempts to create a modern cult of national identity and is consequently rather anthropological in nature. I chose to dwell on this topic because, with the decline of the medieval religious world-view, secularized national cults characteristic of bourgeois societies began to emerge everywhere, and Hungary was no exception. The historical vicissitudes to which forms of national self-representation and national celebration have been subject in Central and Eastern Europe point up the region's distinct character very well. This is largely what lay behind my decision to write about the history of the Millennium Monument in Heroes' Square in Budapest, a symbol of national glory up to the present day, but which has been altered from time to time to accommodate new interpretations of our national history; and about the 15 March celebration, which brings together national values and those of civil freedom, and which was suppressed by the Habsburgs and the communists. I believe that the attempt to create a cult around Queen

Elisabeth of Bavaria, embodying a peculiar mixture of loyalty and resistance, is equally important in this respect.

I am convinced that the problems that Central and Eastern Europe – and so Hungary – is facing today largely originated in the nineteenth century and remain unresolved. I have tried to avoid concentrating exclusively on Hungary in view of the fact that the past, present and future of all the nations of the region are so closely related.

I shall leave it to the reader to judge how successful or unsuccessful I have been in my endeavours, but whatever his judgment may be I would like to believe that the topic itself will inspire further contemplation, dialogue and debate. The Western reader in particular must strive to understand that *the past lives on* in Central and Eastern Europe, posing as much, if not more, of a problem to the present-day societies of the region as to the historian.

Unfair as it may seem, 'bourgeois convention' has it that a book should feature the name of its author only, at the expense of all those without whose contributions and assistance the book could never have come into being. Any expression of gratitude is bound to fall short of the real impact that such contributors have had and it would only be fair to cite them as co-authors in varying degrees.

György Szabad is responsible for the first encouragement I received. My approach was greatly influenced by the work of Péter Hanák, the leading Hungarian authority on the second half of the nineteenth century, the period closest to my heart. The stimulating intellect of Béla G. Németh has also meant a great deal to me. And of course I am deeply indebted to a number of my colleagues and friends for the invaluable help that they have given me, in the form of long discussions on numerous occasions, often debating the merits – or otherwise! – of each others' manuscripts: Miklós Szabó, András Gergely, György Csepeli, János Poór, Iván Sanders, Dániel Szabó, Vilmos Heiszler, Gábor Erdődy, Martha Lampland and János Veliky must all receive special mention.

I am grateful to the Central European University, and especially to its publishing house, which has kindly ventured to publish my book and which has given me every support. And of course I owe special thanks to the translators, who, are really my co-authors.

Last but not least, I would like to express my deepest gratitude to those closest to me, whose patience and love made it possible for me both to embark on and to complete this work.

Budapest, September 1994   András Gerő

Part One

Towards a civil society

1 The Making of Modern Hungary

> Property and liberty are the sweet bonds that tie the citizen to the
> fate of his nation most strongly.
>
>   Ferenc Deák, Delegate of Zala County, around 1830.[1]

Today the 150 year old process of bourgeois development in Hungary has
reached a new stage. We are witness to the re-emergence of a need that has
existed since the 1830s, but which at times has become lost from view.

The fresh start which, in many ways, the fateful events of 1989 represent
could also represent a resumption of a process that had been put on hold –
not, as we shall see in the course of this book, for the first time. But the
question is: resumption of what and by whom? Modern European history
teaches us that although there is no rational alternative to bourgeois development, there are many different forms that such development may take.

Hungarian liberals in the last century viewed private property and political
freedom as intertwined, as much in terms of their actual historical development as in principle. The relations that existed between the supporters and
opponents of bourgeois transformation were responsible for the association
of private property and political freedom under the aegis of patriotism.
Feudal structures, meanwhile, could not be dismantled under pressure from
the people ('from below'), but only from within the political elite ('from
above'). Owing to the continuing strength of the surviving feudal
constraints, there was no substantial middle class in Hungary in possession
of corresponding political influence. It was necessary, therefore, to remove
these constraints *before* the bourgeois development process and the
concomitant formation of private ownership could begin to unfold on a large
scale. It is only one of the many paradoxes which characterize this period
that the victory of liberalism was thus dependent on state intervention. (A
clear demonstration of the underdevelopment of Hungarian society during
the period of voluntary manumission – 1840–8 – is given by the fact that no
more than one in a hundred peasants could afford to buy out their feudal
obligations from their landlords. The required breakthrough did not occur
before the introduction, by a reformed state, of mandatory manumission in
1848.)

The absence of a middle class in Hungary meant that bourgeois transformation could be accomplished only by reaccentuating such liberal values as freedom and private property as essentially patriotic. Another paradoxical consequence of this situation was that the agents of bourgeois transformation had to be the nobility, the only social class whose privilege it was to engage in public affairs, the only peaceful channel through which a new political and social framework could evolve. In contrast with the Western European model of bourgeois development, in Hungary it was mostly the privileged who undertook the representation of new values and the introduction of reforms. The nobility were broadly aware that feudalism had become outdated, and feared that, if left to run its course, it might provoke a violent reaction liable to deprive them of their position and even their lives. After much inner turmoil, the best of the nobility finally made the painful but necessary decision to step forward and demand a diminution of their own privileges, risking condemnation by their families and friends. These members of the nobility hoped that by setting themselves up as the agents of modernization they might be able to preserve their role in society. They realized that in order to achieve this they, too, had to change.

Though to varying degrees, many members of the nobility genuinely wanted to adapt to the requirements of a bourgeois society both in terms of values and life-style. Count István Széchenyi introduced the formal manner of address, did much to popularize sports (such as skating), and – though this might not seem such an important development in an age of hot showers and shampoo – placed great emphasis on personal hygiene; Lajos Kossuth ceased using his noble title, and as Acting President introduced a decree as early as 1849 that did not differentiate between the legitimate and illegitimate children of soldiers who died on active service when it came to the disbursement of compensation; Ferenc Deák insisted to the end of his days that all degree holders should be addressed as 'Your Honour' to give expression to the notion that those with comparable achievements should be treated on an equal footing (he introduced this in 1844); the young Mór Jókay changed his name to Jókai, the suffix -y being reserved only for the nobility; and old Count Miklós Wesselényi was able to make an imprudent match – he married a middle class woman.

Too much should not be made of these developments, but it cannot be denied that in Hungary the bourgeoisie could be defined in terms of its values and life-style as much as by its social or financial status. Those who evolved into the Hungarian bourgeoisie did not simply adapt to an already existing framework, but had to work out a framework for themselves. New models of behaviour, although often inconsistent and inadequate, had the merit of having emerged from a rigorous self-examination and a deep seated desire for progress. Széchenyi, for example, recorded the following incident in his diary. One afternoon he was out riding when a Jew dressed in a long gabardine happened to cross his path. The Count, with the instincts of a feudal nobleman, struck the unfortunate man with his whip. Later that evening, as he reflected on this incident, the Count felt deeply ashamed and subjected this entirely spontaneous reaction to a searching critical analysis.

As clumsy and inconsistent as the formation of bourgeois values in the private sphere was, the liberal transformation of public affairs could be counted a success: although the process was not without conflict and compromise in regard to the extent of the freedoms attained, liberal reformers were consistent in upholding their demand for a combination of private property and political liberty. The bourgeois-transformation process that began in 1848 lacked solid foundations, but the social class committed to introducing and consolidating new public and individual values and structures in Hungary turned out to be strong enough to begin to break up feudal structures and to mobilize the nation.

The period after 1848 in Hungary – as well as elsewhere in Europe – gave evidence that although the bourgeois development process was irreversible, it could be diverted. At the same time, though conservatism may have emerged victorious, absolutism could no longer expect to halt, still less to reverse the advance of private property. On the contrary, it turned out that private property can exist even in the absence of freedom. One of the most important elements of both absolutism and neo-absolutism was to allow bourgeois economic progress – as it was in their own interest – but to prevent its extension to liberal social and political measures. (The development of France in the 1850s – the rule of Napoleon III – proved that even general liberty and universal suffrage do not necessarily go hand in hand with political freedom, and that the absence of political freedom does not necessarily hinder free enterprise.)

In Hungary the situation was aggravated by foreign domination. The introduction, in 1848, of a number of individual bourgeois freedoms (emancipation of the serfs, a more equitable distribution of public burdens, equality before the law) and measures promoting basic bourgeois concepts (such as the elaboration of a penal code) did not in the least change the progressive nobility's rejection of foreign rule and bourgeois development without freedom. In literature, these views are reflected in Imre Madách's play, *The Civilizer*. But according to István Bibó, there was no firm resolution behind this fundamentally emotional stance. For one thing, protection from absolutism could more readily be found in traditional aristocratic forms than in the still-undeveloped resources of the bourgeoisie. The Hungarian nobility had suffered enough from absolutism to have evolved definite views on how it should be combated. The nobility's habitual reaction was passive resistance, a great hindrance to the already slow process by which bourgeois values were being introduced into public life, with its inevitable reinforcement of traditional values and forms of behaviour. We must also remember that the period of absolutism lasted for approximately the same length of time as the Reform Period. Throughout these years, every effort was made to marginalize the devotees of the unity of freedom and private property, with sanctions varying from execution to imprisonment and exile.

The year 1867 brought a compromise between an economically and politically weakening absolutism and a liberal nobility whose bourgeois inclinations had by that time largely run their course. The 1867 Compromise would significantly influence the course of bourgeois development in Hungary up to 1945.

The Compromise not only concerned itself with political power and national issues, but was also a bargain struck about values. Certain aspects of absolutism were to remain unchallenged, with the implication that in public affairs a certain authoritarian attitude would continue to prevail with a strong attachment to an essentially feudal centre – the sovereign – and that conformity to these values would be accounted a fundamental norm. Post-Compromise political structures would therefore incorporate an irremovable and extremely powerful body, any criticism of which would be considered a criminal offence, and the prestige of which was underpinned by hundreds of years of tradition.

Under these circumstances, the nobility's liberal sympathies were hemmed in by a feudal-conservative framework, the inevitable result of which was that their attitudes were distorted into ambivalence, they championed a self-centred patriotism and a marked refeudalization even took place. In socio-historical terms, the nobility was downgraded to the status of a gentry. The dual aspect of liberalism – the considerably transformed legacy of the Reform Period – is well illustrated by the fact that during the premiership of Kálmán Tisza the number of 'tail-mails', an institution providing a kind of feudal protection from market conditions, rapidly increased. The same Kálmán Tisza, however, also took resolute measures to halt the advance of a political anti-Semitism which was attempting to transform proprietary relations in Hungary. Another manifestation of this duality can be found in Deák, who continued to urge liberal reforms after the Compromise with the result that he became more and more estranged from his own party, which was unenthusiastic about civil marriage and the separation of church and state.

At the same time, rapid progress was being made in the economic and private spheres, that is, in fulfilling the other side of the bargain. Bourgeois development, private property relations and private enterprise in Hungary were fully in concordance with contemporary Western norms. Ample proof of growing affluence was provided by the residential neighbourhoods and cultural establishments that were financed and utilized by the Hungarian upper and middle classes, a large part of which was of Jewish origin, having chosen assimilation in order to be part of the bourgeois-development process. I would particularly stress the significance of values in the formation of this new social class, membership of which depended less on financial status than on personal disposition. The bourgeoisie encompassed a wide range of people from the petty bourgeoisie to the upper middle classes, from employees in the private sector to skilled workers who had risen to the lower middle classes simply by virtue of wearing a hat. All these different groups had similar tastes in furniture and clothing, and shared preferences about what they believed was important, proper or shameful. (The ability of middle class taste to set the fashion may be seen in the popularity of the Secession style throughout the Austro-Hungarian Monarchy, and not only as a decorative form of art, but in everyday objects, clothes, etc.) This class also exerted some influence on the political and social elite, but in the public sphere refeudalized, time-honoured forms of behaviour remained dominant. An invitation to a ball in Buda required that men appear in tails, but at the same time all agreed that tails came nowhere near the elegance of traditional festive Hungarian dress. The wealthier (upper middle class) males obtained the right to wear the Hussar dolman, replete with braiding.

Festive Hungarian dress and tails: what better symbol could be found of the two faces of the Dual Monarchy?

Naturally, the middle classes aspired to the gentility of the aristocracy, while the offspring of formerly great noble families – complete with imposing genealogies – did not sneeze at the comfort and intimacy of bourgeois life. Dualism was also manifest in the divisions between the private and the public spheres, in the coexistence of the gentleman and the bourgeois. The same dualism is detectable in the decor of residential buildings. While Hungarian public buildings are without exception fashioned in the likeness of a palace or a fortress – in accordance with the tastes of the sovereign – residential buildings dating from this period are distinguished by the more intimate air of their gateways, balconies and staircases.

The coexistence or even symbiosis of two such contrasting worlds, the moral weakness of the nobility in the face of absolutism, the weakening of a patriotism embodying the unity of freedom and private property: all heralded the rise of disharmony. The gentry still dominated the middle class; at least this was the tendency pursued by the National/Catholic movements which blossomed after the turn of the century, in anticipation of the National/Christian stance of the Miklós Horthy era. In their view, the city was something sinful, and the bourgeoisie (in other words, the Jews) rather than the peasantry was the main cause of the decay of Hungarian society. On the other hand, the number of bourgeois intellectuals – mostly Jews – was also rising. These intellectuals saw the remedy for Hungary's ailments in radical social criticism and correspondingly radical political measures. Many of them rejected not only the genteel liberalism-turned-conservatism, but all refeudalized forms, private property and even

1 Modern Hungary (the new parliament building in 1906)

bourgeois development, as such, in revolt against a bourgeoisie so closely linked with the aristocracy.

The social background of this hostile attitude is to be found not only in the latent animosity between the feudal nobility and the bourgeoisie in spite of their overt inclination to compromise, but mainly in the fact that, by this time, the energy of bourgeois development had outgrown the existing political framework and was seeking new outlets. Such outlets could not be found without undermining existing political structures or repressing already existing bourgeois strata. (For example, growing unemployment resulted in the emigration of 2.5 million people – and political freedoms such as universal suffrage were delayed.)

After the Great War, Hungarian society did everything it could to resolve the political tensions inherent in bourgeois transformation. The Károlyi Revolution sought to widen bourgeois development by reviving the unity of freedom and private property. Political democracy and land redistribution – freedom, the nation and property for the vast majority of the populace. The Hungarian Commune of 1919 suggested that the crisis of bourgeois transformation could be overcome simply by eliminating the bourgeoisie. Dictatorship and collective property represented a new form of 'harmony'.

The ultimately victorious Horthy regime drew on tendencies already in existence at the turn of the century when it put forward – in reaction to previously offered solutions – its programme of partial land redistribution (based on the Nagyatádi/Szabó land reform scheme), anti-Semitism and the repression of the existing Hungarian bourgeoisie: they needed room for more amenable social groups in the education system and the labour market. The tensions arising from bourgeois development did not abate, however, because the prospects of social ascent remained beyond the reach of the masses, particularly the peasantry; this was inevitable, given the fundamental intention of the Horthy regime to maintain a quasi-feudal society resting on the dominance of the nobility, even if an injection of new blood could not be avoided.

Autocratic, National/Christian and anti-Semitic policies were well suited to the desired channelling of tensions. Basic bourgeois values came under threat as the Horthy regime did not hesitate to invade the private lives of the middle class (or at least part of it): the regime claimed the right to decide who could go to university, and at a later stage it even interfered with whom one could marry and who was allowed to own property. Even in comparison with the monarchy's increasing conservatism, this was a backward step. The ultimate outcome was the restriction of ownership in accordance with political considerations. Bourgeois values gradually disappeared from public life and all that remained was a depoliticized middle class distinguished by no more than its life-style and general attitudes and, even then, only up to a point. The bourgeois radicalism or, rather, democratism of the early twentieth century – a natural reaction to the bourgeois-transformation process unfolding during the monarchy – was an expression of the Hungarian bourgeoisie's awakening political and social self-consciousness and focused on the Reform Period concept of the unity of freedom and private property. By the time the Horthy regime had come to power, however, this democratism had been reduced to a scarcely visible rivulet influencing only a fraction of a now large social class.

The example of Újlipótváros (New Leopoldtown, a district of Pest) illustrates the Horthy regime's values. This part of Hungary's capital was constructed in a former milling area in the 1930s and 1940s. The appearance and infrastructure of the district indicate the Hungarian bourgeoisie's sophisticated needs in terms of comfort, life-style and living space in accordance with European standards. This large scale development is dominated by the style of the Bauhaus, distinguished by its simplicity and functionalism. Újlipótváros and Lipótváros, an adjoining area, were, towards the end of the 1930s, renamed Szent István Város ('Saint Stephen's Town') in accordance with the Horthy regime's historo-centric National/Christian ideology. The new name did not catch on, however. (Neighbouring Angyalföld, a working class area, was also renamed, becoming – officially, at least – Magdolnaváros, or Magdolna Town, after Horthy's wife.)

The Horthy regime found an important ideological ally among those who insisted on the social development of the peasantry. Just as the bourgeoisie had established its own independent political representation by the turn of the century, so there emerged a numerous and ideologically heterogeneous group of advocates of peasant development in Hungary between the World Wars. Those who – largely under the influence of the government's National/Christian stance – saw the main obstacle to such development in the Hungarian bourgeoisie, all in one way or another subscribed to the ideal of 'gentleman and peasant united under Hungarian conditions', that is, the ideal of a world without the bourgeoisie. Others – and they were the majority – identified the obstacle in the combination of large landed estates and bourgeois property, and tended to adhere to the doctrine of the 'third way'. From this position, a flirtation both with the Horthy regime's politics – aimed at undermining the existing bourgeoisie and permeated by anti-Semitism – and with leftist formations, opposed to capitalism in any form, logically followed. (The house of the nationalist writer Gyula Illyés was once searched by the security police while he was dining at the house of Prime Minister Gyula Gömbös.)

In the Horthy era, the symbiosis of the social elite and the bourgeoisie became increasingly volatile. The latter had to make ever greater efforts to protect its property, and encountered less and less concern for its freedom; as a consequence it had to be content with being the middle class and relinquish its status as the middle bourgeoisie. The gentry, in turn, was increasingly inclined to encroach upon the domain of the bourgeoisie with the effect of undermining its position even further.

In 1945, a unique opportunity was presented for the resumption of the so frequently interrupted Hungarian bourgeois development process: the demise of the social class which, more than any other, had tried to hinder its progress. The Hungarian gentry fell apart. With this came a freedom-centred democratic movement which first manifested itself in the immeasurably important process of land redistribution whereby 600,000 people were made direct proprietors (in all, at least 2.5 million people were affected). This was the end of the great landed estates, and the way had finally been cleared for the peasantry's social development. At the same time, however – as a consequence of the Holocaust and the mass emigration after the Second World War – the numbers of Hungary's bourgeoisie were considerably reduced. In this period of apparently burgeoning freedom and the redistribution of private property, political formations espousing the complete rejection of bourgeois development thus rose to prominence.

Between 1945 and 1948, growing nationalization and the rising number of politically motivated trials – aimed simply at depriving the accused of his possessions – raised public awareness that there can be no freedom where property rights can be violated at the stroke of a pen. The peasantry, who had only recently acquired private property – and so had their first taste of the prospect of social development – without a significant bourgeoisie to stand in their way, now faced a political force eager to extend the expropriations to them, in its determination to liquidate the bourgeoisie both as a pillar of the institution of private property and as a depository of civilized values. This force was, of course, the Hungarian Communist Party, which enjoyed the support of the latest foreign power to dominate Hungary: the Soviet Union. Despite everything Hungarian society never gave up its aspirations towards bourgeois development; the communists never enjoyed the trust of a majority of the population. Not that this lack of trust was a reflection of nostalgia for aristocratic Hungary. On the contrary: masses of people were faced for the first time with the prospect of becoming masters of their own lives.

While the Horthy era showed that private property does not necessarily secure political freedom, the coalition era that followed showed that freedom turns to dust when the sanctity of private property can be violated without redress. This close relation between freedom and private property, so familiar in the West, highlighted the need in Hungary for bourgeois and social development on a massive scale.

In the course of the 1950s, the ruling political elite correctly recognized that the surest way to guarantee complete control over a people lacking any form of political freedom was to eliminate the last traces of bourgeois development and consciousness, both by way of liquidating all forms of private ownership and by destroying bourgeois values.[2] The post-1948 regime in Hungary tried to promote this principle with the utmost consistency, and the infamous 1950s were much worse years for bourgeois development than the demoralizing enough 1850s. Private property was liquidated with extreme thoroughness, affecting not only urban small industry and the freelance intelligentsia but, above all, the peasantry. We still do not have exact figures on the number of peasants who were slandered, beaten, driven to suicide or imprisoned for the purpose of confiscating their land (although their numbers certainly run to the hundreds of thousands).

An equally ruthless crusade was waged against bourgeois values: many books were banned and cultural policy enforced a stringent censorship. But the real breakthrough came elsewhere. As a result of the liquidation of the private sector and the enforcement of a centralized cultural policy, the intelligentsia in Hungary could look only to the state for employment – in other words it was 'nationalized' just like everything else. So, in the 1950s, not only did the sole political party and the state became one and the same, but the state extended its control over every aspect of society, including the private lives of its members.

The fact that not even violence, the fleecing of the peasantry and the nationalization of the intelligentsia ever entirely succeeded demonstrates, once again, that bourgeois development cannot be uprooted, though it may take different forms.

The nationalization of land forced masses of the peasantry to leave agriculture for industry, the artificial development of which was financed from resources largely stolen from them in the first place. The dispossessed peasantry now constituted cheap labour, just the thing for rapid industrialization.

To all appearances the snake had bitten its tail. The mass migration of the peasantry to urban industry meant the relinquishment of their traditional forms of life, indeed their very status as peasants, however limited urban development may have been to begin with. An urbanized population is always much more susceptible to organization and more highly motivated to develop a political consciousness. In a rural peasant community the individual is extremely vulnerable and defenceless before the Almighty State. In addition, employment in industry often allows greater access to information. The consciousness of a collective fate and the necessity for collective action is easily formed on the basis of daily experience, even in the case of first-generation workers.

From the point of view of bourgeois development, however, it is probably more important to consider how the totalitarian state inevitably comes into conflict with its 'nationalized' intelligentsia, or at least with a large part of it.

Education was a top priority for the communist regime, less from humanistic considerations than from plain necessity. In the early 1950s there were 2.5 times more high-school and 3.3 times more university students in Hungary than before the Second World War. There was an urgent need for a highly qualified intelligentsia for three reasons. First, the Holocaust had dealt a severe blow to the Hungarian intelligentsia (before the War nearly 50% of doctors and 40% of engineers had been Jews). Second, a significant part of the remaining intelligentsia was declared untrustworthy, because of its bourgeois values, and excluded from white-collar career opportunities. Third, excessive industrialization and the overly bureaucratic state administration devoured even the least qualified of the new intelligentsia.

But any intelligentsia is receptive to bourgeois values, by the very force of its professional skills and social role – values capable eventually of undermining a monolithic state establishment. Because of the intense concentration of power characteristic of the communist regime, it was the intelligentsia within the party state's bureaucratic structure which took the first steps towards liberalization. Soon the creative intelligentsia joined in. Demands for freedom – a basic condition of any intellectual activity – paradoxically came from the very persons who owed their rise to the communist regime (for example, the so-called 'Petőfi Circle').

The 1956 Revolution was a reflex of self-defence on the part of Hungarian society, the manifestation of the basic need for bourgeois development and the focal point of a whole range of particular needs: the intelligentsia yearned for political freedom, the peasantry for land and the workers for control through workers councils over industrial assets operated by the state supposedly in their name but without their consent. The demands for freedom and private property once more combined under the aegis of patriotism to oppose a regime dependent on a foreign power – the Soviet Union – which was the apotheosis of unfreedom.

After the post-1956 wave of red terror (a recapitulation of the Austrian General Julius Haynau's suppression of the 1848–9 Freedom Fight), Hungary entered a new phase in its political history (a phase reminiscent of the absolutist regime of Alexander Bach, which had followed the failed revolution a century before) as well as in its bourgeois development. Having learned its lesson, the new political regime tentatively embarked on a very restricted course of bourgeois development, gradually allowing a more liberal economic regime, encouraging greater consumption and the reintroduction of certain limited forms of private ownership. More importantly, citizens were able to acquire extra income to supplement their extremely low fixed wages by operating state assets as quasi-private property, largely at the expense of extreme self-exploitation. This was the so-called 'secondary economy', which by the late 1970s and the early 1980s involved nearly 70% of the country's active labour force. A compromise had also been concluded with the peasantry in the form of the household farming plot. (According to official data, no more than 1 million of the 5 million-strong workforce were engaged in agriculture in the 1950s, though unofficial estimates of the number of actual working hours in this sector arrive at a figure equivalent to the full time work of 3 million people, taking into consideration self-exploitation and the assistance of unpaid family members.) Household farming carried out on only a fraction of the total land under cultivation accounted for nearly half the country's meat and vegetable production.

A new Hungarian middle class was under construction, though once again it was without political aspirations. The new middle class was a heterogeneous formation in terms of both social origins and structure – integrating industrial workers, skilled workers, and high officials – but united in the status symbols it had managed to acquire: a car, a decent apartment, a weekend house, travel, etc. The identity of the Hungarian middle class has changed little up to the present day.

One of the main reasons for the strong orientation towards consumption was the state's attitude to private ownership: for a long time the ownership of two dwelling places by one person was forbidden – it was, of course, still out of the question that a private person could lay claim to ownership of the means of production. The new middle class concentrated its efforts on the achievement of maximum comfort within a political structure which severely limited personal freedom. It was not a good or a loveable regime, but it was tolerable. The reaction it prompted was not rage, but passive submission; not acceptance, but cynicism. The accumulation of wealth was possible, but bourgeois development in the strict sense was not.

The so-called 'consensus' of the 1970s and the early 1980s rested precisely on this social background: on the one hand, the party and state bureaucracy continued to exercise unlimited political control, while on the other middle class consumption continued to evolve alongside widespread recognition that such development was taking place. In considerable contrast to the intended political structure as it was proposed and implemented in the 1950s, this bargain enabled the middle class to relinquish its social and political aspirations in return for being allowed to grow more affluent than the communist 'gentry', the party and the state bureaucracy. The state promised not to interfere in people's private lives if they would reciprocate with a corresponding neglect of public affairs. After a time the holders of highly influential posts began to mix with increasingly wealthy groups – as yet without political influence – forming an increasingly strong and complex symbiosis.

This 'bourgeois development by the back door' – I cannot think of a better term – was later undermined by two things. First, the uncontrolled bureaucracy had ruined the country's economy and was unwilling to shoulder the responsibility for it alone;[3] an attitude encouraged by the Soviet model. With this in mind, the ruling elite began in 1988 to widen the scope of freedom. They hoped to relieve themselves of at least some of the liability for the crisis by adopting a liberal guise. Given that until that time society had been allowed only the freedom of the private sphere, the ruling elite had no serious political rival to challenge its supremacy, and, consequently, nothing changed substantially: the naked emperor merely put on new clothes.

The compromise entered into by the middle class with silent repugnance did not mean that it was uncritical of the political regime which had denied its freedom. Resistance had been growing among the intelligentsia since the 1970s, with varying degrees of intensity and organization. That part of the intelligentsia engaged in teaching and research in the humanities continued to be fully 'nationalized' (the influence of the 1950s continued at least in this respect) and had to face the humiliations of censorship on a daily basis without, however, being able to enjoy the fruits of middle-class affluence in accordance with its needs and tastes. In other words, the scholarly intelligentsia both witnessed the most inflexible aspect of tyranny and was completely dependent upon a political will with which it could not identify itself.

It is not surprising, therefore, that upon the commencement of the communist regime's manoeuvres to redistribute responsibility – thereby widening the scope of political freedom – the literary intelligentsia rushed into politics with elemental force through the newly opened channels. This segment of the intelligentsia came to constitute the leadership of the most influential opposition parties in Hungarian politics, the MDF (Hungarian Democratic Forum) and the SZDSZ (Alliance of Free Democrats). In this new situation, responsibility for bourgeois development fell to them, though with varying degrees of intensity and intentions. This social group, characterized by an extreme sensitivity to freedom, succeeded in undermining the attempts of the party bureaucracy to redistribute responsibility for the social, economic and political crisis. The principal role of the intelligentsia was to revive an ethos of citizenship, that is, to create adequate institutions and, more importantly, social roles for the representation of the bourgeois ideal of freedom. (The distinctions between individual opposition trends should not be blurred: some drew on the legacy of the populism of the interwar period, others on that of nineteenth-century liberalism. What connected these groups, however, was their commitment to bourgeois transformation in the public sphere and in politics.)

As a result of the economic crisis, the lack of middle-class experience in public affairs and the lack of financial resources have once again necessitated state involvement in bringing about a fundamental breakthrough in bourgeois transformation and in the realization of liberal-democratic freedoms. This has occurred despite an apparent contradiction; liberal freedom, by definition, requires not only the separation of party and state functions and political democratization, but also the depoliticization of the state: its transformation from an active political power penetrating a wide range of social spheres into an essentially service-providing and civilizing body .

The question is whether the principles of freedom and private property will come to the fore as universal priorities; whether there will be a bourgeois transformation capable of reviving Hungary's fortunes. It must be remembered that in the old Jewish/German/Christian *Kulturkreis* only those societies were successful which offered a combination of these principles; where the only constraint on liberty was property ownership and, conversely, where these two categories were not only complementary, but mutually constraining.

It is hard to predict what direction bourgeois development will now take in Hungary. If the position of the social strata excluded from the middle-class development of the past few decades rapidly deteriorates there is the danger that an essentially anti-liberal, populist, and authoritarian political movement will gain ground; it matters little whether it calls itself national-populist, red, white and green socialist, or Christian: such a development would amount to nothing less than a return to the Horthy era. If the ruling political elite remains in office long enough to interfere in proprietary relations without the restraint of social control, then bourgeois development may fall victim to the kind of 'tutelary state power' envisaged by de Tocqueville, and, in combination with rampant technocracy, drift submissively instead of evolving self-consciously. This would not be genuine freedom, but making a virtue of necessity and doing as one is told.

In my opinion, everything depends on the intelligentsia now at the forefront of bourgeois transformation and on the still extremely heterogeneous middle class. If the intelligentsia believes that the only option is peaceful transition, it must relinquish any notion of awakening a communitarian mentality on a mass scale. This peaceful transition, however, favours only those who have already mastered the political techniques hitherto in use, and those interested in the revival of bygone phases of bourgeois development. The alternative to peace is not war, but conflict, of which violence is only the most extreme variant. The civic courage and conscious adherence to bourgeois values essential for consolidating freedom in the public sphere generally emerge as a counterreaction to crisis (but not necessarily extreme) situations, rather than during times of social peace and tranquillity. Causes of conflict should not, therefore, be swept under the carpet. Freedom is not a game propped up by institutions, but a mentality, for which a continuous struggle must be kept up – political pluralism in itself is not sufficient. The many forms of civil unrest, ranging from demonstrations to referenda and strikes, are meant to achieve precisely this: to encourage the general public to take a stand, to say 'yes' or 'no', and to experience collectively the taste of civic courage. I am, of course, aware that one cannot expect to make up overnight for centuries of unfreedom and half-hearted attempts at bourgeois development, and that a change in mentality across a whole society is a process generally requiring several generations. At the same time, the widespread inculcation of a sense of personal dignity and an impulse to exercise one's free will must be a priority; otherwise, freedom cannot last.

The role and responsibility of the middle class are enormous in this regard. A great deal will depend on its ability to organize itself and to deal with signs of unrest; on its recognition that a middle class can have other functions and a different mission than those familiar from Hungary's past; and on its acceptance of an important place in the make-up of civil society – unless it wishes to remain dependant upon technocrats and those aiming to adopt old-style authoritarianism in a modern guise.

At the current stage of bourgeois development the kind of joint national effort witnessed in 1848 and 1956 cannot be expected. The adversary is more diffuse and the contemporary social background quite different from what it was. National cooperation based on interest reconciliation is, nevertheless, vital in some form. What is at stake is nothing less than Hungary's future. A failure to cooperate would jeopardize the quality of the lives of all.

What is called for is not beyond Hungarian society's reach. All that would be required is the rational weighing up of some basic truisms. As the Delegate of Zala County said in the 1830s: 'A successful country is not measured by the number of rich people in it, but by the number of the poor.' In other words: 'Property and liberty are the sweet bonds that tie the citizen to the fate of his nation most strongly.' These words once marked the beginning of bourgeois transformation in Hungary, and the process continues.

(1990)

Notes

1 For biographical details of Ferenc Deák and other leading figures mentioned in the text see Biographical Index, pp. 249–74.
2 Those actively participating in the total eradication of bourgeois development inevitably included a large number of persons with a bourgeois background, many of them Jews. In my opinion their motivation was broadly similar to that of adherents of the populist trend who, upon confronting a particular trait of bourgeois development they disliked, came to reject and to contemplate with blind outrage the liquidation of bourgeois development as such. The limited social and political scope of bourgeois development suggested that the Hungarian bourgeoisie itself was not viable and so was to be rejected. Communist ideology and the communist

regime provided an excellent breeding ground for this rejection, as well as for the rise of middle class Jews to whom the previous regime had denied involvement in public affairs. Whatever their ideological commitments may have been, however, many clung on to traditional forms of behaviour and outward appearance rooted in the – bourgeois – past: for instance, Béla Kun's image of the worker dressed in a waistcoat and tie, or György Lukács's conception of the austere man in the habit of smoking a cigar and expressing himself in the sophisticated manner of an intellectual. What characterized the communist intelligentsia was not so much their largely Jewish origin but their reluctance to reject bourgeois tastes and values at the personal level while seeking to eliminate them entirely at the political one. Hence the confusion in the minds of simple sons of the people and their receptiveness to a mode of life which was a cross between the upper middle class and the gentry, transformed into a socialist technocracy.

3 A small linguistic detour: although the ruling elite could not have been farther from embracing genuine democracy and had expropriated all political power for itself, it had a predilection for speaking in the first person plural, washing its hands of responsibility: if something went wrong '*we*' – i.e. the nation – had done it and not *them* – i.e. the party dictatorship. *We* therefore only have ourselves to blame.

2 Industrial Development in the Eyes of Opposition Reformers of the 1840s

Any study of industrial development in Hungary in the first half of the nineteenth century must mention the various pro-industry campaigns that enjoyed wider or narrower public support at the beginning of the 1840s. Although some scholars stress the political impact of such campaigns, while others emphasize above all their economic significance, they are unanimous about their crucial importance. We will begin by trying to fathom what motivated these campaigns and why they were necessary for industrial development in Hungary.

For contemporaries, the call for the nurturing of a 'spirit of association' was a call for an adequate means of expression for the ongoing overall social and economic development, a means which, if insufficient on its own to resolve existing problems, could nevertheless accelerate various processes pointing towards the emergence of a civil society, and hopefully prompt the state to take measures to encourage *from above* the development urged by the opposition. In the writings of Kossuth, this demand is formulated very clearly:

> I by no means overestimate this spirit [of association], or see in it the remedy for all our ills; but I would be deeply disappointed in any man who arrogantly underestimated it. It is a weighty matter that it would be foolish to ignore; it is an artery in which pulsates the very lifeblood of the epoch and an understanding of the nation's interests.[1]

Reflecting further on this question some eighteen months later, Kossuth commented that these campaigns must above all 'serve to cause facts to come into being . . . especially under current circumstances, when the forming of associations and their activities are capable of furthering this or that national interest with the effect of forcing the establishment to take appropriate measures'.[2]

The association campaign was an adequate means of expression for various pressing grievances not only in view of the above, but also in light of the prevailing power relations.

The establishment in Vienna could not take the same measures against such campaigns that it would have in the case of more direct forms of political protest, although it was fully aware of the extent to which the pro-industry associations (especially the Society for Mutual Assistance) were in conflict with its interests. At an earlier period – for instance in connection with the so-called 'national casinos' (a kind of gentleman's club) initiated by Count Széchenyi – the establishment had tried to hinder the activities of such associations, but had failed to stop them altogether. Opposition reformers also had to take into account the distrust of 'the party beyond the [River] Laita' in respect of any social campaign affecting – even indirectly – relations between the two halves of the Austro-Hungarian Empire.

This establishment was foreign in two ways: it was *not Hungarian* (it was located 'beyond the Laita') and it was *feudal*. These two aspects of foreignness were closely related. Naturally, nationalist (bourgeois) and anti-feudal tendencies tended to support each other, just as government policies and measures in this period serving to suppress national development went hand in hand with the maintenance of social and economic backwardness for the purpose of ensuring the continuance of feudalism. In a broader sense, the question arose as to how far the latter could continue to subordinate the former, that is, to what extent a particular establishment or regime could restrain the Hungarian reform movement, or at least impose a compromise upon it; also at issue was the extent to which the divisions within the reform movement itself were a reflection of the restrictive pressures of the state. Any discussion of these questions, however, would take us beyond the scope of this book.

For the opposition to be able to make maximum use of its opportunities, in addition to the utilization of traditional forms of action (such as the meetings of county councils and the Diet), it had to engage in activities that were least likely to give rise to official hostility under the given political circumstances. Among these were the establishment of various pro-industry associations, which, being officially apolitical, were likely to remain free of government interference. What is more, they confronted Vienna with indisputable facts that could not easily be countered. In this period, associations seemingly concerned only with economic progress played a crucial role in the fundamental political transformation of society.

The choice of the association was also necessitated by a desire to forestall reactionaries should they feel inclined to cry foul with accusations of social propaganda. (It remained, of course, a moot point whether it was to be Kossuth, personally, or the industrialization programme as a whole that should be the target of any accusations of incitement to social unrest: in any case, the associations could not be considered revolutionary.) This (conscious) rejection of revolutionary methods naturally went hand in hand with a desire to win the support of those standing for peaceful development within the framework offered by the associations. Success could be attained only if the associations came to enjoy wide public support: they could take effective action against the governing elite only if they operated on a mass basis and could confidently claim to represent public opinion. All associations were therefore open: they did not restrict membership in any way, and many nationalist or patriotic schemes could be characterized primarily by this very determination to involve as many people in their implementation as possible. Such schemes were designed to be expansive – their exclusivity derived solely from their representation of organized socio-economic forces standing in opposition to the official viewpoint – and to serve as a link between the different social strata. These aims found expression in the constitution of the boards and membership of these associations and their essence is reflected in the following two statements: 'In Hungary only socially well-founded movements can secure any hope of a peaceful transition to circumstances that in many other lands could be realized only by way of a revolutionary shake-up',[3] and 'only upon the existing state of affairs can we play the moral tunes of peaceful instigation'.[4]

With this in mind, analyses attributing the emergence of the associations solely to the need for opposition reformers to compensate for the fact that the state held almost all power in its hands seem a little simplistic. Although all pro-industrialization arguments, inseparably connected as they were with other aspects of the emergence of a civil society in Hungary, were the result of an intense struggle with state authority and feudal constraints, the impact of the spirit of association pointed beyond any particular political constellation (though its *timeliness* very much derived from this struggle) because it largely comprised the norms and practices of liberal bourgeois values which were new to Hungary. The emergence of organizations within a feudal society that, by their very nature, would inevitably lead to the *overthrow* of feudal constraints was an inevitable concomitant of *all* bourgeois endeavours. What at the level of everyday politics was an instrument dictated by necessity could at the same time be a vehicle of the basic values sustaining a transition to a civil society. As a concrete political movement these associations emerged as mere instruments for the purpose of reaching a specific goal – the promotion of independent industrial development in Hungary – but they were equally a kind of mediating substance, the form taken by a new set of social values that represented a break from the many constraints of the feudal order.

A closer look at the aims of the associations and how these aims were arrived at may prove useful, not only because it would illuminate *what arguments were used, by whom, against whom and why*, but also because it would clearly illustrate that their activities always had a good deal more to them than their advocates openly declared.

The most important goal was, of course, independent national development. 'The Hungarian people want to be a nation, a nation by the standards of the nineteenth century.'[5] This ultimate objective had, however, to be reached by way of a number of different concrete aims.

In the economic sphere, for example, industrial development went hand in hand with other claims, implicit or explicit, such as the emergence of a middle class and the development of public opinion (creating the social conditions appropriate to a capitalist economy), gaining social recognition for manufacture (promoting the values of a civil society), and the transformation of customs and commercial policies related to Hungary's specific dependence on the Austrian part of the Dual Monarchy, ultimately with the combined effect of eliminating feudal constraints.

The extent to which the attention of opposition reformers focused on the economy embodied two kinds of realization, one general, the other concrete. First, opposition reformers came to understand that 'today, political independence not supported by economic-industrial independence is nothing but illusion and self-delusion which cannot be maintained for long'.[6] The same idea was suggested by an article from the *Moniteur Industriel* – reprinted in *Pesti Hírlap* – which stated: 'Economic facts are the cause and politics is the effect. Economic facts command and politics must obey.'[7] Second, there was throughout the period a rising awareness of the role of industry within a national economy: 'The contribution of a flourishing industry to the status and well-being of a nation is more important than that of military conquest;'[8] and regarding the role of industry in world history in respect to national and bourgeois development: 'All European nations are desirous of establishing their own manufacturing industry.'[9] Industry 'creates and destroys governments, determines war and peace in the world'.[10]

These concrete realizations were a reflection of the interiorization of a truth regarding Hungary's current situation, namely that it was now or never as far as its national development was concerned. At the heart of the matter were Hungary's relations with Austria: failure to create an independent national economy would endanger the very existence of the Hungarian nation. At this period the question of industrialization was little short of a 'matter of life and death'.[11] 'Our nation is beyond redemption unless it develops a sound and flourishing industry.'[12]

These were the main motives that strategically shaped the reform arguments of the opposition.

These realizations did not emerge from nowhere, but had specific antecedents in history and the history of ideas. This was the period in which the Industrial Revolution was at its height in Britain, and on the Continent large-scale mechanized industry was also beginning to establish itself. By this time Britain had already emerged as a world power, a position clearly attributable to its high level of economic development. The emergence of a world market and its day-to-day functioning, most directly visible in the vacillations of the stock market, were bound, sooner or later, to awaken Central and Eastern Europe from its provincial slumber, and to open its eyes to its backwardness and the necessity of matching the achievements that had raised other states to the vanguard of industrial production in Europe (which at that time meant: the world). The impact of the Industrial Revolution and the importance of economic success could not be ignored. At a time when in Britain fundamental changes were taking place at the pinnacle of political power amid intense struggles related to grain prices and customs duties, when one commercial crisis followed another, and the English worker was experiencing the effects of recession in the direct terms of a deterioration of his living standards, it was not possible to hide behind points of law and to restrict one's actions to futile public debates. Instead one had to move forward and to find the means capable of providing real answers to the problems posed by living historical developments.

In Hungary, the question was not, of course, the transposition of the Industrial Revolution and its adaptation to local circumstances, but rather the heightened awareness of the importance of economic evolution brought about by developments abroad, particularly in the political sphere. Under Hungarian circumstances the Industrial Revolution also contributed to the recognition of the importance of industrial development and prompted *conscious* economic development, which had been desired before, but never linked with national autonomy and progress (the establishment of this link made it into a factor of central importance). Emperor Joseph II (and even earlier, Maria Theresa) had already urged the development of manufacturing industry, but their proposals had met with little enthusiasm: the resulting abolition of tax concessions would not have been favourably received by the feudal aristocracy. The following is an extract from the rejected proposal of Joseph II, as quoted by Kossuth:

> Factories in Hungary are not only not protected, they are being crushed . . . If the nobility paid taxes, regulated prices were abolished and military needs satisfied at market prices, malpractice would cease to exist and domestic trade would increase. On this [the acceptance of taxation] alone depends whether Hungary is to enjoy equal treatment with regard to trade with other provinces or is to be regarded merely as a colony in which industrial production is suppressed as much as possible and food prices kept at the lowest possible levels in order to reduce the cost of provisioning the army stationed in the country, so maximizing profits without making the slightest effort to reinvest them in Hungary, because this would be against the interests of the other provinces.[13]

The attachment to feudal privileges prevailed over bourgeois development and the closely related bourgeois national self-determination. How a nation dominated by a tax-exempt nobility could achieve independence was a difficult question, especially when that nobility was determined to hold onto its privileges, even at the cost of national economic progress. It is significant that the questions of industrial development and taxation arose at the same time. Kossuth repeatedly warned that the Hungarian nation was in a 'race against time'. Even after the social foundations of reform had finally been put in place several opportunities were missed, including that of the continuous work of the committees brought into being by the parliamentary session of 1790. The fact that regular work was being done in these committees does, however, indicate that a realization of historic significance had already been arrived at, whether intuitively or otherwise. From the point of view of the enlightened absolutism of Vienna, the linking of capitalist development with abolition of the tax exemptions enjoyed by the nobility did not necessarily entail the encouragement of bourgeois national development. On the contrary. In any case, while during the second half of the eighteenth century Hungary still had some prospect of prosperous natural growth, by the 1840s awareness of a connection between economic underdevelopment and the lack of national independence on the one hand, and capitalist economic development and the emergence of a civil society on the other had become unavoidable.

Hungarian endeavours also had their antecedents in the history of ideas. Friedrich List's *Das Nationale System der Politischen Oekonomie* (The National System of Political Economy) published in German in 1841, and soon afterwards in Hungarian translation, was particularly important for the evolution of Kossuth's thinking.

It is enough to enumerate some of List's main ideas to understand why Kossuth and others accepted them so readily, even at the cost of modifying their views (for example, regarding free trade).

List based his theory not on the individual engaged in some form of enterprise (the 'Robinson Crusoe' of the British model so derided by Marx), but instead on the nation, the goal of economic development being to promote national well-being. List couples economic progress with national freedom and self-determination, supporting his arguments with the historical examples of Britain and France. The most important sector of the economy is industry, upon which the development of all other sectors depends. Regarding the relationship between agriculture and industry, the benefits of industry for agriculture are stressed. Industrial development increases demand for agricultural products, mechanization improves productivity and land prices rise. At the same time, industry supplies those engaged in agriculture as well as processing agricultural produce, and so industry supports and stimulates agricultural development. Industry being the decisive factor, it is necessary to identify trading methods that promote it.

At this point the German perspective begins to emerge. With reference to

Montesquieu, List, somewhat simplistically, cites Poland as proof that 'whole nations have been ruined by exporting raw materials and food and importing industrial products'.[14] List could not identify with the idea of free trade because it required a strong industrial base allowing the export of industrial products. Under the given historical circumstances a 'domestic industrial potential' had to be created and protected. The best method for this was the introduction of protective customs duties. List's 'Holy Trinity' – *(1)* the nation; *(2)* the closely intertwined development of industry and agriculture; and *(3)* a system of protective customs duties – was bound to make a deep impression on Hungarian thinkers because it outlined a possible solution for the problems hindering Hungarian development. This solution was incorporated by Kossuth, in a highly creative and original manner, in his own scheme for industrial development adjusted to Hungarian conditions.

The recognition of the importance of industry was, of course, not the only merit of List's work, nor was it original. What was most striking, particularly in light of the pressing question of national independence, was that List's theory centred on the *nation as the 'teleological' agent of economic activity*. Kossuth and his circle of opposition reformers made a conscious and carefully considered decision to adopt List's approach because it seemed to cover all aspects of Hungarian reality, addressing the vital topics of the day.

The arguments in favour were addressed to the nation as a whole because they concerned issues affecting the nation as a whole. Although Kossuth later came to the sad conclusion that 'in [Hungary] no issue is a national issue, even the most sacred of things is only a matter for party politics',[15] he never entirely abandoned the idea of national unity, remaining resolute in the defence of his principles, and in his famous speech of 20 August 1846 concerning the Association for Mutual Assistance he made specific reference to those opposed to industrialization. The enemies of industrialization were those 'who are currently in power and the recipients of the greatest blessings the nation can give', that is, government supporters. They could be held primarily responsible for the lack of national unity on the question of industrial development. In the same category belong those bound to the fireside in 'pipe-smoking idleness',[16] that is, the conservative county nobility, against whom Kossuth's description of the enemies of this great cause was principally directed: 'Good God! Has anyone seen such a man who, although exposed to reasons as clear as day, would declare himself determined never to be persuaded by them,'[17] simply because, to the enemies of industrialization, 'a graceful smile from Vienna is worth more than the interests of the nation to us all [?]'[18]

Kossuth's style of argumentation, on the one hand addressing the whole nation and on the other labelling its opponents as enemies of national development and 'the interests of the nation', almost going so far as to exclude the latter from the nation, contributed to the widening of the social base of the reform movement and expropriated the notion of the 'true Hungarian', putting those opposed to industrial development on the defensive. This was indeed the purpose of the whole association propaganda campaign.

Having more or less clarified the 'why', the 'with whom' and the 'against whom', we shall now proceed to analyse how the campaign for industrial development was conducted. A significant, if not a fundamental, shift of emphasis took place from the previously dominant public-law approach. One can best characterize this change as an attempt to introduce economic questions into the public domain, or in more general terms, to replace the rationalism of the public-law approach characteristic of the politics of grievances formerly pursued by the nobility (the feudal or landowner approach) with another kind of rationalism focused on the economy (the capitalist-bourgeois approach).

Apart from the inadequacy of the traditional methods of the politics of grievances to questions related to bourgeois transformation, it was necessary to change the whole style of argument once it was a question of targeting the nation (in the sense of a bourgeois nation) in its entirety. Public-law arguments used and understood exclusively by the nobility had to give way to something more accessible. I am not, of course, suggesting that *tables of statistics*, one of the methods introduced, were accessible to everyone, but it is a fact that they broadened the public debate through the participation of a large number of people (for instance, Antal Valero-type capitalists) who had previously been excluded for the simple reason that they were unable to join in the public-law style of argumentation. But the consummation of this change was a somewhat later development: at this stage we can only talk of new tendencies. The reason for the delay was the role played by the nobility in the bourgeois transformation process. (By the way, the same cause lay behind the manoeuvring that generally characterized opposition reformers. They would often not follow an argument to a logical conclusion but would instead stop halfway to take into account the role of feudal constraints – for example, in connection with trade guilds – as well as the expected reaction of the nobility.)

There is another factor that had a major impact on the actions and attitudes of opposition reformers, in addition to more objective factors and influences, and this was Kossuth's personality. Although József Révai is right when he describes Kossuth as 'a nobleman representing the bourgeoisie and a bourgeois representative of the nobility',[19] Kossuth was much more than that. His influence was decisive in terms of both the standard and the dynamism of his argumentation. As regards the level of argument, Kossuth always had a thorough knowledge of the best and most up-to-date European economic thought, as well as an ability to use this knowledge in a creative way. He was familiar with almost all the theoretical achievements of bourgeois economics. Kossuth's thought also benefited from the fact that he never sought to apply theoretical models directly, but always tried to adjust them to prevailing Hungarian conditions.

Kossuth's dynamism may be attributed not only to the urgency of the issues at stake, but also to his astonishing spiritual energy, his identification with the cause, his organizing ability and, last but not least, the rhetorical gifts that ornamented his speeches to dazzling effect. Speaking of Kossuth's methods and impact Domokos Kosáry correctly observed:

> [Kossuth] always tried to establish his arguments on concrete foundations and would illustrate his points with such vivid examples that the description would make the reader's blood boil, finally compelling him to burst out: 'This must not be allowed to go on!'[20]

Through the combined influence of these objective and subjective factors, Kossuth's argumentation was characterized by multiple dualisms: public law and economics, principles and tactics, theory and practice, and reason and emotion. I cannot analyse each dualism in detail, but they are constantly present in the propaganda both of Kossuth himself and of the reform opposition in general.

What sort of arguments were marshalled with regard to the various social movements in pursuit of the development of Hungarian industry? I must point out that the following analysis is somewhat abstract, based on an arbitrary combination of elements. In reality, of course, the same arguments constituted a much more complex whole or appeared in different contexts. Such arbitrariness is nevertheless justified, partly on methodological and partly on theoretical grounds. As regards methodological considerations, in the Reform Period, and particularly in Kossuth's thought, *it is almost impossible to separate one key issue from another*. But in a study such as this an attempt must be made to concentrate on one subject matter at a time and to collect all closely related issues together. As regards theoretical considerations, I shall focus on the social and political aspects of the period.

Just what was understood by the term 'industry' in the Reform Period? In Gusztáv Wencel's definition, 'industry is the totality of activities whereby naturally occurring raw materials are processed and made more apt for human use by way of various mechanical and manual skills and machinery'.[21]

It is important that handicraft was also considered part of industry, although the efforts of the opposition reformers were primarily directed at the development of manufacturing as the very pinnacle of industry. It is interesting to see what contemporaries thought the development of domestic industry would entail, especially in view of the fact that postwar historiography has tended to evaluate such initiatives as autarkic, with the intention of making Hungary a self-sufficient industrial state. Some contemporary commentators also exhibited autarkic tendencies: 'Hungary should never be economically dependent on another nation.'

To begin with, it is necessary to determine what the factors were that in the eyes of opposition reformers determined the course of a nation's industrial development. They included geographical location, population and national temperament: industrial development should evolve organically. The consequence of forced industrial development would be 'an undernourished greenhouse plant' from which 'abnormal interests' would later stem.[22] Kossuth puts it even more clearly when he writes:

> I do not hold the view that a nation should itself grow and produce everything required for civilization and thus close itself off from the world . . . but [I do believe we] should grow and produce what we can with profit and for which we possess all that is necessary.[23]

But views on this were not unanimous. It was Széchenyi who pointed to the contradiction inherent in a desire for a self-sufficient domestic industry (urged in connection with the Association for Mutual Assistance) on the one hand, and active foreign trade on the other. It was not possible only to sell and not to purchase. In other words, an economic policy that wanted to keep all profits within the country at any cost and that reduced foreign trade to export was nothing but a delusion.

From an objective standpoint this was indeed a weak point in the economic and industrial development scheme, but it is equally possible to see it not as a conflict between two fully formulated and opposing views, but rather as coexisting, individually conceived aspirations and requirements (development of domestic industry, prevention of capital outflows, surplus foreign trade balance, increasing independence from Austria), important elements of economic development and independence that could not, however, all be translated into reality at the same time. They did, however, serve as norms, as something to aspire to. This normativity derived from the fact – and this should always be borne in mind – that the arguments and aspirations of the reform opposition were not the expression of an official economic policy implemented under the auspices of the state, but represented the projection of a political movement onto economics. These arguments and aspirations by their very nature had to point beyond particular aims which could be realistically fulfilled, on the one hand because they were part of a larger, more general political concept, and on the other because the phenomena with which they were concerned were a novelty in this region; a domestic industry in Hungary was yet to be created, and even then it would be done against the will of the ruling political elite. It may also be supposed that had there been an active economic policy in the Hungary of the day, that is, if an operating capitalist economy had been in place, the regulatory role of the market would have smoothed out many of the above contradictions.

The carefully prepared statements issued by opposition reformers never featured the concept of an autarkic economy and the contradictions in question were not crucially important for the reasons already given. It would therefore be wrong to assume that representatives of the reform opposition wanted to see an autarkic Hungary.

At the same time, opposition reformers did insist on certain conditions as being vitally important. These could be summarized as the abolition *de facto* and *de jure* of feudal constraints, and the requirement that private property and related political rights be secured. The scope of this study does not allow us to investigate these questions in detail, and in any case what is most important for us in this connection is the attempt to compensate at least partially for the lack of access to executive power in the Reform Period by the organization of various campaigns for industrial development in the form of associations. Here I am referring to the Industrial Association established in 1841, the Association for Mutual Assistance and the Association of Manufacturers established in October and December of 1844 respectively, and the Trade Association, also established in 1844.

The general objectives and related motives that called these associations into being were manifested in the creation of a united national front – by way of raising general awareness of the imminent danger faced by the nation – to serve as a background for the development of industry. Such an objective was evident in the campaign calling people to take a stand in support of the Industrial Association. (The most important objectives of the Industrial Association were the promotion and support by various means of training for those engaged in industry and the organization of industrial exhibitions to publicize Hungarian industry with the ultimate goal of boosting industrial development as such.) The campaign stressed that these objectives 'are in the interest of us all, even if for different reasons'. A list of those whose interests lay in supporting the Industrial Association was appended: the liberal in word if not in deed, the man interested only in wealth, the agricultural labourer and the artisan. The *leitmotiv* of the whole campaign was the argument that industrial development would benefit the whole country and that failure to see it through would similarly lead to the impoverishment of all. 'Those who reject national industrial development leave Hungary beholden to other nations for the supply of what it requires; such indebtedness leads to impoverishment.' [24]

The issue of training was particularly important. The role of industrial schools pointed far beyond the objectives of personal improvement, impressively formulated as 'moral and intellectual betterment' and the abandonment of the 'card table stacked with glasses of beer'. Much more

importantly, industrial schools were meant to create the stratum of professionals so important for industry and repeatedly urged by men like Valero. I
shall return to this question in connection with the middle classes.

Another vitally important role of the Industrial Association was the
organization of industrial exhibitions with the aim of 'creating a forum for
publicizing a scattered Hungarian industry by concentrating its products at
one place and at one time with the effect of demonstrating to sceptics that a
Hungarian national industry does indeed exist, and perhaps even creating the
impression that there is more to it than might actually be the case'.[25]

In my opinion the arguments used by the Industrial Association to justify
its cause best illustrate the reform opposition's commitment to the English
model. I shall discuss this commitment later, but here I would like to draw
attention to the fact that Britain served as a role model for the very concept
of the industrial association and the industrial exhibition (compare the
Society for the Diffusion of Useful Knowledge and the Adelaide Street
Exhibition), although the association and the exhibition played a larger part
in Hungary than in Britain.

The Association for Mutual Assistance served the cause in a much more
direct manner in the sense that, while the Industrial Association was set up
to stand *for* a particular cause, the former was established *against* the protective tariff system unfavourably affecting Hungarian trade, promoting the
cause of Hungarian industry by channelling consumption towards domestic
goods. Although it is not my intention here to describe the various associations, I must make mention of the origin of the Association of
Manufacturers in the not entirely successful but nevertheless extremely
flexible tactics of the opposition reformers. The Association of
Manufacturers sought to win the support of forces not incorporated in the
Association for Mutual Assistance for one reason or other (among them
Széchenyi himself). Of the Association for Mutual Assistance it is sufficient
to say that it was the first organization to provide nationwide coordination
for the efforts of the reformers in a more or less organized way, and with as
many as 146 branches it demonstrated their growing political power.

The effectiveness of the argument is clearly indicated by the fact that the
Industrial Association and the Association for Mutual Assistance – probably
the two most important organizations – managed to create a united front
regarding the question of industrialization with a wide base ranging from
Count Batthyány, Ágoston Trefort and József Irinyi to ordinary people. This
united front manifested itself in various social gatherings at which members
of the aristocracy and the bourgeoisie sat at the same table.

Although it is clear that we are dealing here with an essentially political
issue, opposition reformers nevertheless presented the above associations
to the government as non-political organizations in order to maintain the
legitimacy of their activities and to preserve a unity that was acceptable in

an economic guise but that would have been difficult to manage politically. Just how right they were we shall see later on in connection with the guilds.

The separation of the political and the economic aspects was presented as follows: 'We should make one thing clear: in these pages we are discussing economic and not political remedies. Politics works differently: it uses diplomacy, intrigue, bribery, marriages, alliances and, finally, cannons. Economics does not have such powerful means at its disposal. It can do only what is possible.'[26] Such a separation was also insisted upon in other instances: 'Members should beware of using meetings as battlegrounds for party politics and of holding up the name of our association as a slogan or banner in a field of activities beyond our circle.'[27] Another reason for taking this stand was the wish to avoid alienating the large number of Jewish traders and capitalists, but instead to offer them a forum for political action and to allow them to join the national united front. Kossuth alluded to precisely this in his *Sketch*, where he wrote: 'Theology and politics are excluded.' This was also the only way in which otherwise rather passive aristocrats could be drawn in to promote industrialization. Members of the high aristocracy were among the leaders of the industrialization campaign, and female aristocrats wore with enthusiasm clothes made of coarser Hungarian-made textiles, fashionable at the time, which they would otherwise never have dreamt of exchanging for their more exquisite Parisian creations. In this way, parts of the Hungarian high aristocracy found themselves sharing a platform with the middle aristocracy, the urban bourgeoisie, artisans and even the peasantry.

Furthermore, seemingly depoliticized economic associations made it possible even for those who rejected revolution but sympathized with industrial development to remain within the ranks of campaign supporters. This is the idea behind the passage cited above in which economics is presented as a vehicle of positive reform in contrast to politics. Opposition reformers themselves rejected revolution, regarding 'peaceful legitimate agitation' as the only acceptable means of action, to be used 'with loyalty, but with all our strength deriving from a true cause and the unimpeachable interests of the nation'.[28] At the same time, especially in Kossuth's speech of 20 August 1846, the idea of rebellion was raised repeatedly, only to be dismissed in a gentlemanly manner after it was felt that the government had been sufficiently rattled. In this way, Kossuth sought to recommend the industrialization campaign as an alternative to something much worse. The government's policies 'make even the son of a man gentle as a dove flare up with anger, although there is nothing more dangerous than suppressed anger'.[29] In any case, peaceful agitation served its purpose: 'The number of peaceful reformers has increased.'[30]

Before we can move on to discuss the arguments Kossuth and his circle addressed to particular social groups regarding specific problems of industrial development, we must first briefly address arguments regarding tariff policies serving to support industrial development. This small detour cannot be avoided because without it the campaign unfolded by the Association for Mutual Assistance and the weight and importance of the whole industrial development process in Hungary could not be fully appreciated. The road to industrial development lay through trade and tariffs. In this respect the general assumption was that 'the question of industry in the broader sense, with which the question of trade and tariffs is organically connected, is in our age more important than can easily be expressed'.[31] From the circumstances prevailing in Hungary in the Reform Period it was concluded that because of its tariff system Hungary possessed neither free trade nor manufacturing industry: 'Our national economy is in an unnatural state.'[32] A 'peaceful trade war' would lead to the disintegration of the nation if the existing tariff system were to remain in place. In response, Kossuth first proposed the introduction of free trade, to which he remained faithful up to 1842, after which, under the influence of List's work, he became an advocate of a system of protective tariffs. One could say, somewhat simplistically, that the development of Kossuth's thought on the subject can be presented as a dialectical triad of thesis-antithesis-synthesis. Kossuth's first, natural reaction to the protective tariff system imposed by Vienna was to propose free trade; however, upon realizing the impossibility of carrying this scheme through and that, even if carried through it would lead to national disintegration, Kossuth offered a Hungarian protective tariff system in opposition to the one imposed by Austria; finally, he suggested a compromise solution which would take into account the interests of both parties.

Kossuth saw a direct link between the Austrian protective tariff system in operation at the time and the lack of a Hungarian industry. He opposed Hungary's joining the *Zollverein* (Customs Union), since in his opinion – despite the undoubted short-term benefits it entailed in the form of improved prospects for agricultural exports – it was bound to lead to Hungary's disintegration, eradicating once and for all any chance of stabilizing a Hungarian industry which, as a 'delicate plant', had to be tariff-protected. The *Zollverein*, through forging an artificial unity of material interests by imposing a strictly geographical division of labour within the Austro-Hungarian Monarchy, would have maintained the social and economic backwardness of the less-developed half (namely Hungary) over the long term. The *Zollverein* – acting as a melting pot – would inevitably have destroyed all prospects of forging an independent Hungarian nation.

When putting forth the case for tariffs Kossuth left no stone unturned, making use of everything from statistical tables and empirical data to sentiments of national unity, delving deep into history to the first Hungarian chieftain, Árpád. I would even go so far as to say that in Kossuth's view, the tariff question came before industrial development – although in fact they were inseparable. It was the destructive impact of the tariff system on Hungarian industry that made necessary a particular, socialized model of industrialization for which it was vitally important to win the support of as large a number of people as possible. The tariff question was the contemporary issue that prompted the most heated outbursts: 'But to be merged with Austria? Never – never! If we should really perish, I know death to be far more glorious than a shameful crumbling away, than such cowardly national suicide.'[33] It is probably in connection with the tariff and the industrial questions that the continuity and relation between Albert Berzeviczy and the opposition reformers can most clearly be seen.

One negative outcome of this tense situation was a certain self-delusion which magnified Hungary's opportunities and conjured up imaginary markets for Hungarian-made products in the East and in South America. The short-lived and rather unsuccessful Trading Company was all too evidently a product of such enthusiasm.

At the same time, Kossuth and the opposition reformers around him found ways of compensating for the depressing effects of the tariff system. Kossuth and his circle drew attention to new objectives for Hungarian economic policy (both literally and in the abstract) related to the development of a particular section of the railway (the Fiume/Buccari line), objectives that fitted in well with the socially-based programme of industrial development.

In order to galvanize the whole of society and to win the support of various social strata it was necessary to deploy arguments that not only would not alienate these groups – see above for the case of the aristocracy – but which would ensure their active support, even if an emerging capitalist economy would in fact threaten their very existence.

What kinds of argument were used to target individual social classes and groups?

On the question of the relations of agriculture and industry the argument focused on the fact that Hungary was an agricultural country and likely to remain one. At the same time, in a country where the area of arable land was relatively small, there was a large redundant labour force that could find useful employment in industry. In light of this, only such redundant labour, unutilized by agriculture, should be channelled into industry. Industrial development would in turn stimulate agriculture as the market for agricultural products grew: 'If there is no industrial population, the farmer is forced to sell his few products at very low prices while having to pay very high prices to satisfy his own needs.'[34] In this way the farmer's wealth is limited to a pantry packed full of his own products. To put it another way, prices could only be lowered through the development of industry. To cite a highly evocative example used by Kossuth, even the most primitive agricultural

method – land cultivation using digging sticks – relies on a primitive industrial product, the sharpened stick. *Hetilap* pointed out (as early as 1845) that
'the accumulation of an extensive mechanical and chemical potential' was
required for agricultural development. There was no need to fear famine,
because industry increases agricultural productivity. On this point it was
common to cite Britain as an example: at the period in question approximately 50% of its population were urban dwellers and their supply with
basic agricultural products relied on imports only to a relatively limited
extent. The upshot was that agriculture and industry could not develop
without one another, they together constituted the power and wealth of the
nation, and so 'they must embrace each other with brotherly love'.[35]

The basic idea was that everyone should support industrialization because
it was in everyone's interest: clearly for the *landowner* industrialization
could bring nothing but benefits, while for the *peasant*, scraping a living
from the soil, industry offered employment. This also served as an answer to
those who criticized Kossuth and his circle (a magazine entitled *Magyar
Gazda* and László Korizmics in particular) for neglecting agriculture in their
one-sided pursuit of industrial development. Kossuth and his circle counter-
argued – not without exaggerating certain tendencies observable in Britain
for their own benefit – that a highly developed agriculture could not exist
without a highly developed industry. In addition to economic arguments
linking the interests of the landowner and the peasant to industrial development, they sought to raise awareness of the necessity for a *union* between
agriculture and industry for the purposes of industrialization.

The tendency, previously observed, to portray industrial development as
something congenial and useful for everyone did not lead to a fundamental
change in approach. Such a change was more evident in arguments
regarding the working classes. Industrialization being the aim, opposition
reformers took the capitalist's side, if only because the direct task for the
time being was the creation of a class of industrial workers: 'A class of
industrial workers, without whom domestic raw materials cannot be turned
into marketable products and without whom even Germany, however rich
from agriculture, resembles nothing but a one-armed giant, is yet to be
created.'[36] In response to the conservative argument that manufacturing
industry would lead to the pauperization and demoralization of the working
classes (an indication that arguing for things progressive in themselves –
welfare and morality – does not necessarily go hand in hand with supporting
progress as such), Kossuth and his circle argued that, on the contrary,
manufacturing industry would entail the enrichment and moral development
of the working masses, since it would provide them with a regular income
and allow them to raise their cultural level considerably.[37] *Hetilap* returned
to this question repeatedly in the form of various case studies of humane
conditions in workhouses in America (with only 12 working hours) and the

living conditions of the English worker. According to these case studies, the English worker ate roast beef regularly and several eggs a day, drank whisky and had a significant amount of leisure time. All this in 1845, the year in which Engels published his famous work condemning the situation of the English working classes!

In connection with the prospect of unemployment it was concluded that unemployment existed where industry was essentially export-oriented and where there were wars related to erratic fluctuations in foreign trade. (At this time there had been no war in Europe for over 30 years.) It was argued further that Hungary was not exposed to the threat of unemployment because the domestic economy was primarily oriented towards satisfying domestic demand and so had a constant market. Workers were nevertheless recommended to form 'associations of mutual assistance', just in case, and were ensured of support in their efforts to this end. On the other hand, high wages were frowned upon in connection with Hungarian capital investments (it was pointed out that there were not enough skilled labourers in Hungary and there were calls to allow in foreign skilled workers, in order to cut wages). This also served as one more argument in favour of promoting the industrial training plan of the Industrial Association. At the same time, it was intended to increase domestic consumption, to which end it was necessary to reduce unemployment to a minimum and to maximize job creation. It follows from this that the creation of solvent demand was to be based on widening its scope, maximizing the number of those in employment, rather than on deepening it through higher wages.

It would be easy to take a Marxist standpoint and to condemn the argument outlined above out of hand. Such outright rejection would not, however, bring us any closer to a historical understanding of the situation. I would merely like to point out a recurrent mistake, that of the belief that there exists a direct correlation between an increase in production under the conditions of manufacturing industry on the one hand and an improvement in living standards on the other. Even in Kossuth's time there was ample evidence against this. From a historical perspective, of course, the proposition undoubtedly rests on legitimate grounds: in the case of Hungary low wages were seen as a means to promote general economic and social progress. The problem is that the description of working-class living conditions based on the model of the English working class was an obvious distortion. The reform opposition were not objective even as regards the data they quoted in this connection, quite apart from the differences that divided them from Engels in terms of their basis of comparison and objectives. There are several possible explanations for such misrepresentation. The most important among these is that for Hungary the English model overall represented the goal to be attained. In this context capitalist contradictions were beside the point, given that the capitalist model represented fundamental progress as compared with prevailing domestic conditions: in the struggle for capitalism the benefits outshone any possible disadvantages. (We should remember that Engels also subordinated his facts to political considerations, his aim being to reveal the contradictions of capitalism and, rejecting the capitalist model, to argue for progress by revolution.) In Hungary the unfolding of capitalist development – even in view of merely political considerations – very much needed the drive provided by the example of a Britain then at the peak of its power. It was also necessary to find an alternative to the guilds, by means of which upward social mobility and wealth could become a prospect open to the masses, rather than only to a few individuals such as the guild masters. This was the idea behind the opposition reformers' proposal to raise the social status of industrial labourers. But before we can proceed with this, we need to look more closely at opposition arguments concerning the guilds.

First, to clarify the logic of the argument, let me cite a few statistics. In 1847, the number of factory workers was 23,400, as compared with 78,000 guild workers and apprentices.[38] While these figures indicate that the guilds made up a considerable part of the Hungarian economy, it must be understood that guild workers saddled with handicraft tools and methods were much less productive than their counterparts in the factories. This is an important consideration, given that in this period guilds comprised the majority of Hungarian industrial labourers, and their negative attitude towards industrialization threatened to hinder industrial development. They hindered the circulation of the population within the economy, they were technically underdeveloped, they did not provide adequate training for guild workers and apprentices, using them as semi-skilled labour, and their institutions – such as work by guild masters, the movement of apprentices from master to master and costly feasts – were outdated. The guilds were in need of radical reform.[39]

Given their continued dominance, however, opposition reformers adopted a more conciliatory stance on tactical grounds. In order not to antagonize the guilds, they had separated *Pesti Hírlap*, as a political forum, from the Industrial Association which, of course, had a predominantly economic profile. The idea behind this was not to exclude the guilds from the activities, control and financial support of the Industrial Association. This political division of labour emphasized the positive aspects of the guilds that latently expressed the objectives of the Association, such as a spirit of association, poverty relief and political education, and the fact that in guilds 'an element of people's power is being created for the benefit of society'.[40] The Industrial Association criticized the guilds mainly for the quality and quantity of the training they provided, and proposed that industrial schools be set up instead. The significance of the industrial schools was that with their establishment the monopoly of the guilds on vocational skills would come to an end, despite the Industrial Association's declarations to the contrary.

It is in this connection that the theoretical/practical dualism of the argument can be seen most clearly: the Industrial Association was striving to bring about the natural death of the guild system. The tactics of the Industrial Association were to take training out of the hands of the guilds and to replace the system of feudal privileges first with social then with state controls: in this manner the guilds would gradually run down. At the same time, *Pesti Hírlap* tried to divide the guild masters from the guild workers by acting as a mouthpiece for both the latter and the guild apprentices, taking the view that the position of guild master should be made more accessible. (The Industrial Association at the same time offered guild masters the opportunity to lift restrictions in this regard but only in respect of its own members. The full extent of the anti-guild design is revealed when we add to the above the Industrial Association's arguments about the prospects of better living standards for the industrial working class and its promises to support handicraft workers ('the proudly ramifying tree shall not crush the modest ground plants beneath it'),[41] thus tempting from two directions at the same time the tens of thousands of workers suffering from guild constraints.

Over the many hundreds of years of their existence, the guilds had come to be accepted by feudal society as feudal organizations of production. If industry – which was to acquire a massive scale and become generally accessible under conditions of capitalist development, in contrast to the feudal exclusivity of the guild system – was to be incorporated in the emerging social hierarchy, it was necessary to make use of the emerging bourgeois forms of publicity, the press and public meetings, to campaign for it. Kossuth and his circle showed the utmost consistency in this. They concluded that to be an industrial worker in Hungary was considered degrading, and that when an industrial worker had acquired enough wealth he would want to leave his class and raise his children to better things. This was a tendency that opposition reformers constantly criticized. They did not look for its causes, but instead fought against it on several fronts. One of their lines of argument focused on the financial side of the question, pointing out that leaving industry as an occupation did not usually pay off: 'It is certain that under present circumstances in Hungary industry is a much more profitable occupation than administration.'[42]

The other group of arguments aimed at raising the esteem in which industry was held, from which point of view the industrial worker and the capitalist could be viewed as members of the same group: 'Take firm hold of the tools of industry, and let the wealth and power showered upon our nation by industry be Hungarian.'[43] I would also like to remind the reader of what was said earlier about the focus on the economy and the attempt to transform social values; reformers hoped this could be achieved to the extent that a career in industry would have a higher social status than the legal career generally preferred by the nobility.

The roles of the middle class and of public opinion were central themes of bourgeois transformation. Just as it was essential to dissolve the social basis of the guilds (to distance journeymen and apprentices from them), it was also necessary to create the social basis of capitalist industrial development. In the opinion of the reform opposition centring on Kossuth, the middle class consisted of the following: *(1)* that part of the nobility able to identify itself with the cause of bourgeois transformation; *(2)* the urban population; *(3)* capitalists and smallholders; *(4)* professionals, inclusive of certain catagories of skilled workers; and *(5)* peasants with bourgeois aspirations.

The middle class was thought to be particularly important because industrial development was being hindered by the lack of a class of professionals and the more rational attitudes that usually come with it. This lack was partly responsible for a situation in which 'in this country a judge of the County Court is considered a better designer of roads than an engineer, and economic questions that are essentially financial matters are argued pro and contra by bureaucrats – such a state of affairs is bound to lead to failure'.[44] The same question of the middle class was also raised elsewhere, for example where Kossuth writes about the insufficient involvement of experts in legislation.[45]

Winning the support of the nobility for the bourgeois transformation process was of paramount importance both in reality and at the level of argument. Kossuth concluded: 'That Hungary became and that Hungary is, is [the nobility's] work.'[46] The nobility, as the guardian of constitutionalism, was the foundation upon which the nation's existence rested. The aim therefore was not to discard the nobility in order to allow other social groups to rise, but to fuse the nobility with these groups in one political whole by abolishing the nobility's privileges (primarily its exemption from taxes). Kossuth pointed to the political wisdom of the nobility as the guarantee that this segment of society would be able to retain its primacy: 'Political wisdom is not giving way to necessity but preventing the emergence of necessity.'[47] In return for voluntarily surrendering its privileges the nobility would be able to retain its political supremacy but with a new, bourgeois orientation, in contrast to Joseph II's offer of independent economic development within the framework of a feudal society in return for the abolition of tax exemptions. The trend towards bourgeois development meant that the nobility had to become an open social stratum and to surrender its former homogeneity. Without such economic development a substantial part of the national cause could not be realized. Social progress required the *joint efforts* of society as a whole and this was the function of the middle class: 'We are trying to reconcile the interests of all classes of the population, in other words to carry out reforms that will guarantee and improve the national constitutional order.'[48]

Alongside the emergence of a middle class it was necessary to bring into being a nationwide publicity campaign capable of exerting pressure. This need had arisen in connection with industrial development because industrial associations were the only forum – outside parliament – through which opposition reformers could mobilize society on behalf of their cause. Associations in general, but especially the Association for Mutual Assistance, were ideal vehicles for this purpose. The slogan 'facts should be created' implied not only that public opinion should be prepared, but also that it should be made to take a coherent stand. Efforts to form a public opinion were certainly not devoid of threatening overtones, indicating full awareness of the significance of public opinion and of its potential power. '[Public opinion] shall be a quiet river when that suffices, but it shall be a storm, if necessary, in which the voice of God's judgment can be heard.'[49]

The press also began to be utilized more and more as a means both to express and to influence public opinion, and Kossuth was the first to recognize its true significance. *Pesti Hírlap* (at least until Kossuth was forced to part with it) and later *Hetilap*, which acted as a mouthpiece for the Industrial Association, were the most prestigious organs of the press. *Pesti Hírlap* devoted itself exclusively to political writing, and *Hetilap* also published articles on more general political issues. It was essential for opposition reformers to make use of the press to counter the use anti-industrialization circles already made of them. *Pesti Hírlap*, *Életképek* and *Hetilap* took a stand on the side of the Association for Mutual Assistance, while *Budapesti Híradó*, *Magyar Gazda* and the *Augsburger Allgemeine Zeitung* stood up against it. *Pesti Hírlap* experienced the most rapid development: it increased its circulation from 60 to 5,200 over a period of only three years. *Hetilap*, however, although it did not significantly differ from *Pesti Hírlap*, could never attain a circulation of more than 500 copies.

It is clear that the debate about industry went far beyond its nominal subject matter, like many other reform debates. The industrial question had implications for Hungary's national, social and economic development. The historian can, of course, single out industrial development for study on the basis of a more or less arbitrary separation of the complex issues involved, but he must never lose sight of the wider context.

One of the most important features of the Reform Period, and certainly the most important from the point of view of the topic under discussion, was the way in which different claims and endeavours combined to constitute a complex organic whole. Characteristically, Kossuth's articles always addressed a range of issues, even when they were apparently devoted to a single question. Take, for example, his article entitled '*Adó*' ['Taxation'], published in József Bajza's *Ellenőr*, in which he touches upon virtually every important issue of the day. This cannot be attributed to Kossuth's personality alone. The fact is that individual elements of reform fitted into each other like cog-wheels: set one in motion and all the others would follow. Kossuth put it thus: 'It is the nature of principles that they do not tolerate shackles and can endure as many as five or six transpositions or more. One cannot tell the torch-flame shining in the middle of the great hall of national conviction to cast the full burden of its light into this or that corner rather than the others, like a comet: the hall is illuminated everywhere.'[50]

I believe I have said enough to demonstrate that there existed a close relationship between industrialization and the whole bourgeois national-development process. Contemporary thinkers, too, moved from the notion of the nation to recognition of the importance of economics. No retrospective analysis of the period can write this off as mere coincidence. We must face the fact that a strictly economic approach would not have been adequate in Hungary, where economic questions were so deeply embedded in fundamental political categories. The growing independence of the economy from other spheres, as a historical tendency, unfolded fully only in the period of free market capitalism, and it was not until then that practical and scientific criteria for its interpretation became available. To assume that an economic policy developing more or less independently of the conflicts taking place in the separate world of politics was observable as early as the Reform Period would be anachronistic. For purposes of scholarly reconstruction, of course, it can be very useful to view one period in the light of a later, more sophisticated and historically developed one. The indiscriminate application of this method would, however, obscure what is most essential, which is to investigate the place and role of the subject under investigation within a given complex whole.

As already noted, the study of the various industrialization campaigns provides ample evidence that their importance extended well beyond the economic sphere. However vigorously Kossuth and his circle denied the legitimacy of the adjective 'political' to describe their activities, it is clear that they were in fact involved in an essentially political campaign. (Among contemporaries this was also Széchenyi's assessment.) The same is true of the whole argumentation of reform, given that economics and politics became organically linked both in the public mind and in actual historical processes.

One cannot separate economic questions from politics. In Hungary the most basic economic objectives had a direct political charge: the mere existence of a national economy was a political demand and, one might add, inevitably so. ('In this country it is a question of politics even whether someone buys Brunn cloth or cloth of a domestic make,' as the popular phrase had it.)

This explains why Kossuth chose List's theory, with the nation at its centre, for adaptation to Hungary, rather than Adam Smith's, which is patently more germane to free market capitalism. List's, and so Kossuth's, theory incorporated a political category, the nation, and fitted everything else around it. As already stressed, the whole argumentation of the reform opposition focused on the economy, but this was mostly to attain political ends. These arguments sought to enable social strata otherwise excluded from the political sphere actively to participate in it. To summarize, reform opposition arguments were decisively characterized by political rationality and a determination to win the support of all social classes.

Our conclusions could also bring us closer to understanding the question of feudal and bourgeois nationalism that has given rise to so much polemic. Briefly, and most importantly, reform opposition arguments served to promote bourgeois transformation; in order to achieve this, it was necessary to move forward from feudal conditions, but only insofar as this did not alienate the nobility, the reform opposition's own most important constituent element. As we have seen, this dualism gave rise to a number of contradictions and constraints but it nevertheless succeeded in promoting its aim. In the given political circumstances society could no longer retain its feudal structure in a pure form, but neither was it ready to become fully bourgeois. In this period feudal nationalism could exist side by side with bourgeois nationalist trends, depending on what social issue was being addressed. This was an inevitable by-product of bourgeois transformation.

In this situation the politician acted as a synthesist for a number of different endeavours; he had to incorporate, penetrate and resolve problems over the full range of social and economic life. In such an environment the economy could function only if it was directly politicized, and, conversely, all political thought was projected onto the economy. Bourgeois and *citoyen*, a duality which as an abstraction represents a theoretical aid to an understanding of capitalist development, were not two different entities in the Reform Period but, on the contrary, were united in the shared need for independent bourgeois national development in Hungary.

(1978)

Notes

1 *Hetilap* (hereafter *HL*), 1845/1.
2 Adolf Gyurmán (ed.), *Magyar Szózatok* (hereafter *MSZ*), Hamburg, 1847, p. 79.
3 *MSZ*, pp. 79–80.
4 *MSZ*, pp. 79–80.
5 *HL*, 1845/8.
6 *Pesti Hírlap* (hereafter *PH*), 1842/150.

7 *HL*, 1845/58.
8 Domokos Kosáry, *Kossuth és a Védegylet* [Kossuth and the Association for Mutual Assistance], Budapest, 1942, p. 37.
9 *HL*, 1845/2.
10 *MSZ*, p. 84.
11 *MSZ*, p. 84.
12 *MSZ*, p. 137.
13 Dr. Gyula Viszota (ed.), *Gróf Széchenyi István írói és hírlapi vitája Kossuth Lajossal* [The Debate between Count István Széchenyi, as Writer and Publicist, and Lajos Kossuth], Part II, Budapest, 1930; Lajos Kossuth, 'Adó' [Tax], p. 889.
14 Friedrich List, *Das Nationale System der Politischen Oekonomie,* [The National System of Political Economy] (Hungarian transl.: József Horn), Budapest, 1940, p. 251.
15 *MSZ*, pp. 72–3.
16 *PH*, 1842/150.
17 *HL*, 1845/8.
18 *MSZ*, p. 69.
19 József Révai, *Marxizmus, népiesség, magyarság* [Marxism, Popularism, Hungarianness], Budapest, 1948, p. 121.
20 Domokos Kosáry, 'Kossuth Lajos harca a feudális és gyarmati elnyomás ellen,' in *Kossuth Emlékkönyv* [Memorial Volume], Budapest, 1952, Vol. I, p. 19.
21 *HL*, 1845/26.
22 *PH*, 1845/15.
23 *PH*, 1845/150
24 *HL*, 1845/90.
25 *PH*, 1842/150.
26 *HL*, 1845/90
27 *HL*, 1846/1.
28 *MSZ*, p. 77.
29 *MSZ*, p. 71.
30 *PH*, 1845/22.
31 *MSZ*, p. 84.
32 *HL*, 1846/41
33 *MSZ*, p. 159.
34 *HL*, 1845/25.
35 *HL*, 1845/34.
36 *PH*, 1843/293.
37 *HL*, 1845/18.
38 Elek Fényes, *Magyarország leírása* [Description of Hungary], Pest, 1847, Part I, p. 71.
39 *PH*, 1841/89.
40 *PH*, 1845/20.
41 *HL*, 1845/8.
42 *HL*, 1845/53.
43 Kosáry, *Kossuth és a Védegylet*, p. 7.
44 *HL*, 1845/58.
45 *PH*, 1843/293.

46 Viszota, *Gróf Széchenyi*, Vol. II, p. 877.
47 Ibid.Vol. II, p. 879.
48 Ibid.Vol. II, p. 857.
49 *MSZ*, p. 76.
50 *Pesti Hírlap*, 1841/22.

3 The Emergence of Bourgeois Thought: Arguments in Favour of the Polish Uprising at the Hungarian Diet of 1832–6

When the Hungarian Diet opened in 1832, the guns were already silent in Poland. The uprising which had broken out at the end of 1830 had been mercilessly suppressed by the Russian army. After the defeat at Ostrolenka, Warsaw capitulated on 7 September 1831. Empowered by his victory, Tsar Nicholas I could declare in his 'Organic Statute' what he had been striving to achieve ever since his coronation in 1825: the dissolution of the Polish Diet, army and ministries, the incorporation of Poland in the Russian Empire, and thereby the abolition of the Polish Constitution created by Alexander I after the Congress of Vienna. The Tsarist regime, even if it did not increase its territorial possessions, significantly strengthened its empire in respect to the powers of absolutism.

While the leading powers participating in the Congress of Vienna did not lift a finger to help Poland – despite the strength of public opinion in favour of action – the Hungarian reform opposition, though lacking a significant power base and the influential voice in world affairs that would come with it, launched a pro-Polish campaign, culminating in a debate on the 'Polish question' in the Lower House of the Diet in November 1833.

The political environment at the time did not favour – to say the least – effective pro-Polish measures. What is more, in September 1833 a secret agreement had been concluded between Austria and Russia. In the Münchengrätz Agreement, the two sides agreed to guarantee each other's territorial integrity, to exercise surveillance over those who had participated in the uprising and to inform each other of anything which might serve to threaten their mutual peace. Finally, the two sides agreed to assist each other in case of war, be it civil or international. But it was not necessary to be aware of this secret diplomacy to understand that, under the current circumstances of European grand politics, foreign intervention in whatever form on the side of Poland against Tsarist absolutism would not be tolerated. The delegate of Szatmár County in the Hungarian Diet – the poet Ferenc Kölcsey – wrote in his diary on 11 January 1833:

> Men of that dejected country! We bear your grief in our hearts; we shall make bold and brilliant speeches in your favour; our petition may awaken the sympathy of the ruler towards you; but what is the use? When Louis Philippe and his people have let you down, when in Wilson's land there is none who would take up arms to defend you, what can you expect from a nation that wears only a blunted sword, and then only on the occasion of pompous ceremony?[1]

It was not only recognition of the limitations of Hungarian foreign policy that inspired such a view. In response to the goodwilled and pompous words of László Palóczy to the effect that in Borsod County – for which he was the delegate – thirty thousand noblemen were ready to take up arms in support of the Poles, Kölcsey remarked: 'The thirty thousand noblemen of Borsod that Palóczy referred to, even the seven hundred thousand that may be found in the whole country, would soon disperse as soon as actions rather than words were required. My good friends! We don't seem to know each other well enough. When you see a chest that does not mean that there is also a heart within it.'[2] Kossuth also hinted, as early as 1831, that there was not much chance of taking effective action – although in his case the obstacle was the resistance of the royal court – referring to 'the doubtful success of our petition'.[3]

In view of all this, one would be justified in asking: what motivated the Hungarian reformers to intercede for the Polish people? Why was this issue important to them? Answering these questions will also reveal whether their action can be counted as a success or a failure. As so often with the reform movement the whole affair has implications well beyond the nominal point at issue. The political action taken by Hungarian opposition reformers offered very few prospects from the very beginning, so the fact that they nevertheless embarked on their campaign must be attributed either to ignorance and naiveté – which can be excluded – or to motives which are not immediately apparent. What is important here is not so much the actual course of events as the set of arguments underlying them; only the latter can provide us with the key to understanding the causes and assessing the consequences.[4]

The first petition to the sovereign in support of Poland from Bars county is dated 3 May 1831. The petition emphasized that although Vienna had been saved from the Turks with the Polish King Sobieski's help, the Habsburg Empire had as a rule been left to its own devices in its struggle with the Ottomans. The petition continues:

> And indeed, if we summon up memories of the once-great power of the Ottoman Empire and its wars with the Byzantine Empire, we cannot fail

to recollect the sad fact that the latter was abandoned and so crushed by the force of Turkish weapons, and that now its fate has been handed down to us. The many vicissitudes that our homeland has gone through and the recurrence of historical events should serve as a warning that it is time at last to restrain the Northern Colossus located so close to us, not by succession or the free choice of the people but by armed force. And so, if we pay back Poland for having once fought dauntlessly for our independence and survival, we are at the same time protecting our own interests; if we now abandon the Poles, not yet defeated but severely outnumbered by the enemy, our posterity may find themselves in a similar peril and unable to stand up to this same enemy and they shall then bitterly regret that Sobiesky is no more.[5]

It was further demanded that the Diet be summoned and orders hindering Hungarian/Polish trade or resulting in the closure of borders between Hungary and Poland be revoked. The petition submitted by Bars County – which was initiated by their delegate János Balogh in the Lower House of the Diet – was dominated by a desire to halt the expansion of Russian influence and to promote the county's commercial interests. This petition did not make particularly telling points concerning domestic policy, but it is of considerable significance because of its orientation towards the protection of particular economic interests and its intention to influence foreign policy with likely ramifications for the whole nation. The wording of the petition suggests an opposition not simply to Russian expansion but to absolutist and militarist regimes as such. The moderate wording of the Bars petition, however, contributed to the fact that 33 counties finally came out in support of it.

Some of these counties, while supporting the 'Polish cause', introduced new elements and put a new slant on the matter. On 23 June 1831, Kossuth delivered a speech at the Zemplén County Assembly in Sátoraljaújhely. This speech on the one hand foreshadows the tone of the debate which was to commence two years later in the Lower House of the Diet, and faithfully reflects the endeavours of the Hungarian reform opposition overall.

[The Poles] . . . in their struggle with the formidable power extending its autocratic rule over one-sixth of the territory of the known world, are giving their lives by the thousand in a desperate battle, not only for their homeland but for the freedom of the whole of Europe threatened by the shackles of the Northern Colossus, and for the triumph of civilization, which the northern barbarians have reduced to savagery. Europe and anyone who loves freedom and the rule of law, who loathes the leaden scourge of absolutism and falls into despair at the mere thought of the danger threatening all Europe's thrones and peoples, cast their abhorring gaze upon St Petersburg, in fear that if the heroic Poles should fall, the hideous ruler of the Arctic Ocean will build bridges from their corpses to carry its countless hordes while they flood the more gentle parts of Europe – the Polish cause is the cause of Europe.

And, Kossuth's speech continued:

> We believe ourselves to be free citizens of a constitutional state and not slaves. One of the most sacred legacies that we have is freedom of thought and its natural companion, the right to freedom of speech. Deceit is more effective when it can work under cover of darkness: the free Hungarian nation should have the right to speak its mind; we are loyal subjects of the King but also part of the majesty of the legislative body, and if we are entitled to inner courage and care of public welfare, we are all the more entitled and, what is more, it is our duty to monitor the barometer of our country's foreign policy, and it is expedient to consider constitutional ways of averting any danger threatening the stability of the throne or our independence. Our steps should never be guided by merce-nary aims alone, but when we want to restore the ancient heritage of the heroic Polish nation of which they could be stripped only by sacrilegious force bearing the mark of political vice, their interests merge with our interests and so the interests of the whole of Europe. The Hungarian people are right in believing that by showing humane feelings and grati-tude they are fulfilling their duty to the good of their nation and king. If a nation freely stating its sovereign opinion deserves respect I regard the assertion of the people's will as the fulfilment of our civic duty to the homeland, and accordingly, cowardly silence would be a civic vice.[6]

The basic tone of Kossuth's reasoning is set by a very distinct liberal-bourgeois consciousness – in considerable contrast to the tone of the Bars application it was seeking to support. Kossuth's argument focused upon the civil rights which go together with the bourgeois condition; individual rights become collective rights and are manifested in representative national sover-eignty. From this it follows that the nation has the right to express its opinion on both domestic and foreign policy; what is more, it is its duty to do so. Civil freedom and national sovereignty are the key concepts in his assessment. In this way he supported the reform opposition's endeavours to bring about the emergence of a civil society through the introduction of civil values into Hungarian feudal conditions.

Discussion of the Polish question was one way of expanding freedom of speech in Hungary, and it allowed political self-determination to become a matter for parliamentary debate. Russia represented a threat not only because of its size and territorial ambitions, but because it was an absolutist regime, the most bitter and dangerous adversary of liberal-bourgeois devel-opment. The significance of the Polish liberation movement for those committed to civil freedom, therefore, was not only that it opposed the army of a great power, but, most importantly, that it thereby carried on the struggle against despotism. The geographical proximity of Russia made the Hungarian transformation process vulnerable. Congruence of European and Hungarian interests was possible only if a bourgeois transformation took place in Hungary and if expansionist Tsarist absolutism stood in the way of the formation of an appropriate political framework for bourgeois development. To take a political stand against autocratic Russia was to take a stand in favour of the emergence of a civil society in Hungary, and – regardless of its success or failure – was likely to lead to a curbing of domestic absolutist tendencies and promotion of the slowly emerging free will of the nation. Quick success being far from guaranteed, political demands were sublimated into a moral commandment: 'A nation with moral integrity must never let itself be guided by expediency; it should only take care that whatever it does is dictated by duty and good conscience.'[7] It is obvious that the triad of civil freedom, a national interest formulated in its spirit and the taking of a moral stand, each supporting the others, was directed towards the realization of bourgeois political norms and the constitution of bourgeois consciousness as a political morality.

By the time of the Diet, the 'Polish question' had already given rise to the expression of grievances in the Lower House because the Emperor had failed to respond to county petitions on the subject. This left no doubt that, for the Metternich regime, the rebels represented a far greater threat than those trying to suppress them. Many minor details seem to support this interpretation, such as the anti-Polish closure of Hungary's northern border and the unfriendly attitude towards Polish refugees. In addition, the Palatine, the highest administrative dignitary in feudal Hungary, was less than enthusiastic about committing himself to the Polish cause, given that since the death of Tsaritsa Alexandra he had been drawing an annuity of two hundred thousand forints. His sole interest in pro-Polish activities was in finding out what he had to put a stop to.

Coming, as it did, after the suppression of the Uprising, the debate of the Polish question in the Hungarian Diet was inevitably restricted to symbolic actions. The Polish question was first brought up at a district session of the Diet on 28 December 1832. At this meeting, some speakers voiced their general disapproval of official policy, and Palóczy, the Borsod County delegate, said: 'When one king dies all the other kings go into mourning, so how can all free nations not go into mourning over the moral death of another free nation?'[8] This was, however, not enough to persuade the Diet to debate the Polish question as a grievance of its own. This had to wait until November 1833.

At the district session of the Diet held on 20 November 1833, Balogh, the Bars delegate, brought up the Polish question again. His speech was far more radical than the petition that he had worded two and a half years before and pointed essentially in the same direction as Kossuth's Zemplén speech. National freedom and constitutional rights he interpreted as natural rights which must be protected even when they were not granted by kings and emperors. He continued in a rather elevated style:

> I would ask you: what has become of the nation which has been murdered four times in a single century, partly as its undeserved fate and partly as a result of the low standard of European politics? The answer is as follows: those who owed their lives and everything they had to their homeland and who later on sacrificed all this to maintain the violated Constitution now inhabit the wilds of Siberia; those to whom future generations will build memorials are now forced to live as beggars in foreign lands. But they are forbidden even that much by cowardly politicians, and if we asked of the deadly silence now hanging over Warsaw: where has the heroic Polish nation gone, the answer would be: at the hearth of this once free and great nation the uncouth Muscovite now warms himself. Can we close our eyes to all this, can we cold-bloodedly watch as the first strongholds of European civilization are destroyed, thereby breaking down the gate and opening the way for the realization of Russian expansionist desires? The most important guarantee of the constitution of a free nation is the maintenance of the freedom of its neighbours; the termination of the freedom of one inevitably leads to the shaking of that of the others, and this is how free nations acquire brotherly love and compassion for one another. How can our homeland expect other free nations to support and protect it if it plays the part of a mere spectator in this national tragedy whose finale is the hideous suppression of the sacred rights of humankind?[9]

It is interesting how specific features of Hungarian bourgeois development are incorporated in this line of argument based upon natural law. The passage on the one hand calls for solidarity with the Polish nobility fighting for their constitutional rights, and on the other makes reference to the requirements of reciprocity. Hungary's bourgeois transformation process might also find itself in a tight spot in which the support of the Poles, now defeated in their struggle against a common enemy, might be needed. Beyond the implications that the outcome of the Polish struggle against absolutism had for the present, the long-term prospects were of fundamental importance. Where there existed an alliance between absolutist regimes, those in pursuit of constitutional rights could not afford to overlook similar relations.

At the same district session, Kölcsey also appealed to natural law when he said the following: 'A free nation must ask its king to protect its freedoms; in doing so we are fulfilling our natural duty before God and Man and this is both a profitable and an honourable thing to do.'[10] That is – as I pointed out in connection with Kossuth's Zemplén speech – the sovereign *must* represent the will of the people as embodied in their parliamentary representatives, and this is not only his constitutional but his moral duty. Here we encounter once more the transformation of the bourgeois ideal of freedom into a moral category; and vice versa, morality dictated that a stand must be taken for bourgeois freedom. The two are closely connected: ethics and political interest on the one hand, and the representation of values on the other, were mutually legitimizing.

Finally, the Polish question was discussed at the national session of the Diet on 23 November 1833. This was an excellent forum for the confrontation between reform-opposition arguments and those of their opponents. The tone of the debate continued to be set by the desire – on the part of both the royal court and the majority of county delegates – to ignore the Polish question. The problem formulated by Kölcsey himself therefore arose once again: 'Why petition His Majesty the King when we know in advance that our request will fall on deaf ears?'[11] What is more, the opponents of reform listed a number of effective and very pragmatic arguments. The Chief Justice began his speech with the assertion that, for one thing, there was no hope at all of any proposal going through, and furthermore:

> When the Estates debate the good of the homeland and are engaged in the making of laws the effects of which may be felt for centuries to come, they cannot divert themselves with foreign countries; the real power of the nation lies in its sound inner structure and it should be assured that this inner structure serves the flourishing of the homeland. When this has been secured, [the Chief Justice] will fear nothing because . . . our constitution will be able to withstand any danger.[12]

He therefore proposed on behalf of the royal court that the debate on the Polish question be dropped: 'We were elected [to the Diet] to strengthen our own constitution and not to concern ourselves with those of other nations. Freedom itself does not allow us to interfere with the affairs of other nations.'

The delegate from Esztergom County, the conservative József Andrássy, representing the views of the counties opposed to a debate on the Bars proposal, urged the House not to deviate from its regular work:

> As a private individual I too looked in amazement at the heroic deeds of the Polish nation humbled by a mighty power and at its efforts which seemed to surpass what was humanly possible and I very much regretted the sour fruits of these efforts. As a legislator, however, my attention must be directed to at least two things: (1) should, and (2) can the independence of the Polish nation be restored by the Hungarian Diet or as a result of its intervention? The answer to the first question is a clear no. My right

honourable friends, what could we do to assist the Polish nation in achieving its independence? What could we request from his Majesty in our petition? Should we enter into a war for the Polish cause? I believe my right honourable friends to be wiser than to want to rekindle a fire in Europe from sparks now buried beneath the ashes, a fire that could rage for centuries, so endangering the whole continent, and our homeland with it. Even if I were to assume that my right honourable friends were unaware of the weakness of our position and that therefore diplomacy was the only thing left for us, despite the fact that I am little knowledgeable on matters of diplomacy, the little knowledge I have tells me that the path of diplomacy and paltering with public opinion do not usually attain the desired effect. If we were to make a petition we would no doubt seek an affirmative answer, thereby putting our government into a difficult position. Each of us can see for himself and it is my firm conviction that this would do more harm than good to the Poles. Or is it that my right honourable friends intend to use this petition as a mouthpiece for our desires without expecting an answer? I would find this irreconcilable with the nation's dignity: I do not support Bars County's proposal and indeed I find any such approach to be ill-advised.[13]

In Andrássy's view the counties brought great discredit upon themselves by persisting with the Polish question in defiance of the fact that it was hopeless from the outset. Although he considered what was happening in Poland regrettable, Andrássy remarked: 'Nations come into being and nations pass away.' However regrettable it might seem, espousal of the Polish cause would be little more than a pointless rebellion against the laws of history, quite apart from any more concrete and extremely unpleasant consequences that might ensue.

In regard to the call for the Diet to devote itself to home affairs instead of foreign politics, opinions differed. It is worth looking at why the Sopron County delegate, the openly conservative Pál Felsőbüki Nagy – from a more consistent conservative foreign-policy standpoint – believed it important to curb Russian expansion and, more generally, to take a stand on questions of foreign policy. According to Felsőbüki Nagy, the Russian action was in breach of the resolutions of the Congress of Vienna because it threatened stability in the region. Felsőbüki Nagy condemned:

. . . the dangerous teaching in accordance with which even the holiest alliance is only binding until brute force dissolves it. On this basis how can nations be expected to respect agreements concluded between them and between their sovereigns when these sovereigns hold each other in contempt? Finally, I would ask: does not the subversion of the Polish constitution and the incorporation of that country in the Russian Empire bring down the reputation of his Majesty, who at the Congress of Vienna was, as King of Hungary, the most committed of the sovereigns present to the maintenance of neighbouring Poland's independence? Who can blame us Hungarians if, when debating our domestic affairs, we cannot overlook foreign acts of bravery and look to neighbouring lands anxiously, when a great power which three years ago we knew only distantly and by its hunger for new territories now stretches along three-quarters of our border. Now that Poland has been destroyed this power has encircled us even further and I say it is indeed time for us to wake up. If his Majesty, who is personally respected by all European sovereigns, could live forever and the Ministry continue to do all that lies in its power to preserve peace, our worries might be misplaced, but if this cannot be done and if not this but another Tsar were to extend his territories so much further that Austria had to take up arms crying 'non plus ultra!', would not then our beloved Homeland become the stage of hideous war or even prey to a victorious enemy?[14]

As is clear from Felsőbüki Nagy's comments, the right to influence foreign policy, and the existence of an outlet for public opinion, were essential also for those not directly involved with the political establishment but concerned about political and – in connection with this – social stability. These demands were by no means abstract; after all, a great power had suddenly loomed large on Hungary's borders. In Palóczy's view the main point was also the direct threat to Hungary:

What weight is there in the objection that some have already made in the British and the French parliaments, their words however falling on deaf ears? They are not as concerned as we [Hungarians], because can the British, the favourites of Neptune, have any reason to fear that this growing power in the north will snatch the trident from their hands? They are turning their gaze to Tiflis, Yerevan and Tehran, to ensure that they cannot be cut off from India in the east. Why should the French army numbering 1,000 battalions fear this northern power so far away? . . . And their government too is turning its gaze more to the south-western penin- sula than anywhere else. Let us take a look at the map of Europe. From Olmitz to Zimony, at the frontiers of the Austrian Empire, the Northern Colossus is encountered everywhere. I heard at the district session of the Diet that some counties have ordered their delegates not to dabble in anything else, but to press on with their regular work. Our home affairs come first and we are not to worry about the troubles of others. It is easy to say this, but to what does it lead? It is true enough that the preparation of a nationwide petition would take weeks or even months and that regular legislation alone can lay the foundations of the prosperity of our Homeland, but is this everything? . . . What about our obligations abroad? Are they not one of our most sacred duties?[15]

Palóczy took a stand in favour of greater concern with foreign affairs not only in view of the very real expansionist threat, but also because of his commitment to bringing foreign policy under the control of the legislative body: he regarded foreign affairs as just as much an organic part of national sovereignty as domestic self-determination. In response to Andrássy's objection he said: 'Are we indeed doing great harm by submitting a petition; is there nothing to be gained from it? I believe the opposite to be true. The quill of ministerial diplomacy is more weighty and more influential when it expresses the joint will of the sovereign and the nation.'[16] In this way Palóczy took a stand in favour of the public determination of foreign policy by a representative body, as opposed to court diplomacy behind closed doors. The public debate of political issues he regarded as unquestionably the best method, adherence to which would lead to more consistent and open policymaking. Such an approach also entailed the reaching of consensus on government policy between sovereign and parliament, thereby eliminating, among other things, absolutist tendencies in domestic affairs.[17]

This line of reasoning brings us back, once again, to the relevance of the Polish question to Hungarian domestic politics: nothing less than bourgeois political freedom in Hungary was at stake. For the sake of this freedom it was necessary progressively to eradicate absolutist tendencies within Hungary, if necessary by turning public opinion, however powerless, against it. As Balogh put it: 'Does not the murder of the neighbouring Polish nation shake our constitution to its very foundations? My right honourable friends, we pass even the best laws in vain when a Hydra with a hundred heads is curling around our hearts, only one of whose hungry mouths could easily devour us. The duty of a legislative body is not only the making of prudent and timely laws, but the safeguarding of the constitution in every way . . . '[18] The metaphor of the 'Hydra with a hundred heads' – as the political jargon of the time had it – was an obvious reference to the absolutist regime, the exercise of power without public accountability. Kölcsey's diary entry for 15 June 1833 makes this clear:

At some sessions of the Diet a grievance about anonymous traitors was aired. These anonymous traitors are none other than the 'geheime Polizey' as they are called in the sacred Austrian language, aptly referred to in Diet documents as 'the Hydra' as early as 1825. The heads of this thousand-times cursed hydra are multiplying from year to year and by God's will we have lived to see them head our highest and a considerable number of lower offices; and even outside the sphere of state administration the multitude of the breadeating nation is swarming with them. We should not think that this multitude is devoid of order and spirit, because this immoderately ramifying hydra, as it spreads invisible to the eye, keeps returning just as invisibly to the same centre which directs its every movement. It is hardly necessary for me to talk about this centre in more detail.[19]

Here the Polish question once again turns out to be closely intertwined with the domestic constraints faced by the Hungarian reformers. And the more, in these circles, that free expression came to be regarded as natural, and the more opportunities to propagate bourgeois values they took advantage of, the less room to manoeuvre the 'Hydra' found itself with.

Viewed in this light, even the making of demands doomed from the outset was not in vain. Taking up a position as the opposite pole to authority was functionally very important, and their lack of power was merely temporary. What became important was how successfully the opposition fulfilled their mission and how ably they recognized opportunities and risks lying ahead. On the Polish question the opposition reformers passed with flying colours. The problem was most clearly formulated by Dénes Borsiczky, the Trencsén delegate:

> Not only shall the Polish constitution granted by the Congress of Vienna descend into the grave together with the Polish nation – the overall plan is to crush the constitutional principle altogether. Although I am fully aware of the majestic virtues of our good sovereign, and I do not fear that the Hungarian constitution will be crushed (while divine providence allows him to remain with us for our greater good), and although I wish with my whole heart that he should live and reign over us for many centuries to come, I am sad when I recall that even his majesty is merely mortal and so the Hungarian constitution, now guarantied by his person, will have to be strengthened by further guarantees for the future. It is therefore our duty to observe the pattern of events currently unfolding in Northern Europe, because at a time when all other constitutions are being overthrown we have no reason to believe that the Hungarian constitution would alone survive.[20]

The 'export' of Russian absolutism – given the fact that even in Hungary there were some who were by no means averse to it – represented a fundamental threat to Hungarian bourgeois transformation. Resistance to it was an essential concomitant of any political intentions towards the emergence of a civil society. Resistance to the export of Russian absolutism meant the rejection of all non-constitutional, autocratic regimes, without, however, losing sight of the realities of the current political situation. What was required were guarantees furnished by institutions and the popular will, rather than by individuals. At the same time, it was important to combat the widespread but illusory notion of an 'island of constitutionality': it was absurd to believe that Hungarian constitutionality could survive in an ocean of absolutism.

The recognition of political interests was very much enhanced by liberal political values. In this case – and in many other instances involving Kossuth and his circle – these abstract values dictated a particular ethical standpoint, in connection with which a commitment to liberal political values and interests thus became defensible and, what is more, imperative. The picture of a harmonious combination of ethical and political commitments emerges clearly from the words of Kölcsey and Ferenc Deák. Kölcsey was referring to his political actions' lack of direct impact when he said:

> It is not the habit of a compassionate man to calculate with mathematical precision the success of his benefaction; instead he must readily undertake what the movement of his heart dictates. If a man whose possessions were ravished by an enemy, fire or some other mishap, were to come and ask for help, would it be humane to answer him in this manner: Poor devil! I cannot give you much and that little would not help you: therefore you shall not get anything from me. My right honourable friends, is it not the will of humankind that we should give this man what we can, because when a little is given by many, enough is given in the end?[21]

Deák responded to Andrássy's historical and philosophical lucubrations by saying:

> Nations die, nations are born. These are the words of the respectable delegate of Esztergom County. I do not think, however, that he meant to say anything original with this because history provides us with an abundance of examples of one nation rising while another declines: but the history of the world does not teach us to stand coldly aside when another nation is in danger of sinking into an abyss. Because individuals are born and die, too: and it is then our duty to do everything in our power to save our fellow men in extreme peril or suffering from destitution.[22]

Both Kölcsey and Deák were speaking from a moral conviction deeply embedded in European culture and based on the teachings of the Bible. They ascribed traditional values such as humanity and decency to the struggle for freedom. Their arguments put the holders of power onto the moral defensive. They well knew that to challenge the moral legitimacy of the actions of those in power was an important step towards the wider acceptance of a new system of values. Equally, if not more importantly, they equated ethical behaviour with the liberal expansion of rights and the shaping of a liberal consciousness. This suggested that an affinity with certain political values should be based on moral conviction, and that an ethical commitment should result in an understanding of political interests with implications beyond the present.

This was a new kind of pragmatism, turning away increasingly consciously from short-term success and driven by conviction, an approach with much better prospects of political success. The concordance emerging between bourgeois humanist moral conviction and political commitment strengthened the position of those with a critical mind, arming them with a manifold sensitivity and greater effectiveness. The novelty of this pragmatism was its theoretical edge. And however strange it seems to talk of 'theoretical pragmatism', it was in great contrast with a politics incapable of seeing beyond the task of daily survival.

One could, of course, object that it is all too easy to advocate high principles when one is in opposition and that these same principles would vanish into thin air as soon one ascended to power. But such a view would be too simplistic. The emergence of theoretical pragmatism established a norm *for itself* as much as for anybody else because it introduced into the political sphere bourgeois values binding on *all*, rendering everyone accountable for his actions the instant he deviated from them. The separation of ethics and politics would result in the stabilization of the prevailing attitude of 'naive daydreaming' and 'cynical self interest', as a consequence of which only one kind of pragmatism would be possible. In the case under discussion, a successful attempt was made to harmonize values and interests, so making possible the resolution of the conflict of roles and the integration of the principle of theoretical pragmatism into the world of politics as a viable basis for action rather than as an alien element. The Hungarian reform opposition did their country an invaluable service when they brought about this concordance and focused their efforts on the creation of a system of political institutions within the framework of which these new political norms could become universal and so direct all political action.

The Polish question provided a suitable platform for the discussion of a whole range of wider issues, broadening the scope of domestic political action. At the same time, it allowed the adherents of bourgeois development to make use of lessons learnt from the Polish question in their scheme to bring forth a civil society. In November 1834, Balogh once again raised the question of the Polish Uprising. In connection with a debate on questions of socage he said the following in support of manumission:

Poland was the only remaining country, before it was crushed by the Northern Colossus, in which serfs were doomed to eternal servitude, but I am probably not mistaken in saying that it would have liberated its serfs prior to the national uprising if it had followed the example of Kosciusko, an outstanding figure whose heroic actions will forever be recorded in the book of world history as so many irrefutable principles, and who in his letter of concession written from Solothurn granted eternal freedom to the serfs who had been given to him by the state: had the Polish nation followed his example the heroes of Poland would probably not now have to freeze in Siberia nor would they be forced to try to warm themselves at the fireplaces of other nations. Because a nation can be great, free and strong in spite of oppression if each class shakes hands with the others and they all shout together: Long live the Constitution![23]

A critical approach to the uprising in Poland suggested that a reconciliation of interests was required and was linked – similarly to all other arguments on the Polish question – to the struggle for the emergence of a civil society in Hungary.[24] This was not simply anti-feudal rhetoric, but also meant taking an active role: the Diet served as a weapon against feudal absolutism and a vehicle to introduce social norms incompatible with it, with the end of making liberal freedom and representation the norm.

The indirect significance of the Polish question lay precisely in this. In a broader sense, one could say that it lay in the *emergence of bourgeois thinking*, in the creation of moral and political values. For this purpose it was essential consciously to improve the nation's philosophical and political understanding, and allow it to discern more clearly where the future lay amidst the many changes that were taking place at the time, thereby enabling it to transform itself. New norms of political and personal behaviour had to be introduced to assist in the transformation of the subjects of an absolutist regime into citizens. This new way of thinking was firmly opposed to absolutism and so represented one of the major subversive factors in its decline. ('Let us slowly corrode it', in Kossuth's slogan.) Furthermore, such thinking had the great advantage that once it had become generally accepted it was likely to act as a major obstacle in the way of any future autocratic scheme. So, the emergence of bourgeois thinking by its very existence altered reality, widening the scope of political freedom.

I believe there can be no doubt that the outcome of the Polish question – although, of course, it eventually had to be abandoned – was a success rather than a failure for Hungarian domestic politics. Debates on this issue accelerated national self-determination, gave rise to new values and played an important part in the formation of a group of highly skilled politicians who knew exactly what they wanted and who were able to recognize the dangers threatening the Hungarian bourgeois transformation process, such as the absolutist regimes at home and in Tsarist Russia, an external threat to the whole of Eastern Europe. Speeches made in the Hungarian Diet on the Polish question took on tragic overtones when the same country that had sent troops to Poland in 1832 ordered intervention in Hungary in 1849. The general who had occupied Warsaw was the Russian field marshal, Count Paskievich – the same man who would, as commander of the Russian army, help defeat Hungarian Freedom Fighters. But before we surrender to feelings of regret or despair, this was not the end and even less was it the moral of the story.

(1984)

Notes

1   Szauder József and Szauder Józsefné (eds.), *Kölcsey Ferenc összes művei* [The Complete Works of Ferenc Kölcsey] (hereafter *KFÖM*), Budapest, 1960, Vol. 2, p. 396.

2   *KFÖM,* Vol. 2, p. 370.

3   István Barta (ed.), *Kossuth Lajos összes munkái* [The Complete Works of Lajos Kossuth] (hereafter KLÖM), Vol. 6; *Ifjúkori iratok – Törvényhatósági Tudósítások* [Municipal Records], Budapest, 1966, p. 225.

4   For a detailed study of the events in question, see Endre Kovács, *A lengyel kérdés a reformkori Magyarországon* [The Polish Question in Reform Period Hungary], Budapest, 1959. An earlier publication with a reliable index of sources is the work of Adorján Divéky, *Magyarok és lengyelek a XIX. században* [Hungarians and Poles in the Nineteenth Century], Budapest, 1919. For an assessment see: Mihály Horváth, *Huszonöt év Magyarország történelméből 1823–tól 1848–ig* [25 Years of Hungarian History from 1823–48], 2nd Edition, Pest, 1868, Vol. 1, pp. 260–6 and 344–50. Several memoirs contain references to the Polish issue, e.g. *Újfalvi Sándor emlékiratai*, Kolozsvár, 1941; József Madarász, *Emlékirataim 1831–82*, Budapest, 1833; Ferenc Pulszky, *Életem és korom*, Budapest, 1880. For a study of international conditions, see: István Diószegi: *Klasszikus diplomácia – modern hatalmi politika* [Classical Diplomacy – Modern Power Politics], Budapest, 1972, pp. 72–6. On the uprising in Poland see: Zuzanna Stefaniak (ed.), *History of Poland,* 2nd Edition, Warsaw, 1979.

5   Divéky, *Magyarok és lengyelek* [Hungarians and Poles], pp. 105–6.

6   *KLÖM*, Vol. 6, pp. 223–5.

7   *KLÖM*, Vol. 6, p. 225.

8   Lajos Kossuth, *Országgyűlési Tudósítások* [Parliamentary Records] (hereafter *OGyT*), edited (I–III) by the staff of the Institute of Historical Studies, (III) István Barta, (*KLÖM*, Vol. 1), Budapest, 1948, p. 42.

9   *OGyT*, Vol. 2 (*KLÖM*, 2), Budapest, 1949, p. 402.

10   *OGyT*, Vol. 2, pp. 403–4.

11   *OGyT*, Vol. 2, p. 433. On the national session of the Diet see: *Az 1832–ik esztendőben, karácson havának 16–ik napjára rendeltetett Magyar ország gyűlésének jegyzőkönyve* [Protocol of the Hungarian Parliament for the 16 December 1832 Session], Pozsony, 1832/33, V., 143th session, pp. 433–59. Quotations are taken from Kossuth's *Országgyűlési Tudósítások*, partly because I could not find a significant difference between it and the original, and partly because the Kossuth edition is supplemented with explanatory footnotes and is therefore more comprehensible.

12   *OGyT*, Vol. 2, p. 418.

13   *OGyT*, Vol. 2, p. 436.

14   *OGyT*, Vol. 2, pp. 448–9.

15   *OGyT*, Vol. 2, p. 449.

16   *OGyT*, Vol. 2, p. 426.

17   The delegate of Arad County, Ravazdy, strengthened this position by saying: 'My answer is yes to the question of whether this is a suitable place to discuss

the affairs of other nations. The nation has a right to do so, because if the government can intervene in the affairs of other nations in Bologna, Ancona, etc., then the free nation who pays for the army must also have a say.' *OGyT*, Vol. 2, p. 446. Ravazdy objected to the use of troops – partly financed by Hungary – to suppress revolutionary movements in Italy and called for foreign policy to be controlled by the Diet.

18 *OGyT*, Vol. 2, p. 418.
19 *KFÖM*, Vol. 2, p. 581.
20 *OGyT*, Vol. 2, p. 445.
21 *OGyT*, Vol. 2, p. 434.
22 *OGyT*, Vol. 2, pp. 441–2. See also: *Deák Ferenc beszédei* [The Speeches of Ferenc Deák], collected by Manó Kónyi, Budapest, 1903, Vol. 1, pp. 43–6.
23 *OGyT*, Vol. 3 (*KLÖM*, 3), Budapest, 1949, pp. 702–3.
24 The scope of this study does not allow me to deal with the effect of the uprising in Poland as a whole on the Hungarian reform movement and its organization. The mobilization of the counties, the injection of a reform element into the politics of grievances, the formation of an information network, the role of the younger generation of parliamentary representatives, etc., were all important factors deserving consideration. Kölcsey's diary contains a number of entries on the subject of the difficulties encountered in the course of shaping the profile of the opposition. This question is particularly exciting because the period of the 1832–6 Diet was crucially important for the formation of the reform opposition as a group.

4 Count Széchenyi and the Conflicts of Modernity

Posterity has analysed and assessed both the person and the work of Count István Széchenyi from various points of view and on the basis of different tables of value.[1] As a result, we have a colourful picture of the Count's personality and achievements, befitting a great historical figure.

But there is a particularly important aspect of Count Széchenyi that the ramified and sometimes absurdly interwoven texture of these historiographies, cults and countercults has never disputed, namely that he was the embodiment of the great modernizer. From whatever angle they are looked at, the Count's actions reveal a man dedicated to the modernization of Hungary. Even the influential monograph by Gyula Szekfű, in which Széchenyi is described as a conservative reformer 'in the name of God', does not call this into question.[2]

Modernity and modernization are sometimes equated with the process of civilization and on this basis the Count could also be dubbed the 'Hungarian civilizer' *par excellence*. But it is very important to recognize Széchenyi's contributions to the infrastructural or material as well as the 'spiritual' sides of this process.

Under the former may be listed the regulation of waterways, bridge and railway construction, the introduction of steamboat navigation and the elaboration of a scheme of transportation, to mention only a few. If we complement this notion of material civilization with the notion of the *civilized man* as it was understood at the time – primarily on the English model – Széchenyi's labours are no less impressive. The aspects of 'spiritual' civilization to which the Count contributed include such diverse matters as personal hygiene, fashion, leisure activities (skating and rowing were introduced to Hungary at around this time), a more refined use of the vernacular, the emergence of linguistic norms based on different forms of social contact (with, for example, separate forms for formal encounters), and new forms of social life for the middle and upper classes.

2   Count István Széchenyi, 1835

The emergence of both the material and the spiritual aspects of civilization goes hand in hand with a fairly clear understanding of what is undesirable if civilization is to develop smoothly: backwardness and traditionalism, regardless of their embodiment (materially, the dust and mud on the streets of Pest; spiritually, a quasi-Asian mentality). Széchenyi rejected these as strongly as he advocated their counterparts.[3] Indeed, in the name of the new and the modern, he tended to reject the past as a whole. In his book *Credit*, he writes: 'I do not, I confess, look back into the past as assiduously as many of my fellow men, I rather look ahead; I care less to know "what we used to be" than to look into "what we are and what we could become."'[4] Indeed, the famous concluding line of *Credit* – 'Many think that Hungary has been; I like to believe that it will be!' – may be interpreted as an expression of Széchenyi's rejection, in the name of a putative and much desired modernity, of a pervading orientation towards 'tradition' prompted by recollections of past greatness and glory.

As far as material development is concerned, Count Széchenyi was always an unyielding adversary of traditionalism. In respect to spiritual civilization – the existing nature of which hindered the consistent enforcement of norms of 'civilized human behaviour' – Széchenyi took up a position against the traditional feudal-aristocratic world-view, life-style and behavioural norms as a matter of principle, though perhaps not without a certain inner hesitation.

His position was made somewhat easier by the fact that the conflict between modernity and traditionalism is an 'external' one, in the sense that for the advocate of modernity there can be no doubt about what is to be rejected, at least from an ideological and rational standpoint. Such thoroughgoing rejection is not so easy at the political and the personal levels.

The matter becomes more complicated when the modernizer and agent of civilization is confronted by the *internal* conflicts of modernity, particularly when they are also a historical novelty for his society. Internal conflicts are inherent in both the development of material civilization and the desire to facilitate it. Anyone calling for the establishment of a modern system of credit as an indispensable structural element of a modern, industrial society and who finds that its emergence is being blocked by aristocratic privilege; or embarking on a project of bridge construction, only to face the absurd situation of being unable to collect tolls from members of the aristocracy – an essential element in the financing of the project – because of their traditional exemptions, cannot avoid taking up politics. The source of internal conflict here is not the political goals to be achieved: they are a logical product of taking a stand in favour of modernization. The right to buy and sell private property, equitable distribution of taxation, equality before the law and other related demands have no source of conflict in themselves. Conflict here is a result of the fact that some individuals take longer than others in drawing these logical conclusions. The logical and the historical principles are different in nature.

The principal internal conflict of modernity lies in the determination of who shall be called upon to 'set right' time that is 'out of joint', and how. Methodology and agency are intrinsically related issues: does the road to a modern, civilized Hungary pass through liberalism or absolutism? More generally, does liberalism or absolutism form an organic part of modernity?

In the grip of liberty

We know the answer, based on the development of Great Britain, the United States and Germany in the nineteenth and twentieth centuries: modernity can emerge both under liberty and under absolutism. This political – and so personal and ethical – ambivalence lies heavily on modernity and has been the main source of its inner conflicts.

Széchenyi was destined to experience modernity under both liberty and absolutism in nineteenth-century Hungary. The public liberties of 1848 and the neo-absolutism of the 1850s both accepted – if with different points of emphasis – modernity, or at least the civilizing intent of its material aspect. Széchenyi therefore experienced directly what is probably the greatest dilemma of modernity and felt a constant urge to respond to the challenge. Furthermore, it was Széchenyi's generation that was the first in Hungarian public life to encounter this dilemma with complete innocence and inexperience.

The physical rather than the theoretical reality of modernity, combined with public liberty, forced Széchenyi to react in March 1848. On 3 March 1848 Kossuth presented a proposal to the Diet in Bratislava (Pozsony). Among other things, the proposal stated: 'Our laws designed to develop constitutionalism and promote the spiritual and material good of our nation can breathe in life and reality only if their implementation is entrusted to a national government independent of foreign interference, responsible to the majority under the Constitution.'[5] In this speech, Kossuth committed himself to eliminating the existing – outdated – political regime and, at the same time, expressed a readiness to 'carry out a reconciliation of interests with the Austrian provinces . . . on the condition that our independent national rights and interests are not violated'.

On the same day, Széchenyi made the following entry in his diary in connection with Kossuth's speech: 'Stupidity has received unanimous approval.'[6] On the following day, Széchenyi contemplated what it would be like if he were to become plenipotentiary. Széchenyi listed his conditions in a casual but quite detailed manner:

Ten thousand forints to be paid by the state plus five thousand forints per month current expenses to be calculated for each meeting, such as lighting, paper and heating.

The Grand Cross of Saint Stephen.

A document drafted by me granting me full powers and to serve as a guarantee.

A free hand in the selection of those I wish to employ.

Everyone must obey me.

All necessary resources.

The Army.

No orders must contradict me – until I am recalled.

Secrecy.

Parliament in 6 months . . .

All opposition circles and political clubs must be dissolved.[7]

The contours of despotism may be discerned here along with an apparent yearning for financial reward and a medal supposedly ensuring moral esteem. This Széchenyi believed that the cause of modernization was only viable in combination with absolutism – as opposed to liberty.[8] Széchenyi's reaction is quite understandable, considering his prominent role in the feudal regime (in 1845, Széchenyi was head of the transport department at the council of the Governor-General); when the council resorted to autocratic means to curb feudal constitutionalism (for example, the 1846 institution of a system of administration) Széchenyi did not feel compelled to resign.

Events rapidly gaining pace, however, prompted him to make an unambiguous choice between the two alternatives and he committed himself to absolutism. On 24 March he made the following entry in his diary: 'As things stand, Man has to give up either himself or others. To hang or to be hanged. What difficult alternatives!'[9]

Difficult alternatives indeed! And what is more, his choice stands in sharp contrast to Széchenyi's self-image as recorded on the same day: 'I have been a reformer. I have never incited anyone to anything. Did not Jesus Christ preach love?' Imagine the reformer, the disciple of Christ, as he hangs Batthyány and Kossuth with the Great Cross of Saint Stephen on his chest and ten thousand forints in his pocket; imagine the Saviour as he kills and the reformer as a dictator with bloodstained hands. Imagine the omnipotent dictator of nation-saving continuity and of nation-saving transformation! The self-image – while remaining imaginary – is at least logical, for all its absurdity. But the demands of realizing this role, with all its inner tensions, would be unbearable, and anyone called upon to play it would surely be broken.

Healthy self-protection alone would be enough to compel one to resolve the absurdity of such a situation, even if no organic link could be established between modernity on the one hand and autocracy or liberty on the other. On 27 March, three days after writing the diary entry about his dilemma, Széchenyi wrote an article, entitled 'What shall become of us Hungarians?'. The article was published in *Pesti Hírlap* and *Jelenkor* on 8 April. Although it makes repeated allusions to the need for order and a solid environment, the article expresses a clear commitment to liberty, constitutional government and personal participation therein. 'A beautiful morning has dawned upon our homeland which has suffered under oppression for so long', Széchenyi wrote. He continued:

> Behold! Within a strictly constitutional framework almost all political conflict has now been stamped out, one Hungarian will sincerely shake hands with another, and look how rapidly we have been moving towards perfection in our development.
>
> A responsible Hungarian government is now in place, millions in our homeland are secure within the ramparts of a constitution, and enjoy benefits which will undoubtedly win the sympathy of the heavenly powers – their benevolence being well deserved – for the Hungarian race. An annual parliament is held in Buda-Pest, its powers resting on the broadest possible consensus through a free press and, consequently, free debate: these are the only certain antidotes to subversion. Who would not rejoice at such an outcome?

Then, turning to personal confession, Széchenyi wrote:

> I idolize liberty, and unlike many others who only wish it for themselves, I wish it for all my fellow-men. I am hoping for the best and only regret my appointment as minister because many will now say: it is easy for him to speak as Cicero pro domo. I would have much preferred – and I am sure the time for that too will soon come – to serve as a common soldier and to exercise bourgeois virtues without being rewarded for it with a medal. That would be just as noble an occupation and just as sacred a duty as my position in the front rank of the state!

But another diary entry contradicts this expression of regret:

> I am feeling more relaxed. People will say that I have played my cards well, à la Talleyrand: I am now a minister . . . and even had Apponyi [i.e. the Metternich regime] won I could have stayed on as a minister. However, I did not play my cards for my personal advantage; zeal was the only vis motrix in me. That is what guided me. And that, why I fell on my feet instead of my behind.[10]

I would argue that the lines in the diary concerning Széchenyi's behaviour, self-image and public role should be given credence, at least in part. Széchenyi did not take the sides of both absolutism and liberty because he was guided by momentary vanity (although vanity was by no means absent – witness the constantly recurring motif of the medal): Széchenyi oscillated between the two extremes because he could not connect the modernity of which he was certainly a representative with either one system or the other. He was entirely sincere in his contradictory commitments as well as in his contradictory choice of roles (plenipotentiary and common soldier).

It is this very sincerity, working at cross-purposes, that suggests that we should also take these diary entries with a pinch of salt. It is particularly doubtful whether the passage in which Széchenyi boasts about his own adeptness ('I fell on my feet') should be taken seriously.

As absurd as the role of hangman-modernizer may be, equally absurd is the sincerity of a 'schizophrenic' mind shaped under the influence of the internal conflicts of modernity. But while the former is immediately apparent, the latter points to the slow destruction of a personality. In the final analysis, this is exactly what happened as Széchenyi was tortured by his dilemmas again and again until September 1848. No one could have coped with the strain of living under such inner tension. Széchenyi's dilemma was inherent in the ambivalence of modernity itself and cannot be explained away on the basis of so-called 'class constraints', political changes, personal ambition, virtues and vices.

The strain on him was so great that at the beginning of 1848 Széchenyi repeatedly tried to commit suicide. His physician sent him to a lunatic asylum.

In the grip of absolutism

By 1856, Széchenyi had recovered from his mental disturbance. While in Döbling he saw that the at once dreaded and beloved demon of liberty had gone, to be replaced by absolutism. One would expect Széchenyi to have been essentially tolerant towards absolutism given that neo-absolutism had nothing against modernization, even if he rejected particular manifestations and excesses. Under the rule of absolutism, railways were being built, legislation on manumission was being introduced and the principle of the equitable distribution of taxation was making headway in Hungary. The situation as seen with the eyes of a modernizer was far from tragic, although it is true that modernization went hand in hand with Germanization which – from a nationalist point of view – called for a negative reaction. One might therefore expect that Széchenyi would sharply condemn Germanization but accept modernization under the auspices of absolutism.

Széchenyi soon had the opportunity to put his views on neo-absolutism in writing in *Önismeret* (Self-knowledge) as it is known in the literature, and then in *Nagy Magyar Szatíra* (Great Hungarian Satire), and in *Blick*.[11] In

Önismeret, certain elements of Széchenyi's dilemma of 1848 regarding the reality of neo-absolutism were once more discernible. Széchenyi wrote: 'Will not people come to esteem democracy of the gallows type higher than the sickening display of stars and ribbons with which the Xerxian army of bootlickers, spitlickers and ass-kissers not long ago became particularly saturated . . . ?' Széchenyi's criticism became ever more ferocious until it extended even to 'hypocrisy and the Austrian system of government founded on lies'.[12]

His words, erupting with the power of a volcano, spared no one: Prince Felix Schwarzenberg, for instance, the deceased 'father' of neo-absolutism was an 'impotent, half-rotten' character. The climax of criticism, however, came with Széchenyi's condemnation of the ruler of Hungary, Franz Joseph. Széchenyi, who had been brought up in a spirit of loyalty to the ruling dynasty, wrote about the Emperor in a manner which is, on that basis, beyond belief. He is described as 'fat, disdainful, heartless, dull-witted, blood-thirsty'. And on top of all this: a murderer. Such a 'person stinking with human blood is despised in their heart of hearts by everyone and there is no praise, ceremony, pomp, festival, bought or forced enthusiasm that would be aromatic enough to suppress the stench of this carrion'. If he died, 'probably not a single human being would feel sorry with the sole exception of his embittered mother – and even that is doubtful'.[13]

One could quote many similar passages from the *Satire*.[14] Strong expressions are recurrent in Széchenyi's assessment of the Emperor. But although we are not furnished with a full and systematic account of current political conditions, Széchenyi's coarse criticism, contravening all accepted standards of decency, gives us strong grounds to assume that the Count rejected the whole of Habsburg neo-absolutism and not just particular elements of it, such as Germanization. This assumption seems to be supported not merely by the tone of the writing – it was not meant to be published – but also by the fact that, under the conditions of neo-absolutism, the Emperor was not only a symbolic figure but the source and manifestation of all power. Széchenyi was fully aware of this. I am not arguing that the reality of absolutism had transformed Széchenyi's views to such an extent that he was now a supporter of unconstrained liberty. Rather, his writings suggest that, just as the liberty which emerged in 1848 had given rise to a deep ambivalence in him because of his personal experience of the resulting conflicts of modernity, absolutism prompted an identical response.

This assumption is supported by an article intended for publication in *Blick*,[15] replying to an official publication glorifying the regime of Alexander Bach which read: 'There is no province in Europe that could boast greater and more rapid cultural development for the admiration of the world.'[16] Modernity and its manifestations were directly linked in this official publication to absolutism, that is, to the Bach regime itself. Such attempts to establish a connection between modernity and absolutism provoked Széchenyi to speak out, and his writings on this subject give evidence that he by no means considered the relation between modernity and any particular political regime a question to which an easy solution could be found.

The ambivalence in Széchenyi's attitude is amply demonstrated by the following two statements: 'There would be nothing more beneficial for the development of a society than inspired and wise absolutism permeating all aspects of life'; however, 'absolutism goes hand in hand with folly'.[17] When *Blick* made the folly of absolutism the object of ironic criticism it was taking a stand against absolutism manifested, despite the fact that it did not denounce the absolutist regime in principle.

The edge of Széchenyi's criticism was softened somewhat by the fact that he made the all-powerful minister rather than the Emperor the focus of his ire. Such softening was merely a tactical ploy, however – as the example of the *Satire* shows – since the intended effect would otherwise have been greatly diminished: his article would have been interpreted not merely as a critique of absolutism but as a direct call for revolution, so deterring a great many readers, not to mention the risk it ran of becoming the source of further ambivalence.

The question arises once again: which Széchenyi should one believe? The Széchenyi who committed himself to absolutism or the Széchenyi who called it into question with almost every sentence he uttered, thereby inevitably committing himself to its opposite, that is, popular liberty?

The answer – similar to the one given in connection with 1848 – is that his sincerity is beyond question both pro and contra. Modernity itself cannot help one to decide whether absolutism or liberty would be a better environment for it. Hungary's experience in 1848 and the 1850s serves as ample evidence that this dilemma cannot be easily resolved.

Intellectual or politician?

Széchenyi had been driven mad by liberty and he was driven to his grave by autocracy. He suffered because he saw the realization of the modernization he advocated come under serious threat from both directions. In the period of liberty, he both rejected and identified himself with the principle of liberty from a position of power, while in the period of absolutism, when he had no power at all, he accepted absolutism in principle but rejected its actuality.

Széchenyi embodied a dilemma of historical magnitude. As an important member of the ruling elite, mere identification with the cause of modernity was for him a politically significant act. But while as a politician he was compelled to make a choice between liberty and absolutism, as an intellectual he was aware that any such choice must be arbitrary. An intellectual is always ambivalent, constantly switching from one alternative to another. Széchenyi's dilemma was whether the roles of politician and intellectual could dwell side by side in one person.

He could find no answer to this question, since such a conflict of roles is inherent in modernity, and with that Széchenyi was at one.

(1991)

Notes

1 For a survey see Zoltán Varga, *A Széchenyi-ábrázolások fő irányai a magyar történetírásban 1851–1918* [The Main Trends in Hungarian Széchenyi Historiography 1851–1918], Budapest, 1963.

2 Gyula Szekfű, *Három nemzedék* [Three Generations], Budapest, 1920. Szekfű presents his view on Széchenyi in the chapter entitled 'The Conservative Reforms of István Széchenyi'. For an evaluation of Szekfű's view see András Gerő, 'A *Három nemzedék* Széchenyi-képének logikai-fogalmi struktúrája' [The Logical and Conceptual Structure of the Image of Széchenyi Developed in the *Three Generations*], in *Tájékoztató* 1982/4; also Ferenc Glatz: 'A *Három nemzedék* története a hetedik nemzedék szemével' [*Three Generations* in the Eyes of the Seventh Generation], Preface to the 1989 edition of *Three Generations*.

3 On the ideology of modernity, see András Gergely, *Széchenyi eszmerendszerének kialakulása* [The Formation of Széchenyi's Thought], Budapest, 1972.

4 Count István Széchenyi, *Hitel* [Credit], Pest, 1830, p. 270.

5 For an interpretation of Kossuth's speech see György Szabó, *Kossuth politikusi pályája ismert és ismeretlen megnyilatkozásai tükrében* [Kossuth's Political Career In The Mirror Of His Thought And Actions], Budapest, 1977, pp. 112–13.

6 For an analysis of Széchenyi's role in the events of 1848 see György Spira, *1848 Széchenyije és Széchenyi 1848-a* [Széchenyi in 1848 and 1848 in Széchenyi's Life], Budapest, 1964. Spira's analysis influenced in several aspects the material of the debate entitled 'Negyvennyolcas forradalom kérdései' [Questions of the 1848 Revolution] and held on the occasion of the 125th anniversary of the 1848 Revolution. The text of the debate was published in 1976.

7 The hitherto most complete edition of Széchenyi's diaries is linked with the name of Gyula Viszota (*Gr. Széchenyi István Naplói* [The Diaries of Count István Széchenyi], Vol. I–VI, Budapest, 1925–39). In the following, I shall quote from the Diary in Ambrus Oltványi's selection (Budapest, 1978) due to the fact that this edition gives Széchenyi's sentences, originally formulated in foreign languages, in Hungarian. This particular quote is to be found in: István Széchenyi, *Napló* [Diary], selected and edited by Ambrus Oltványi, Budapest, 1978, p. 1202 (hereafter *Napló*).

8 Széchenyi's standpoint was at least partially motivated by the current political situation, but it must be pointed out that the same idea had occupied him for a

long time – regardless of whether there was a need for it in actuality. Széchenyi had already voiced his reservations concerning liberty in his polemical debate with Kossuth at the beginning of the 1840s, although his ambivalence on this issue goes back even further. He wrote in his *Hunnia* (written in the mid 1830s, banned, printed in 1858 and published in 1860): 'It is common knowledge that absolute rule is probably the best due to its simplicity', but he also wrote: 'How often humankind has been blackmailed by the mercilessness of absolute rule.' Thus there were substantial antecedents to the formation of a 'system of representation' which cannot be corroded by 'the bitterest of slanders'. See: Domokos Kosáry, *Széchenyi Döblingben* [Széchenyi in Döbling], Budapest, 1981, p. 170.

 9 *Napló*, p. 1215.
10 *Napló*, pp. 1217–18.
11 For the whole text see Vilmos Tolnai (ed.), *Gr. Széchenyi István döblingi irodalmi hagyatéka* [The Döbling Literary Remains of Count István Széchenyi] , Vols. 1–2, Budapest, 1925. (Hereafter *DH.*)
12 *DH*, Vol. 3, p. 669.
13 Quoted by Domokos Kosáry in: *Széchenyi Döblingben* [Széchenyi in Döbling], p. 110.
14 For more detail on Széchenyi's attitude towards the Emperor see András Gerő, *Ferenc József, a magyarok királya* [Franz Joseph, King of the Hungarians], Budapest, 1988, pp. 88–91.
15 *Ein Blick auf der anonymen Rückblick*, London 1859. Unfortunately only one translation of this article exists in Hungarian: K. Papp Miklós: *Széchenyi István gr. Blickje* ['Blick' by Count István Széchenyi], Kolozsvár, Hungary, 1870.
16 Quoted by Kosáry in: *Széchenyi Döblingben* [Széchenyi in Döbling], p. 130.
17 *DH*, Vol. 3., pp. 171–2. Text quoted by György Szabad in: 'Az önkényuralom kora' [The Age of Absolutism], in *Magyarország története 1848–90* [The History of Hungary 1848–90], VI/1, Budapest, 1979, pp. 650–1.

5 Liberalism, 1830–67: Reformer Roles and Social Awareness

Liberalism is not an ideology of social awareness. Historically, one of the most frequent objections levelled against liberalism is that it is not conscious enough of social tensions; that it formulates its objectives in legal rather than social terms. As critics of liberalism aphoristically put it: the millionaire and the beggar are equal in their right to sleep under a bridge. From the second half of the nineteenth century, various intellectual movements and their political offshoots launched a series of attacks on this front, promising a decisive breakthrough. The justice of these criticisms was, however, recognized and, what is more, the criticisms were precisely formulated by a considerable number of liberal theoreticians and politicians. A Hungarian example is József Eötvös's *A XIX. század uralkodó eseményeinek befolyása az államra* (The Influence of the Events of the Nineteenth Century on the State). In this work, Eötvös discusses, among other things, the irresolvable antagonism between the principles of freedom and equality. That this was more than a merely theoretical problem was amply demonstrated by the large number of anti-liberal social and political movements that emerged after the complete or partial victory of liberalism. Throughout Europe attempts were made – and not without success – to transform nineteenth-century political regimes founded in the spirit of liberalism into absolutist states or dictatorships on the basis of slogans largely emphasizing social issues.

While this is in many ways a specifically nineteenth-century issue, its historical relevance points well beyond that period, and in the twentieth century – indeed up to the present day – it has undergone important new phases of development. For the purposes of this study, we shall focus on a relatively narrow range of questions, confining ourselves to an interpretation of Hungarian liberalism in light of the question of social awareness. I shall attempt to prove that Hungarian liberalism in the Reform Period was in fact possessed of a unique and extremely effective social sensibility.

Names and emphases: the theoretical profile of liberalism

During the roughly two decades now known to historians as the Reform Period those advocating change were subject to a whole range of intellectual influences. Here, however, I shall highlight only those most relevant to liberalism, outlining four main trends (or rather *emphases*), each of which underwent changes in both accent and internal dynamics, but nevertheless remained clearly present at all times.[1]

One of these trends was the French Enlightenment and the liberal ideas directly stemming from it. This was a trend towards the accomplishment of classical liberalism with a sense of justice, this being fundamentally best able to call into question feudal structures and promote their transformation. As the Enlightenment in Western Europe had by the eighteenth century theoretically undermined the feudal worldview, subsequent liberal demands sought to do the same at the political level (in terms of political structures and practices). References to natural law and the notion of the social contract had a powerful anti-absolutist thrust, similar to the ideas of Montesquieu in justification of the separation of powers. Although nothing could be less applicable to Hungarian public life than the French notion of *laissez-faire*, this environment nevertheless proved highly receptive to the new liberal law-based approach. The emergence of such a sensibility within Hungary was the result of a manifold necessity, rooted in tradition as well as in political reality, in a way that seems to indicate that liberalism was more than just an intellectual import. Liberalism was the European answer to a need squarely rooted in Hungarian soil.

The politically minded nobility consisted almost exclusively of law graduates. The institutional framework of, and arguments used in connection with, the feudal politics of grievances provided an ideal environment for a law-based approach, that is, for the enforcement of new – liberal – principles of law within a feudal establishment. Furthermore, the Hungarian nobility – which as a group believed strongly in its own constitutional legitimacy – having at the end of the seventeenth century waived its right to effective resistance as laid down in the *Golden Bull* (the nobility's Charter of Rights issued in 1222), could now use only legal means to oppose the absolutism of Vienna.

If one representative of Hungarian liberalism springs to mind it is Ferenc Deák.[2] The rapid and widespread acceptance of this man is a good example of how the amalgamation of a traditional framework and mentality and a new element in the end resulted in a very potent mixture. Deák formulated radically new arguments and demands based on natural law, with a traditionalist pathos.

Paradoxically the most shocking – or if you will, stimulating – effect came not from law-based classical liberalism derived from the French

3   Ferenc Deák, c. 1872

Enlightenment and most in concordance with Hungarian feudal traditions, but from English liberalism dominated by utilitarianism. In this case, the distant remove of English liberalism's origins had its advantages: it was evident what England had achieved after it had freed itself from the bonds of feudalism and adopted a largely utilitarian form of liberalism. The enormous achievements of the Industrial Revolution and of industrial and bourgeois civilization were paramount, especially when compared to conditions in Hungary.

The most outstanding representative of this trend towards English liberalism was Count Széchenyi.[3] I am aware that such a categorization pidgeon-holes Széchenyi's thought and personality somewhat, but my object is to identify the dominant features of Hungarian liberalism in the Reform Period.

A glance at the chapter titles of Széchenyi's *Hitel* (Credit) will suffice: 'The Hungarian landowner is worse off than he should be, given his estate'; 'Hungarians do not live as well as their circumstances allow'; 'The Hungarian landowner cannot make his estate flourish as it should'; and 'Hungary does not engage in trade'. Széchenyi was clearly preoccupied with utilitarian considerations and therefore well on the way to adopting most liberal principles. Of course, when such utilitarianism came to be embodied in actual politics, it inevitably turned out to be quite different from Deák's theoretical liberalism. Széchenyi believed that certain utilitarian demands could be met within the framework of conservatism and so, in accordance with the English model, he did not mind restraining liberal principles somewhat. Deák's theoretical liberalism could not accept this approach and sought to maintain liberal principles even at the cost of making compromises. In practice, these two trends supplemented rather than confronted each other because by their very nature and scope of action they focused on different issues and so were able to meet different sorts of challenge. The two trends thus overlapped not merely in time but also in terms of content.

The point of crystallization in this context was the third kind of liberalism, which in Europe was most characteristic of Germany. The key to German liberalism was the nation: liberalism was necessary in order to improve the overall condition of the nation, and so it had to assume the lineaments of a nationwide programme and a force beyond the circles of the privileged. This orientation potentially went beyond the principal demands of liberalism because it was also directed at the creation of a modern public opinion; that is, of a wider public discourse. This variety was represented in Hungary above all by Kossuth.[4] It is not that law-based and utilitarian liberalism overlooked the concept of the nation – on the contrary, this was what united them. The differences that existed between these three kinds of liberalism related, instead, to the degree of their political and ideological openness. These differences appear especially relevant when it is understood that the emergence of a civil society in the full sense of the term was probably the best way to ensure national development. National liberalism therefore was far more expansive both politically and socially than the law-based and utilitarian varieties. National liberalism was also more open in respect to the relation between the nation and political self-determination. With this approach, the implementation of liberal principles was to be a national programme, prepared to go beyond utilitarianism in the narrow sense, when necessary. The national element was present in all three forms of liberalism, but each interpreted it in its own way and attached a different emphasis and different theoretical and political values to it. In this manner, the national element was something that both joined and divided the various forms of liberalism.

One should not forget, however, that there existed another Western influence, rooted in the values of civilized Europe and characteristic of a particular phase of bourgeois development. The transformation of Christian morality into liberal ethics was both enhanced and given life by the intellectual atmosphere surrounding Romanticism. This was an aspect present in all three forms of liberalism mentioned so far, even if it manifested itself slightly differently in each. In its most emphatic formulation, liberal ethics held that it was one's moral duty to stand up for certain principles and that to take a stand on such principles should not be dependent upon considerations of political strategy. The most outstanding representative of this approach was the poet Ferenc Kölcsey.[5] His activities and writings represent a synthesis of Christian values and liberal ethics. The functional importance of ethics lay in the fact that liberalism – of whatever variety – was fundamentally an opposition ideology and as such offered its adherents the moral high ground. Moral principles permeated Széchenyi's formulations just as much as those of Deák or Kossuth. They all wanted to see the *Hungarian nobleman* replaced by the *noble Hungarian*. Overemphasizing questions of morality had both its benefits and its drawbacks. There emerged the prospect of a fourth form of liberalism, sensitive to human affliction and vulnerability and so determined to resolve social tensions. Strict adherence to this approach could, however, lead to isolation from public life for years at a time.

The four forms of liberalism existed side by side. Hungarian liberalism was always a mixture of various elements and these four forms never really crystallized into separate ideologies; the identification of a different representative for each is therefore somewhat artificial. It is also clear that these different types of liberalism emerged in the context of external influences – intellectual and otherwise – and domestic exigencies. We cannot, however, remain content with such a schematic categorization: to do so would be to indulge in a kind of insubstantial gaming with the history of ideas, differentiating Hungarian liberalism from other kinds by weighing on a pair of imaginary scales the ideological elements constituting individual mixtures. It would be more fruitful to reflect upon the following simple proposition: liberalism exists only where there are liberals who, under the conditions of a given political establishment, occupy a certain position and have a certain scope of action. This must obviously have repercussions for the substance and quality of any particular variety of liberalism. It was this positional and political context that was largely responsible for the incorporation of a social awareness by Hungarian liberalism in the Reform Period. The forms of liberalism – emphasizing the law, utilitarianism, the nation and the strict maintenance of moral principles – allowed openness between social strata only to a limited extent, and by no means guaranteed its realization.

Reformer roles: the prospects of social awareness

In the Reform Period, a liberal was also a reformer irrespective of which variety of liberalism he adhered to. The choice of a particular form of liberalism was, however, relevant in respect to whether a reformer also joined the opposition; only the utilitarian variety had any chance of penetrating the establishment, provided that the individual reformer considered the Metternich regime a suitable vehicle for the satisfaction of utilitarian goals that perforce came to be interpreted in an ever narrower sense. For representatives of the other forms of liberalism, however, legitimate opposition was the only possible political role, given that the notion of radical upheaval was rejected by them all. The stands adopted by the opposition on questions of law, the nation and ethics were completely unacceptable for the reigning political elite. Those restricting the scope of reform to technical modernization could at least count on the conditional sympathy of the establishment; those reformers who committed themselves to more substantial change could expect a difficult struggle.

The alternatives in question were, of course, largely theoretical; in reality, reformer roles were shaped by a combination of establishment exigencies, legal and other circumstances and the temperament of the individual. For aristocratic reformers the feudal establishment offered direct scope for action because they were entitled to participate in the work of the Upper House of the Diet. The aristocracy was such an interweaving of dynastic and familial relations that its members could usually count on some form of direct access to the holders of central power; this, at least, offered the possibility that utilitarian reform plans could somehow be used to modernize the state from within. In other words, eligible reformers were allowed limited involvement in a political regime that itself wished to appear modernizing and reforming. Being an aristocrat was, however, no more than an entrance ticket into the world of grand politics. This led to the emergence of a kind of exclusionism, the aim of which was to contain reform ambitions within the existing political and social framework. As already explained, such a role was attractive mainly for the representatives of utilitarian liberalism and, even then, it involved an inevitable narrowing of the scope of utilitarianism by the ruling elite ('No more is possible under the present circumstances,' etc.). This narrowing of the meaning of utilitarianism led in turn to a narrowing of access, preference being given to as limited a social stratum as possible by those in power. The representatives of utilitarianism in turn focused their attention on those possessing genuine influence, and the holders of high office. Their ability to realize their aims was dependant on their retaining insider status, rather than on broadly-based social pressure. It will readily be comprehended that – on the liberal side – the utilitarian reformers who managed to penetrate the higher levels of political power were those least likely to display a social awareness.

Variations were, however, not excluded: a given individual could play a number of reformer roles at the same time. Public figures in the Reform Period cannot be divided into strictly defined categories. They were all subject to a number of social influences and apt to display a mixture of reformer orientations. Utilitarian reformer-aristocrats saw themselves as a social elite and any 'openness' they might be inclined to display was limited to their own class. Széchenyi was the typical representative of this breed. While the casino (or gentleman's club) pointed beyond the feudal regime, membership was restricted to the upper classes. Only those able to present recommendations from influential persons and possessing sufficient wealth could expect to join. Members of the bourgeoisie could in principle become eligible for casino membership but the stringent entrance criteria obviously excluded the great majority. While the casino was a conscious attempt to replace a sense of feudal affinity with an elitist one, it must be pointed out that the 'elite' comprised persons as far apart ideologically as the liberal Széchenyi and the conservative Metternich.

Elitism inevitably led to social exclusionism – no ideological conflict worth debating could exist outside the higher social classes. Social exclusionism gave rise to political exclusionism from the 1840s onwards. It was a natural development that Széchenyi came to apply the principle of elitism to the sphere of political power. This was partly psychologically motivated (being one of the social and political elite conveyed a sense or at least the illusion of personal security) but that is not the main point. What is more important is that changes affecting the country as a whole were to be carried out by way of deliberately excluding from their consideration and implementation most of society. 'We' shall make decisions about 'Them' – and without their interference. The position under consideration was justified by its adherents on the grounds that the vast majority of the population were at that time too ignorant, passive and easy to manipulate to be allowed a substantial say in social change. (It is interesting that the reformers most conscious of the limitations of the masses were those most distant from utilitarianism.) But however much we moderns might balk at this line of argument, neither it nor a demagogic appeal to a 'national' ethos was an answer to the underlying problem. It would be more fruitful to look at the advantages and disadvantages of being an elitist reformer.

The main advantage for an elitist reformer was that he was in a position to influence political events directly; on the other hand, his scope of action was restricted to what could be achieved by way of personal and social connections. Someone *consciously* choosing to take up an elitist stance and to become an insider for the sake of the protection that it entailed, risked becoming overdependent on those under whose wings he sought shelter.

Furthermore, elitism meant condoning the ignorance and vulnerability to manipulation of the masses and surrendering any hope of their gradual involvement in political affairs. The wish to maintain social and political involvement as the privilege of the chosen few (even a differing chosen few) could not but result in the narrowing of the broad scope of reform that I have already emphasized. This reformer role was doomed to increasing isolation because it was unable to go beyond particular schemes (such as the introduction of steamships and horse racing, or the construction of the imposing Chain Bridge in Budapest) to conceive of fundamental and comprehensive reform. I do not mean to underestimate the role of economic progress in social reform, but even the most outstanding technical achievements can never resolve chronic social and political problems such as those that beset Reform-Period Hungary; I would even go so far as to say that technical modernization tends rather to preserve outdated political structures.

Exclusionism attracted many supporters by virtue of the aesthetic appeal of peaceful transition. It held up the promise of reform without bloodshed, cataclysms and painful conflicts, gradually changing conditions and unforcedly precipitating compromise. The lack of a wide social base, however, blinded elitist reformers to the need for gradual change and encouraged a belief in reform as a personal affair rather than an objective exigency. Emphasis upon the freedom of personal decision was another element of the aesthetics of elitism: it rejected any notion of setting the whims of the Great Unwashed over the more weighty considerations of their betters and instead upheld the ideal of the 'autonomous personality' – as we would now put it – the individual with a secure financial background, conscious of his social standing and able to command esteem.

The role of the elitist reformer – although understandably attractive for a highly accomplished individual – was in reality hard to live up to, with all the consequences and contradictions it entailed, and could easily crush those who committed themselves to it. First, the role of the elitist reformer did not offer any prospect of short-term success; indeed, the chances of *any* success – for the reasons given above – were doubtful, and dependant least of all upon the individual reformer. The combination of an ideological orientation (utilitarian liberalism) with a particular social and political role (elitism and exclusionism) inevitably led to a reduced social awareness; what social awareness its adherents did have was largely restricted to a fear of the masses. And given that all social and political change tends to work against elitism and exclusionism, the representatives of this reformer orientation constantly saw their fears confirmed. This is why, in Széchenyi's *Stádium*, the classical liberal concept of representation as a guarantee of the enforcement of reform endeavours is not developed; at no point does he describe with any precision how this might be implemented. Elitism requires restricted representation: it could not possibly retain its essential exclusivity if, even in principle, anyone at all could have a say in public affairs. Wider representation would also go against the essence of exclusionism which is attracted to broad representation only when its own interests are at stake. To dwell on questions of representation would at some point inevitably lead to a challenge to liberal principles: the distinction between conservatism and liberalism would gradually disappear and the very difficult question would arise of whether it is possible to come to liberalism by way of conservatism. (The English model of development is usually cited to prove that this is indeed a possibility, but the question is not as simple as it might seem. The problem is that those advocating such a transition take as their point of departure the period of consolidation following the English Revolution rather than the Revolution itself – the rebellion culminating in the beheading of the English King is conveniently forgotten.) Széchenyi's increasing isolation, beginning in the early 1840s, indicates that committed reformers were not satisfied with the hard-fought, piecemeal achievements of utilitarian liberalism and had decided that other reformer roles would suit their purposes better.

And alternative roles were already available. The Lower House of the Diet, and the system of county assemblies, each nominating two delegates to it, were legitimate representative forums for reform endeavours. These alternative reformer roles – given the structure under which they had to operate – had both advantages and disadvantages. From 1818 onwards county assembly representatives were elected by majority vote, in contrast to the previous method of appointment. While a county assembly nominee had the right to attend meetings of the county assembly, his participation in sessions of the Diet depended on the outcome of a political struggle. Even when a member had been elected by the county assembly, there was a risk that a new mandate would require that he give up his reform endeavours (Kölcsey, for example, stepped down because he was not prepared to carry out such a mandate). Electoral practice was often electoral malpractice, rendering victory morally bankrupt (Deák refused to accept his election on these grounds). On the other hand, the position of delegate offered an opportunity for the free expression of one's opinions, and personal and political independence from the central authorities. This was a reform position offering legitimacy, legality and the chance to exhibit moral fibre.

Reformers committed to law-based liberalism were, at first, opposition members without exception. In the Lower House, liberal views could legitimately be held in the context of a parliamentary opposition with centuries of tradition. While the liberals constituted a minority, the emergence of genuine conflict was not a likely outcome. Such conflict could not arise before the liberal reformers had acquired a majority in both Houses, regardless of the fact that the doings of the Lower House had a significantly greater political impact. Representatives of the legitimate reform opposition were fully aware of this, as is clear from the arguments they marshalled in connection with the court proceedings against Miklós Wesselényi.[6] By making a distinction between the sovereign and the government they were not only defending Wesselényi and upholding a crucial liberal principle, but were also emphasizing that the composition of the government might not remain the same even if continuity was maintained in the person of the sovereign and in the form of government. And by accepting that the composition of the government might be subject to change, one also accepted that the opposition might one day acquire a majority and take power. Legitimate means existed to resolve a constitutional crisis, as the events of the spring of 1848 show. Opposition members committed to legitimate reform took power without resort to exclusionism.

Such a reformer role could not, of course, remain free from compromise; indeed, it could not be avoided with both the sovereign and the electorate. This type of compromise did not, however, require the abandonment of one's principles, because one's position was not a matter of intrigues and personal favours, but rather depended upon a number of institutions and the minority-majority power relations behind them. Compromise based on intrigue could affect who received what appointment, but not the issues and principles at stake. In this manner, ethical and political liberalism did not come into conflict with each other. It was certainly a weak point, however, of this particular reformer role that, like exclusionist liberalism, it offered slow progress, and its appeal was dependant on whether its representatives behaved ethically. Its drawbacks were therefore both political and personal: on numerous occasions, this reformer role had a restraining effect on its representatives and was not free of disappointment. These drawbacks, paradoxically, only made this role more attractive, given that they led to the working out of a comprehensive programme during the Reform Period and consequently increased the moral credibility and attractiveness of reform politics.

The legitimate reform-opposition role – as previously mentioned – went hand in hand with law-based (and ethical) liberalism. This was entirely natural given that the wheels of legislation were far too slow and clumsy, especially when the stimulus for change had to be exerted by the opposition. Feudalism and the politics of grievances in their highest form were, however, the ideal setting for a reformer role with a radically new substance and objectives, and resting on natural law. The outdatedness of feudal conditions, however, reduced in large measure the social accessibility of this reformer role, legitimate action being possible only within the framework of feudal privileges. Nevertheless – and this is another paradox – the same reformer role also acted as a stimulus towards greater social openness, or, one might also say, social awareness. (This duality was one of the causes of the inner conflicts which went with this reformer role.)

Social awareness and openness comprised a number of things. First, the need to be 'elected'. In order for someone to acquire recognition in a county he – personally or through his family – had to participate in local affairs, be well acquainted with local conditions and, whatever our assessment might be of elections in the Reform Period, face some kind of public appraisal. A liberal county reformer had a double mandate: while it was inevitable that he would outstrip his local community in his political and social aims, it was essential that he did not lose touch with the mood in his constituency. Of course, these are to some extent general rules of politics, but it is important not to underestimate the extent to which a thorough knowledge of local conditions was necessary. A detailed examination of the careers of liberal delegates from the Reform Period reveals that, almost without exception, they had gone through a schooling in county affairs before they were elected to the Diet, supplying them with a substantial knowledge of social circumstances in Hungary and ensuring that they remained free of doctrinairism. If, in addition to this, the nobleman had liberal views, from this combination emerged a political attitude that took a global view of political opportunities and acute social problems, whether consciously or otherwise. Ultimately, it was the interaction of social awareness and political opportunity that allowed reformers within the Diet to go beyond the existing social and political feudal framework even if they did not challenge feudal laws.

Social awareness was also enhanced by the prospect of a constitutional crisis, measures for the prevention of which took the form of a proposed separation of powers; that is, separation of the government and the sovereign. A solution built entirely on theoretical and ideological foundations could be effective only with wide social support. In the absence of this, the likelihood was that any reform action initiated in the Diet would have become a target for ridicule or even persecution, or would have condemned its perpetrator to perpetual opposition; a further possibility would have been a move towards revolution, a development irreconcilable with the concept of legitimate action widely adhered to by county reformers. It was therefore necessary to look for new reformer roles capable of going beyond the possibilities offered by the existing regime, while at the same time enjoying the wide social and political support necessary to improve the prospects of opposition reform.

New reformer roles (we shall examine two) were called into being both by necessity and by favourable circumstances. It must again be stressed that there was no clear dividing line between the various approaches: individual circumstances, personal character and political room for manoeuvre made these roles partially overlap. Minor differences of emphasis need some elucidation, however, as they were largely responsible for any conflicts that existed between attitudes towards social awareness.

One of these new reformer roles, in particular, was directly influenced by

liberalism. The liberal world-view provided an intellectually coherent explanation of the economic, social and political problems facing Hungary, and
served as material for political debate between representatives of the utilitarian, exclusionist and legitimate-opposition reform tendencies. As the
feudal regime neared its end, the need arose for a reformer role oriented
towards the substitution of ability for privilege. Intellectual refinement, high
professional standards, European erudition and little affinity for power
politics were the characteristic features of this role – which may be termed
the 'contemplative-professional' role – which was most popular with
centralists.[7] It was also an opposition role, but since it was not primarily
political in orientation it was not combative in spirit; it was characterized by
the description and understanding, rather than the sharpening of conflicts.
(The key to its success was that it spoke for abstract rationality and was a
combination of many features attractive to the contemporary intelligentsia: it
was critical but not radical, political but at the same time maintained a
certain distance from politics, abstractly intellectual but also pragmatic.) Its
weak point was that it was unable to reach political solutions for the
problems with which it concerned itself. It was therefore inevitable that this
role should shift towards intellectual elitism and a post-feudal, essentially
'academic' approach to the problems faced by Hungarian society.

   This ideology was not homogenous; it combined various liberal trends.
The representatives of this reformer role took a critical approach to the
emergence of civil societies in the West, as well as to the environment
which sustained parliamentary-opposition reformism. The social issues
which concerned them covered a wide range, from prison conditions to
destitution. Eötvös's study on poverty in Ireland (1840) and his literary
works (*A falu jegyzője* [The Village Notary] published in 1845 and
Magyarország 1514-ben [Hungary in 1514] published soon afterwards), as
well as studies such as *Nyomor és óvszerei* (Destitution and its Remedies)
serialized in 1847 in the magazine *Pesti Hírlap,* show that the author
possessed a strong social conscience. Such publications widened the scope
of liberal thinking in Hungary. The place of centralism within the available
reformer roles was somewhat ambivalent, inclined as it was both to opposition and exclusionist reformism. Centralist ideas could not be implemented
without a corresponding increase in the influence of opposition liberals, but
the manner in which centralists spoke and the role from which they did so,
bolstered their influence intellectually rather than politically. But since they
were not subject either to the paralysing logic of exclusionism or committed
to parliamentary political solutions alone – which often tended to slow
things down and to descend into pettiness – and they were able to glean
freely among liberal principles, they were able to develop a more or less
explicit social awareness. At least as far as can be documented, a social
awareness was much more characteristic of centralists than the majority of

their fellow reformers. The ambivalent nature of their reformer role, however, rendered this awareness somewhat sterile. It was left to others to draw on what was usable in this reformer role.

The intellectual impact of the liberal opposition in the Diet increased with the addition of the intellectual capital of the centralists, and what the 'contemplative-professional' reformer role could provide in the political arena was largely unimportant to it. This is well reflected in the fact that while there were arguments over minor details, it was never a matter of dispute that all concerned were committed to reform. The question was whether liberal-opposition reformism – on the one hand bound by the law and on the other politically interested in dissolving the feudal order and in gaining wide public support – would be able to find a reformer role capable of sustaining it. It formed a minority in the Diet, and given that it represented a political standpoint substantially different to that of the feudal regime, it was in its interest to foster an incipient public opinion.

One of the intrinsic conditions of public opinion is the existence of differences between the players in the political arena; in the case of Hungary, these differences stemmed largely from the existence of the reform opposition. It had a chance of becoming a majority – provided that it did not think in revolutionary terms: an eventuality excluded for reasons previously elaborated – and of attaining the constitutional enforcement of a majority, if only it could obtain sufficient public support. For this purpose it required publicity, which in turn entailed the acquisition of a reformer role outside the political structure of feudalism, though not isolated from it. This role could be operational in two areas: in the associations (see Chapter 2) and in the press. The publication of *Országgyűlési Tudósítások* (Parliamentary Records), the subsequently discontinued *Törvényhatósági Tudósítások* (Municipal Records), the *Pesti Hírlap* and the various associations (first the Industrial Association and, from 1844, the Association for Mutual Assistance) – which functioned with some success in the 1840s – document the particular forms taken by this structural necessity. The most important feature of this emerging reformer role was its need for public acceptance, an acceptance that became more or less tangible as time went on. It derived its position not from the feudal establishment but from a perception of genuine social need and from the self-organizing forces of society – such a standpoint was, of course, oppositional by its very nature. Its activities were largely directed at what it most required: to constitute a broad-based public opinion, to achieve acceptance for its views, and to mobilize the value-formulating forces of society.[8] This was inevitably an expansive role, as it sought to disseminate its views, to win people over and, at the same time, to represent particular interests. Because it was not dependant on the feudal institutional framework and its inner workings, it had an ambivalent relationship with the law: while it very much favoured lawful transformation, it was relatively outspoken in pursuit of its aims. Its expansivity, or openness, gave preference to national goals among the issues dear to the various forms of liberalism. This did not, however, mean that it was willing to sacrifice freedom. On the contrary, it expanded the concept of liberal freedom from the individual to the nation as a whole, applying the general ideological premises of liberalism to the question of national or state self-determination. Any reformer role wishing to exercise influence beyond the existing feudal – and elitist – framework required a new style of behaviour and expression: it could not turn to tradition for its 'aesthetic materials'. One of its fundamental characteristics was that it served as a mouthpiece for public opinion, the will of a majority both feudal and post-feudal. It derived all its strength from this, which was also the basis for its dedication.

The typical representative of this role adhered to the ethos of 'one man speaking in the name of millions'. This new kind of political figure was capable of arousing strong dislike, not only because it was not traditional, but because the role itself was burdened with contradictions difficult to resolve. For example, how could someone claim to be a mouthpiece for the will of the majority when, under the feudal regime, there were no established means to determine who and what the majority actually was, given that the lower classes did not even have political rights? How could someone claim to be giving expression to public opinion – a concept, by the way, so alien to the feudal way of thinking – when he was clearly shaping that opinion at least as much as he was voicing it? Irritation was further heightened by the fact that the public opinion-oriented reformer role we are discussing strongly rejected the kind of bureaucratic politics characteristic of exclusionism. It was also frowned upon by those for whom the absolute measure of Man was his intellectual achievements: this role saw its function as the creation of a pragmatic political force committed to clearly defined aims, rather than the formulation of abstract truths or descriptive interpretation. Such pragmatism did not exclude a more contemplative approach, but this was clearly of secondary importance. To sum up, there was an intellectual element in this reformer role but – as distinct from centralism – it was combined with a strong social awareness. The intellectual fruits of this position differed from the achievements of contemplative-professional reformism less in their level of accomplishment than in their substance.

This role is linked primarily with the person of Kossuth, although he later outgrew it. In Kossuth's case, we are dealing with a uniquely fortunate combination of reformer role and personal talents. Apart from Deák and law-based opposition reformism, in no other person did such a harmonious combination occur. For the less fortunate, there was always some conflict between personal temperament and role: it is sufficient to mention Széchenyi, for whom it was increasingly difficult to find a place, let alone

4   Lajos Kossuth, 1877

tranquillity, and Eötvös, who left us with an account of his own 'disloca-
tion'. The criticism directed at Kossuth was often an expression of dislike
towards the role he represented, a role which followed naturally from his
commitment to liberal reform and the improvement of the prospects of
reform politics.

From the point of view of the ruling political elite, public opinion-
oriented reformism was the most vulnerable of all – as far as its origins were
concerned – but also the most dangerous. The initial vulnerability of this
reformer role was a consequence of the fact that it did not have the direct
protection or support of the feudal regime. It was also a modern reformer
role with a substantially new content, being the only reform position
expressly rooted in and deriving its legitimacy from 'society'. Hence its
dangers for the regime: it was capable of mobilizing the masses, a force

which was becoming increasingly difficult to control. This explains why the authorities at first resorted to drastic measures to suppress public opinion-oriented reform – Kossuth was the only member of the 1848 government who had served a term of imprisonment – and why many reformers were unwilling to support it. (For instance, the co-editor of Kossuth's *Parliamentary Records*, a certain Orosz, decided to look for a new job with the government.) It is beyond doubt, however, that this reformer role, especially when represented by someone possessing the right temperament, could ultimately be very effective and have a political impact beyond what had originally been intended for it. This explains the dislike which this reformer role gave rise to, particularly within the reform camp, although it should be pointed out that the irritation caused by its success only developed into outright disavowal when the person rejecting this reformer role had himself moved away from the spirit of reform.

This reformer role had a number of advantages and disadvantages, although the latter were comparatively insignificant. Its function was to overcome feudalism and elitism, and in return it won nationwide recognition and influence. All this, of course, could be achieved only by being truly open – by involving in public life and politics representatives of social strata which had not been allowed such involvement before. The civil-association movement – especially the Association for Mutual Assistance – was also successful from this point of view. It becomes clear, however, how important the interaction between social role and personal make-up was: personal deficiencies affecting the formation of associations in many instances left unutilized a great deal of potential for social collaboration (for example, in the case of the *Kereskedelmi Társaság* [Trading Company]). From 1841 onwards, a social awareness could clearly be discerned in the pages of the *Pesti Hírlap,* a popular move – judging by its circulation and influence – capable of interesting all social groups in the liberal concept of bourgeois transformation.

The success of *Pesti Hírlap* – even if various civil-association movements remained disjointed – demonstrated the viability of public opinion-oriented reformism, and helped its most important representative, Kossuth, to assume yet another reformer role, as a member of the parliamentary opposition. His new parliamentary-opposition role did not, however, spell the end of public opinion-oriented reformism, but contributed to the modification of all previous reformer roles by making social awareness a central issue and a dominant feature of Hungarian liberalism. Other reformer roles, with the exception of exclusionism, were, at least to a limited degree, receptive to social concerns.

The outcome of interest reconciliation

A number of different reformer roles, coupled with various forms of liberalism, created a constellation which allowed Hungarian liberalism to acquire the distinctive feature needed for it to be successful. As we have seen, the social awareness which was essential for the working out and implementation of interest reconciliation was primarily based on a political logic embodied in particular reformer roles, rather than in liberalism's overall ideological content. In this respect, public opinion-oriented reformism achieved the most, not because it was 'superior' to other forms but because it was organically related to the legitimate parliamentary-reform opposition and so was able to influence it significantly. Public opinion-oriented reformism in itself was – as we have seen – rooted in society and so the source of a considerable degree of social openness. Of the four reformer roles we have dealt with, only exclusionist reformism proved incapable of identifying with the cause of interest reconciliation. The 'contemplative-professional' approach was reluctant to become involved in interest reconciliation, as in everything else, although at certain stages it provided significant intellectual support. The most harmonious relationship was formed with parliamentary opposition reformers and to this we owe the fact that, in 1848, political changes took place in Hungary in a lawful manner.

The radical role, which was given the opportunity to act in the spring of 1848, played a great part in the political acceleration of the changes. It was, however, less important overall than might be imagined. Although the radicals gave a political 'push' to the concept of interest reconciliation, they did not modify it. Apart from anything else, they were unable to do so because the great majority of the reform camp had no intention of breaking with those to whom the reforms applied; socially, interest reconciliation did not leave any inflammable material to the 'rear' of the reformers. (Apart from the national minorities, but that is another question – see Chapter 6.)[9]

Ultimately, in 1848–9 – the moment of truth for Hungarian reform liberalism – only two reformer roles succeeded in establishing any kind of durable power base capable of forming a government. Neither exclusionist nor 'contemplative-professional' reformism could handle the conflict-riven implementation of interest reconciliation and reform. The ideological framework of liberalism slowly began to work its way into the inner logic of the reform process. It was stated more and more often that the notion of interest reconciliation had to be reformulated on a democratic basis. Historical events and the success of foreign military intervention prevented a domestic political decision on this question which clearly represented a watershed in Hungarian history.

After 1849, the neo-absolutist regime, making preparations for long-term rule, wanted to eliminate reformer roles that were independent of it, partly because it planned to leave in place some achievements of the policy of interest reconciliation – it would in any case not have been able to revoke them – and partly because it regarded itself as an agent of reform and the source of all progress, a belief that outraged Széchenyi. If Hungarian public opinion could not be brought to believe them, however, the ruling political regime's reformist claims were in vain. This lack of credibility is attributable to two things, both related to the activities of Hungarian liberals, both in 1848–9 and in the Reform Period generally. First, the Josephinist dilemma could not be repeated. It was no longer possible to enforce a choice between the modern and the national, largely because interest-reconciling liberalism – public opinion-oriented reformism having acquired political dominance – had made clear the interdependence of national and reform values: that personal, social and national freedoms were intrinsically linked and that private property could lead to prosperity for individual and nation alike only when combined with freedom. Interest-reconciling liberalism also managed to incorporate utilitarian elements, so that when absolutism promoted utilitarian aims – but in the absence of liberalization – it called down upon its head the disapproval even of former exclusionist reformers. It found sympathy only where 'contemplative-professional' reformism was dominant, although the ruling political elite never really required such services. This is the other element in the ruling political elite's lack of credibility. How could an executive power not tolerating the existence of independent reformer roles claim to be a supporter of reform? No reforms can take place – whether it comes from the ruling power or from the opposition – without significant change and the active criticism necessary for the purpose of sustaining the reform process. In order for reform to take place in a peaceful manner – without a revolution – reformer roles must be available and independent of the control of the current executive authority. The Reform Period showed how fragile the exclusionist reformer role was and the extent to which its inner logic worked against substantive reform. Hungarian liberalism took special care to ensure that property rights went hand in hand with civil freedom, and its activities throughout the Reform Period and 1848–9 give evidence that it was committed to seeking legitimate opportunities for criticism and change. It was not only his commitment to legitimate means, but also to interest-reconciling liberalism that caused Kossuth not to quit the Diet, even in the vexing year of 1849. Furthermore, one was not persecuted for one's political views – provided one did not advocate armed conspiracy.

Absolutism took a very different approach and consequently failed to make its commitment to reform appear credible.

The radical elimination of reformer roles (as previously mentioned, only 'contemplative-professional' reformism was in any way amenable to the regime) led to deep divisions within the seemingly united Hungarian reform camp and Hungarian liberalism. They rejected the existing state of affairs – as the Diet of 1861 proved[10] – but their ways parted on how to proceed. The absolutist regime deprived public opinion-oriented reformism of its element so that its representatives – if they escaped execution or imprisonment – were forced to emigrate. Although they used their years in exile to work out a new concept of democratically based interest reconciliation (Kossuth's Draft Constitution of 1851 put together in Kütahya and the document written by the *Dunai Szövetség* [Danube Association], published in 1862, in which it tried to extend rights to the national minorities spring to mind) they were forced into a fundamentally different position: their commitment to the creation of a broadly based public opinion and a free country now forced them into the adoption of unprecedented and illegal methods, so bringing their ends and their means into radical contradiction. In addition to many other – international and personal – reasons, this made the democratic enforcement of interests increasingly difficult.

For liberals deprived of public opinion-oriented reformism, thinking in terms of a defensive, lawful – and so restrictive – social awareness seemed appropriate given that both absolutist oppression and the limitations imposed upon their reformer roles pushed them in this direction. These influences prompted them to seek scope for action exclusively in legal and constitutional means, without any thought of reviving the policy of interest reconciliation. In turn, this cautious and defensive attitude inevitably exploded the unity of individual, social and national freedom, because this unity could be maintained and reinstituted only through interest reconciliation. Compromise could be reached only through capitulation to the absolutist regime.

The Compromise of 1867 strengthened the law-based, utilitarian trend within liberalism and, despite all Deák's efforts, toned down its ethical content. The compromise reached excluded – by its very nature – the synthesis of national and liberal contents. This meant, among other things, that there was no longer room within Hungarian liberalism for an interest-reconciling trend characterized by social awareness. A small window remained through which these values could have been reintroduced, but from this point on, the viability of interest reconciliation was no longer a question for Hungarian liberalism, the 1867 Compromise having forced it into a conservative role from both a national and a social point of view.

Developments after 1867 posed this question differently for the long term: Could Hungarian society step onto the road to democratic development?

(1990)

Notes

1   For an overall history of liberalism see G.Ruggiero, *Geschichte des Liberalismus in Europa* [The History of Liberalism in Europe], München, 1930, and J.S. Schapiro, *Liberalism: Its Meaning and History,* London, 1957. A contemporary Hungarian summary on the subject is: János Benczur, *A szabadság és társadalmi rend elméletei* [Theories of Freedom and Social Order], Pest, 1848. A North American travel diary published in 1834 by Sándor Farkas Bölöni and de Tocqueville's work on American democracy published in 1841–3 were also highly influential. Several writings by István Barta address intellectual influences in Hungary, such as '*A magyar polgári reformmozgalom kezdeti szakaszának problémái*', [Problems related to the Initial Stages of the Hungarian Bourgeois Reform Movement], *Történelmi Szemle*, 1963, 3–4; '*Széchenyi és a magyar polgári reformmozgalom kibontakozása*' [Széchenyi and the Unfolding of the Hungarian Bourgeois Reform Movement], *Történelmi Szemle*, 1960, 2–3, and *A fiatal Kossuth* [The Young Kossuth], Budapest, 1966. In the pre-war literature a comprehensive work on the subject is Zoltán Varga's, *A szabadság eszme a XIX. század első felének magyar államszemléletében* [The Ideal of Freedom in Hungarian Political Theory in the First Half of the Nineteenth Century], Századok, 1938, Melléklet, Hungary. For a more recent account, see János Varga, *Kereszttűzben a Pesti Hírlap. Az ellenzéki és a középutas liberalizmus elválása 1841–42-ben* [*Pesti Hírlap* under Fire: The Parting of the Ways for Opposition and Centrist Liberalism 1841–2] Budapest, 1983. In a broader context see the same author, *Helyét kereső Magyarország. Politikai eszmék és koncepciók az 1840-es évek elején* [Hungary in Search of its Place; Political Theory in the Early 1840s], Budapest, 1982. A number of works on the history of literature also concern themselves with the influence of liberalism. For a list of these see the notes to the most recent comprehensive study: '*A magyar liberalizmus születése*' [The Birth of Hungarian Liberalism], in András Gergely, *Egy nemzetet az emberiségnek. Tanulmány a magyar reformkorról és 1848-ról* [A Nation for Humanity. Studies on the Hungarian Reform Age and 1848], Budapest, 1987. An unpublished manuscript that I received from András Gergely entitled '*A liberális eszmék és a valóság 1848 Közép-Európájában*' [Liberal Theory and Reality in Central Europe in 1848] I found very useful, although it takes an approach rather different from my own. I would like to take this opportunity to express my gratitude to Gergely for his help.

2   Deák's views can be discerned clearly in his speeches, the fullest edition of which was the one published by Manó Kónyi, *Deák Ferenc beszédei* [The Speeches of Ferenc Deák], Vols. 1–5. Budapest, 1903. For the most detailed biography of Deák see Zoltán Ferenczi, *Deák élete* [The Life of Deák], Vols. 1–3, Budapest, 1904. For a detailed biography and the latest research findings see *Zalai Gyűjtemény 5* [Zala Collection], Zalaegerszeg, 1976. An interpretation of Deák's life is given in György Szabad, '*Deák Ferenc három politikai korszaka*' [The Three Political Periods of Ferenc Deák], *Magyar Tudomány,* 1976/11.

3   There are countless works on Széchenyi and most of his writings are available in

the *Fontes* series under the editorship of Béla Iványi-Grünvald, Zoltán Ferenczi and Gyula Viszota. Széchenyi's thought is analysed – though not taking account of his life as a whole – in András Gergely, *Széchenyi eszmerendszerének kialakulása* [The Emergence of Széchenyi's Thought], Budapest, 1972.

4 Some of Kossuth's work was published, edited by István Barta, under the main title *Kossuth Lajos Összes Munkái* [The Complete Works of Lajos Kossuth]. But as there is no single complete edition the incomplete edition edited by Ignác Helfy and Ferenc Kossuth should also be consulted: *Kossuth Lajos Összes Munkái* [The Complete Works of Lajos Kossuth], Vols. 1–13, Budapest, 1880–1911. Compare György Szabad, *Kossuth politikai pályája ismert és ismeretlen megnyilatkozásai tükrében* [Kossuth's Political Career in the Mirror of his Thought and Actions], Budapest, 1977.

5 The complete poems of Kölcsey were published in three volumes by József Szauder, Budapest, 1960. The last comprehensive monograph on Kölcsey was written by József Szauder and published in 1955.

6 Compare Zsolt Trócsányi, *Wesselényi Miklós,* Budapest, 1965. See also by the same author, *Wesselényi Miklós hűtlenségi pere* [The Treason Trial of Miklós Wesselényi], Budapest, 1986.

7 Compare István Sőtér, *Eötvös József,* Budapest, 1953; István Schlett, *Eötvös József,* Budapest, 1987; and István Fenyő, *Haza és tudomány* [Nation and Science], Budapest, 1970, and *Nép, nemzet, irodalom* [People, Nation, Literature], Budapest, 1973.

8 For an analysis see: György Kókay (ed.), *A magyar sajtó története* [The History of the Hungarian Press], Vol. 1, 1705–1848, Budapest, 1979.

9 Compare András Gerő, '*A magyar politika és a nemzetiségek 1848–49-ben*' [Hungary's Policy on National Minorities 1848–9], *Társadalmi Szemle*, 1987/6, pp. 125–44.

10 See György Szabad, *Forradalom és kiegyezés válaszútján (1860–1861)* [At the Crossroads of Revolution and Compromise (1860–1)], Budapest, 1967, and on the curtailment of the reformer role, *Miért halt meg Teleki László?* [Why Did László Teleki Die?], Budapest, 1985.

6 Politics and National Minorities, 1848–9

In July 1848 an armed conflict broke out between Serb rebels and Hungarian troops in the Szerémség region near Karlóca. There had been isolated conflicts before, but this time the fighting was persistent. In September, the Croatian minority also resorted to armed action to express their dissatisfaction with the concessions they enjoyed and their refusal to acknowledge the Hungarian government in Pest. Even the usually calm Felvidék (Upper Hungary) began to stir: Slovakian irregulars penetrated Hungary from Moravia halting only when they realized that ethnic Slovakians in Hungary would not support them. In October, civilians were killed in Transylvania and the Romanian uprising began. Raging civil war claimed the lives of thousands, both soldiers and civilians.

What led to this bloodshed and was it inevitable? Was it impossible for Hungarians, Serbs, Slovaks, Croats and Romanians to peacefully coexist?

* * *

In the spring of 1848, the time had come for the liberal reformers who had finally ascended to power to realize their dreams and enact a political agenda gradually hammered out over 20 years. The liberal model of bourgeois transformation manifested itself in new laws on popular representation, accountable government, equitable distribution of taxation and other public burdens, freedom of the press and, probably most importantly, the emancipation of the serfs. It seemed that their grand design – the bourgeois transformation of Hungarian society by way of gradual reform – could be successfully and relatively painlessly accomplished.

The bourgeois-transformation process rested upon a carefully elaborated notion of interest reconciliation: in other words, compromise. The events of the spring of 1848 heightened hopes that no major conflicts would arise to threaten its success. Interest reconciliation centred on three things: political power, social issues and the national minorities. In the case of political interest reconciliation, there were hopes that armed conflict with the Habsburg Empire could be avoided. It was envisaged that Hungary would remain under the rule of the Austro-Hungarian Emperor, but acquire national sovereignty – independence in regard to its internal affairs – whereby it would become a politically and economically much stronger and so more useful supporter of the Habsburg dynasty than a Hungary deprived of constitutional and other institutions that would serve to promote bourgeois development. It was widely believed that if Hungary could persuade the Habsburgs that it was also in their interest to acknowledge the reforms of 1848, conflict could be avoided. Regarding social issues, the peasants were to be relieved of their feudal obligations not by the Emperor but by the Hungarian National Assembly, largely made up of members of the nobility (the latter were to be compensated by a compulsory fee absolute, that is, by funds raised by a general tax). This provided the reformer nobility with a social base and a leading role grounded in ability, social status and tradition rather than feudal privileges: the introduction of the fee absolute and the corresponding halt to major feudal obligations were an attempt to ensure that the peasantry would not be incited against the nobility even if the political interest-reconciliation process should fail. The interests of the peasantry and the nobility did, of course, continue to diverge, but what brought them together was more important than what divided them.

Interest reconciliation represented a genuine compromise, both sides gaining as well as giving up something in return. The Habsburg dynasty had to relinquish its dream of a homogeneous empire and come to terms with radical constitutional limitation of the sovereign's powers. At the same time, Habsburg authority over the whole of the realm would remain unchallenged in its enjoyment of the free and absolute loyalty of the Hungarian nation. In addition, it was perceived that a Hungary undergoing dynamic social and economic development would increase the international standing of the Habsburg Empire.

However, given how intolerant Metternich had been towards anything that challenged feudal power even indirectly, the prospects for interest reconciliation were doubtful. By the spring of 1848, Metternich was no longer around, however, and the sovereign reluctantly gave his blessing to laws transforming relations between the Habsburg Empire and Hungary. The Habsburg Dynasty would have preferred that things stay as they were, but it had also come to realize that no Hungarian politician even considered a complete break from the Empire and, paradoxically, that the crumbling Empire could be held together only if the basis of the Dual Monarchy were reconsidered.

Vienna's attitude was partly the result of a growing awareness that large masses of the Hungarian peasantry could no longer be counted on to turn against their reform-oriented nobility. Although the emancipation of the serfs did not bring complete relief (landlords were to retain lesser feudal usufructions), it was sufficient to legitimize the nobility's political supremacy.

The weak point of the liberal reform programme was the third aspect of their interest reconciliation scheme: the national minorities. While political and social reforms could work on the basis of a rational exchange of concessions, the same model could be applied to the national minorities only to a very limited extent. Individual members of the national minorities were treated on an equal footing with Hungarians, but they had no collective rights. It was assumed that social interest reconciliation combined with political freedom would cause individuals to forget about collective issues.

Although the interest-reconciliation scheme did not directly target the needs of national minorities and did not take into account their existing and potential grievances, it did promote their interests: freedom of the press, for instance, opened the way to greater cultural and political initiatives. However, the whole programme was in the hands of Hungarian liberals imbued with national feeling, liberal values having become indistinguishable from national independence in the minds of many, and this was enough, in itself, to prevent the national minorities from identifying with it.

In its turn, liberal nationalism derived its main strength from its ability to transform non-political calls for modernization into a struggle for the realization of national values, and by doing so to give an emotional colouring to its anti-feudal agenda. The still ongoing language reform, the foundation of a National Academy and the nurturing of national cults (for example, that of Miklós Zrínyi) were cultural phenomena which contributed greatly to the declaration in 1844 that the Hungarian language would henceforth be the sole official language of Hungary. These were all steps along the road to the emergence of a modern bourgeois nation. Needless to say, national feeling cutting across the feudal hierarchy of social classes – and thereby creating an affinity between speakers of the same language, regardless of their social standing – was the cornerstone of social interest reconciliation, consistent anti-feudalism and constitutionalism. To be able to build on this national feeling, it was necessary first to reconstitute Hungary's territorial integrity, lost in 1541. Whole regions of Hungary were still under the direct rule of Vienna. Had this continued, political interest reconciliation would have suffered; in case of conflict, these territories could have been used to blackmail the Hungarian government. This is why reunion with Transylvania was urged with such vehemence and why the Habsburg Dynasty entered into dispute with the ministry in charge of the so-called Military Border Region regarding administrative competence over it.

Under bourgeois constitutionalism, it was unacceptable that different rules and conditions should prevail in Transylvania or the Military Border Region from the rest of the country. The liberal nobility wanted to see universal, bourgeois freedom replace individual freedoms that could be easily manipulated to set one social group or nationality against another. National feeling was more than emotionally motivated enthusiasm: it was based on the recognition that anti-feudalism and liberalism went hand-in-hand. The minorities question was a weak point in the interest-reconciliation scheme, partly because it was difficult to reconcile the new, bourgeois national outlook emphasizing universal values with the separatist claims of the national minorities, and partly because, in this case, rational interests were mixed with irrational motives. It must also be remembered that in spring 1848, a new group of politicians came to power committed to liberalization; although this new political elite could not do a great deal more for the national minorities than its predecessor had, its very political orientation raised expectations that it might consider the creation of collective rights, including rights for the national minorities, at some time in the future.

In the spring of 1848 the political scene in Hungary was fraught with difficulties, but little indicated that tragedy was imminent.

*   *   *

The national minorities reacted differently to the events leading to the introduction of basic freedoms in Hungary, motivated by three factors: first, the level of development of the particular minority, that is, how far they had gone beyond the cultural phase of 'national emergence' (this also indicated their level of social development); second, the minority leaders' assessment of the political situation; and third, their population structure. In areas with a diffuse or mixed population nationalist initiative tends to be weaker than in areas where an ethnic population forms a compact block.

The Croatians were the most compact ethnic group of all. They coexisted within the Hungarian state, but did not mix with Hungarians. Given that the Croatians had a well-established and traditionally autonomous system of local administration and were familiar with the concept of public law, it might be expected that relations with them would have been easy. Kossuth proposed at the Hungarian Diet as early as 22 March 1848 that Croatians should be able to use their ethnic language in local administration and that the use of Hungarian should be restricted to Croatian-Hungarian relations. (Kossuth had made a similar proposal in 1842, when he was still a member of the opposition.) The next day the court appointed one of its most trusted men, Baron Josip Jellacic, Viceroy of Croatia. At this time no approval from the responsible Hungarian ministry was required to confirm the appointment, because such a ministry had not yet been formed.

The Croatian National Assembly at its 25 March session called for bourgeois transformation, unification of Croatia, Slavonia, Dalmatia and the Military Border Region, unlimited use of the Croatian language and the formation of a responsible ministry. The Emperor, in his reply to the National Assembly at the end of the month, promised to consider reasonable requests, but emphasized that he would not meet any demands violating the territorial integrity of the Hungarian Crown, so making it clear that he would allow neither complete autonomy for Croatia nor the annexation of the Military Border Region. Croatia nevertheless continued to lay claim to considerable non-Croatian territories. In the person of Jellacic, however, Vienna had a Viceroy absolutely loyal to the Habsburg court, and on whom it could rely even if political interest reconciliation with Hungary should fail. At the same time, its large claims made Croatia a useful card in the hands of Vienna, one that could be played at any time against a Hungarian revolution.

In March one national minority after another came forward and stated its demands.

On 24 March 1848, Simion Barnutiu presented a petition to ethnic Romanians in Transylvania inviting them to demand a national assembly and the recognition of Romanians as a fourth nation (in the feudal sense of a recognized ethnic group with particular rights). On 27 March, the Serb National Assembly in Újvidék (Novi Sad) demanded the recognition of Serbs as an autonomous nation (again in the feudal sense) and the right to use their native language in local administration. They also demanded the abolition of feudal conditions in the Military Border Region. (On 4 April, Serbian borderguards made similar demands in their petition to the Emperor.) At the Slovakian county assembly held on 28 March in Liptó, Milán Hodza demanded the use of Slovakian in county administration and education. On the same day, members of the Romanian intelligentsia demanded in Cluj (Kolozsvár) that Romanian be introduced as the official language in counties with a Romanian majority.

At this stage territorial questions were not raised, other than by Croatia, though it was likely that the Serbs would come forward with similar demands.

Between 28 March and 3 April, while the national minorities were busy formulating their claims, an important debate took place at the Hungarian Diet concerning a law on political representation. Kossuth expressed the view that if the Diet was to be transformed on the basis of the principle of public representation, the county assemblies should be, too. Széchenyi was against the idea: he warned that such a reform would considerably empower the national minorities. Kossuth maintained that political representation for counties was desirable precisely because it was in the nation's own interest to promote political representation for national minorities in their own localities. Kossuth was no doubt largely motivated by recognition of the importance of interest reconciliation at a national level, especially in view of the possibility of failure to reach political compromise with Vienna. The proposal concerning political representation nearly brought about the collapse of the Batthyány administration, at this time only temporarily entrusted with government. In the end, Kossuth backed down and a decision was made in accordance with a compromise solution suggested by Deák: the nobility were to retain their majority position within county assemblies, at least until the next session of the Diet, despite the fact that the principle of political representation was already supposed to have been implemented in the counties. Under the law on political representation, Hungarian was to be the working language of all county assemblies with the exception of Croatian and Slavonian counties.

The uncertainty this dispute created was largely responsible for diminishing public trust in Hungarian liberal policies.

This was the situation when Kossuth received a Serb delegation led by Kostic in Bratislava (Pozsony). At this meeting, Kossuth talked about his vision of public freedom and did not reject the idea of unrestricted use of Serbian in local (village and town) administration, as well as in cultural and religious matters (this was also to be supported by the abolition of all forms of discrimination against the Greek Orthodox religion), but he refused to recognize Serbia as an autonomous nation. Kossuth rejected even more strongly the Serb demand for the formation of an autonomous Serb region within Hungary. There is no reason for us to believe that Kossuth acted in any way against his principles, but – in the light of the aforementioned dispute over political representation – he must also have been aware that, apart from anything else, if he were to show any leniency to Serb demands on questions of autonomy and sovereignty he was bound to cause a split within the Hungarian reform camp and jeopardize the whole bourgeois transformation process.

The Serbs were quick to respond. In mid-April, the Serb National Assembly in Karlóca demanded that an autonomous *Vajdaság* (district governed by a '*vajda*' or '*voivode*') be created, covering the regions of Bácska, Temesköz, Szerémség and Baranya. Voivodina – as it was to be called – would have 690 thousand Serbs living alongside 350 thousand Hungarians, 400 thousand Germans and 560 thousand Romanians. The Serb demand was far-fetched not only because it violated the principle of national unity that the reformers were dedicated to restore, but also because it involved a claim for large territories beyond those where Serbs formed the majority. The Hungarian government could not create a precedent for other national minorities and it was determined to reject territorial claims from other minorities without legitimate grounds.

The Serb National Congress summoned in mid-May, again in Karlóca, after having stated its commitment to the idea of a Serb Voivodina, appointed Josif Rajacic as Patriarch, and Colonel Stefan Supljikac as Voivode. It must be understood, however, that not all Serbs supported this idea. Those who opposed it lived mostly on the territory of Hungary proper (excluding Croatia). It is noteworthy that there were Serbs who sought to avoid confrontation with the Hungarian government and, instead, saw the ultimate solution in a Greater Serbia, in the way of which stood Turkish feudal supremacy. Even in decline, Turkish rule could not be overthrown without external assistance. It seemed an obvious choice to seek such assistance from the Hungarian government with its openly anti-feudal orientation. In order to bring into being a Greater Serbia, it was necessary to neglect the question of Voivodina, which was only of minor importance in any case. In the long term, this scheme foreshadowed a conflict between ethnic Serbs in Hungary and the Hungarian population, but in the short term, conflict was to be avoided.

Anti-Hungarian attitudes were nevertheless being encouraged among Serbs in Novi Sad, while the Serb government was reluctant to break with the Turkish occupiers for fear of the consequences of an irreconcilable conflict. The Serb government, under pressure from Serb public opinion, incited nationalist feeling among Hungarian Serbs and occasionally – taking advantage of the independence of the Military Border Region from Hungarian administration – resorted to armed action to point up its political claims.

On 27 June 1848, Hungarian Romanians led by Eftimie Murgu, a solicitor freed in Pest by the revolution, demanded the creation of an autonomous Romanian area, promising in return armed assistance to the Hungarian revolution. In addition, a large number of ethnic Romanians protested against their membership in the same Church that had supported the Serb cause.

Conflicting territorial claims on the part of Hungary's national minorities threatened to set them against each other – Serbs against Croats, and Serbs against Romanians because of the Serb claim to Temesköz – not to mention the threat to the Hungarian government. This complex issue cannot, therefore, be reduced to a conflict between the inflexible minorities policy of a Hungarian government out of touch with both reality and legitimate nationalist claims. The Habsburgs themselves realized the great political potential in the situation and managed to exploit it by fuelling nationalist controversy and setting minorities against each other as well as against the government.

The situation was also becoming volatile in Transylvania. Here Hungarians had a majority in the feudal parliament seated in Cluj (Kolozsvár) and there was no doubt that they would be able to push through a decision in favour of reunification with Hungary. But there was also strong opposition to reunification: many Transylvanian Saxons did not want to see their feudal privileges threatened by the introduction in a reunified Transylvania of legal changes emerging from the Hungarian bourgeois transformation process. Romanians – the majority in Transylvania – feared the minority status reunification would bring; they were not directly represented in the parliament of Transylvania, as it was.

In mid-May, the Romanian National Assembly had demanded recognition as a nation, proportional representation in parliament and a renegotiation of reunification, this time with Romanian participation. The peasantry insisted on land redistribution. A national council was also set up, headed by Greek-Orthodox Bishop Andrei Saguna. Many of these demands were entirely unacceptable to the Hungarian government. The so-called April Laws could not be enforced before the declaration of reunification. Only a legal solution could ensure the success of reunification and reconcile competing interests, so preventing a breach between the Austrian imperial court and the Hungarian government. The introduction of proportional representation in the parliament threatened to upset the nobility to whom the concept of universal suffrage was unacceptable, so putting in jeopardy the whole interest reconciliation process in which they were to play the leading part – the prospect of Hungarians becoming a minority in their own parliament was equally unacceptable. Resentment about reunification grew among the Romanian minority as their most important claims came to be rejected. When it was finally announced at the end of May by the parliament of Transylvania, reunification was endorsed only by Greek-Catholic Bishop János Lemény on behalf of the Romanian minority.

In such a threatening situation, the Hungarian government could only hope that manumission – a cornerstone of social interest reconciliation – would win peasants from ethnic minorities over to the Hungarian transformation process with the result of curbing, at least for a time, their nationalist tendencies.

This expectation was best fulfilled in relation to ethnic Slovakians. On one occasion, a radical evangelical priest, Jozef Hurban, reproached Slovakian peasants for neglecting equality for all nationalities in favour of the benefits they enjoyed from serf emancipation. Although isolated instances of nationalist action continued to take place even after the introduction of manumission, and irregular troops encouraged by the Habsburg Emperor would take up arms every now and then, ethnic Slovakians as a community never rose against the Hungarian revolution. The reluctance of Slovakians to break away from Hungary for the sake of demonstrating their national identity may be attributed to the fact that Slovakians and Hungarians had much in common in terms of religion and culture.

It was a different story in Croatia. Jellacic, who was installed as Viceroy of Croatia in Zagreb on 18 April, announced the emancipation of the serfs on 25 April as a measure independent of Hungarian law, seeking to win the loyalty of the peasantry to himself and the Emperor, and to prevent Croatians from making a connection between the improvement in their fortunes and events taking place in Hungary. Jellacic, having strengthened his own position by taking credit for interest reconciliation – manumission, for example – began to defy the Hungarian government. He was encouraged to do so by his allies at the Habsburg court who were committed to scuppering political interest reconciliation with Hungary. Any assistance he could give to this end would be well rewarded.

Currying favour with Vienna was the motive behind Jellacic's actions and the cause of the whole protracted controversy about his position as Viceroy (although suspended on the Hungarian government's request – but later restored – his authority at no time diminished). One way out would have been for Hungary to offer Croatia full autonomy and to satisfy any related claims, so removing the Croatian question from the agenda of court politics. In this scenario, Croatia would secure its nationalist agenda without bloodshed, whereas if Vienna were to become involved, military action could not be avoided. At the end of August, the Hungarian council of ministers passed a resolution offering full recognition of Croatian autonomy to the extent of secession. The Habsburg court reacted by officially restoring Jellacic to Viceroyship on 4 September. Jellacic went into action without delay: on 11 September, his main troops crossed the Drava river in the south of Hungary and in the Emperor's name marched against Hungary's capital city and the Hungarian government. The crumbling political interest-reconciliation process finally collapsed. Croatians acting in the belief that they were fighting for their own cause were in fact being used to promote the political and personal interests of others.

There was a chance that conflict with ethnic Serbs in Hungary, at least, could be avoided. The Serbian peasantry had benefited from serf emancipation and were appeased to the extent that they were repeatedly criticized at the Serb National Assembly for being largely indifferent to nationalist concerns. The prospect of a Serb uprising diminished even further when, on 30 May, the Hungarian government abolished feudal obligations for the Temes Military Border Region and other territories. Radical nationalist Serbs headed by Rajacic made every effort – in collaboration with the local feudal administration which had remained virtually unscathed by reform – to misrepresent the situation and to spread false rumours suggesting that the population could rely solely on the Habsburg Emperor for concessions and the protection of their existing privileges, but should not trust the Hungarian government. They were, of course, secretly supported by the Habsburg court; the prospects of cooperation with the Hungarian government looked increasingly grim. In addition, officers of the imperial army who had little loyalty to Hungary did nothing to prevent the influx of political agitators and armed irregulars into the country.

At the same time, the Hungarian government did not have sufficient forces in the Serb region – a deficiency that virtually invited an uprising. The Hungarian army could not resist even smaller rebel forces, and the Serb minority had little to lose and much to gain. Armed conflict, in turn, was likely to mobilize the otherwise passive part of the peasantry living outside the border region. The Serbs saw the weakness of the Hungarian army and believed that their defeat by the Habsburgs was imminent, after which they expected to receive Voivodina as a reward.

By June, intention had ripened into action and the first wave of armed conflicts broke out. Events seemed to support Serb expectations, as the rebels extended their control over more and more territory. By November, their acquisitions were so large that they felt able to set up the so-called 'supreme *odbor*', the highest institution of Serb civil government. The Serbs were, however, internally divided; there was even a Serb military commander, János Damjanich, fighting on behalf of the Hungarian government.

The Romanians were also divided: Hungarian and Transylvanian Romanians reacted quite differently to the unfolding events. The leaders of the Hungarian Romanians (Murgu and Jan Dragos) were personally committed to the freedoms introduced by the Hungarian revolution, while the peasantry had benefited greatly from social interest reconciliation and serf emancipation. In addition, the new and extremely ambitious Serb nationalism represented a direct threat to the Romanians in the Temesköz. Under such circumstances, it was not in their interest to seek military confrontation with the Hungarian government, although this did not prevent them from formulating nationalist demands. When the situation required, Dragos – a Romanian member of the Hungarian Diet – acted as mediator between the leaders of the militarized Transylvanian Romanians and the Hungarian government.

Relations continued to be strained with the Transylvanian Romanians, however, and for a combination of reasons confrontation could not be avoided. In Transylvania, the conditions of socage were significantly different from those in Hungary. The laws were contradictory, and the situation was further aggravated by the fact that individual landowners and the more reactionary politicians hindered and delayed even the enforcement of existing regulations. Significant numbers of the peasantry were left uncertain about how they would be affected by the reforms of 1848. The situation played into the hands of the Church elite who were loyal to the Viennese court and were able to manipulate the peasantry almost at will, portraying the Hungarians as the enemies of all Romanians, who could rely for help on the Emperor alone. In the eyes of the politically uneducated peasantry, these accusations were realized in the form of the small Hungarian and Székely units specially chosen by the anti-Hungarian military command of Transylvania to suppress peasant uprisings in the region. Everything about the behaviour of the Transylvanian military command suggests that it condoned anti-Hungarian and anti-revolutionary action. It succeeded in combining nationalist claims with social grievances, and with loyalty to the Habsburg court and ethnic clergy. Supported by the Habsburg Emperor – first secretly, then openly offering an alliance – and encouraged by the general anti-Hungarian atmosphere dominating Transylvania (partly in connection with the discontent among Transylvanian Saxons), the Transylvanian military command welcomed such developments. In any case, the Hungarian government did not possess sufficient military force in the region to ward off confrontation. Finally, legitimate grievances deliberately aggravated by the political manipulations of the Transylvanian military command culminated in a Romanian uprising.

*   *   *

By the autumn of 1848, antagonisms between the Hungarian political establishment and a number of the national minorities under its jurisdiction had developed into armed conflict. By the time of Jellacic's incursion it was too late to widen the social base of interest reconciliation – for example, by abolishing the so-called 'vine tithe', one of the most severe of the remaining feudal obligations – and to emphasize social interdependence: the rebels either did not learn about these measures or chose to ignore them.

The failure of political and social (ethnic and national) interest reconciliation brought the Hungarian revolution to the brink of crisis. The Hungarian military command was helpless in the face of the Délvidék (Novi Sad) uprising. The situation was similar in Transylvania where the joint efforts of the imperial army and the Romanian rebels challenged Hungarian supremacy. From the end of November, General Jozef Bem came to lead the Transylvanian army, but any improvement from this change of command was not soon forthcoming. Slovakian irregulars, meanwhile, repeatedly attacked the Felvidék from Moravia. Another Serb National Assembly held in Karlóca demanded equal legal status with Croatia for Voivodina. In its peace efforts, the Hungarian government was now prepared to grant virtually any concession to the Serbs except this recognition of Voivodina. By the end of December, the Austrian Prince Windischgrätz's troops reached the outskirts of Pest. The national council of defence and the Diet were forced to flee to Debrecen.

In such dire circumstances, there was no choice but to surrender to nationalist demands and offer peace. This is exactly what General Bem did in Transylvania: in a proclamation, he assured the Transylvanian minorities that they were to enjoy greater freedom in using their own language. At the end of December, Bem issued another proclamation, offering unconditional amnesty to any rebels who surrendered. However, on 8 January Romanian rebels massacred 600 people in Nagyenyed and set fire to symbolic receptacles of Hungarian culture, including the Nagyenyed library and archive, making reconciliation psychologically impossible.

The time had come when only national solidarity based on cooperation between the nobility and the peasantry could save the country. Accordingly, national feeling emerged as a prime virtue. Under the circumstances, any major concessions to national minorities who had become allies of the political enemy threatened to upset the social interest-reconciliation process and to demoralize the classes who provided the social foundation of national self-defence. The prospects for compromise were gloomy: no one was likely to make concessions to a political elite which seemed on the way out.

Habsburg absolutism used classic 'divide and rule' tactics: it fuelled and maintained armed conflict between the nations it meant to bring under its rule. And so the fighting continued. But despite the machinations of the Hapsburg court, the Hungarian army was winning one victory after another over the imperial army. By March, Bem had liberated Transylvania, with the exception of Gyulafehérvár and Déva Castle, which were still held by the imperial army. At this point the Romanian uprising was restricted to a few highland areas. By early April, General Mór Perczel had taken the military centre of Serb resistance. The supporters of an autonomous Voivodina were forced to retreat to the Titeli plateau.

Social interest reconciliation had passed the test with flying colours. In an atmosphere of victory, the Hungarian government was able to offer the national minorities a compromise settlement; to pass a national minorities act acceptable for all concerned and to do so with grace, representing the inevitable as a voluntary initiative.

After the announcement of its Declaration of Independence, Hungary had to come to terms with its national minorities if it was to take a republican and democratic stance, emerge as a strong and independent state and prevent political restoration. Immediate action had to be taken, particularly because the constitution issued in early March in Olmütz by the Austrian Emperor – one of the things preparatory to the Declaration of Independence – offered some minorities a complex settlement, including a declaration of equality for all national minorities, the transformation into autonomous regions of Serb Voivodina (composed of Bácska and Temesköz), Transylvania with its Parts (*Partium*), the Military Border Region and the union of Croatia, Slavonia and the coastal region. All these regions were to form part of a single and indivisible Austrian Empire.

The rebellious national minorities had mixed feelings about the Olmütz Constitution. It did not fully satisfy the territorial claims of Croatia, and Serbian expectations were also disappointed. The Romanians were even more dissatisfied: the Constitution made no mention of their claims at all, although Bishop Saguna – in a memorandum presented to Franz Joseph in February – had demanded that all Romanian-populated areas should be transformed into an autonomous territory. The more liberal wing of minority politicians was growing increasingly concerned about their future within the framework of an Austrian Empire that was slowly revealing its true absolutist orientation. Many felt betrayed in what they actually received from the Habsburg court in return for their loyalty.

Hungarian politicians recognized the potential of this situation. As the Olmütz Constitution neglected Romanian nationalist claims above all, Kossuth sent Dragos, a member of the Hungarian Diet, to enter into negotiations with Avram Iancu, leader of the Romanian rebels. Kossuth offered, in addition to promises already made about religious and cultural freedoms, use of the Romanian language in local administration and their recognition as a nationality in their own right. Dragos, however, could not accomplish his mission. In early May, negotiations ground to a halt after an ambush by a Hungarian irregular unit led by Imre Hatvani. The rebels reacted by executing Dragos.

Count László Teleki, special envoy of the Hungarian government in Paris, urged the transformation of the Hungarian state into a federation and conducted negotiations to that effect with émigré political representatives of the national minorities. In the meantime, Kossuth, as government commissioner, authorized measures to meet the social demands of Romanian and Serbian border guards and briefed Perczel, who was then fighting Serb rebels, on the terms on which he should initiate a settlement.

Although a number of individual initiatives were taken, no law on national minorities yet existed, and the committee in charge of working out a new Hungarian Constitution – which might also have dealt with the matter – had not yet commenced work. The country's ruling political elite was largely responsible for the failure to take advantage of the circumstances prevailing during the month that elapsed between the Declaration of Independence and the Russian intervention. Such inaction cannot be justified, especially as, by this time, the national minorities were themselves seeking a compromise with Hungary, being more under threat from Central Europe's mightiest absolutist regime than from the Hungarians.

Although the Hungarian government was not entirely remiss, its response was too slow, a delay which did not help to maintain an atmosphere of trust in its competence. Particular initiatives could not substitute for a comprehensive act on national minorities. On 14 July, Kossuth and Balcescu signed a Hungarian-Romanian Draft Peace Plan which now included a provision on the bilingualism of counties with a Romanian majority in addition to other local concessions. Regardless of the peace plan, however, an 8–10 thousand-strong army under Bem's command continued in its attempts to suppress the Transylvanian uprising, at a time when Hungary was under threat from Russian intervention forces and needed every single soldier on Hungarian soil. Finally, on 21 July, the Government presented an Act on National Minorities, which was passed by the Lower House on 28 July. The act declared that all national minorities had the right to autonomous development, unrestricted use of native languages in their settlements, municipal assemblies, local administration, courts of law, schools and churches. Career advancement was to depend on merit, regardless of nationality and religion. The law declared an amnesty, and Article 15 opened the way to further improvements by declaring: 'The Hungarian government shall be authorized and entrusted especially to pay attention to all the justified demands of Serbs and Romanians and to alleviate all their legitimate grievances either by its own decree or by way of submitting a draft law to the National Assembly.' However, by this time it was already too late. Less than two weeks later, the main body of the Hungarian army was forced to surrender at Világos.

The Hungarian revolution and freedom struggle were suppressed by the joint efforts of two armies. Hungary's defeat on the battleground, however, was to a great extent attributable to its failure to resolve the national minorities crisis in due time, so preventing its escalation into civil war. Although this failure was partly the fault of the revolutionary government which acted too slowly, the thoughtless actions of the impatient minority leaders fatally undermined the position of the only government and politicians in the region likely to meet their demands.[1]

(1987)

Notes

1 The period of 1848–9 and, particularly, the national minorities question is covered by an extensive literature both in Hungarian and in other languages, including both general surveys and studies of particular questions of interest. Source books also offer a great deal of material on the subject. Many of the views one encounters in this vast literature are controversial, given that the minorities question cannot be viewed independantly from national and ideological considerations. Interested readers should note two essential reference books which have appeared recently: Endre Kovács (editor-in-chief), László Katus (ed.), *Magyarország története 1848–90* [The History of Hungary 1848–90], Budapest, 1979, Vol. 2, esp. pp. 1577–8 and pp. 1592–3 – György Spira is the author of the chapter on 1848–9 – and Béla Köpeczi (editor-in-chief), Zoltán Szász (ed.), *Erdély története* [The History of Transylvania], Budapest, 1986, Vol. 3, pp. 1798–1806. (The main reference is the work of Ambrus Miskolczy.)

Part Two

The emergence of civil society
at the crossroads of liberalism
and conservatism

7 Mamelukes and Zoltans: Elected Representatives under the Dual Monarchy

The chosen ones

In 1848, after the first general elections, Pál Nyári declared that: 'Transformation in Hungary may be theoretically complete, but it is certainly not so in reality: the same people continue to sit in parliament as before.'[1] A statistical analysis shows that he was right. Parliament, destined to control the bourgeois political-transformation process, was still dominated by the landed nobility, which comprised 64% of its elected members, while 12% were civil servants and 24% members of the urban bourgeoisie. Among the latter final group, many were professional people, primarily barristers and municipal civil servants; most were also members of families with a noble background. Only two members of parliament were landed serfs, despite the fact that all smallholders (with a minimum one-fourth holding) were now entitled to vote and were themselves electable from the age of 24. There is nothing surprising in these data, considering that political skills had traditionally been the domain of the nobility. The nobility constituted the Lower House of Hungary's feudal parliament – the Diet – and only noblemen could be members of county assemblies. What is remarkable, however, is that very few members of the genuine aristocracy (in ascending order of rank: barons, counts, dukes, and archdukes) were successful in the first general elections – they constituted no more than 6% of all Members of Parliament, with 16 counts and 10 barons seated.

The make-up of the body of elected representatives changed throughout the Dual Monarchy;[2] the role of the aristocracy was only its most striking aspect. The percentage of aristocrats in the Diet varied, as follows, between 1861 and 1910:

1861	1865	1869	1872	1875	1878	1881	1884
13.3%	16.5%	10.6%	8.6%	10.8%	11.0%	12.4%	12.8%

1887	1892	1896	1901	1905	1906	1910
13.3%	16.4%	13.4%	13.6%	14.4%	11.1%	15.7%

In the last full year of the Monarchy, 1917, aristocrats constituted the largest single group of MPs – 16.9% – as a result of the by-elections following the general election of 1910 (there were no elections in 1914 because of the outbreak of the First World War). They were elected in particularly large numbers in years when the country was facing major political decisions, as was the case in 1867, when the Hungarian parliament endorsed the Austro-Hungarian Compromise; in 1892 – a time of intense political controversy concerning the separation of church and state; and in the 1910s – the years before and during the war.

The involvement of the aristocracy in the Lower House in such relatively high numbers is surprising, given that they already had their own hereditary institution – the Upper House – in which all members of the aristocracy were entitled to a seat by birth. In 1886, however, property qualifications were introduced (Act VII of 1885), restricting the number of those qualifying for membership of the Upper House. At the same time, membership was extended to holders of certain state offices and a limited number of persons appointed by the King. But even after these reforms, 70–80% of Upper House members were aristocrats. (It must be added, however, that as a protest against property qualifications and appointed membership, many hereditary members chose to stay away from the House; as a rule, no more than 40–50 members of the 350 were ever present.) In this study we shall restrict our attention to elected institutions of representation in which the aristocracy also wished to participate directly; a wish, given the prevailing electoral system, which was easily fulfilled. The majority of such MPs represented regions dominated by national minorities.

The numbers and wealth of the aristocracy assured it direct and sizeable – and predominantly pro-governmental – representation in the Lower House. (Franz Joseph I and Karl IV distributed 204 aristocratic titles between them. Forty per cent of new aristocrats were Hungarian, 18 of Jewish origin, 22% German, 14% Slav, 18% and 6% from the other national minorities.) Rich new aristocrats (Jewish barons, among others) merged with ancient families, thereby further consolidating existing power relations and a democratic system under which one-fifth of all adult aristocrats became elected representatives. The interests of this class were further promoted by the legal counsellors, barristers and stewards whom they helped to elect.

The landed nobility completely dominated parliament in 1848, although their proportion gradually decreased thereafter. Parliamentary almanacs first referred to them as a social catagory in 1884. In the 1860s and 1870s, this social class provided about 60% of all elected representatives, though later on their proportion fell to around 30–35%. There were both pro-government and opposition landed nobility in the Diet, the former having a slight majority. The liberal opposition was dominated by the landed nobility whereas the government party was overwhelmingly constituted of aristocrats. Landed nobles, many of whom were wealthy enough to finance their own political careers, were usually elected to parliament by areas with a majority of ethnic Hungarians (as opposed to aristocrats, who found their support among the national minorities). The divisions within the landowning nobility between the governing party and the opposition indicates an ambivalent political identity.

Another sizeable group within parliament were the middle classes or professionals – civil servants, barristers, freelance intellectuals, teachers and journalists. This group felt most affinity with the landowning nobility in terms of both values and aspirations. They sought to ascend to the status of gentleman, and chose to call themselves the 'genteel middle classes'.

In the Diet, 12–14% of representatives were barristers (many of noble origin), and 7–14% civil servants, also of noble origin. There were hardly any representatives of peasant origin, nor were there many representatives of the industrial class.

The Lower House was far from being dominated by a gerontocracy, as the following tabulation shows (%):

	1887	1892	1896	1901	1905	1906	1910
Under 40	36.6	30.0	29.1	28.6	27.1	36.1	28.1
41–60	49.1	56.9	56.9	55.7	57.9	53.2	56.7
Over 61	14.3	13.1	14.0	15.7	15.0	10.7	15.2

The lead was taken by middle-aged representatives combining solid skills with experience; but the younger generation were also present in considerable numbers.

It was inevitable that the aristocracy – with its extensive power base – would retain its political dominance; this time, in the name of liberalism, but in the same spirit of feudal privilege. The continuity of its social and political influence boosted the aristocracy's confidence, reinforcing its belief in its feudal supremacy, in the light of which the emerging social classes felt inclined to accept a subordinate role. No wonder the aristocracy was disdainful of popular representation, given its knowledge of how little the political system had to do with representing the people's interests. The aristocracy looked at popular representation from above and outside. Exceptional moral strength would be required of them, not only to realize the preposterousness of this situation, but to voluntarily reject the political role that followed from it.

In 1867, the Lord Chief Justice refused to be sworn in by the Minister of Justice because of the latter's inferior social origins (the Minister was the son of a cobbler). The King had to intervene to ensure that the constitution should prevail over feudal pride.[3] Under conditions of increasing liberalism, however, the aristocracy had to assume more democratic forms of behaviour. An incident that took place in the Upper House in 1885 illustrates the more refined ways in which the aristocracy managed to maintain an air of superiority:

[Cardinal] Haynald buoyantly made his way to the gallery reserved for the press to have a chat with Zsigmond Singer, correspondent of *Neue Freie Presse,* who was himself to become a member of the Upper House at a later date. The correspondent of *Pester Lloyd*, Bernát Pataki, hung around in the hope of catching what his Excellency was going to say. Our friend Pataki, a prime example of journalistic confidence, suddenly turned to the Cardinal, asking casually:
'Excuse me, your Excellency, could you by any chance tell me the time? My watch has stopped.'
His Excellency looked at Pataki, a mild but ironic smile playing on his lips. He took out his beautiful, enamelled gold watch, placed it carefully on the edge of the gallery and walked out without uttering a word.
Singer snarled at Pataki for having behaved so tactlessly and told him to apologize to the Cardinal immediately and to return his watch.
Pataki, of course, pretended not to understand what he had done.
Nevertheless, he hurried out to catch up with the Cardinal. He found his Excellency in the hall. There he apologized and handed his watch back with a deep bow. The same smile appeared again on his Excellency's face, who took out a red handkerchief, wiped his watch and carefully slipped it back into his pocket.[4]

At the same time, there were genuine efforts to introduce more democratic relations among members of parliament. For instance, it was decided that the elected parliament would retain the informal manner of address in use among members of the feudal Diet, all members of the nobility. In these changed circumstances, this form of address gave rise to some very awkward situations. On one occasion a baron – no doubt reluctantly – addressed a commoner in the informal manner. In his confusion the latter failed to return the compliment and used the formal manner of address usually required of a person speaking to his superior. This caused the baron to burst out angrily:

'Do you refuse to address me in the manner now customary in the Lower House? Do you not think me worthy of it?'
'Your Excellency, if you will allow me', the commoner replied apologetically.
'There is nothing for me to allow' – the baron interrupted impatiently – 'I am entitled to demand that you follow what is common practice among representatives!'[5]

The aristocracy used its social connections and dominance to strengthen its political power. The National Casino – the aristocracy's habitual venue for social occasions – was a place where many political discussions occurred and many important measures were decided, and it functioned as an important, if unofficial, factor in Hungarian politics. As József Kristóffy remarked, those who came here:

> . . . were convinced that nothing could take place without their consent, because at this time the political power base of Hungary was still the *latifundia*. Kálmán Tisza and his successors, being well aware of this, never failed to consult the '*Skuptsina*' in the Casino when facing important political decisions and faithfully followed their instructions. The '*Skuptsina*' [political slang for a gathering of wise men, or elders] were the politicized members of the Casino – mostly the Casino's elders, whence this gathering derived its name – who met in the evenings in the Deák Hall and discussed, among other things, public affairs.

In this period *latifundia* – the catagory of the largest land-holdings – with an area of one to ten thousand *hold* (an archaic Hungarian unit of measurement: 1 hold equals 1.42 acres) constituted 32%, while latifundia of over ten thousand *hold* constituted 7.4%, of Hungary's territory. This explains the political authority of the '*Skuptsina*', despite the fact that they never openly engaged in politics.[6]

The Casino would not, however, hesitate to come forward when its political privileges were under threat. On one occasion, a newspaper owner and editor dared to write harshly about the Casino, calling its members 'a gang dressed in tails'. One of the most hot-headed of the Casino's members provoked the editor to challenge him to a duel, in the course of which the editor was severely wounded in the stomach. This incident gave rise to public demonstrations lasting several days, in protest against the aristocratic disdain that the Casino embodied. In the end, two men were shot by the army, and the Casino's influence remained undiminished.[7]

The Casino was, in fact, almost omnipotent, with the right to judge and punish the actions of its members in whatever way it saw fit. The merest allegation of improper behaviour was enough to incur excommunication, and enforced resignation from parliament or the army; it could even lead to the loss of one's life in a duel. The Casino could bypass the law, parliament, the sovereign and the army. Its tyrannical rule extended over the whole country.[8] Parliament was also powerless against the Casino's influence: the Lower House was dominated by the aristocracy, and derived its political legitimacy from a regime dedicated to feudal consolidation.[9]

The power of the aristocracy rested on such solid foundations that it did not even matter if some of its members joined the opposition. No attempt was made to prevent the opposition from acquiring a majority in parliament

5   Kálmán Tisza, c. 1890

(in 1906), even, for the simple reason that the opposition was harmless; like everyone else, they were in the hands of the almighty aristocracy and would not even dream of challenging its undisputed authority.

It was, of course, in the aristocracy's interest to perpetuate the regime under which it enjoyed unparalleled political control and flourished in every conceivable manner. This was the motivation behind its efforts to obtain seats in both houses of parliament. As a group, the aristocracy – given its expertise, erudition and traditional political leadership – had little competition from other social classes in the political arena. In the period under consideration, however, the social composition of parliament was considerably more varied than it had ever been before, making it much more difficult for individual members of the aristocracy to become MPs.

In the initial stages of the political selection process, that inevitably began within the aristocracy itself, those with the best prospects for election to the post-1867 Lower House were those who had played an outstanding role in the feudal Diet and/or in public affairs – with special importance placed on their involvement in the political events of 1848–9. Political imprisonment or exile during the years of absolutist repression that followed the defeat of the Hungarian Revolution and Freedom Fight were now invaluable in forwarding one's career. Those who had been sentenced to detention or even death for involvement in the revolutionary events – many of them outstanding statesmen, poets and writers – were now revered as national heroes and enjoyed the wholehearted support of the population. In other cases, political authority rested on influence, noble origin, personal talents and the confidence of the King.[10]

In the period after 1867, Ferenc Deák was the most popular political figure in Hungary. Most prominent public figures joined his party or, after 1875, the Liberal Party led by Kálmán Tisza. Kálmán Mikszáth, a popular writer of the time, remarked with more than a hint of irony:

> The lives of these eminent Hungarians are tediously similar . . . They all took part in the 1848 revolution, were imprisoned for ten years in Olmütz or Kufstein, released in 1861, elected to parliament where they sat around for a while, joining the opposition before ascending to the title of Your Excellency, but at least obtaining membership of the Upper House, which nowadays resembles a waiting room for the graveyard more than anything else.[11]

The less prominent of these politicians joined the independent opposition in which they played a leading role. Although they did not rise to high social positions, they could at least get a secure seat in parliament.

Despite the national hero-worship of former freedom fighters, some of the Revolution's former enemies managed to remain in political life and continued to play a part for some time after 1867. But the old generation of politicians was gradually dying out, and a new generation was on the rise, drawing its political capital from a firm rejection of repressive Austrian imperialism. Kálmán Tisza, who eventually rose to the rank of Prime Minister, first became famous for his attempts to revoke the short-lived Constitution adopted in 1861 by the Habsburg Empire, the so-called 'Imperial Patent'.

Tisza's career points to yet another important means of political selection: family relations and social contacts. Tisza was related to some of the most influential figures in Hungary, among them Count László Teleki, a leading Hungarian émigré and head of the Resolution Party until his death by suicide in 1861. Tisza's father had himself been a prominent Hungarian politician since the Reform Period. The younger Tisza did not have to follow his father's political orientation to find his entry into politics an easy one.[12]

A new way of making a career began to emerge in the period – delineated by the consolidation of the constitutional regime – after 1867. Although some professional men had previously made their way into politics, they had met with limited success. One such person was Károly Csemegi, one of the greatest legal authorities in Hungary and author, in 1878, of the country's Criminal Code (he would go on to become a three-term Prime Minister). Csemegi began his career in 1870 in the Finance Ministry, gradually climbing the professional hierarchy until, finally, he became an MP. Competence was, however, not enough to take someone to the top: political loyalty was of equal if not greater importance. The political establishment, on the whole, guarded itself carefully against the dominance of professional people, as it was feared that their personal qualities would prevent or hinder the implementation of policy on the basis of pragmatic considerations. This is probably the reason why Csemegi – despite his internationally recognized expertise – never emerged as a candidate for the post of Minister of Justice. (The fact that he was a Jew may also have played a part in this.[13])

Political careers often depended on favours done for one's superior, even if they involved breaking the law. An example is the case of Gábor Baross, a State Secretary under Prime Minister Tisza. Tisza was involved in a court case concerning liability for the construction of a bridge, in which the final ruling went against him. Baross, whose final approval was required, overruled the adverse decision – and shortly afterwards was appointed Minister of Public Works and Transport.[14] The outcome of this incident was paradoxical: a highly competent person ascended to an important post by transgressing the law and surrendering the interests of the plaintiff (a village) to his personal ends. This was the kind of political loyalty (or 'flexibility') without which talent was unlikely to be suitably rewarded.

Whenever professional expertise was required, a minister or government MP could consult ministerial experts; opposition MPs were compelled to acquire the necessary knowledge themselves, because of the government's policy of monopolizing recognized experts in its employ. No wonder parliamentary debate often revealed widespread ignorance of the issues at stake, especially when economic matters were being discussed.

While talent and professional qualifications could help forward a career only to a limited extent, it was open to anyone to exploit a notable act of heroism or even scandal – on the principle, 'There's no such thing as bad publicity' – for the purpose of getting into parliament.

For instance, in 1870, a previously unknown young man called Gábor Ugron left Hungary to join Garibaldi's army; the publicity from this daring exploit brought him nationwide fame. In 1877, during the Turkish War, Ugron managed to heighten his reputation further by mobilizing troops to attack the Russian army from Romania, motivated – so he claimed – by a desire to avenge the 1849 Russian intervention in Hungary. The operation failed, but Ugron's celebrity in Hungary was secure and, in 1878, he became an MP.[15]

Another example is that of Miklós Bartha who, beginning with his entry to university, consciously prepared the way for a future political career (among other things, he became a journalist at an independent Kolozsvár newspaper). After he had been defeated in two parliamentary elections by the Liberal Party candidate, he decided to take matters into his own hands. On the basis of information he had received from some Hungarian students, Bartha published an article in which he portrayed a particular Austrian officer – a certain Dienstl – in a very bad light; Bartha claimed that this officer had dubbed junior Hungarian volunteers under his command 'Hungarian dolts', among other things. The outraged officer challenged Bartha to a duel which the latter refused, pointing out that he had received his information from a reliable source and that the most the accused could do was to seek legal redress. The officer, dissatisfied with this solution, walked into the newspaper's offices with a fellow officer on 12 November, where they repeatedly slashed the defenceless Bartha with their swords, leaving the victim bleeding from several wounds. This incident gave rise to a great deal of protest: a demonstration, a question in parliament and a deputation to and subsequent declaration by the sovereign – in fact, all that Bartha could have wanted. As a result, he emerged a Hungarian patriotic hero. He had suffered 24 wounds and his right hand was paralysed. The two officers were sentenced to 30 days confinement to quarters, though later Dienstl was promoted and restationed. Rustov – Dienstl's fellow assailant – left the army and found employment in the court of Archduke Prince Albrecht.[16] In due course, Miklós Bartha became an MP.

University strikes and demonstrations offered similar publicity and an opportunity for making useful contacts. Béla Barabás, a 22 year old student, helped to organize a demonstration held in 1877 – on the birthday of Prime

Minister Tisza – in front of the Prime Minister's office in the Buda Castle. The programme: the smashing of windows. A number of prominent opposition figures were also present. The same student was also the chief organizer of a demonstration scheduled to be held on the anniversary of Franz Joseph's 1848 accession to the throne. The Prime Minister, having learnt of the demonstration, called Barabás in for questioning. What more could Barabás have dreamed of? True, he was punished and failed his exams that year, but in return he became famous and, some time later, an MP.[17] This was self-promotion on a market basis, that is, strictly in terms of personal achievement (usually of a scandalous nature) and risk-taking. The hunt for sensational stories, then as now, was a central concern of the press.[18]

Other means of selection were self-nomination, bribery and corruption, and taking up service with the landowning aristocracy. The patrimonial political system ensured that the country's political establishment was made up of dependant and easily controllable individuals. In regard to personal contacts, there were well-established institutions all over the country, including the casinos (gentlemen's clubs) with the National Casino at the top. There were also a number of other forums for the making of contacts that could be used to promote individual political aspirations.[19]

This atmosphere of personal dependence and loyalty to actual and potential benefactors rather than to the electorate was further enhanced by the practice under Tisza's prime ministership of frequently moving members of parliament from constituency to constituency within Hungary, so preventing them from developing roots and local influence, with the result that they became ever more receptive to instructions from above and to corruption. In addition, 176 of the 329 government MPs were former district magistrates who owed their parliamentary seats to Prime Minister Tisza and the authorities directly responsible to him. This army of faceless 'Mamelukes', as they came to be known – who referred to Tisza as the 'general' – formed the bulk of the Lower House of Parliament.[20]

The system of political selection had three effects. First, a large number of elected representatives owed their political careers to personal favours rather than to personal ability.[21] As a result, these MPs willingly subjected themselves to party discipline and were reluctant to take a firm stand on principle. Second, politics became an arena for personal contests and conflicts, with little room for competing opinions or political agendas. Third, this patriarchal approach to politics made a mockery of political representation and created an atmosphere of deep cynicism. Characteristically, professional politicians – mostly emerging from the workers' movement after the turn of the century – as well as intellectuals could not get into parliament. Popular representation in this period was only nominal; the government could easily be controlled, directly and indirectly, by powerful interest groups.

* * *

What about the financial status of members of parliament? Before 1893, Hungarian MPs were closest to their Belgian counterparts in terms of pay; after a radical pay increase, however, their financial status became similar to that of French members of parliament, the highest paid on the Continent.[22]

It cannot be said that the leaders of the nation were anything but generous with themselves. In 1848, MPs were awarded a daily fee (under Act V, Article 55) disbursed on extremely generous terms: even when there was only one parliamentary session, they were paid for the whole month at the same rate (parliament was generally in session for 9–10 months a year), averaging an annual 2,100 forints. Parliamentary minutes keepers received double the rate under the standing orders of the House, while the sergeant-at-arms received an annual 1,200 forints extra in addition to his daily fee. Members were further entitled to a housing allowance (in 1870 this allowance was doubled, in the end totalling an annual 800 forints). The head of the Lower House received an annual 12,000 forints (and was to be addressed as Your Lordship), equal to the pay of a minister (who, in turn, was to be addressed as Your Excellency). During parliamentary sessions held in Austria, members of the Hungarian delegation received a 10-forint daily allowance in addition to travel fees. A regular MP would, therefore, receive an annual 3,200 forints (or 6,400 crowns) altogether.

For the sake of comparison, someone with an annual expenditure of 5,000 forints (or 10,000 crowns) was accounted a very wealthy man in Hungary.[23] At the other extreme, the lowest paid labourers – cottagers – had to survive on wages of as little as 1 crown a day, and usually could not count on more than 200 working days a year.[24] Skilled workers earned 445 forints (or 890 crowns) a year on average (as shown by a survey conducted in 1906, covering 300,000 people).[25] Around the turn of the century a district magistrate – an almost omnipotent source of local authority – received a salary of 826 forints, while a senior district magistrate (or chief constable) received 1,234 forints.[26] The highest paid employee on the public payroll was the Prime Minister with 30,000 forints per annum.

MPs enjoyed an upper-middle-class standard of living, especially after 1893, when their remuneration was substantially increased.[27] This was little more than pocket-money, however, for most of them: during Tisza's period in office over one-third of all MPs had landed estates larger than 1,000 *hold*, and consequently, had large private incomes.[28]

As a group, large and medium landowners, rich businessmen and the most sucessful members of the intelligentsia (for example, the foremost writers), enjoyed very different material circumstances from the group composed of elected representatives coming from a poor background – primarily members of the intelligentsia – and bankrupt landowners. Nevertheless, for many representatives on both sides of the political divide, political influence was a valuable investment. Posts in any way related to railway construction were particularly sought after.

Ferenc Deák – one of the outstanding political figures of the Reform Period – was strongly committed to the ideal of an independent political domain and used all his powers and moral authority to curb the practise of abusing parliamentary membership in exchange for personal advantage. His task was not easy, since corruption and 'personalism' (justice, government contracts and career opportunities meted out on a personal basis rather than objectively) permeated the political system from top to bottom. Financial and other interest groups had come to regard bribes as a semi-legal way of dealing with the state administration at all levels. In 1869, for instance, two Belgian engineers seeking – with support from a Hungarian financial consortium – a government licence for the construction of a railway line, filed an application with the State Secretary of Transport (also an MP), and enclosed a cash cheque for 40,000 forints, drawable on a Brussels bank should they be successful. But the Belgians had fatally misjudged the State Secretary, who – unlike many of his colleagues – happened to be a perfectly honest man; instead of accepting the bribe he immediately reported the incident to the Minister of Transport.

There were, of course, many cases in which officials showed integrity, but they were not frequent enough to counterbalance the norm. To express his disapproval, Deák boycotted parliamentary sessions whenever matters known to involve corruption on a wide scale (e.g. the licensing of railway construction) were being debated and ostentatiously remained outside, taking a seat in the corridor. In 1868, when a draft law on conflicts of interest was being elaborated, some urged the exclusion of persons directly employed by the government from involvement in the economic sphere. Deák, however, was not satisfied with such a one-sided solution: 'I cannot agree to rule out the exclusion of anyone seeking parliamentary approval and authorization for any particular enterprise. To do so would lead to a greater infringement of the independence of the members of this house than any influence from the government could achieve.'[29] Deák was extremely consistent on this matter, and in 1873 supported a proposal by József Madarász – an independent MP – that no member of parliament should be allowed to sit on the board of directors of the Discount and Commercial Bank then being set up:

This is crucial, partly because it could be the first step on the road to an independent and more rational political order. I do not mean to suggest of course that someone sitting on a corporation's board of directors cannot be independent, as if I were calling into question the patriotism of those who take up such offices. Not for all the world. It is nevertheless the case that the bank in question will be involved with the State in a number of different ways and its interests may well come into conflict – whether only apparently or in reality – with those of the State. I cannot imagine anything worse than a *collisio officiorum* (conflict of interest). People – and especially statesmen – must be spared such an experience.[30]

In the early 1870s, some of the older generation of politicians were still around to exercise strong moral control, partly under Deák's influence.[31] But the temptation of lavish rewards proved too great and soon quietened the conscience of those guilty of abusing political influence.

From its ascent to power in 1875, the Liberal Party gradually lifted restrictions on the involvement of MPs in business activities. Judging by the speed and extent of such liberalization during the years of Liberal-Party rule, it would appear that lobbying was readily allowed or even encouraged. Even when an act on conflicts of interest (Act I of 1875) was finally introduced, it was never meant to be enforced. The only aim of the governing party was, at least at the beginning, to prevent members of the opposition from enjoying any financial benefits which might otherwise – if they were to toe the line – accrue from their political careers. In fact, there were instances when deliberate attempts were made to bring about the financial ruin of opposition members. Ernő Simonyi was one such victim. Simonyi was a leading member of the independent opposition who, during his years of exile, had become the representative of a British trading company. After his return home, in 1868, he retained his post as representative of the Sheffield firm for Hungary and Austria. But neither the Hungarian government nor the companies under its control ever gave an order to the Sheffield venture, despite the fact that the Austrian Railway Company made major procurements from it. Even Hungarian companies (producers of railway machinery and equipment) with which Simonyi had formerly had excellent relations, ceased all communication with his company as soon as they were nationalized. The situation did not improve in 1875: the newly installed Tisza government – at least at this stage – was equally ruthless with the opposition. Simonyi was finally rescued from financial crisis by fellow party members and a few members of the governing party itself.

By the 1880s, infamous sinecures had become more widely available.[32] A member of the opposition wrote, with sinister intent:

> Tisza . . . is careful to ensure that no one gets too large a piece and that the less important members get smaller bites to satisfy their appetites. He manages his parliament like a fish-pond: worm-eating rainbow trout, brandling-eating tench, sharp-toothed pikes and big-bellied catfish swim about in separate tanks . . . each being fed in accordance with its needs.[33]

There were many ways in which one could grow fat on government connections: sinecures at financial institutions and ventures, procurement of licences and state subsidies, and an intricate web of mutual favours. The Prime Minister was careful not to dirty his own hands, and was therefore able to maintain an appearance of neutrality and manipulate his subordinates from a solid moral position (having absolute control over his subordinates by allowing or preventing them from obtaining sinecures, etc.).[34] His son, István, was not so choosy: he was president or non-executive director at six large companies, all at the same time.[35] This was the Hungary of the 1890s and the turn of the century. Even Ugron, the boisterous Székely nobleman and former reckless fighter for Hungarian independence, became involved in some very fishy oat procurement deals with the treasury. Ugron proved himself dishonest even in the details of the transaction, double-crossing his partners on the difference between the wholesale and retail prices. The same man, meanwhile, continued to make passionate onslaughts on all forms of corruption in the House.[36]

Because it was not backed by the appropriate sanctions, the 1875 Act on Conflicts of Interest could not curb the domination of politics by financial interests in all their versatile forms. Between 1897 and 1900, the Lower House debated 130 cases of conflict of interest, of which 123 ended in acquittal. Only 7 cases resulted in the expulsion of MPs, their transgressions having been too flagrant to overlook.[37] In less obvious cases, whenever there was even the slightest opportunity, the wording of the law was usually twisted until it finally suited the interests of the accused politician. When, for instance, István Tisza was accused of a breach of the 1875 act, the court – although it could not ignore the fact that Tisza had entered into a contract with the Rimamurány-Salgótarján Metal Works – nevertheless acquitted him, on the dubious grounds that the Metal Works could not be regarded as a corporation.

Personal dependence on the government and the political system was widespread in the governing party and the opposition alike; but it was particularly disappointing that the opposition should have surrendered to the power of money and that there was so little action behind their frequent criticisms. From the 1890s, those members of the so-called 'independent' opposition who were big on words, but whose interests went no further than their own careers, were labelled 'Zoltans'. Mamelukes and Zoltans were the two political tendencies which came increasingly to dominate the Lower House. As a contemporary put it with biting sarcasm:

A member of parliament, if he behaves himself and – even as a member of the opposition – 'barks but does not bite', is allowed to 'glean the corn' every now and then. He can be made to oblige by promoting one of his family or friends, a favour he simply must return. Another is secretly handed some of the spoils, as a cook would reward her soldier sweetheart. A third is silenced by threats to disclose some former blunder if he should 'act foolishly'. Others are rewarded by lucrative receiverships and court cases, others by a cosy position as non-executive director. And there are countless others who are happy just to be left alone in their electoral districts and to receive a modest daily allowance (5 forints and 25 kraitzars). Irányi has made a secret agreement not to interfere with the government's affairs as long as his own affairs in Békés are not interfered with. Gábor Ugron is openly striking deals in Transylvania: he has put in claims for two constituencies, one for himself and another for his friend, promising to lie low if he gets them . . . What motivates these people in their immorality is their awareness that the government cannot be overthrown in an open election; under such circumstances it is only wise to embed themselves in either the governing party or the opposition.

And in relation to the governing party:

. . . The Right Honourable Members are busy building, expropriating and trading. This is the politics of log-rolling, a source of much evil, whereby Parliament has turned into a commodities market and the commodities market into Parliament; whereby constitutionalism is used as a means for enrichment and elections are no more than a disguise for a sham constitutionalism.[38]

The sale of political influence in return for financial and other benefits was a well-established but, of course, illegal practice. Exposure of individual cases ended in political scandal and the resignation of those found guilty. Individual perpetrators may have been duly punished, but no resolute action was ever taken to root out the heart of the evil.

In Hungary, the political system disguised rather than reflected the prevailing power relations; hence the false legitimacy to which we have referred so often. The outcome was mutual dependence between the business sphere and members of the political establishment. Businessmen sought political leeway and politicians sought the capital that was essential to finance and maintain their positions. No law on conflicts of interest could be enforced because the ruling political elite would thereby have undermined itself. Sadly, MPs were generally independent only of their electorates, since the latter did not even have the option of impeachment. It is not surprising, therefore, that the 'nation's representatives' adopted a very condescending attitude towards the very people whose interests they were supposed to safeguard. Relations between the two were usually limited to political presentations delivered by MPs in their electoral districts and the lobbying of more influential electors, portrayed as interest representation on behalf of the district. Direct contact was infrequent, except when an election campaign was approaching and MPs suddenly began to show an interest in those whom they otherwise so badly neglected. If ordinary electors contacted an MP about something, he would usually excuse himself, saying that he had to depart on some urgent engagement without delay; if that was not possible, he would promise to do almost anything just to be left alone.[39]

Members of parliament also developed a craving for titles. They were proud to breathe the same air as ministers and the holders of other distinguished titles, and to be able to address them as equals, in the informal manner. False political legitimacy and the forms of behaviour described previously combined gradually to strip parliamentary membership of its original liberal content.

By contrast, at the end of the Reform Period and in 1848 there was a general tendency to reject honorific titles. Some family names with spellings reserved for the nobility were changed (for example, names ending in -y: the contemporary writer Mór Jókay changed his name to Jókai) to eliminate the air of social superiority such a distinction conveyed, while others refrained from using their noble titles (as did Kossuth). Some titles, however, lived on, such as 'Your Lordship' (*'tekintetes uram'*) for members of parliament, county officials, and – from 1844 – university graduates.

Politicians' love for honorifics can best be understood as the side-effect of an emerging civil society.[40] This was a transitory period: although people had not yet managed to break away completely from feudalism at the same time there was a clearly discernible – if not yet widespread – tendency to move towards more straightforward and democratic forms of social contact. This dual consciousness among the rising bourgeoisie was detectable for instance in the coexistence of both feudal (Your Excellency) and more liberal (Your Lordship) forms of address. Deák consciously encouraged the latter, but he did not succeed in making his attitude prevail. In fact, towards the turn of the century, the craving for imperial titles (which only the King could bestow) was so great that it led to a revival of the nobility. For many, the height of personal aspiration was to become a count, a baron, a member of the Upper House, a privy councillor, or a royal chamberlain. Formal feudal attributes were worth more than one's position within the constitutional hierarchy. Feudal titles formed the basis of one's public relations value: on the occasion of royal receptions members of parliament were seated according to title, rather than political rank, so that chamberlains received more prestigious seats than those without such a title, even if the latter happened to be more important public figures.[41] Feudal attitudes also found expression in a condescending attitude towards representatives of bourgeois constitutionalism. What a sad contrast with the Reform Period and the year of the Revolution, hallmarked as they were by a conscious distancing from exactly this kind of servility and unconditional loyalty to the sovereign and an obsolete political system.

The behaviour of Károly Eötvös on the occasion of Kossuth's death, in 1894, amply illustrates the survival and revival of traditional attitudes.

Eötvös held the hand of the dying Kossuth – who had become a national symbol of independent democratic thought in his own lifetime – to the end. When death finally came, he kissed it, and proceeded to write Kossuth's obituary. As his pen wrote the name of the deceased, it came out as 'the King's Lajos Kossuth'.[42] Kossuth would, of course, have passionately protested against such an appellation, contradicting as it did everything he stood for; but it was the entirely spontaneous – and so all the more striking – outburst of a past still very much alive.

Another manifestation of the general desire for social advancement was the craving for medals.[43] In the Reform Period, Deák had refused to accept medals on principle and many followed his example up to the early 1870s. In 1873, there was a diplomatic reception to which a large number of Hungarian MPs had been invited. They arrived in understated tailcoats and without medals, as their invitations had specified. It was highly unusual that, among a crowd of several hundred, the foreign guests should be distinguishable by their decorations. A Prussian gentleman was also surprised and enquired of József Szlávy, Hungary's Prime Minister at the time:

> 'Pardon me, Your Excellency, but is it not the custom in Hungary to wear medals on such occasions?'
>
> 'It is, and those who have them wear them most readily. But it is not the custom for a Hungarian to ask for or to accept medals', the Prime Minister remarked with a great deal of dignity, no doubt under Deák's influence.[44]

But these resolute assertions of personal independence and integrity – that had even come to be perceived as part of the Hungarian character – were slowly eroded over time. Under Kálmán Tisza's premiership the prestige of orders of merit and decorations once again began to rise. This time, the process combined personal and party interests: the ruling Liberal Party received a small 'contribution' from all those granted a noble title or medal while it was in power. For the party, this was an important source of revenue, while for the individual it was a matter of social prestige.

As has already become clear, a peculiarity of the Hungarian bourgeois-transformation process was the assimilation of the newly arisen bourgeois to the feudal upper classes. The prevailing social structure did not support political autonomy. The parliament was the only place where autonomy would have been at least theoretically possible, on the assumption that MPs were elected rather than appointed, and so independent of the sovereign and the good will of the executive authorities – their high social status was no more than a democratic confirmation of their personal competence. In reality, as we have seen, no effort was spared to undermine all democratic foundations. Under these conditions, success largely depended on assimilation to the upper classes who, of course, held executive power. Political representation, having failed to break with the old regime, could not ensure the survival of the ethos of representation that had originated in the Reform Period and in 1848, with the aim of facilitating the autonomous manifestation of the public will. On the contrary, the political and social atmosphere of the 1880s and of the late monarchy clearly promoted and rewarded unconditional loyalty, subservience, and the surrender of one's principles. Political representation being largely independent of the electorate, widespread conformity to the political elite and the sovereign inevitably emerged, with the effect of heightening their prestige. This, in turn, made conformism universally accepted so that any attempt at political autonomy seemed utopian or deviant, and not only the objective but even the subjective preconditions of autonomy were prevented from becoming the norm.

The absurdity of this situation lies in the fact that, although the whole structure of political authority rested on the lower classes, they were made to feel as if an enormous favour had been granted them should the political elite ever condescend to acknowledge their existence. Enslaved by social prestige and traditional political norms, MPs, by and large, cared only for being seen as important figures in the country's political establishment. They had little interest in genuine progress and development, being much more concerned with the privilege of treating their social superiors as equals and being seen as part of their circle.[45]

Most prestigious in this regard was the delegation in charge of the Monarchy's joint departments, the highest forum of political representation. Anyone who became a member of this delegation, which was comprised of 40 members from the Lower House and 20 members from the Upper House, could count himself one of the elite of the elite and acquired such privileges as reception at court, an introduction to the sovereign and invitations to royal banquets. As a result, competition for delegation membership could not have been greater. 'When the Lower House debated nominations for delegation membership, both secret and open patronage and the full arsenal of other means of self-promotion were put in motion, and those who happened not to be included among the chosen few would take serious offence and make many envious comments', wrote Béla Barabás, president of the delegation in 1908.

At the turn of the century, the keeper of minutes of the delegation wrote:

The delegation had no other important task than to vote. This is how it had been since 1867. It was not really possible to voice criticisms or to make speeches. If one of us wanted to speak, he first had to ask the Prime Minister's permission, which as a rule was refused. It was the general desire of the most prominent Hungarian statesmen that things should run smoothly, because this was how His Majesty preferred it. No wonder that over time the Delegation was reduced to a mere puppet and was kept alive solely by its external glamour; it had never had a truly and essentially political substance.

What then was all the fuss about? According to Barabás, 'membership of the Delegation was a glamorous, gentlemanly appointment'.[46] This same Barabás, who headed the Hungarian delegation to supervise the handling of joint administration – which did little to enforce true Hungarian interests – and who sat next to his Majesty the Austrian Emperor and Hungarian King at royal banquets, was at the same time one of the leaders of a political party the main policy of which was to contest joint administration. Was this situation a farce or a tragedy?

Politics and ethics

The reign of Franz Joseph was a period of vehement autocracy. Parliament was permitted to debate only issues and draft laws that had already been approved by the King (see the Cabinet Decree of 17 March 1867).[47] The sovereign's absolute powers were undiminished even by the Act on Political Compromise – for instance, he remained commander-in-chief of the Hungarian army. And if democratic parliamentary elections did not go as the sovereign wished (his fear prevented him from seeing that the opposition was ready to make far-reaching concessions and to abandon its political programme), he was perfectly entitled to appoint his government from a minority party, so ignoring all mandatory liberal procedures. This actually happened in 1905; when parliament protested, on 19 February 1906, the King used his cavalry to disperse the assembly and ordered its closure.

In this way, constitutional order was severely restricted. Under these circumstances, there was no hope for a democratic political transformation based on the constitution and political representation. The conservation of the previous regime necessarily went hand in hand with false legitimacy and a series of political lies. After a while, actual political power was no longer a question of political authority, and control of the armed forces depended solely upon their unconditional loyalty to the regime and its embodiment in the person of the sovereign. With such political attitudes constituting the norm, the hard facts of power politics were glossed over and transformed into an ethereal atmosphere which pervaded everything. On the other hand, because this regime was based on assimilation to a social and political elite and failed to reflect the true interests and structure of society, it was ultimately doomed to failure.

As István Bibó wrote in 1948:

The whole situation brought about a deterioration of the ruling elite's political rationality, while the political rationality of ordinary Hungarians was kept in abeyance by the constant, pervasive and thoroughly demoralizing abuse of elections. Anyone accepting the Political Compromise also accepted electoral fraud: in the spirit of the Compromise advocates of neither absolute independence nor social revolution, not to mention national autonomy, were allowed to emerge as a majority. This is how the institutions of constitutionalism which in the spirit of 1848 were meant to be institutions of political education emerged as instruments of obscurantism.[48]

The dynamic history of the post-1867 period is that of an anti-liberal political regime under which political representation was severely restricted or even entirely absent. Only the press, groups of politicized intellectuals and agrarian and workers' interest groups active from the turn of the century truly represented the country's socio-political structure. These groups were, of course, barred from the official political establishment. In this manner, authentic political pluralism in the Hungary of the post-1867 period was almost exclusively extra-parliamentary.

The complete absence of market principles in politics indicates that liberalism is not a necessary concomitant of bourgeois transformation. The post-1867 period was a period of political modernization accompanied by the emergence of bourgeois society and capitalist economic development. But while development in the economic sphere rested on market principles, the modernization of political and individual behaviour unfolded under severe restrictions or even under the exclusion of these same market principles. Both Hungarian and European experience shows that a market economy can live in perfect harmony with and, what is more, can be used to finance market-free politics.

The basic principle of anti-liberal Hungarian politics was formulated by a Hungarian politician, in 1882, as follows: 'In Hungary you can have opposition attitudes but opposition ideas must never prevail.'[49] At the level of the individual, this meant that if someone was to remain faithful to his principles, he had either to commit himself to the governing party or to resign himself to permanent opposition. Even those able to maintain high principles risked becoming demagogic, because their ideas were never put to the test. The seemingly hard-core opposition was thus permeated by both political naivity and, what was perhaps even worse, by a calculating attitude.

Under the conditions of a merely theoretical political pluralism, when elections did not function as an instrument facilitating the healthy rotation of political power, the differences between the governing party and the opposition were audible rather than visible: there were more similarities than differences between them. Although the opposition was denied any scope of action, it nevertheless deluded itself that its day would eventually come and, in the meantime, satisfied itself with eroding the governing party's powers instead of developing a positive stance of its own. In this way, both the governing party and the opposition derived their legitimacy from the same political regime and were equally interested in its consolidation and survival. Competition between political tendencies was substituted by personal rivalry. At the same time, both sides engaged in the formulation of countless theories to justify their actions (or inaction), ranging from exclusionist declarations to complete commitment to and outspoken belief in the status quo.

The first person to discover the springs of this political mechanism was Kálmán Tisza, who became the first and, in his own way, the most gifted, connoisseur of its operations. In 1868 the party headed by Tisza still believed that its primary task was 'to ensure that all laws violating the country's independence be nullified, to terminate the institution of the delegation and the Joint Ministry, and to obtain diplomatic recognition of Hungary's independence in its military, financial and commercial affairs'.

However, as a first sign of 'flexibility', the party's programme went on to say:

> The party established for this purpose will not be diverted from its aims but will rationally consider the due time and constitutional means necessary for its actions, avoiding all appearance of indecision, as well as any stirring of emotions that might jeopardize the constitutional process and so represent a threat to Hungary.[50]

By 1873, Tisza was able to make the following exclusionist comment, reflecting his commitment to changing things from within: 'If the walls of Jericho cannot be brought down by our shouting from outside we shall simply go around them.'[51] On 3 February 1875, in a parliamentary debate on the state budget, Tisza insisted that in the present economic crisis all attention must be focused on questions of finance and, for the time being, all constitutional issues must be put aside.[52]

Needless to say 'for the time being' came to mean the lifetime of the Dual Monarchy, including the 15 years of Tisza's government. Ten years after the transformation of his views, Tisza – still Prime Minister – reflected in the Lower House on his decision:

> I only want to say one thing in connection with what is said about many, but primarily about my humble self. It is said to be a sign of moral decline when someone changes his political views. Honourable Gentlemen, I am not afraid to say what I think about this. In my view, if someone changes his political views without sufficient reason, he is indeed contemptible. On the other hand, if someone comes to realize under the influence of some crucial event that his views do not stand up or that the road he has taken is not leading to good but is on the contrary harmful for the public

cause, and he does not confess his mistake, that person is no patriot, giving preference to the appearance of his own righteousness over the public good. Look around and see what kind of person will not change his views with the times. How many people were still loyalists in March – I won't mention of which year – but in December had already taken up the flag of revolution. Did they not change their political views? It seems to me that they changed considerably. Perhaps the events that have taken place in the meantime justify their actions and so no one will condemn them for it. Honourable Gentlemen, I do not intend to defend myself here but I am determined to speak out against the view that any change in one's political views signifies a decline in ethical standards. I remember very well what I said ten years ago and I also know what I have done since. I take full responsibility before Man and God, because my soul tells me that if I had done otherwise, I would have been a consistent Kálmán Tisza, but not a good patriot.[53]

Tisza's self-justification might have been credible had he not played such an active role in extending the regime, improving its efficiency and firmly rooting it in Hungarian soil.

In such circumstances, devoted opposition members – their numbers were not high – had no choice but to shun political representation. This is exactly what Ottó Hermann, a radical independent, did in the second half of the 1890s, leaving the opposition party and his seat in parliament. An opposition member who followed his example had good reason to write to Hermann in 1906 about the parliament, led, for the first time, by the opposition: 'We can but congratulate ourselves for not being in this Parliament, as there has never been a worse.' Hermann wrote about the opposition in power, with full justification:

It has distinguished itself from the Tisza coalition only by a tendency towards self-delusion: the government stood on the platform of 1867 and the opposition was also forced to 'suspend' its principles and to pass laws in accordance with the principles of 1867 and to participate in institutions based upon them. Their self-delusion derives from the belief of Ferenc Kossuth and his circle that the signing of an agreement with the King [the Compromise] would automatically lead to the demise of the previous order. The notion of suspending principles on which the body of a living and developing state has rested hitherto is a curious one; frankly, it is an absurdity . . . On the other hand, the principle of independence is not there simply to be represented by the Prime Minister, it is to be implemented; when this does not happen, historical continuity is broken, and this principle is suspended.[54]

From our point of view, it is a question of marginal importance whether

1875 and 1906 can be distinguished by the presence or absence of self-delusion (in all probability they cannot), but it is a fact that a process of the isolation and voluntary marginalization of unofficial political models was unfolding in contrast with the Tisza/Kossuth trend. (Those who, against all the odds, remained in the opposition had either become museum exhibits or were unable to keep to their principles, like Gyula Justh who had stymied the realization of his political aspirations by ascending to the presidency of the inferior Lower House.) It is paradoxical in the extreme that he should first have to resign in order to remain consistent with his opposition views; in other words, an MP should have to give up the means (parliamentary membership) which, in theory at least, provided the widest scope for political action. This is further proof that parliamentary political representation in Hungary was during this period based on the exclusion of market selection.

There is, however, yet another paradox here. As it became more and more obvious that only individuals – not trends – could have a political future, and as the number of those seeking a political career on these terms increased, a competitive market emerged from which the ruling political elite could pick and choose: a counterselective market in the absence of a free one. At the level of political culture, this unhealthy situation led to a lowering of the standard of political debate to the level of personal insults on the one hand, and to a peculiar two-way openness of the otherwise-closed political power structure on the other. Regarding the second result, openness to competition manifested itself, among other things, in the lowering of the average age of politicians – the absence of normal political selection offered unparalleled opportunities for the younger generation. Such a juvenescence of the political spectrum did not, however, signify the introduction of a spirit of fundamental transformation in the political establishment, but instead served as an instrument for the consolidation of an outdated political model. Individual competition was, of course, a poor substitute for political liberalism and flexibility.

Another form of 'openness' was, especially from the 1890s, the invention of ever-new restatements (in terms of individual styles) of the same old political content. Under Tisza's premiership, individual competition was not tolerated, although the atmosphere thawed somewhat towards the end of his term of office. At the same time, Tisza's government was in no particular need of such competition: by this time, the opposition had been sufficiently tamed into acceptance of their new role as operatives and doorwardens of the status quo. As competition became tougher, the personal factor lost its significance for the government: one hopeful was as good as another, since every player in the political arena could be trusted to exhibit unconditional subservience and loyalty. It did not really matter to whom the country's political leadership was entrusted, whether it was the grey bureaucrat Count Gyula Szapáry, the provincial, crude and cunning Dezső Bánffy, Kálmán

Széll, whose style of government did not differ from the management of a factory, the feudal warlord Károly Khuen-Hédervary, Sándor Wekerle, the grand Western capitalist with exquisite manners, or the obstinately consistent Count István Tisza with his policy of iron discipline. An almost endless list may be drawn up of the different political personalities and styles which characterized the era. In fact, the range of personal styles became more and more colourful as political representation declined. The most marked personality of them all was István Tisza, who, from the beginning of the twentieth century, tried mercilessly to maintain what was doomed to failure. In the end he had no choice but to give up and to dissolve his administration, just as his father had in the mid-1870s, though under much worse conditions, and employing even more extreme measures.[55] But for the son, this did not cause any particular crisis of conscience, because all he had to do was to act in the interests of the existing regime. His attempts to ensure its survival in the face of ever greater problems were hopeless, though not impossible. Gyula Szekfű in his *Három generáció* (Three Generations) published in 1920, saw Tisza's ethical antagonist in Endre Ady, who was neither prime minister, nor an MP, but a poet and essayist.[56] It is not surprising that Szekfű was unable to choose an alternative *political* figure. Within the political establishment, itself, differences went no further than an individual's degree of consistency and method of maintaining the existing regime.

The political morality dictated by this regime was a totally unsuitable model for either a private or a public morality. The separation of private and public morality is a natural concomitant of the emergence of a bourgeois society, but there must be some overlap between the two, if only because politicians must practice both. What we are interested in here, of course, are the rules dominating both spheres. In this pursuit, it would be useful to cite some political slogans and proverbs from the period. Examples include the favourite slogan of Pál Szontágh, an MP of the 1890s who went from opposition member to government supporter: 'He who cannot twist and bend will be broken'; a comment by Lajos Csernátony, Kálmán Tisza's right-hand man: 'One should always treat one's friends on the understanding that they may turn out to be one's enemies tomorrow'; the simple invitation by the nobleman Imre Ivánka, the former army officer turned Tisza devotee: 'Trust appearances!'; the warning of Frigyes Podmaniczky, president of the Liberal Party which ruled Hungary for 30 years, to the members of his party: 'My sons, you should stick to voting and refrain from thinking – thinking is bad for you and the nation will not benefit from it either'; and finally Kálmán Tisza's famous dictum which sums up perfectly the public morality we are endeavouring to describe: 'If someone throws mud at you, don't try to clear up the mess; wait for it to dry and it will fall off of its own accord.'[57] All these statements suggest that a twisted or broken backbone does better service for a political career than a straight one – though these twisted ethical norms must be clearly distinguished from the willingness to compromise which is the essence of politics. The players in the political arena, given the absence of normal selection criteria, were regularly forced to surrender their principles, in which circumstances only one sort of compromise was possible, that contributing to consolidation of existing conditions. Those unable to reconcile themselves to this had either to resign or to not enter the system in the first place.

Politicians seldom identified themselves completely with the political regime they represented. Much more characteristically they suffered from a kind of schizophrenia. They could tolerate the rules of the game by adopting either a cynical or a fanatical view. As I have already pointed out, public morality could be justified only by one thing: acceptance – whether on rational grounds, on faith or by a combination of the two – that the political regime founded on the Compromise was in the nation's best interests. Rational defence of this attitude broke down at the point where it had to be admitted that a large part of the population had no interest in the achievement of this ultimate good. In this case, the nation faced either the wholesale rejection of a political solution – regardless of what was assumed to be in its best interest – or the enforcement of policy against the public will. In Hungary there was little chance of a radical popular rejection of their leaders' decision, since the Compromise had been preceded by a failed revolution and a period of absolutism (lasting approximately as long as the reform period during which the development of revolutionary forces had taken place). Needless to say, one of the primary aims of absolutism was to restrict or even to eliminate all forms of radicalism. Every political measure of the absolutist regime served to bring about the acceptance of a political viewpoint that would – even under conditions of compromise – keep Hungary under Austrian rule. The Compromise did ameliorate some acute social grievances, but it lacked the active support of the majority of the population which was needed to go further. One of the main historical outcomes of absolutism, and the compromise settlement which succeeded it, was that, having given up the ideal of full emotional acceptance, it transformed accommodation into a way of life. This, in turn, provided the supporters of absolutism with a basis on which acceptance for the existing political regime within a constitutional framework could be won, despite its failure to win acceptance even from a number of those who had initiated it. This basic contradiction could be resolved only by stressing that the Compromise – although it left a lot to be desired – was nevertheless a political necessity and of great benefit to Hungary.[58]

Given this lukewarm reception, the political elite believed it could not afford to be choosy in regard to how it would procure acquiescence. This is why so few took the fanatical approach; even István Tisza, who otherwise showed so little restraint in the practice of deceit that he estranged some of his own party, refrained. Dishonesty in politics did not, however, spill over into the public domain, if only because politicians were fully aware of how inadvisable it would be to reveal their cynicism to the electorate. Political ethics were such that, while it was quite acceptable for the opposition to give up its principles in return for entry into the domain of political power, it was not acceptable for it to sell its political influence for a set price – as we shall see in connection with a particular 'transaction' aimed at persuading the opposition to give up all attempts at political obstruction. Similarly, while this behaviour commonly turned political influence into a source of financial gain, violating the relevant clause of the Act on Conflicts of Interest, the opposition would never have agreed to drop the Act on Conflicts of Interest altogether.

While this political schizophrenia could, to a certain degree, be concealed, the blurring of the distinction between public and private ethics could not. From the late 1880s, the number of political duels sky-rocketed, partly as an expression of intensifying political competition – concentrated on the personal level – and partly because the state of public morality at the time bore an obvious relation to the crumbling of the ethos of political representation. The more widespread the cynicism in public and political life, the more political duels were fought in an attempt to cover up the decline of political liberalism with a facade of gentlemanly conduct; that is, by projecting private values onto politics. Although duels were fought to demonstrate one's possession of the moral high ground, in reality, they revealed more similarities than differences between the combatants. Such a transposition of private values to public ethics was suitable neither for the purification of public ethics, nor to compensate for their decline. It is possible to calculate the personal consequences of a public disagreement – a duel at worst – without in any way contributing to halt the crumbling of public morals: although duels were usually not fought to the death, the mere parade of bravery drew a veil over the gravest public crimes without preventing their recurrence. The duel functioned as a form of public confession with the promise of redemption. An increasing sensitivity to personal honour went hand in hand with the loss of public decency. One is led to wonder how it was possible that so many men who professed to hold their honour in high esteem could commit so many underhand tricks in the public sphere. But, of course, this was an inevitable side effect of a corrupt political regime. There is a Latin proverb which describes this situation very well: 'The senators are good, but the Senate is a beast.' While Hungarian politicians were by and large decent and honourable, as a group – the rules of which they felt obliged to follow – they left much to be desired.

The blurred distinction between private and public was only one of several manifestations of double standards that characterized public morality.

Another, and probably the most marked, instance of the same phenomenon was the political double standards rooted in the double role that almost all members of parliament had to play. First, with its bogus legitimacy, the majority was in fact a minority, and vice versa. Second, the use of dishonest political practices ensured easy parliamentary victory for the governing party and the subordination to its interests of the opposition. Third, as the public did not accept the Compromise, popularity could be achieved only by demonstrating strong national feeling rather than by exhibiting support for the monarchy. Consequently, the spirit of 1867 penetrated the thinking of a large part of the generation of 1848, and vice versa. Speaking from the Mameluke standpoint, Jenő Szontagh aptly wrote: 'In the hearts of many Hungarian Mamelukes there is still a trace of the spirit of 1848, although they allow it to show itself only in the safety and familiarity of their own homes.'[59] The spirit of 1848 did, from time to time, find expression in the public domain, examples of which include Antal Tibád, State Secretary of Domestic Affairs, who betrayed plans for the wreathing of the Hentzi memorial, and the Mamelukes who protested against the clauses of the Defence Act restricting the use of Hungarian in the army. For the generation of 1867, openly declared or covert nurturing of the ideals of 1848 played a very important role. These ideals compensated somewhat for the levelling effect of party discipline aiming to suppress individual initiative, and provided a useful pretext for demonstrating one's attachment to popular national values. The latter was especially important because the political structure of the Dual Monarchy frustrated full satisfaction of Hungarian national interests. The legacy of 1848 was also important as a means of moral self-justification: the 1867 generation of politicians used 1848 to demonstrate that they had a moral backbone, after all, thereby redeeming their habitual inconsistencies and political subservience. In this way, the legacy of 1848 turned into a sterile, polished symbol and became the source of a politics devoid of a sense of responsibility. This formal attachment to the memory of 1848 engendered high sensitivity to all 'sacred' matters related to that year, but it did not encourage further development of the ideals underlying it or a rethinking of its political legacy. Characteristically, the governing party could be cornered most easily by criticisms made in the spirit of 1848, but its fundamental legitimacy never came under question. Such instances included the Jansky and Hentzi affairs, which occurred because the Compromise required the Hungarian army – subordinate to the sovereign – to pay homage to those who had died for him, many of whom also happened to be enemies of the Hungarian Revolution. Such paradoxical situations followed directly from the very notion of the Compromise and were usually greatly exaggerated by the press to the governing party's great disadvantage. The position of the governing party was extremely difficult: its official duty was, as in this case, to endorse the tribute paid by the army to the war dead of the monarchy; at the same time it was profoundly irritated by the disdain for Hungarian national feeling this implied.

Of all the demonstrations of the continuing influence of the ideals of 1848 on the generation of 1867, the most striking was Kálmán Tisza's resignation. Tisza, weary after 15 years of active government, staged his own fall in a manner worthy of such a consummate statesman and, as a result, was able to leave the post of an 1867-generation Prime Minister as a man of 1848. In his New Year's speech of 1890, Tisza scorned the cult of Kossuth; he had, however, already completed the script of his resignation speech, the aim of which was to bathe in the glory of 1848. By the terms of Act L of 1879, Hungarian expatriates failing to report to an Austrian-Hungarian consulate before having lived abroad for 10 years would lose their Hungarian citizenship. The provisions of this law were, of course, also binding on Kossuth. Then living in Turin, Kossuth declared, in an open letter dated 20 December 1889: 'I have never been and I shall never be a subject of the Austrian Emperor and Hungarian King Franz Joseph, not even for a second. This is my position.'[60] On 22 November, Tisza had said that Kossuth, who was a freeman of several Hungarian cities, would automatically retain his Hungarian citizenship. On 11 December, Tisza said that he would modify the Residence Act to this end. Tisza's decision was welcomed by Kossuth but not by Franz Joseph. On this occasion, however, Tisza refused to give in to the King's wishes and, on 9 March, he handed in his resignation, which was accepted.

Tisza was, of course, aware that his political position depended much more on the King than on Kossuth's sympathy, and his resignation was obviously a calculated decision rather than the involuntary consequence of his firmness of principle. Tisza demonstrated that he was a conservative adherent of the ideals of 1848, so creating the illusion that he possessed a strong moral backbone. This kind of reference back to 1848 was the customary means to this effect in the post-1867 period. Tisza knew his age as well as anyone and was aware that a split moral consciousness, the product of an inevitable compensation mechanism, was a useful political weapon. By the second half of the 1890s, the two tendencies were officially combined when the events of 1848 were made the object of national celebration. The date of the national holiday was carefully chosen. Instead of 15 March – signifying the revolutionary phase of these events – the choice fell on 11 April, in honour of the constitutional consolidation of the achievements of the Hungarian Revolution in the promulgation of the so-called April Laws. It turned out, therefore, to be a state rather than a national holiday (see Chapter 13). The events of 1848 and what they signified were, then, celebrated twice: on 15 March in the form of private commemorations, and on 11 April, the official national holiday.[61] This was yet another example of a split social consciousness.

On the other side of the coin, the majority of those who participated in the events of 1848 were gradually integrated into the political atmosphere and establishment of the post-1867 period. This was a passive acceptance of the Compromise, but nevertheless it opened the way to moral inconsistency on a large scale. The most obvious sign of this acceptance was the demonstration of loyalty to the sovereign and growing acceptance of authoritarian principles in connection with the desire to assimilate to the higher social classes. Very few remained unaffected by these tendencies. The absence of an opposite tendency strengthened the identity of the social elite. This reduced the prospects for the kind of democratic processes envisaged in 1848, as well as for the related forms of public conduct and morals. Naked ambition often instigated indignant calls for a general reshuffle. Behind such emotive actions lay, more often than not, coldly calculating private and business interests or simply envy and vindictiveness stirred up by the absence of such opportunities. This was a world made up of independent Zoltans who had loud voices but poor moral credentials, members of the opposition who had overestimated their own powers and party leaders looking for compromise; a world that would not change even as a consequence of the frequent divisions of the political parties: like hydras' heads they would always return in a new form. This was an environment in which opposition attitudes characterized by 'ressentiment' and secret rancour flourished.[62] And here was the point at which the split consciousnesses of the governing and opposition parties met: the conservative adherence to 1848 values by the post-1867 generation weakened the political rigidity of their times and, vice versa, the pragmatism of the post-1867 generation smoothed the harsh opposition of the majority of the 1848 generation.

This situation, which manifested itself most clearly in the early part of the twentieth century, had a profoundly regrettable consequence: almost every parliamentary party lost its moral credibility. Not one of them was able to pursue its political agenda by ethical means. Attempts were, of course, made in this direction but they always failed, leading to nothing more than a series of scandals the consequences of which did nothing to prevent their ever happening again. The accumulation of political blunders led ultimately to the discrediting of the institution of parliament itself which, despite the magnificence of the building it came to occupy in 1904, never seemed more powerless than during the wave of anti-obstructionism. Public morality in Hungary suffered incalculably from the absence of a political party with an interest in safeguarding it. Without the protection of such institutional interests, moral values can remain no more than wishful thinking. Under the conditions of a political regime dedicated to modernization, the public will has a positive value only if it finds institutional form. Political representation, which was destined to perform this function, fell victim to its false legitimacy so that there was no party in parliament (not even the opposition) that could have ensured the maintenance of moral standards in politics. This is one of the reasons why no autonomous political behaviour could emerge institutionally in Hungary. All players in the political arena participated in the great political lie in one form or another, and with varying degrees of involvement and responsibility. The consistent misrepresentation of the country's true social make-up and, therefore, of its political power structure led inevitably to the regime's demise.

(1986)

Notes

1 Dénes Papp, *A magyar nemzetgyűlés Pesten 1848–ban* [The Hungarian National Assembly in Pest in 1848], Pest, 1866, Vol. 1, p. 107.
2 Sources of the data below: Ernő Lakatos, *A magyar politikai vezetőréteg 1848–1918* [The Hungarian Political Elite 1848–1918], Budapest, 1942; Rezső Rudai, *A politikai ideológia, pártszerkezet, hivatás és életkor szerepe a magyar képviselőház és a pártok életében (1861–1935)* [The Role of Political Ideology, Party Structure, Vocation and Age in the Life of the Hungarian Parliament and Parties, 1861–1935], Budapest, 1936; Adalbert Toth, *Parteieren und Reichstagswahlen in Ungarn* 1848–1892, Munich, 1973; *Revolution in Perspective* (Andrew C. Janos and William B.Scottmann, eds.), Berkeley/Los Angeles-London, 1971; and Andor Csizmadia, *A magyar választási rendszer 1848–1849-ben* [The Hungarian Election System in 1848–9], Budapest, 1963. The proportion of national minority representatives never exceeded 10%, and in certain periods there were very few in the Lower House. The majority government on whom the Compromise settlement rested obtained their votes to a great extent from majority national-minority populated counties. In this context, certain national minority groups played an important part in the Compromise process (primarily national bureaucracies). Consequently, national minorities were largely responsible for the continuity of the political regime which, after the collapse of the Monarchy, has so often been described in the darkest of colours. Hopefully the time will come when the political behaviour of individual ethnic minorities is studied and evaluated in the light of their social structure. This would be a great contribution to ending the predominance of one-sided and even false portrayals of the Hungarian and East European social and political scene, the purpose of which is generally to put the blame on others for one's own misfortunes.
3 Lajos Beck, *A régi Magyarország* [Hungary Under the Old Regime], Budapest, 1944.
4 Mór Szatmári, *Húsz év parlamenti viharai* [Twenty Years in Parliament] Budapest, 1928, p. 66 (hereafter Szatmári).
5 László Tar, *A délibábok országa* [A Country of Mirages], Budapest, 1976, pp. 149–50.
6 József Kristóffy, *Magyarország kálváriája. Az összeomlás útja. Politikai emlékek 1890–1926* [Hungary's Tribulations: On the Road to Collapse, Political

Recollections 1890–1926], Budapest, 1927, p. 161 (hereafter Kristóffy). On the economic basis of the aristocracy's political influence before 1890 see Timdeon (Beksics Gusztáv), *Legújabb politikai divat* [The Latest Trend in Politics], Budapest, 1884, pp. 97–110.

7 Szatmári (1928), p. 41, and Tamás Vécsey, *Tisza Kálmán. Politikai és publicisztikai tanulmány* [Kálmán Tisza: A Political and Publicistic Study], Celldömölk, 1931, p. 127 (hereafter Vécsey).

8 Specific instances of this are described in: *Ady Endre publicisztikai írásai* [Endre Ady's Publicistic Writings], selection and notes by: Erzsébet Vezér, Budapest, 1977, Vol. 1, pp. 269–70 (hereafter Ady). It is worth recalling a particular incident as a typical example of a tendency widespread at the time: 'Count Miklós Berchtold allegedly lent one hundred forints to Count Antal Forgách at a party. Forgách later insisted that he had never borrowed anything from Berchtold. Berchtold then took out a lawsuit against Forgách, but both the court and the court martial of honour rejected Berchtold's claim. Berchtold then proposed that the National Casino expel Forgách. In response, Forgách tried to resign from the National Casino, but his resignation was not accepted and he was expelled anyway. The explanation behind the whole affair is that the whole incident was invented as an electioneering trick.' (Ady, Vol. 1, p. 653).

9 It is not only that the aristocracy had a dominant presence in parliament, but it was also an aristocracy whose sense of its own superiority was never challenged. This is why Baron Géza Fejérváry could reproach the Minister urging the introduction of universal suffrage: 'And you want to see universal suffrage and democracy in Hungary! Don't you know that in this country everybody bends over backwards to please even the most insignificant magnate?' Kristóffy, p. 195.

10 Károly Eötvös, *Magyar alakok – kortörténeti rajzok* [Hungarian Figures – Contemporary Sketches], Budapest, 1904, p. 84 (hereafter Eötvös).

11 Judit Garai and István Rejtő (eds.), *Mikszáth Kálmán Összes Művei* [The Complete Works of Kálmán Mikszáth], Vol. 74, Budapest, 1979, pp. 16–17 (hereafter Mikszáth).

12 For an informative case study on making use of family relations see: Baron Feilitzsch Berthold, *Emlékeimből* [From My Memoirs], Budapest, 1933.

13 The incident was reported by Károly Eötvös, in Eötvös, pp. 182–3.

14 Kristóffy, pp. 12–13.

15 László Cs. Szabó, *Ugron, a székely (A székely puccs ismertetése)* [Ugron And The Székely *Coup d'État*], Budapest, 1940. For a more recent adaptation of the Ugron story see: Tibor Cseres, *Foksányi szoros* [The Foksány Defile], Budapest, 1985.

16 See: Szatmári pp. 11–15.

17 Béla Barabás, *Emlékiratai (1850–1929)* [Memoirs: 1850–1929], Arad, 1929, pp. 30–5, 53–7 (hereafter Barabás).

18 On the conscious use of publicity see Ady's article: *X úr* [Mr X], written in 1900 (Ady, Vol. 1, pp. 94–5). For a more substantial account see: Domokos Kosáry and G. Béla Németh (eds.), *A magyar sajtó története 1867–1892* [A History of the Hungarian Press 1867–92], Vol. 2/2, Budapest, 1985.

19 About life in the National Casino see: János (József) Bognár, *Három évtized egy úri kaszinó életéből* [Three Decades of a Gentlemen's Club], Budapest, 1927.

20 For an assessment of Tisza's personnel policy see: Gusztáv Gratz, *A dualizmus kora* [The Age of Dualism], Budapest, 1934, Vol. 1, pp. 207–8; Gyula Szekfű: *Egy nemzedék és ami utána következik* [A Generation and its Heritage], Budapest, 1938, p. 235; *Magyarország története 1849–1918* [The History of Hungary, 1849–1918], university notes, Budapest, 1972, p. 226.

21 If in 1872 Dezső Szilágyi was concerned that the introduction of universal suffrage would result in the lowering of the standards of parliamentary work, then by the 1880s his fears were realized as a direct result of this method of political selection. Mikszáth writes about this in a witty sketch entitled: '*Párbeszéd egy ángliussal*' [Dialogue With An Englishman], (Mikszáth, Vol. 74, pp. 30–2).

22 Mikszáth, Vol. 73, pp. 148–9.

23 Béla Kempelen, *Útmutató az összes nemességi ügyekben* [A Guide to All Matters Concerning the Nobility], Budapest, 1907, p. 59.

24 Kristóffy, p. 196.

25 *Magyar munkásszociográfiák 1888–1945* [Sociographical Studies on Hungarian Workers, 1888–1945], Budapest, 1974, pp. 86 and 158; the writings of Manó Somogyi and Jenő Varga and the article by Róbert Braun in: *A szociográfia első magyar műhelye* [The First Sociographical Workshop in Hungary], selection and introduction by György Litván and László Szűcs, Budapest, 1973, Vol. 2, pp. 107–29.

26 Béla Mezőssy's speech delivered in the Lower House on 16 January 1901.

27 Eötvös, pp. 7–9. He illustrates the value of an MP's remuneration with the example of Dániel Irányi.

28 *Magyarország története 1848–90* [The History of Hungary, 1848–90], Budapest, 1979.

29 *Deák Ferenc beszédei* [The Speeches of Ferenc Deák], collected by Manó Kónyi, Budapest, 1903, Vol. 6, p. 137 (hereafter DFS).

30 DFS, Vol. 6, p. 369. This incident is quoted by József Madarász, pp. 447–8.

31 Eötvös, pp. 45–6. József Madarász – who once exclaimed: 'How dare a member of parliament enter this House when his pay is about to be frozen the next day, whom Jews execrate and Germans seek to bribe: how can I let the future of this country rest in such hands?' (Eötvös, p.15) – is another example of such high ethical standards.

32 Kálmán Mikszáth, *Jókai Mór élete és kora* [The Life and Age of Mór Jókai], Budapest, 1982, p. 283.

33 Gyula Verhovay, *Az álarcz korszaka* [The Age of the Mask], Budapest, 1889, p. 126 (hereafter Verhovay).

34 Before 1875 Tisza was vice president of the North-Eastern Railway run under the presidency of Baron Pál Sennyei (a peculiar economic coalition involving a moderate left-wing and a conservative aristocrat). Tisza became very wealthy from manumission compensation: he inherited from his father's family 20,000 hold. In 1868, he increased his estate by another 8,000 hold, which in the 1880s he transferred to his son István. As Prime Minister he earned 30,000 forints annually. Later, Kálmán Tisza divided his fortune among his children, after which time he lived on a pension of 8,000 forints a year and an annual 44,000 forint in allowances from his wife (Countess Ilona Degenfeld-Schomburg).

35 These were the following: Adria Shipping, Bihari Local Rail, Hungarian Industrial and Commercial Bank, Central Land Bank of Hungarian Savings Banks, Rimamurány-Salgótarján Metal Works, and Arad Wagons. In Sándor Balogh, *Érdekösszeférhetetlenség* [Conflicts of Interest], Budapest, 1901. This was common knowledge among contemporaries; one MP – Oszkár Ivánka – in fact, read out this list in the House of Representatives in 1898, at the 356th National Assembly. Sándor Várnai also used this as an example when drawing up a study on the 1875 Law on Conflicts of Interest. Sándor Várnai, *A képviselői összeférhetetlenség elvei és gyakorlata* [Conflicts of Interest Involving Members of Parliament (Act I of 1875) in Theory and Practice], Budapest, 1897. An influential political post could generate not only extra income but other benefits such as preferential loans: in 1896 several MPs received substantial loans (50,000, 15,000 and 5,000 forints each) at a very low rate (5.25%) of interest from the Hungarian Agricultural and Stocks Bank. See also György Szabad, 'A hitelviszonyok,' in István Szabó (ed.), *A parasztság a kapitalizmus korában 1848–1914* [Credit Relations in The Peasantry in the Age of Capitalism, 1848–1914], Budapest, 1972, pp. 234–5.

36 Sándor Pethő, *Politikai arcképek. Az új Magyarország vezéregyéniségei* [Political Portraits: Leaders of Hungary Under the New Regime], Budapest, 1911, pp. 98–9.

37 Árpád Zeller, *Az országgyűlési képviselők összeférhetetlenségéről. Az 1901 évi XXIV. tc. keletkezése, magyarázata az eljárási szabályok és az eddigi joggyakorlat alapján* [On the Conflicts of Interest of Members of Parliament: Drafting and Interpretation of Law 24 of 1901, Based on Legal Procedures and Legal Practice Hitherto], Budapest, 1930, pp. 89–90. Also: Konrád Imling, *Az 1901 XXIV tc. az összeférhetetlenségről* [Law 24 of 1901 on Conflicts of Interest], Budapest, 1901.

38 Verhovay, pp. 119 and 126. See also: *Az ország urai* [Rulers of the Country], Budapest, 1890. But Verhovay, again, was one of those the credibility of whose criticism of social and political malpractice was called into question by his own actions. Verhovay is believed to have been involved in the disappearance of public funds donated for the resettlement of the Csángos (ethnic Hungarians in Romania), as well as funds donated for the erection of a monument to Kossuth.

39 On the right of electors to recall MPs, and for a description of their legal status see: Ferenc Pecze, *A magyar parlamenti jog intézményei a 19.sz. második felében – különös tekintettel a képviselői jogállásra* [Legal Institutions In The Hungarian Parliament, With Special Reference To The Legal Status of MPs], PhD. Dissertation, Budapest, 1974. By the way, the conditions were in place for the creation of a law on the legal standing of MPs (similar to the one on conflicts of interest), although the only effect of such a law would probably have been an increase in the level of bribes paid to MPs.

40 On diverging opinions on the subject see: János Török, *Magyar életkérdések, összhangzásban a közbirodalmi érdekekkel* [Hungarian Interests Corresponding to Imperial Interests], Pest, 1852; Lajos Mocsáry, *A magyar társasélet* [Social Life In Hungary], Pest, 1855, contrasting the alternatives of conservative and liberal-democratic bourgeois development; (Kálmán Kenessey, *Egy-két őszinte szó társadalmi viszonyainkat illetőleg* [A Few Frank Words Concerning Our

Social Conditions], Pest, 1857). On the social impact of this trend see: György Szabad, *A társadalmi szerkezet átalakulásának kérdései az abszolutizmus korában* [Questions Of Social Transformation In The Age Of Absolutism], in *Történelmi Szemle*, 1958, No. 1-2, pp. 252–60; by the same author, *A társadalmi átalakulás folyamatának előrehaladása Magyarországon 1849–1867* [The Unfolding Of Social Transformation in Hungary 1849–67], in *Valóság, 1976/5*, pp. 1–15; on their political impact there is a comprehensive monograph: *Forradalom és kiegyezés válaszútján (1860–61)* [At The Crossroads Of Revolution And Compromise (1860–1)], Budapest, 1967. The debate continued after 1867. On this subject see also: *Kákay Aranyos (Aurél Kecskeméti) politikai-társadalmi tragico-humoristicus krónikája* [Tragi-Comic Socio-Political Chronicle By Aranyos Kákay], Pest, 1869; Gyula Schwartz, *Magyarország helyzete a reálunióban* [Hungary In The Real Union], Pest, 1870; Tamás Lipcsei, *Néhány szó a magyar társadalomról* [A Few Words About Hungarian Society], Pest, 1872.

41 Albert Apponyi, *Emlékirataim 1899–1906* [Memoirs 1899–1906], Vol. 2, Budapest, 1934.

42 Gyula Krúdy, *Kossuth fia* [Kossuth's Son], Budapest, 1976, p. 49. It must be admitted that in the end Eötvös destroyed the obituary, precisely because of the noble title used in it. But this only underlines that Eötvös's behaviour was motivated by a deeply embedded reaction in the first place.

43 Lajos Alleker, *Az osztrák-magyar monarchia rendjelei* [Medals of the Austro-Hungarian Monarchy], Nyitra, 1890; János Szerencs, *A főrendiház évkönyve 1900* [Yearbook of the Upper House 1900], Budapest, 1900.

44 Eötvös, p. 47. János Arany's extreme reluctance to accept a Saint Stephen Cross on the occasion of the Compromise is a faithful reflection of general sentiment at the time. (*Arany János leveleskönyve* [Letters of János Arany], selected and edited by: Györgyi Sáfrán, Budapest, 1928, pp. 591–5). This incident demonstrates that no one committed to the ideal of freedom could accept a medal in the light of the public opprobrium he would incur. The same sentiment is reflected in the following stanzas by Arany:

> Title holders come to see me,
> Offering me a title:
> 'Forgive me, my lords,
> But I have no inclination'
>
> All that is shiny in it
> Has been earned by literature;
> All that is slippery in it
> Belongs to me alone
>
> I suffer from a stomach ache
> They send me a medal;
> I would rather sleep with a good conscience
> Than receive a medal.

45 Verhovay, p. 133; also: Lajos Hentaller, *Politikusaink pongyolában* [Our Politicians In A Bathrobe], Budapest, 1886, pp. 7–8.

46 Barabás, p. 117; Kristóffy, pp. 57–58; Barabás, p. 117.
47 Herczeg, p. 226; Gyula Krúdy, *Kossuth fia* [Kossuth's Son], Budapest, 1976, p. 265. It is indicative of the importance of the King that annual costs related to his person exceeded the operational costs of parliament by four times, even at the most conservative estimate.
48 István Bibó, *Eltorzult magyar alkat, zsákutcás magyar történelem* [Deformed National Character and the Hungarian History of the Cul-de-Sac], in *Bibó István Összegyűjtött munkái* [Collected Works of István Bibó], Vol. 1, Edited by: István Kemény and Mátyás Sárközi, *Európai Protestáns Magyar Szabadegyetem* [European Protestant Hungarian Open University], Bern, 1981, p. 268.
49 Lajos Degré, *Pártok és vezérek az országházból* [Political Parties And Leaders In Parliament], Budapest, 1882, p. 26.
50 *Hazánk* [Our Country], April 2, 1868, in *A magyar politkai pártok programjai (1867–1918)* [The Programmes Of Hungarian Political Parties (1867–1918)], compiled and edited by: Gyula Mérei, Budapest, 1971, p. 71.
51 *Ellenőr,* September 3, 1873, cited in: Viktória M. Kondor, *Az 1875–ös pártfúzió* [The Party Fusion of 1875], Budapest, 1959, p. 114. On the fusion process see also: Gyula Oláh, *Az 1875–ös fúzió története* [The History of the Fusion of 1875], Budapest, 1908.
52 *Magyarország története 1848–1890* [The History of Hungary 1848–90], Budapest, 1979, Vol. VI/2, p. 864.
53 Quoted by: Vécsey, pp. 108–9. It must be pointed out that there is still no comprehensive monograph available on Kálmán Tisza. Vécsey's work, although it provides a lot of valuable details, is primarily a panegyric.
54 Quoted by: Gábor Erdődy, *Hermann Ottó és a társadalmi-nemzeti felemelkedés ügye* [Ottó Hermann and Social-National Progress], Budapest, 1984, pp. 164–5; on Hermann's conflict with his own party see: Ottó Hermann, *A pokol cséplője* [Thresher Of Hell], selected and edited by: Gábor Erdődy, Budapest, 1983, pp. 335–82.
55 Péter Hanák, *A dualizmus válságának problémája a XIX.század végén* [The Crisis of Dualism at the End of the Nineteenth Century], in *Magyarország a Monarchiában. Tanulmányok* [Hungary Under The Monarchy: Studies], Budapest, 1975, pp. 223–87. On Tisza's use of increasingly harsh measures see: Ferenc Pölöskei, *A koalíció felbomlása és a Nemzeti Munkapárt megalakulása 1909–1910* [Collapse of the Coalition and the Formation of the National Labour Party 1909–10], Budapest, 1963; and by the same author: *Kormányzati politika és parlamenti ellenzék 1910–1914* [Government Politics And Parliamentary Opposition 1910–14], Budapest, 1970.
56 Gyula Szekfű, *Három nemzedék* [Three Generations], Budapest, 1920.
57 Lajos Hentaller, *Politikusaink pongyolában* [Politicians in a Bathrobe], pp. 39, 49 and 55; *A T. Ház humora. Kivonat a parlamenti naplókból* [The Humour of the Honourable House: Extracts From The Protocols Of Parliament], foreword by Géza Szüllő, Szeged, 1943, p. 107; Ferenc Molnár, *Szülőfalum, Pest* [My Native Village], Budapest, 1962, p. 92.
58 Endre Nizsalovszky, *Eötvös József két levele Haynald Lajos érsekhez* [Two Letters by József Eötvös to Archbishop Lajos Haynald], in *Irodalomtörténeti közlemények* [Literary History Reports], 1967, No. 1, p. 76.

59 Jenő Szontagh, *Arcképek I. Ferenc József korából* [Portaits from the Age of Franz Joseph I], Budapest, 1936, p. 37.
60 *Kossuth Lajos iratai* [The Writings of Lajos Kossuth], Budapest, 1904, Vol. 10, p. 320.
61 Péter Hanák, *1898. A nemzeti és állampatrióta értékrend frontális ütközése a Monarchiában* [1898: The Clash of National and State Patriotic Values under the Monarchy], *Medvetánc*, 1984/2–3, pp. 55–72.
62 Miklós Szabó, *Nemzetkarakter és resszentiment. Gondolatok a politikai antiszemitizmus funkcióiról* [National Character And Ressentiment: Ideas on Political Anti-Semitism and Its Functions], *Világosság*, 1981/6, pp. 361–2.

8 The Two Houses of Parliament: History of a Changing Atmosphere

The forum of political representation in Hungary under the Austro-Hungarian Monarchy was the Lower House of parliament, the focal point of political life. The press provided continuous coverage of parliamentary debates and the most prominent speakers were national figures. The House was in session throughout the year with only short recesses, and under the prevailing press laws no one could be held legally accountable for reporting what was said there. The Lower House was the 'treasurehouse' of the country's elite, featuring aristocrats in large numbers, despite the fact that they had their own forum of representation in the Upper House. Despite fundamental reform in the mid-1880s, every twentieth male aristocrat had a seat in parliament. Over one-third of all members were members of the landed nobility. The rising bourgeois intelligentsia, including several outstanding literary figures, also gained seats in parliament. Politics, the press and the wide participation of the country's social elite made Hungary's parliament the centre of national attention.

Interest in parliamentary politics never abated, but the atmosphere of the House changed considerably over the years. These changes were mainly the result of the fact that parliamentary representation did not reflect the electorate (suffrage narrowed over the period, electoral manipulation became increasingly prevalent, the system of representation was undemocratic and political selection was subject to outside influences).[1] It also became clear that the political regime had no intention of allowing any alternative: access to power and influence was dependant upon competition at a personal level, rather than upon competition over political principles. The patriarchal orientation of the feudal regime had gradually been replaced by a merciless jockeying for position in which participants readily resorted to finger-pointing in an attempt to discredit competitors. The Hungarian political system rested on the rotation of persons, rather than of differing political views. The principle that one could only keep his head above water by drowning all the others came increasingly to dominate the changing atmosphere of the Lower House.

The seat of parliament

A great many of the most notable parliamentary events took place in the Sándor Utca Palace, a house in Sándor Főherceg utca (Archduke Sándor Street) near the National Museum (today 8 Bródy Sándor utca, home to the Italian Institute). Parliament was moved to its present location on the bank of the Danube only in 1904, and the imposing building has remained almost entirely unchanged ever since.

The Sándor Utca Palace provided a rather intimate setting for the activities of the House.[2] The building did not stand out from its neighbours, apart from the Hungarian coat-of-arms which decorated its facade. On entering, a visitor would first see the porter in a tall bearskin hat. To the left of the entrance was the cloakroom, where members of parliament could leave their coats and hats – each member had a place allotted to him marked with a nameplate.

After the cloakroom one reaches the corridor. Groups of MPs are engrossed in debate, the air filled with cigarette smoke, cigarette ends scattered everywhere on the grey carpets. Not a particularly dignified, but a most lively scene. The clamour of many voices emanating from figures both strange and familiar strikes one immediately; there are more Mamelukes – the governing party's lustreless supporters who generally prefer to stay out of the spotlight – than celebrities. This army of Mamelukes is waiting anxiously for an encouraging look or word from Prime Minister Kálmán Tisza – or the 'general' as they familiarly call him – who is just about to leave the chamber. They buzz around, chatting to ministers, seeking to obtain smaller or greater favours for themselves or their *protégés*.

This is where the private debates of members of the opposition and the governing party take place. There are separate corridors for governing-party and opposition members, but MPs tend to mingle, with habitual meeting points maintained for individual parties and their factions in window niches or entrances. Life on the corridor is made more pleasant by the presence of a buffet where the waitress is changed from year to year to protect confidentiality. The gentlemen can treat themselves to *pogácsa* (small savoury cakes), and the more affluent can enjoy the best caviar and ham. Sherry and a variety of wines are also very popular. The relaxed atmosphere of the buffet is congenial for the collection of signatures in support of charitable causes and for the asking of personal favours.

We are nearing the end of our tour of the Sándor Utca Palace. But before we describe the heart of the whole establishment – the chamber itself – let us

6   The old parliamentary chamber in the Sándor Utca Palace

take a brief look at the facilities, such as the post office and the telegraph agency: a rapid and ever more accelerating flow of information was a basic requirement even in those days. The Speaker of the House was entitled to a separate room, while ministers congregated in the Red Reception Hall, named after its beautiful drapery. The entrance to the Reception Hall was guarded by an attendant who would peep through the door, left slightly ajar, to see whether a minister was ready to receive an MP seeking to present a petition. There was also a library, established in 1866 on the basis of a contribution of 1,000 forints. The library was first housed in the National Museum and, from 1873, in the building of the Lower House itself. As the library's collection grew books came to be stored in the corridor and even the buffet. At the same time, the members cannot be said to have made much use of them: very few of the hundreds of MPs ever visited the library. A separate room was occupied by stenographers who were frequently visited by MPs wishing to make a speech. It was here that they could have their manuscripts corrected, copy-edited and prepared for publication in the Parliamentary Journals.

A large crowd on the corridor and in the buffet was a sure sign that a dull speech was being given in the chamber. An electrical device kept those outside the chamber constantly informed of what was going on inside. One ring meant that a new speaker was about to commence; two rings signified that a minister had risen to make a speech. Several rings called the members in to vote, upon which everyone rushed inside. Later a so-called 'logometer' was installed to indicate the names of the current speaker and his successor.

Now we must enter the centre of all legislative activity: the chamber. The hall is lit from three windows in the roof (gas lighting was introduced later). Around the walls run rows of oak benches upholstered in green leather. The focal point of all the benches is the seat of the Speaker of the House; above it are ruffles of green drapery, the national coat-of-arms and a clock which often runs late. On the high lectern, the only adornments are a bell and a container of ink. In front of the rows of benches stand the red velvet seats of the ministers. In the centre there is a separate desk for stenographers and a large oak table: the Table of the House. This is where MPs deposit petitions from their constituencies and their recommendations, while parties and ministers can deposit their bills and draft laws. There is room for over four hundred MPs but the house is rarely full. In front of each seat there is a nameplate. One seat has remained empty since 1867: it is dedicated to the memory of Ferenc Deák.

Looking around, MPs could see the public eye upon them in the form of the two galleries behind the green benches reserved for the press (with 20 seats in each) and a further eight galleries above.[3] Members of the Upper House were entitled to 24 seats of their own. Seats in the so-called 'special gallery' could as a rule be taken by former members of the House. Foreign visitors could sit in the 'foreigners' gallery'. The so-called 'medium gallery' was situated behind the lectern of the Speaker, who took personal charge of its 36 seats. Every MP had a kind of parliamentary invitation card written out in his name: anyone in receipt of such a card could gain admission to the so-called 'members' gallery' reserved for 100 persons. Furthermore, MPs could apply for tickets granting admission to the 'ladies' gallery' with 142 seats, the pearl of the House, which often attracted more attention from members than the issues they were there to discuss. There was also a separate gallery with 22 seats for the younger generation, probably in memory of the Parliamentary Youth who actively participated in the events of 1848. The 'young persons' gallery' was supervised by the elected head of the university reading circles. Finally, there was the 'open gallery' which could be entered without a ticket. Although the House rules ordered all visitors to be silent in crucial debates, speakers were greatly stimulated by the knowledge that they were being watched by hundreds of outsiders, possibly including someone whose opinion might be important for their public career and private wealth.[4]

Parliamentary security was maintained by policemen who were, however, not allowed to enter the chamber. The House rules – and, most importantly the atmosphere that characterized parliament – did not tolerate the presence of armed officers within the legislative body. Their posts were at the entrance of individual galleries and the main entrance to the building. As a rule, the security force numbered eleven. On 28 January 1889, the last day of debate on the controversial Act on the Armed Forces, some MPs noticed – as the speech of Kálmán Tisza was nearing its end – that some police detectives had sneaked into the galleries. Cries of protest could be heard from the opposition: 'What are policemen doing here? We refuse to talk before informers! The session must be closed! Shame! Disgrace!' Declarations of disapproval came also from the backbenches of the governing party. The Speaker of the House announced that he would take immediate measures to remove any unauthorized persons. The affair came to an end on the following day, when it turned out that the detectives were there to supervise pro-opposition university students who were against the act being debated. The Speaker suggested that the House let the matter drop but at the same time promised to ensure that the incident would never be repeated.[5] In the rows of the governing party sat István Tisza, who just a quarter of a century later would adopt an entirely different attitude.

'Those were the days'

The changing political atmosphere and the unwritten rules of parliamentary representation – how patriarchalism was replaced by merciless personal attacks and naked competition for political power – are the subjects of this chapter. But before we begin, it is important to provide a general definition of patriarchalism and personalism. These terms might suggest an origin in some sort of conservative nostalgia, that is, something vaguely positive. However, these traits were deeply embedded in political and historical reality, and their abstract treatment would be misleading. We are dealing with a complex phenomenon. Patriarchalism and personalism were related – especially at the beginning of this period – to the important role played in society by personal authority acquired as a consequence of some outstanding personal achievement. This was the source, for example, of Deák's authority and of that of a number of other politicians, including those temporarily or permanently in opposition (Kálmán Ghyczy, Dániel Irányi, and Ernő Simonyi to name only the most well-known). Personal dignity and decency tended to strengthen such authority further. At the same time, there was a tendency towards the formation of social castes – with the nobility at the top – on the basis of common behaviour. This was the foundation of the almost mandatory custom among members of parliament to address one other in the informal manner (not in public, of course, but certainly in the privacy of the House), and of such exclusive social venues and occasions as the casinos and table parties.[6]

A third aspect of the same phenomenon was the institution of so-called 'party clubs' that were supposed to compensate for the party discipline that had been introduced to curb the advance of personalism in politics.[7] The Liberal Club housed in the Lloyd Building was not so much a venue for political discussion – in fact, such discussion went into a decline as the number of Mamelukes continued to grow (see Chapter 7) – as a means of fostering the illusion of social equality when most politicians were, in fact, losing their personal and political integrity. This was a place where minor political figures could engage in confidential exchanges with the mighty and defeat at the card table those on whom they were normally so basely dependent; where a sense of humour and charm could make someone into a leading figure at his party's social occasions – and so provide him with compensation for failing to emerge as an important political figure. The corridor of the House was in a way an extension of these political clubs. Here, governing-party and opposition members could freely mingle and the humblest opposition MPs could feel themselves on an equal footing with the mightiest statesmen. This atmosphere was further strengthened by the intricately woven fabric of family connections and economic interests.

It was personal authority, above all, that ensured – at least in the early years – that political debate was conducted with a modicum of decorum. General respect for opposing views did not, of course, rule out heckling – this was, in fact, promoted by the informal atmosphere that reigned in the House – but the most malignant personal attacks were outlawed or at least curbed in favour of rational argument. With the demise of personal authority, however – partly as a result of the deaths of leading figures and of causes related to the consolidation of the post-feudal political regime – such mutual respect also declined. It became increasingly difficult to both acquire and maintain personal authority. As the substance was eroded, the outward ceremonies of social class coherence – patriarchal forms of social behaviour and social ceremony – became mere empty formalities, the bleak masks of a caste-based society suffering from the deep internal ruptures caused by intensifying personal competition.

In parliament itself, the same members worked together for nine to ten months a year, which further promoted an atmosphere of increased personalism. Cabs parked in front of the House were a frequent sight: they were waiting to collect MPs from nearby taverns to rush them to parliament by the time they had to cast their votes. Members as a rule were together from 10 a.m. to 2 or 3 p.m., and in the case of debates on more important issues their presence was mandatory. Parliament was a workplace, but because of its intimate arrangement, also served as a social venue. Countless scenes illustrative of the personalism and sense of confinement instilled by the House were played out in its focal point: the chamber. Kálmán Mikszáth wrote:

> But is it possible to hit a body which is constantly in motion: what is a foot one minute turns into an elbow, and what yesterday was a mouth is now an ear? The House changes like time: it is never exactly the same but never quite different.[8]

And this is how Sándor Wekerle saw the House in 1896:

> As regards behaviour, it is different from the United States where [members] can eat, drink and smoke in the chamber; it is also different from the English model where [members] sit with their hats on, squashed together on benches with no tables and where there are less seats than members; as regards procedure it is different again from the German model in that the atmosphere here is more lively – there are more comments, expressing both approval and disapproval. It is broadly similar to the French and Italian parliaments in that nowhere else is there to be found such indifference towards non-political matters and such enthusiasm for politics. It is also similar to the English parliament in that long and grand speeches are held in high esteem, with the cultivation of the neo-classical style of diction and the poignancy specific to each period. Finally, the Hungarian parliament has an unparalleled and most honourable feature, the familiarity, ease and warmth of communication between members. All shades of feeling and temperament are represented here. The Lower House always has its humorists and willing speakers who, with varying degrees of wit, provide a serene atmosphere; its pessimists who carry on their shoulders, not only a deep concern for the homeland, but also the troubles of the whole world; there are irascible members who find fault with everything and see the world in dark colours, but whose hearts flutter whenever they find their enemies in trouble; it has its *enfants terribles* who throw out their chests and pose as the competent and exclusive agents of all that is good, noble, gentlemanly, proper and decent; its gossips who sneak around awfully well-informed, spreading rumours that are seldom complimentary; and there is the vast majority who observe the handling of public affairs with a cool head but rapt attention, who are seldom carried away and never despair, who observe events with the tranquillity of the East but begin to stir, rise and electrify others whenever public affairs or an ideal, feeling or desire deeply rooted in the national spirit appears to be in danger.[9]

This is the atmosphere of personalism and intimacy that Mikszáth described in hundreds of his parliamentary sketches, the atmosphere that up to the early 1880s still characterized the House of Representatives although, by then, it was already on the wane. The same atmosphere was also reflected in rhetoric – the main instrument of parliamentary activity – and in the behaviour of politicians.

Speech and behaviour in parliament were regulated by the House rules. For instance, speakers had to sign up in advance to speak on a particular item on the agenda. Furthermore, speeches could not be read out, they had to be learned by heart. An MP could speak on matters off the agenda, if his contribution concerned the House rules or his own person. The Speaker of the House was obliged to reprimand any speaker making an indecent comment concerning the House or one of its members. It was also the duty of the Speaker to ensure that a speaker was not interrupted. These were the written rules.

Reality was somewhat different, however, and this is where the unwritten rules entered into play. A speaker's contribution to a debate could be disturbed in many ways other than by straightforward verbal interruption: provocative indifference or equally provocative attention were powerful means to make a speaker feel ill at ease.[10] Some would stretch their legs so that their feet stuck out into the aisle between the benches while their fingers beat a disconcerting rhythm; others would theatrically engross themselves in reading instead of paying attention. Messages expressly designed to provoke laughter would be circulated. The target of such ridicule would, of course, be the speaker himself. At the same time, MPs were continually entering and leaving the chamber or walking up and down within it. Those with poor hearing would move closer to the speaker, look for an empty seat and sit down with some noise. This was the habit of the opposition member István Csanádi who walked around with his hands held to his ears for amplification. Others would take a seat in front of the speaker and theatrically show how bored they were, punctuating their display with the occasional yawn. Naturally, loud-voiced professional interrupters would not sit back: they would encourage or annoy speakers by their braying, deliberately talking loudly to put them off.

The sometimes overcomplicated style of speech used in parliament was partly attributable to the requirement that speeches be delivered as if *ex tempore* and not merely read out. Many would put down their speech in writing and memorize it, keeping a copy of the written text in front of them in case their memory faltered. Some MPs would incorporate in the written copy anticipated affirmative exclamations from the audience, and present them to the stenographer in this 'ready' form.[11] Others would put down their speech but diverge from it in the heat of the debate. It became common to incorporate references to the 'previous speaker' in an effort to create an appearance of spontaneity. Astute interrupters, however – if several 'previous speakers' had already spoken – would hasten to enquire to whom the current speaker was referring, often to his considerable embarrassment.

'It was . . . what'shisname', the speaker would mumble, his attempt at spontaneity having blown up in his face. Those who began by saying: 'I did not intend to speak today, but . . . ', and who nevertheless glanced continually, if surreptitiously, at a carefully prepared manuscript throughout, would be equally sure to displease their audience.

Given the fact that speeches had to be made without notes, effective speakers were those who had not only prepared their topic well, but who also had the ability to respond to the speeches of those preceding them and were always ready with a witty riposte to turn aside the jibes of opponents. A brief but felicitous rejoinder could often undo the most carefully prepared argument, as in the case of the MP who supported his speech in favour of prolonging the license of the Austro-Hungarian Bank – as against introducing an independent Hungarian National Bank – with a mass of statistical data. In reply, a member of the opposition dryly remarked: 'Anything can be proved by statistics. One could, for example, argue that it is better to suffer from typhoid than to be a millionaire: according to statistics only 40% of typhoid sufferers die, whereas millionaires are doomed to "shuffle off this mortal coil" without exception.'

Although a ready wit was a formidable weapon, the best speakers were those who could deliver long but enjoyable speeches and take the arguments of their rivals to pieces with relentless logic. One such person was Dezső Szilágyi who never spoke for less than one or two hours. He prepared his 'act' days in advance, thinking through every possible counterargument, frequently asking friends to marshall arguments against him which he would then try to refute. His speeches usually attracted a full house. In the mid-1890s, Albin Csáky nicknamed him the 'Great Thresher' for his role in the debate on religion. Csáky humorously admitted that he could only count on reaping one of the first ears of corn because the Great Thresher – and here he pointed to Szilágyi – would inevitably claim the lion's share.

Albert Apponyi was another speaker who always attracted a large crowd with his aristocratic appearance, cultured style of speaking, pleasing voice and high erudition. Apponyi had distinguished himself in 1873 with his maiden speech on the subject of financial support for the establishment of a Music Academy. He had drawn up a detailed list of all the things likely to lead to the success of a maiden speech in parliament: choose a cultural or humanitarian topic; don't contradict the views of influential politicians; be brief; stick to your topic; and do not talk about yourself.[12] Apponyi gratefully acknowledged later in life that both sides of the House had greeted his first speech with benevolence and had observed the provision of the House rules according to which a maiden speaker should not be interrupted. Apponyi also laid down five golden rules for the ideal parliamentary speech: avoid forced populism; aim at simplicity and transparency of formulation; support your argument with facts and figures; take the general feeling about an issue as your starting point; and keep the attention of your audience by inserting appropriate anecdotes.[13] He wrote:

> It is no small thing to have experienced – particularly when I reflect upon my difficult first years in Parliament – the sudden filling of the chamber and the descent of silence upon my being invited to speak; how the galleries would be filled to overflowing at the prospect of hearing one of my speeches; and that in the hour during which my speech lasted I possessed total control over the feelings of my audience. Let he who has never fallen victim to such vanity cast the first stone of criticism![14]

It is difficult today to imagine the effect that his words must have had since we are unable to reproduce his diction, tone of voice or appearance, though the substance of his speeches was reported in detail by the press: detailed parliamentary reports were a regular feature of the newspapers of the day.

The heroes of a particular parliamentary session could acquire national fame, often becoming a major topic of coffee-house and club conversations. The physical presence of the public eye in the galleries, and indirect forms of publicity embodied in enthusiastic or condemnatory press reports, brought a number of speakers to the forefront of public debate. The majority of MPs – especially of the Mameluke persuasion increasingly gaining ground within the House – did not excel in speechmaking, going to the House merely to vote. When the Speaker invited members to cast their votes it was as if 'a forest had begun to move': MPs voted by rising to their feet. As parliament became more and more of a voting machine (and after the 1880s, it was little else),[15] parliamentary speeches were reduced to only two functions: to influence public opinion and to heighten the speaker's reputation.

This glimpse into the atmosphere of parliament indicates that, at least up until the 1880s, although heated political debate was an integral part of political life, expressly personal abuse was non-existent. Parliamentary etiquette did not allow any behaviour liable to violate the dignity of the House. Of course, political conflict inevitably involved two or more conflicting persons, but the limit was never reached beyond which the integrity of political representation itself was jeopardized. One final illustration of this is the example of Ghyczy, Speaker of the House between 1875 and 1879, who once silenced an overexcited MP clamouring for permission to speak by declaring: 'What the Right Honourable Gentleman appears to want to say is almost certainly unparliamentary and so I would ask him to sit down!'[16]

A new era

The idyll could not last long. The emergence of Mamelukes in large numbers, and public awareness of dishonest electoral practices, had a corrupting influence on public morality to the extent that the activities of political interest groups and the corrupt methods employed in election campaigns came to be regarded as more valiant than vicious.[17] Such practices were not publicly condemned. Mamelukeism evolved into a form of morality, best formulated by the liberal MP Ernő Urbanovszky who, when told of the crushing defeat of the government, asked with perfect composure: 'But there will be *some* government left, won't there?' This tendency got into full swing in the 1880s, along with an increased orientation towards financial gain. As an anonymous parliamentary poet put it: 'Your fixed income is like your lawful wedded wife. But you must also have a mistress.'[18]

Growing disillusion with the legitimacy of political power and a related atmosphere of cynicism did not leave the unwritten rules of political behaviour unaffected. The transfiguration of a dubious political legitimacy into a kind of gentlemanly valour was accompanied by renewed emphasis on personal honour, representing a return to feudal forms, a tendency generally justified on the basis of continuity and tradition. The ruling political elite used this historical patina as a screen to conceal the moral deterioration of public life and the increasing lack of substance of political representation.

From the 1880s onwards, this tendency manifested itself in two principal respects: the radical degradation of parliamentary debate, and the increasing number of duels fought between MPs. Duels were further proof that political representation was failing to provide enough of a counterbalance to feudal public manners. Besides, duels tended to attract rather lenient sentences: although Section 19 of Act V of the Penal Code of 1878 punished duels with incarceration in a state prison for political offenders, in practice imprisonment was very brief, sometimes no more than a couple of days. The absence of a genuine deterrent encouraged the resorting to duels in order to settle political arguments. The institution of the duel, which saw a revival after the 1880s, paradoxically strengthened the sense of gentlemanly superiority of those involved by reinforcing their sense of belonging to the same social caste.[19]

The lowering of the tone of parliamentary discussion – and the re-emergence of the duel that resulted – at first assumed a rather benign appearance. In 1882, a clash involving two MPs – Mór Wahrmann, a Jewish member of the governing party, and the leading anti-Semite Győző Istóczy – culminated in a duel, although their seconds avoided injury by handing the fighters defective pistols. Personal conflicts, however, began to get more serious as the decade progressed. The sharp disagreements that threatened to tear the House apart could no longer be contained. On 13 December 1883, the independent MP Sándor Almássy suddenly shouted at Ottó Hermann, another independent: 'A villain! That's what you are, a villain!'[20] Those present were deeply shocked at this unprecedented attack.

Still, a sense of balance prevailed between the old and the new morality, as the 1883 case of Füzesséry versus Polónyi demonstrates. On 16 April 1883, the independent MP Géza Füzesséry put a question to the Minister of the Interior:

> Is the Honourable Gentleman aware that in the middle of February the Graz police sent a certain constable Glavostnik to Budapest to investigate a gang of thieves allegedly hiding here? Is he also aware that the list of gang members in the possession of the Graz police features the name of a member of this House?[21]

Füzesséry accused a fellow member of the House – without naming him – of complicity in a crime, an announcement which naturally gave rise to considerable excitement. In a public-spirited effort to satisfy calls to identify the guilty party, the independent MP Verhovay whispered audibly to a neighbour that the man in question was another independent MP, Géza Polónyi. It turned out later that this accusation was entirely groundless and had been brought forward with the sole purpose of blackening Polónyi's character. A wave of condemnation promptly engulfed the chamber: József Madarász, the 'Father of the House', commented that such behaviour would have been unimaginable in the parliament of his youth. He proposed that until the case had been satisfactorily closed, the House should go into recess: since nothing less than its moral integrity was at stake, his proposal was unanimously accepted. Finally, Füzesséry apologized to Polónyi before the House and Kálmán Tisza, then Minister of the Interior, warned members that the dignity of the House depended, above all, on their moral integrity and that no moral code could ever repair the damage should it be compromised. The Speaker also warned MPs not to abuse parliamentary privilege in this fashion.

This affair points to the emergence – principally within the opposition – of a new willingness to further one's career at the expense of others, almost without constraint. Instead of seeking to discredit a rival's political views in an open and honest contest, the adherents of this new political credo sought to banish their opponents from the political arena altogether. Such tendencies are present in any parliamentary regime to a greater or lesser extent, but they are likely to prevail chiefly where political change is reduced to the rotation of personnel within an entrenched ruling elite, that is, where there is no prospect of constitutional reform. The greater the number of those prepared to abandon their principles for the sake of ensuring the survival of the regime, the wider the scope for personal confrontation became: as principles ceased to shape politics career opportunities tended to entail the removal of rivals at whatever cost.

This tendency got into full swing during the 1890s and at the turn of the century. By this time it was no longer the custom to listen to a maiden speech in silence. Furthermore, the informal manner of address within the House was no longer practised by all MPs. Members of party cliques were largely engaged in attempts to undermine each other's credibility. In 1898, Nándor Horánszky tried, with some success, to discredit the Prime Minister by saying that 'there is no casino or readers' club in this country that would suffer such a member'.[22] The rest was a matter for the seconds; only the Emperor's refusal to give his permission prevented the country's premier politician from becoming involved in a duel. In the second half of the 1890s, Gábor Andreánszky crossed swords with the Minister of the Interior in parliament and the latter did not fail to demand satisfaction for the injury he had suffered. What a glorious moment in the history of the Hungarian parliament, when the head of the police publicly violated the Penal Code![23] In 1905, after parliament had moved to its present location, Count István Keglevich was insulted by another member with the observation that he 'should be put out to grass'. The ensuing duel ended tragically when Keglevich died of his wounds.[24]

This alarming decline did not pass unnoticed by contemporaries. In 1890 Vilmos Vázsonyi (who in 1901 would become an MP with democratic inclinations) wrote:

In our parliament sit most of the country's unregistered tradesmen and registered cavaliers. More thorough statisticians could provide exact figures to prove that the increase in the number of MPs experiencing conflicts of interest has been directly proportionate to the increase in the number of duellists. There was a time, in the period of constitutional restoration, when there were hardly any MPs to be found on the boards of banks and other companies, and when the unscrupulous politician trading in political influence was a rare bird. Duels were also few and far between; to demand satisfaction through arms was not the fashion in Hungarian public affairs. The filling up of the reception halls of banks, ministries and cavalry barracks with members of parliament was a sudden occurrence. The new economic order and the duel appeared on the scene together.

There are two laws in particular that the Children of Modernity have turned upside down in the most brazen manner possible: the Law on Conflicts of Interest and the one prohibiting duels. The ruling social elite, which from time to time simulates a fit of moral pique, has freely consented to this. It is true that the Penal Code has hypocritically been amended to make duelling a criminal act; but the legislators themselves were the first to transgress it. Events in parliament also provide ample evidence that the rise in the number of duels has gone hand in hand with a general lowering of standards. The more nullities have penetrated the House the more chivalrous escapades there have been. To cap it all, even ministers have stooped to fighting duels and so to the nadir of ridicule: the minister in charge of the police and internal affairs has even fought a duel under the protection of his own policemen! The Right Honourable Gentlemen discuss their duels with astonishing tranquillity, while the protocols of individual matches are quoted word for word in the press. The time is not far away when the cavalry barracks will be as integral a part of the House as the buffet. The wave of duels sweeping through our country indicates two things: first, Hungarian politics lack sincerity, all political trends are hypocritical and, at the end of the day, amount to little more than gallantry without substance, whatever guise they might assume; and second, feudal rule has been restored and what is more, having now won the support of the *nouveau riche*, it is stronger than ever.[25]

At this point it would perhaps be in order to quote from two articles by Endre Ady, one of Hungary's foremost poets, both written in 1902. The first was composed on the occasion of the announcement by the Serbian MP Ljubomir Pavlovic that he had reached an agreement with representatives of the other national minorities to refrain from duelling. Ady wrote in fitting appreciation of this decision:

> We can see that Pavlovich is a true representative. He is the elected representative of his people and he acknowledges no other authority. He has refused to be terrorized by foolish casino attitudes . . . I wish our Hungarian members of parliament were able to attain such high principles; but no, they will remain what they have always been: as soon as more radical action threatens they all play the same tune.

The second piece relates to the same Vázsonyi who had bewailed the parliament's lawlessness. On one occasion, the Jewish Vázsonyi, an MP known to oppose duelling, was prevented from speaking in parliament in a manner characteristic of the spirit of unrestrained personalism which at times led to the flaunting of both the written and the unwritten rules of the House. Ady hastened to respond:

> Our noble country with its glorious past yesterday succeeded in plumbing the depths of Balkanization with a farce which, provoking us to laughter for all its ignominy, is sure to go down in the history books . . . This latest scandal of our most Balkanized of parliaments has shed a terrible and merciless light, unveiling a secret that we would have been better off never learning. We have discovered that the various offspring of the Hungarian parliament are deep down all the same, whether they swear on the claws of the double eagle, Kálmán Széll's weeping pimple, Lajos

Kossuth's hat, or the slippers of His Holiness the Pope. One need only lightly scrape the hard shell of their confused brains to see them swarming before us in all their deplorable glory . . . They regard Hungary as a nation of high culture. They recognize our inability to progress, how we sprawl and quibble in the middle of Europe with our Samoyed values, like a relic from the Middle Ages, they see that we are light and empty, that our notion of great achievements does not stretch beyond a little Jew-bashing, and as we begin to come to our senses we hasten to drink deeply of the tarted up glory of our thousand year history; finally, they see that we are layabouts and good-for-nothings; and that the great fortress of other nations, the parliament, is in Hungary only something to be discredited. Where will this end, my noble brethren? [26]

These contemporary reactions draw our attention to two things: first, that honourable political views did exist in defiance of what threatened to become the norm; and second, that by the turn of the century some observers had become aware, if not of the complete progression of causes and consequences, at least of the ever increasing homogeneity of their politicians.

The shattering of appearances

To all appearances, there had never been a more unbridgeable chasm between political trends than in the 1890s and around the turn of the century. This was the period when obstruction, the most radical tactic of the opposition, emerged as a persistent element of parliamentary politics. Obstruction meant, above all, filibustering: debating government bills to death, thereby delaying or even preventing their enactment. Under House rules such obstruction was quite legal. Although it was the only means the opposition had to make its voice heard, it had the absurd consequence – under a nominally liberal political system – of allowing a minority to control the majority by making it impossible for it to govern.

From 1889, one wave of obstructive behaviour followed another, apparently the manifestation of the growing readiness of the opposition to assume power. They succeeded in portraying themselves as a strong and resolute element within parliament when the reality was quite different. But the opposition's seeming formidability was enough to mislead the ruling elite – including the sovereign – as to the true extent of its internal decay and lack of moral fibre. As the events of 1905–6 would show, the substance of the opposition was rather more smoke than fire.

While obstruction entered the parliamentary scene largely as a result of the crisis of political representation, in its turn it contributed to a deepening of that crisis and a further deterioration in the level of personal attacks.

Obstruction by its very nature rendered members of parliament clowns in the eyes of the public and thereby discredited the very institution of parliament. The following passage, from 1899, illustrates this principle:

> Of what obstruction was like in practice I can give the following description:
>
> Inside the chamber there were no more than a handful of people. At the Speaker's lectern sits old Madarász, with a notary on duty on either side. On the far left Gyula Justh, President of the Dispute Settlement Committee, is in charge. He is not presently engaged in the settlement of disputes, however, but is busy casting for the next parliamentary scene. He is handing a piece of paper to some opposition MPs. The piece of paper contains a petition signed by 20 members of this august House. No palaver is required. The petition must simply be read out and presented to the Speaker of the House who will then invite MPs to cast their votes.

The procedure is as follows. After the opening of the session, one of the notaries reads out the minutes of the last session. János Hock then stands up and proposes that the word 'session' be replaced by 'assembly' in the minutes. Another opposition MP now hands over another piece of paper to the Speaker in which 20 MPs request that a roll-call vote (in which each member is polled individually on the floor of the House) be held on Hock's proposal. Under the House rules, the Speaker must now invite members to vote.

After three such roll-call votes have come and gone the first day of obstruction is over. On the following day, different tactics are employed. István Fái proposes that the date of the session be recorded in the minutes not in figures but in words; Lajos Hentaller in turn proposes that the phrase 'the debate having come to an end' be modified to 'the debate having ended'. Lajos Bíró and Lajos Holló will present similarly weighty proposals. And each proposal is followed by the presentation of two sheets of paper each signed by 20 MPs, one requesting a roll-call vote and the other that the vote be postponed until the following session. The Speaker of the House is bound by the House rules to honour these requests. In this way, the dispute settlement committee makes sure that roll-call voting takes up a great deal of time in the next session too. And this is how it goes, for weeks on end. Every so often, the eternal round of senseless voting is interrupted by the occasional speech on an issue of personal concern to a member, or a question is presented to a minister on an issue of concern to the opposition.

Votes are, as a rule, cast in the same ratio: 'No' votes are cast by 114 MPs and 'Yes' votes by only four. It is clear that it was not necessary for the whole opposition to be present when voting took place; it was enough if those four or five MPs were present who had forwarded the motion. In contrast, the governing party had to ensure that at least a 100 of its MPs be present, the minimum required to constitute a quorum. Otherwise the governing party would be playing into the hands of the obstructive opposition, not to mention laying itself open to possible surprises.

Strategic obstruction sometimes led to the most absurd situations. On one occasion, Ferenc Blaskovics requested leave to make a point of order. However, 20 MPs had requested a roll-call vote and another 20 that the voting be postponed until the next session. The ridiculous outcome was that the House could not decide before the next session whether Blaskovics should have been allowed to make a point of order on the previous day.[27]

The strategy of obstruction would, from time to time, be enlivened by speeches which could last for four or five hours. Needless to say, such orations were little more than the modulated expulsion of hot air.

Such clowning inevitably brought the already heavily mortgaged image of parliament into further disrepute. Ferenc Herczeg wrote in 1896 that:

[When] I took my seat in the old House in Sándor utca, I could not really rejoice at my new role. Electoral malpractice, with the memory of which the country was still resounding, and the depths to which obstruction had lowered the standard of Hungarian public affairs had tainted my joy. I was haunted by the terrible suspicion that we might not even be genuine members of parliament.[28]

Herczeg was probably right to question the legitimacy of parliament under prevailing conditions. But he and many others were mistaken in their belief that the standard of Hungarian public affairs had been lowered by obstruction alone. Obstruction was rather an – undoubtedly theatrical – consequence of the lack of legitimacy which characterized post-Compromise politics, and it was far from being the only one. Obstruction was no more than a time bomb deposited by an already profoundly flawed system.

In this world of appearances, however, it was no wonder that the consequences were taken for the cause. The erosion that had begun decades before had worked slowly and invisibly to undermine the edifice of political representation. Ironically, the representatives of a political regime responsible for the destruction of parliamentarianism and its transformation into a mockery of democratic representation could in good faith pose as its saviours. The sacred cause of defending democratic representation in turn provided moral justification for a complete disregard of the rules of parliamentary politics. The logic which regarded obstructionism as not merely the consequence, but the principal cause, of the decline of political representation did not lead to an understanding of the fact that – as a first step – the false legitimacy of the feudal-conservative regime should be purified by the introduction of universal suffrage and the secret ballot; only then should

7   István Tisza, c. 1915

particular abuses have been addressed. But such an approach is unlikely to have worked, in any case: fundamental reforms would have led to the demise of the regime that the whole system of political representation was meant to prop up. It was, therefore, inevitable that fundamental reforms should be put aside, to be supplanted by minor corrections serving to ensure political continuity.

These 'corrections' were made by Count István Tisza. The scene: the chamber of the impressive new parliament building. The time: 18 November 1904. Tisza was the director of the show the undoubted stars of which were Gábor Dániel, a governing-party MP, Dezső Perczel, Speaker of the House, and a number of liberal MPs. Dániel proposed an amendment to the House rules with the intention of curbing strategic obstruction and establishing deadlines within which so-called 'state priorities' (the budget and mustering of the armed forces) must be addressed. The opposition, naturally, resorted to the very weapon which the motion sought to remove from their hands for good. This was the point at which the director entered the scene. Tisza, in the spirit of Kossuth and Deák, launched a passionate attack on 'these profligates of national values'.

The time had come when a choice had to be made between leaving the country to its fate and putting an end to the farce of obstruction. Tisza's intervention was the signal for the Speaker of the House to indicate with his handkerchief that those present should cast their votes. The liberals had been waiting only for this: they rose as one and voted to accept Dániel's proposal before the debate had even ended, in violation of the House rules. The session was then adjourned in accordance with an ordinance obtained in advance from the sovereign.[29]

It is characteristic of the whole situation we are attempting to describe that established parliamentary procedures had to be violated in order that the principle of parliamentarianism itself could be salvaged. This was the culmination of the absurd quandry into which political representation in Hungary had got itself. The counterattack was not long delayed. On 13 December, the opening of the new session of parliament, the opposition smashed the furniture and fittings of the chamber of the House to pieces. Bánffy, a former Prime Minister and now a member of the opposition, outdid himself in devastation. Tisza, however, had managed to estrange the majority of the adherents of 1867 by his insistence on radical measures to preserve the existing regime, measures which brought out into the open parliament's advanced state of decay. Naturally, this conflicted with the interests of those who had hitherto successfully employed public affairs as a cover for their private interests. The exposure of the insubstantiality of political representation was resisted at every turn. The split that occurred within the 1867 camp happened because the supporters of the post-Compromise regime had been reduced to mere marionettes. After this split, the wing of the 1867 camp which felt comfortable in the environment created by the decay of parliamentarianism – but which was unwilling openly to admit its transgression of the principles of liberalism – and the 1848 camp, which had long since accepted its role as upholder of the status quo, finally formed a coalition. They were quite happy at the prospect of governing Hungary for four years and were determined not to change anything.

The epilogue to the history of obstructionism – and of liberal-parliamentary practice – came in 1912, after the fall of the discredited coalition, with the active participation of István Tisza, who in 1910 had regained some of his influence. On 22 May 1912, Tisza was elected Speaker of the House. Tisza's coup d'état of 1904 had curbed obstructionism only partially, insofar as it affected priority affairs of state. On 4 June 1912, the opposition once again attempted to exercise its parliamentary rights and requested that a closed session be held. On this occasion, however, Tisza denied the request and ordered voting to proceed, in blatant violation of the House rules. He went even further, ordering the removal of the outraged opposition MPs by the police, and making the immunities committee pass a resolution suspending them from parliament for 20 days. Many refused to

8 The police invade parliament

acknowledge the resolution and defiantly made their appearance in the House as usual.

The following eyewitness account describes the subsequent scene:

What now happened in the House on a daily basis was both horrible and humiliating. When the police entered the chamber opposition members would rush to the centre, linking arms to protect their suspended fellows. The police would nevertheless remove them from the crowd one by one. Bearers of the most respected names in the country would be dragged out by their collars. This was the nadir of the authority of the Hungarian political elite. Among the first MPs to be dragged out, his clothes torn and his tie creased, was Count Mihály Károlyi. And yet the opposition MPs believed that they were fighting to uphold Hungary's thousand year old Constitution as firmly as the members of the governing party.

The willpower of the Speaker of the House was hardened by a kind of fearful fanaticism. His party followed him, terrified of the unforeseeable catastrophe that might erupt at any minute. They obeyed their leader almost against their will, subdued by his terrible spell. I was, I must admit, awestruck by these shocking scenes repeated day after day. I have never seen the dignity of the legislature in a more rumpled and besmirched state. But Tisza knew neither let nor hindrance – he proceeded undaunted and hauled his whole party on behind him.

On one occasion a police officer defied his orders and refused to lay hands on such 'excellent patriots'. His fellows also hung back, not knowing what to do. Members of the governing party would normally leave the chamber while the police were at work but on this occasion I witnessed events from the gallery reserved for the press. I saw that the policemen had ceased grappling, had taken off their helmets and kept wiping their damp foreheads, conferring with each other in a group. It seemed that Tisza's plan was about to collapse. I walked out onto the corridor and there caught sight of the Speaker. When I told him what was going on inside, he suddenly turned to the Minister of the Interior who was standing beside him and asked:

'How many gendarmes do you have in Budapest?'

He was obviously considering using the gendarmes [provincial policemen] to arrest the defiant [Budapest] policemen; but at no time did he think that he might have to withdraw.

Later Tisza decided to surround parliament with a military cordon – soldiers were ordered not to allow the entry of the suspended MPs.

As a result, the scene of scandal shifted to parliament square. The whole of the opposition congregated in front of the cordon, hurling abuse at workers' party members entering the building; the noise and excitement filled the city. On many occasions I myself was subject to the shameful ordeal of having to pass between rows of my fellow MPs shouting hoarsely with distorted faces.[30]

The opposition's reaction was not long in coming. On 17 June, Gyula Kovács, an opposition MP, fired three shots at Tisza. At the end of October, a law was passed extending the powers of the Speaker of the House (which in practical terms meant the complete elimination of obstructionism), and the setting up of a parliamentary guard entitled to use force against MPs should it be necessary.

All this happened just 23 years after the detectives caught sneaking around the galleries in pursuit of unruly students had been driven out of parliament amidst the general outrage of all MPs. The loss of political autonomy suffered by individual politicians had been followed by parliament's loss of political autonomy as an institution.

(1988)

Notes

1 I tried to present the whole of the process in my *Az elsöprő kisebbség. Népképviselet a Monarchia Magyarországán* [The Decisive Minority: Political Representation in Hungary Under the Dual Monarchy], Budapest, 1988.

2 I based the description of the interior on Mikszáth's sketches about parliament.

3 The description of the galleries is from: *A képviselőház háznagyának és a háznagyi hivatalnak hatásköre és ügyrendje* [Functions Of and Procedures Used By the Sergeant-at-Arms of the Lower House], Budapest, 1886.

4 On House rules, among other things, see: József Kun, *A parlamenti házszabályok* [The House Rules of Parliament], Budapest, 1902. On a comprehensive description of mechanisms underlying the internal workings of parliament see: Rezső Mantuano, *A magyar törvényhozás* [Legislation in Hungary], Budapest, 1900.

5 For a description of the incident see: Mór Szatmári, *Húsz év parlamenti viharai* [Twenty Years of Storms in Parliament], Budapest, 1928, pp. 102–4 (hereafter Szatmári).

6 On the Hungarian Casino see: János (József) Bognár, *Három évtized egy úri kaszinó életéből* [Three Decades In The Life Of A Gentlemen's Club], Budapest, 1927. Ferenc Herczeg too wrote on the subject of the casino (*Emlékezései. A gótikus ház* [Memoirs: The Gothic House], Budapest, 1934 (hereafter Herczeg). On social life see: Szilárda Veres Rudnayné, *Emlékeim 1847–1917* [Memoirs 1847–1917], Budapest, 1922 (hereafter Rudnayné). On table parties see: Szatmári, pp. 140–6 and Lajos Hentaller, *Politikusaink pongyolában* [Politicians in A Bathrobe], Budapest, 1886 (hereafter Hentaller).

7 Much has been written on the clubs, including Hentaller, pp. 6–7; Tamás Vécsey, *Tisza Kálmán,* political study, Celldömölk, 1931, pp. 132–3; and

Herczeg, p. 106. On the question of party discipline see: Károly Szász, *Egy képviselő naplójegyzetei az 1856. december 10-én megnyílt országgyűlés alatt* [Diary Entries of a Member of Parliament During the Session Which Opened on 10 December 1856], Budapest, 1866 (an account of Deák's party in the initial stages), and: *Kecskeméthy Aurél naplója 1851–1878* [The Diary of Aurél Kecskeméthy 1851–78], editing, introduction and notes by: Miklós Rózsa, Budapest, 1909; and Gusztáv Beksics, *A szabadelvű párt története* [The History of the Liberal Party], Budapest, 1907. A valuable but eclectic collection is: *Politikai Magyarország* [Political Hungary], chief editor: József Szász, Budapest, no date, Vols. 3–4.

8 Kálmán Mikszáth, *A tisztelt Ház* [The Honourable House], Budapest, 1887, p. 83 (hereafter Mikszáth, The Honourable House).

9 Sándor Wekerle, '*A magyar parlament*' [The Hungarian Parliament] in Mór Gelléri (ed.), *Az ezeréves Magyarország múltjából és jelenéből* [From the Past and Present of the Thousand Year Old Hungary], Budapest, 1896, pp. 47–54, quoted in: László Tarr, *Az ezredév* [The Millennium], Budapest, 1979.

10 Details of the description were based on Mikszáth, *The Honourable House*. The comments and ironic replies were borrowed from: *A T. Ház humora* [The Humour of the Honourable House], extracts from Protocols of Parliament, introductions by: Géza Szüllő, Budapest, 1943 (hereafter Szüllő).

11 On the history of stenography in parliament see: László Siklóssy, *Az országgyűlési beszéd útja* [How A Speech Was Written in Parliament], Budapest, 1939. See also Dezső Zelovich, *Adatok a parlamenti napló, általában a parlamenti nyilvánosság történetéhez* [Materials for Study of the History of the Protocols of Parliament and Parliamentary Representation], Karczag, 1928; and *Az Országgyűlési Napló története* [History of the Protocols of Parliament], Budapest, 1936.

12 Albert Apponyi, *Parlamenti működésem emlékei* [Memories Of My Years In Parliament], Budapest, 1912.

13 Albert Apponyi, *Emlékirataim* [Memoirs], Vol. 1, Budapest, 1922, pp. 68–9.

14 Albert Apponyi, *Emlékirataim. Ötven év* [Memoirs. Fifty Years], Budapest, 1926, pp. 116–17

15 *Magyarország története 1848–1890* [The History of Hungary 1848–1890], Budapest, 1979, pp. 216–17. The relevant chapter is the work of Zoltán László.

16 Mikszáth, *The Honourable House*, p. 120.

17 Szüllő, p. 106.

18 Gyula Verhovay, *Az álarcz korszaka* [The Period of The Mask], Budapest, 1889, p. 128.

19 Geiza Farkas, *Az úri rend* [The Gentlemen's Regime], Budapest, no date, p. 18–22. On the history of duelling see: Géza Kacziány, *Híres magyar párbajok* [Famous Hungarian Duels], Budapest, 1889. In parliament, the leading expert on duels was Lajos Hentaller, who acted as second in 96 duels.

20 Szatmári, p. 44.

21 Szatmári, p. 70. This incident is described on pp. 69–78. The balanced coexistence of personalism and the tendency to try to eliminate one's rivals is shown by the following anecdote relating to the session of parliament that passed the Defence Act on 20 January 1889. The opposition made every effort to prevent

the draft law from being adopted, including a sleaze campaign directed against Kálmán Tisza and the mobilization of university students. After the session, in question a group of opposition demonstrators awaited Prime Minister Tisza in front of the parliament building. Some of the governing party MPs directly responsible for inciting the demonstration offered to walk between the Prime Minister and the mob, but Tisza refused.

22 Szatmári, p. 212; Herczeg, p. 130. Two weeks after Bánffy's resignation a fight took place involving Gábor Ugron in the army barracks in Üllői út. Antal Balla (ed.), *A magyar országgyűlés története 1867–1927* [The History of the Hungarian Parliament 1867–1927], Budapest, 1927, p. 220.

23 Rudnayné, p. 191. Considerations of personal honour were not a hindering factor. István Tisza fought a duel with Mihály Károlyi in 1912, while Speaker of the House. (Mihály Károlyi, *Hit illúziók nélkül* [Faith Without Illusions], Budapest, 1977, pp. 52–3).

24 Miklós Bánffy, *Megszámláltattál . . .* [Having Been Measured and Found Too Light], Budapest, 1934, pp. 212–13.

25 Vilmos Vázsonyi, *Beszédei és írásai* [Speeches and Writings], Budapest, 1927, Vol. 1, pp. 67–70.

26 Endre Ady, *Publicisztikai írásai* [Publicistic Writings], Budapest, 1977, Vol. 1, pp. 211–12.

27 Szatmári, pp. 218–19. It is indicative that the number of writings addressing the phenomenon of obstruction in parliament increased at the beginning of the century, including: Viktor Jászi, *Clotüre és obstrukció* [Cloture And Obstruction], Budapest, 1903; Imre Hodossy, *Az obstrukció* [Obstruction], Budapest, 1903; Gyula Fayer, *Parlamenti dolgok* [Parliamentary Affairs], Vols. 1–3, Budapest, 1908. The obstructionist viewpoint is elaborated in: Ferenc Sima, *Az obstrukció, mint parlamentáris fegyver* [Obstruction as a Parliamentary Weapon], Szentes, 1897.

28 Herczeg, p. 105

29 *Magyarország története 1849–1918* [The History of Hungary 1849–1918], Budapest, 1972, p. 397.

30 Herczeg, pp. 321–3.

9 Liberalism, Conservatism and Political Legitimacy under the Dual Monarchy

The motivations of liberalism

The political regime that emerged in 1867 considered itself a liberal one. The governing party, associated with the name of Deák, and the coalition which ruled from 1875 to 1905 both claimed liberalism as their political credo. The governing party formed in 1875 under the leadership of Kálmán Tisza, indeed, called itself the Liberal Party.[1]

The choice of liberalism was an obvious one, prepared as it had been by the whole course of recent Hungarian history. The political elite – faithful to the spirit of the Reform Era and the 1848 Revolution – pursued their careers with all the political and ideological baggage of the Hungarian bourgeois-transformation process. As has been emphasized so often in this work, the need to overcome feudalism and to forge a modern national identity were closely related. The Habsburg court was the principal stronghold of the feudal order and so stood in the way of Hungarian national sovereignty and self-determination. The events of 1848 were a balanced amalgamation of liberal values and the craving for national autonomy.[2] The ideology and politics of neo-absolutism that followed the suppression of the Revolution in 1849 left this balance essentially unchallenged, although troubling signs were already apparent. Neo-absolutism claimed that certain liberal values – such as the equitable distribution of public burdens, compulsory manumission, equality before the law and proprietary rights – could stand alone, rendering unnecessary such things as responsible government and the freedoms of speech, association and the press. The advent of neo-absolutism in Hungary in the form of foreign political domination, in broad terms, did not challenge the marriage of liberalism and national feeling.[3] In 1867, when Hungary's sovereignty crystallized in the Compromise Settlement, a more liberal political orientation seemed inevitable. All the more so, because the loosening of the grip of neo-absolutism was possible only through fundamental reform.

The choice of liberalism was also motivated by the experience of partially accomplished bourgeois transformation. The transformation process began with the April Laws of 1848 and its progress was not halted during the period of neo-absolutism. Post-1849 developments showed that the emergence of bourgeois private property was a historical inevitability: while its progress could be slowed down, its ultimate victory was assured (the strongest possible evidence for which is provided by the Imperial Patent which sought to reregulate the institution of manumission). It also turned out that political oppression was self-defeating. During the period of absolutism, economic development began to advance (for example, the railway network increased from 178 km in 1848 to 2,160 km in 1866), but on the whole, enterprise was curtailed and economic potential left unutilized. This was an inevitable result of the absolutist state's positive discouragement of any initiative undertaken by private citizens.

The maintenance of repressive institutions of power and the extensive bureaucracy needed to control society was very costly. (In the golden days of absolutism military expenditure devoured 31.5% of the state budget, while per-capita expenditure on the police exceeded similar costs in Great Britain by 300%. By contrast, agricultural development and culture accounted for no more than 4.5% and 0.65% of the state budget, respectively.) The state could finance its overspending only by drastic tax increases and extensive borrowing. In 1850, taxes collected in Hungary amounted to 23 million forints, but by 1864 this had rocketed to 75 million. The national debt increased by more than two and one half times as compared to the pre-1848 period.[4] Such a negative experience coupled with a number of other lessons learned from Hungarian history further strengthened the move towards liberalism.

The foundations of conservatism

Alongside the ideological advance of liberal ideas there were, however, practical constraints which worked to curb liberalism and to promote more conservative outcomes. Hungarian conservatives, though, played little part in this process: some discredited themselves with their reactionary views, calling into question even the necessity of manumission, while others were too eager to cooperate with anti-Hungarian absolutism. The main cause of anti-liberalism was, instead, the obvious connection between the existing political regime and the prevailing social crisis.

The conservative position was strengthened above all by the sovereign's absolute powers. His scope of authority included not only unrestricted control over the army but also the right of arbitration in the joint affairs of Hungary and Austria under the Monarchy, provided that no agreement could be reached between delegations from the Austrian and Hungarian parliaments. Besides, the Austro-Hungarian Emperor and Hungarian King could not constitutionally be made to abdicate. His role as ultimate arbiter, free of constitutional constraints, demanded obedience to the sovereign's will – and ascertaining the sovereign's will required little ingenuity. The cabinet meeting of 17 March 1867 invested the sovereign with the right of 'presanctification': a government bill could be debated in parliament only on the condition that it had previously been authorized by the sovereign.

Another conservative constraint on liberalism was the continuing lack of regulation of the conditions governing the Compromise Settlement. To be more precise, it was agreed that – as with the economic compromise – the political compromise should be renegotiated every ten years. But unlike the economic compromise, which had given rise to passionate debates as the two sides jockeyed for position, there was no legitimate way in which the political compromise could be terminated or amended. This brought about a situation in which any attempt to introduce liberal reforms into the political structure of the Compromise was inevitably illegal.[5] This situation, in turn, dictated the subordination of liberal principles to preservation of the status quo, a subordination manifest in everyday politics as well as in legislation.

As we have seen, until the turn of the century the majority of Hungarian citizens were from national minorities – even after the turn of the century, native Hungarians were only marginally preponderant. This was another factor which significantly reduced the prospects of liberalism in Hungarian politics: the radical extension of political freedoms in combination with majority-led politics could, it was feared, undermine or bring to its knees the governing regime.

With the suppression of the Revolution of 1848–9, the process by which feudal conditions were slowly being eliminated had suffered a major setback. From 1867 onwards, however, political freedoms were slowly rediscovered which had already been introduced as a result of the events of 1848. (Continuity was a major concern of those who concluded the Compromise on the Hungarian side: they insisted on the enforcement of the April Laws of 1848 as a precondition of the settlement.) As a result of the suppression of the 1848–9 Revolution, Hungarian politics had been thrown back eighteen years. Absolutism offered no more than token resistance to feudal tendencies, concentrating on the conservation of a large number of feudal elements deemed useful for restraining liberalism.

Legitimacy

For liberalism the main source of legitimacy is the will of the people. For feudal conservatism, on the other hand, the source of legitimacy is the grace of God. The conflict of these two principles has on more than one occasion demanded the heads of both rebels and kings. The conflict can be resolved in two ways. Either the conservative principle overrides the liberal principle of legitimacy (this is the approach adopted by absolutism) or liberal legitimacy overrides its feudal counterpart (at the very least reducing it to a mere formality). In the spring of 1848, liberalism prevailed in Hungary: feudal legitimacy was reduced to a shadow of its former self. Under a constitutional monarchy the sovereign has only formal power, while effective political rule is the task of a government founded upon a parliamentary majority. In Hungary, however, the sovereign was dethroned in 1849 and stripped of all political authority. 1867 signified a compromise, the partial restoration of the sovereign's powers. But the feudal principle on the basis of which the hereditary sovereign derived these far from merely formal powers, was restored in its entirety. Once this had been reestablished, liberalism could either accept its subordination or struggle along in permanent and legally irresolvable conflict.

A liberal regime is founded upon universal suffrage, elections, parliament and a government responsible to parliament. At the local level, it must be supported by municipalities whose actions do not violate the laws passed by the majority of the nation's representatives, and the structure and operations of which are fully integrated into the country's political and legislative framework.

One of the essential tenets of nineteenth-century liberalism was that politics could no longer remain the privilege of a feudal elite. One of the first laws passed after the 1848 Revolution (Act V) increased the scope of suffrage from 2.5% to 7–8% of the population.[6] Suffrage – in accordance with the liberal views of the time – was based upon property qualification, the so-called 'census'. The census was meant to ensure that only a homogenous group of mature men with appropriate financial means could influence the running of the country. (Under the new policy those who had enjoyed hereditary suffrage rights under the old regime were declared a dying class and their offspring could vote only if they could satisfy the property qualification.) In 1848, Hungary was in the European vanguard as far as suffrage was concerned.

Electoral rights were amended by Act XXXIII of 1874, in accordance with which all elections under the Dual Monarchy were henceforth conducted. Under the law, the number of those entitled to vote actually fell. By the turn of the century, the fall in the number of voters was so great that a regulation deleting those with tax arrears from the electoral register had to be abolished. With the introduction of Act XV of 1899 – which abolished the above restriction – the number of voters suddenly increased by 118,000. The percentage of the popluation entitled to vote in the 1870s was just over 14%, but by the turn of the century this figure had fallen to 5–6%.

According to the relevant data, the census of 1874 – based largely on taxation figures – could barely find enough eligible males to make up for the reduction in the number of 'old' voters (who could no longer meet the property requirements).[7] In 1905, 6.2% of the Hungarian population were entitled to vote, while in Austria the figure was 27%, in France 28%, in Germany 22%, in Great Britain 16%, and even in Italy, where the toughest census in Europe was in operation, the figure was 8%. Other statistical data illustrate even more strikingly the unworkability of the Hungarian electoral system. Under Hungarian law only 2 million of Great Britain's 40 million people would have been entitled to vote, while under British law the figure was 7 million; only 2.7 million of Germany's 11 million voters would have enjoyed the same right under the Hungarian system.[8]

The other major component of the electoral system – proportional representation based on electoral districts – was also totally inadequate. New regulations governing electoral districts were laid down in Act X of 1877. This law – with minor amendments – remained in effect until the end of political dualism (the fall of the Austro-Hungarian Monarchy).

The number of representatives was not proportionate to the number of voters in the electoral district which elected them. In 1896, the smallest electoral district in Hungary was Abrudbánya, with 181 voters, and the largest was Homonna (in Zemplén County), with 6,210. In 1905, Felvidék and Transylvania with a combined population of 6.2 million elected 182 representatives, while the 8.3 million people living in Transdanubia and the region between the Danube and the Tisza elected only 136.[9] The ruling political elite stubbornly clung on to an electoral system widely condemned as unfair and unworkable, a fact which even they had to acknowledge.

Act XIV of 1913 was introduced to regulate elections, but was not legally implemented until after the First World War; Act XVII of 1918 was introduced to regulate elections, but was never implemented. The 1913 Act – after many years' delay – finally increased the electorate by 28%, raising the number of those eligible to vote from 1,272,755 to 1,627,136. Suffrage was now the privilege of 8.7% of the Hungarian population.

The 1913 law ordered that secret elections should be held in municipal towns accounting for 66 of the 435 electoral districts. Open voting continued in the remaining electoral districts. Vilmos Vázsonyi's bill – which would become Act XVII– was presented to the House in 1917 and proposed that the number of those entitled to vote be increased temporarily to 3.8 million and ordinarily to 3.4 million, but retained the reformed census with its less demanding property qualifications and the combination of open and secret voting. The final version of this bill reduced the proposed number of voters by 437,000.[10] The law was approved on 11 September 1918. Less than six weeks later the Monarchy, and with it Hungary under the old regime – the so-called 'historical' Hungary – was dissolved.

In light of the inflexibility and disproportionate nature of suffrage – the foundation of liberal political legitimacy – electoral and parliamentary structures were required that would leave unchallenged the legitimacy of the half-liberal and half-conservative political regime and avoid a crisis in this political formation aiming to uphold the Compromise.

The rules governing electoral practice and the extent of suffrage were one way of halting the advance of political forces whose programmes were built around national grievances related to the conditions of the Compromise and the question of independence. The most powerful opposition groups at this period were the various independent party formations, the number and names of which were subject to constant change.

The electoral laws restricting – for the foreseeable future – the number of those entitled to vote had a particularly bad effect on majority-Hungarian areas. In these areas, the minimum payable land tax for eligibility to vote was set higher than elsewhere. This measure affected 60–70% of those entitled to vote (apart from which, the structure of electoral districts could not have been more disadvantageous for the Hungarian population). At the 17 June 1896 session of parliament, Prime Minister Dezső Bánffy, in connection with the land census, said: 'The census is highest of all – I must emphasize this – in majority-Hungarian areas, particularly the Alföld. In counties populated by Slovaks, Russians and especially Transylvanian Romanians the census is significantly lower.'[11]

According to 1906 data, the ethnic composition of the Hungarian electorate was as follows (the figure in brackets gives each group's percentage of the population according to the census of 1910): Hungarian 56.2% (54.5%), German 12.7% (10.4%), Slovakian 11.4% (10.7%), Romanian 11.2% (16.1%), Subcarpathian-Ukrainian (Ruthenian) 2.9% (2.5%), Croatian 1.2% (1.1%), Serbian 2.8% (3.0%), and other 1.6% (1.7%).[12]

It may easily be seen that Germans were heavily overrepresented, while Romanians were even more heavily underrepresented; other nationalities were marginally overrepresented. To obtain a more balanced view, however, the considerable differences that existed between the levels of social development of the various ethnic groups must also be taken into account. The most highly developed were the Germans, followed by the Hungarians. Furthermore, 30–40% of voters obtained suffrage on the basis of an entitlement other than landed property, including members of the intelligentsia, a group containing persons proclaiming themselves Hungarian in very high numbers. Hungarians were represented in this electoral system only in accordance with their numbers – their level of bourgeois development was not taken into account at all. The contrast with which we are concerned was greatest between Hungarians and Subcarpathian-Ukrainians. Although the latter were commonly recognized as the least advanced ethnic group, their electoral representation was the same per capita as Hungarians. Paradoxically, the fact that a higher property qualification was established for majority-Hungarian areas than for other areas is in itself an indication of their higher level of bourgeois development. These facts reveal the government's true aim, hidden behind the facade of a hypocritical national ideology: the preservation of its own power and authority. Hence its interest in minimizing the number of Hungarian voters, traditionally sympathetic to the opposition.

Control over suffrage was of course not the only way in which liberal legitimacy could be adjusted to the requirements of feudal conservatism and the consolidation of its powers. Actual elections and events in parliament also provided many opportunities.

Until 1887, the elections which followed one another in cycles of first three, then five, years were open: there were no secret ballots. Various mechanisms rapidly evolved in these circumstances with the purpose of manipulating the outcome of elections. The spread of corruption was made even easier by the fact that the turnout at elections was generally not higher than two-thirds of the electorate. The Hungarian electoral system was based on the 'first-past-the-post' principle. This meant that even a handful of votes obtained through corruption could make all the difference. One should not, however, overestimate the role of corruption. Electoral districts seldom changed their political orientation: majority-Hungarian areas voted with the opposition; districts with a majority of national minorities (though many Hungarians also lived there) as a rule voted for governing-party candidates. There were, however, certain electoral districts – characteristically in locations sandwiched between solidly opposition and solidly governing party areas – where corruption did, indeed, often decide on which side ambivalent electoral sympathies would come down.[13]

Parliament also exhibited the same mixture of liberalism and conservatism, and this had a profound effect on its operation. Legislative work was conducted in the two Houses of parliament. The feudal Lower Chamber came to be replaced by the Lower House (of parliament) with 413 members (plus 40 Croatian representatives under the Hungarian-Croatian Compromise) within the framework of political representation based on census suffrage. From 1848 the feudal Upper Chamber was known as the Upper House, although its fundamental reform, or even its elimination, was already being considered. The Upper and the Lower Houses were formally on an equal footing, but in reality the latter was clearly dominant.

The Upper House was the last important institution of feudal conservatism. Membership was, of course, hereditary. The reform of the Upper House constantly urged by Deák did not take place until 1885 (Act VII), 12 years after he had first demanded it and 9 years after his death. But reform was not only significantly delayed, its eventual scope was so narrow that it failed to have any impact on the essentially feudal structure of the Upper House. The core of the reform measure was to restrict membership to male aristocrats paying a minimum 3,000 forints annually in direct state taxes. Although Deák insisted on the liberal principle of separating church and state, so excluding religious representation from the structure of the Upper House, his demands were not met. On the contrary, religious representation was extended to encompass all religious denominations. Reduced representation for the Catholic and Greek Orthodox Churches went hand in hand with the extension of representation to the bishops of the Protestant Church (and later to Judaism). Lord Lieutenants were excluded from the Upper House only to be replaced by high ranking officials. The sovereign was invested with the right to appoint 50 members of the Upper House himself, based on the recommendations of the Cabinet of Ministers. This measure opened the way, at least to a limited extent, for those who had managed to distinguish themselves in public affairs to obtain membership of the Upper House. The Upper House remained an essentially feudal institution of Hungarian legislation, which – although its powers were lesser than those of its counterpart – was still strong enough to curb the prospects of liberal transformation.

The half-liberal, half-feudal conservative basis of political legitimacy also determined the political role of members of the Lower House.

The essence of the so-called House rules was freedom of speech for members of parliament with only minor restrictions.[14] Parliamentary representation rested on the liberal principle that members of parliament were representatives primarily of the nation rather than of political parties. (This democratic principle also contrasted with the feudal principle of representation by delegates who were merely entrusted with carrying out the orders of their county assembly.) The freedom of speech enjoyed by members of parliament might seem an entirely liberal principle, but given the peculiarities of political legitimacy in Hungary, this freedom was not untainted.

A dual process was taking place. The principle of feudal conservatism demanded that the government ensure political continuity in elections, electoral law and parliamentary power. To this end MPs had to be strictly controlled in order to prevent the emergence of extremist tendencies and to ensure their submission to the will of the parliamentary majority. Prime Minister Kálmán Tisza employed a skilful combination of threats and favours for this purpose, a policy which gave rise to the political phenomenon known as 'Mamelukeism' (described at greater length in Chapter 7) based on the principle of 'Don't think, just vote'. Members of the governing party slavishly executed the Prime Minister's instructions and gave up any claim to a direct influence over government affairs. Tisza was, of course, known by the members of his own party as the 'General', a paramilitary rather than a liberal-constitutional title.

As described in Chapter 8, the opposition sought to compensate for the submissive Mamelukeism permeating all aspects of parliamentary work by making full use of their rights under the House rules to obstruct the governing party. The more persistent this policy of obstruction became, the tougher the defence mechanisms adopted by the governing party, culminating in an attempt to break the opposition's resistance and even to exclude liberal principles from politics altogether.

This task fell to István Tisza, who as Prime Minister was more of a 'general' than his father had ever been. First in 1904, and later in 1912, regulations were introduced which severely restricted the scope of parliamentary debate. Protesting members of parliament were suspended from the House even if police had to be brought in to remove them.[15] These measures marked a challenge even to the pretence of liberal legitimation within parliament itself.

Conflicting principles of legitimacy

The coexistence of feudal conservatism and liberalism within the political system inevitably led to conflicts, with now one side and now the other prevailing.

Liberalism is committed to the separation of church and state. This separation can take a number of different forms, but the underlying principle is the same: religious beliefs are a private affair and, as such, must not be criteria for discrimination; a concomitant of this is that no church should seek to interfere in politics. Although the political representation of various religious denominations survived in the Upper House, bourgeois development brought with it an acute need for reform in areas which were formerly the exclusive domain of the church, such as marriage and the registration of births, to bring them within the competence of the state. With the growth of individualism, marriage for life was an ideal increasingly difficult to uphold, while the fact that different churches were subject to different marriage laws made questions of property and inheritance overcomplicated and sometimes chaotic. In Hungary, as many as nine different matrimonial codes were in operation at the same time.[16]

This is ample evidence that urgent reform of matrimonial law was demanded by pragmatic considerations at least as much as by liberal notions. Liberals such as Deák[17] and the opposition MP Dániel Irányi urged the introduction of civil marriages which had been legal in France since 1791. Although the proposed law, while liberal in orientation, did not directly challenge the authority of the regime, the feudal-conservative foundations of the latter tended to hinder liberal reform of religious matters. The sovereign, a devout Catholic, succeeded for a number of years in preventing the presentation of bills of this kind to parliament, using the previously described right of presanctification. The Upper House was also opposed to such reforms. As a result religious reform – including marriage legislation – was delayed for years, despite the fact that it had supporters in the governing party as well as in the opposition camp. The political trump card, however, was in the hands of the Prime Minister, Sándor Wekerle, who told the sovereign that any further delay would endanger the Hungarian government's position, and with it the stability of the Austro-Hungarian Monarchy. This was too great a risk to take – he argued – for something that would not represent a direct challenge to the status quo. The sovereign finally consented and in 1894 newly appointed members of the Upper House, on a free vote, passed legislation governing mandatory civil marriages, state registration of births and reciprocal acceptance of mixed marriages. In 1895, Judaism became an established religion. The same law outlawed political discrimination on the basis of religious beliefs, declaring that political rights must not be dependant upon religious affiliation; it also contained a provision on freedom of religion.

Another conflict highlighting the limitations of liberal legitimacy occurred in early 1905, when for the first time in the history of the Dual Monarchy the opposition were elected with a majority – though they owed their ascension largely to the governing party's inept tactics – on a platform challenging the very foundations of the Dual Monarchy. But the victors were prevented from forming a government. The sovereign – the supreme representative of feudal legitimacy – simply disregarded the outcome of the elections, appointed one of his former Guard commanders as Hungary's Prime Minister and at a five minute audience tersely informed the representatives of the winning parties that he had rejected their programme.

If the sovereign were to allow the defeated party to form a new government, such blatant disregard for the public will might incur civil unrest. In view of this, a plan was drawn up for the military occupation of Hungary, entitled *Kriegsfall U*.[18] Invasion would have been perfectly legal given that the Austrian Emperor was the head of the joint army, one of the most important elements of feudal conservatism.

Submitting to the public will which had manifested its liberal sympathies in the elections would have opened the door to the transformation of the political structure of the Monarchy – including the restriction of the sovereign's powers – and this possibility was dismissed out of hand. In 1906, the sovereign ordered a royal military commissioner to dissolve the Hungarian parliament, the building was occupied by the army and MPs were refused entry.

The winners of the election could do nothing other than submit to feudal authority and relinquish all claims that could be regarded as a threat to the regime. The outcome of the 1905 election made it clear that, regardless of the ideology espoused by individual parties, conservatism was, and would remain, part of the political substance of Hungary.

Political parties in the grip of a political structure

In the period after 1867, political parties tended to define themselves as either for or against the Compromise (and its consequences).[19] Their detailed programmes did not, however, represent genuine alternatives. The opposition was unable to implement its policies, which it had to surrender in order to be allowed any role at all in government, though it would not be induced to submit at the point of a gun until 1905. (Kálmán Tisza, one of the first representatives of an opposition founded on public-law issues, was also among the first to bow to the inevitable and to put aside his political programme – the so-called 'Bihar Points' – in order to become Prime Minister.)

The governing party was equally constrained. A number of national grievances – an independent bank of issue, the army – enjoyed widespread popular support, but since the governing party was unable to pursue even these reforms, it became immensely unpopular with the Hungarian people. The more unpopular the government's policies became, the more the government was compelled to keep suffrage to a minimum in order to avoid defeat, resorting to electoral manipulation and corruption. In this way they fatally undermined their own liberal foundations, the only guarantee against the excesses of feudal-conservative rule.

The widening gulf between liberalism and conservatism became unbridgeable, and the political spectrum heavily fragmented. Liberal and conservative values were not the exclusive property of the parties which nominally espoused them. As a result of the situation which had emerged from the coexistence of two contrary sets of values within the same – fragmented – structure of political legitimacy, various political formations associated themselves with liberal or conservative values purely from strategic considerations. Regardless of what ideology they professed, all political parties had to operate in the same undemocratic environment, their survival depending upon their ability to accommodate themselves to it. As a result, liberal progress within the existing political structure was permanently blocked. Having come to accept a feudal-conservative role, Hungarian liberalism became blind to new political challenges.

Both the opposition and the governing party were prisoners of the same situation: a liberalism that was forced to take on the role of feudal-conservatism and that regulated the political roles and activities of both parties, in and out of parliament. A Catholic People's Party established in 1895 and distinguished by a militant conservatism, both old and new, and an anti-liberalism foreshadowing the Horthy era, made its appearance in parliament. The largest extra-parliamentary opposition group, the Hungarian Social Democratic Party (founded in 1890) which evolved from the General Workers Union (1868), almost emerged as an ally of feudal legitimacy during the 1905–6 crisis when it was fighting for the introduction of universal suffrage. The Democratic Party (1906), a bourgeois party aiming at the transformation of liberalism into democracy, remained marginal and never became an important factor in parliamentary politics.

All political parties were effectively prevented from representing national interests – neither agrarian nor the working-class questions were debated on their merits. By contrast, debates could last for several days on such trivial issues as the use of particular flags, and scandals related to the laying of wreaths at memorials.

It was, once again, liberalism that suffered most from the general discredit into which parliament and the very institution of parliamentary democracy were brought. At the same time, because of its extreme inflexibility and inability to correct itself, the existing regime was becoming increasingly anachronistic.

The Compromise – which had been intended to settle the differences bisecting an empire – in the end turned out to be a compromise between two opposing principles of legitimacy. The coexistence of such irreconcilable principles resulted in a situation in which liberalism was tolerated only up to the point at which it posed a challenge to conservative legitimacy. Whenever such a threat emerged, liberalism was immediately suppressed or press-ganged into upholding the very feudal-conservative policies to which it was nominally so adamantly opposed.

(1992)

Notes

1 See Pál Móricz, *A magyar országgyűlési pártok küzdelmei a koronázástól a Deák és a balközép pártok egybeolvadásáig (1867–1872)* [The Struggle between the Political Parties in the Hungarian Parliament from the Coronation to the Merger of the Deák Party with Moderate Left-Wing Parties (1867–72)], Budapest, 1892; István Toldy, *Öt év története 1867–1872* [The History of Five Years: 1867–72], Pest, 1872; Miklós Rózsa (ed.), *Kecskeméthy Aurél naplója 1831–1879* [The Diary of Aurél Kecskeméthy 1831–79], Budapest, 1909.

2 András Gergely, *Egy nemzetet az emberiségnek. Tanulmányok a magyar reformkorról és 1848-ról* [A Nation For Humankind: Studies on the Reform Age and 1848 in Hungary], Budapest, 1987.

3 Béla G. Németh, *Létharc és nemzetiség* [Struggle For Existence and Nationhood], Budapest, 1976, and by the same author, *Türelmetlen és késlekedő félszázad* [An Impatient and Dilatory Half-Century], Budapest, 1971.

4 György Szabad, '*Az önkényuralom kora'* ['The Age Of Absolutism'] in *Magyarország története 1848–1890* [The History of Hungary, 1848–90], Vol. 1, pp. 525–71, Budapest, 1979.

5 *Magyar Törvénytár* [Corpus Juris Hungaricus], 12 of 1867 and 14–16 of 1867.

6 Andor Csizmadia, *A magyar választási rendszer 1848–1949-ben* [The Hungarian Electoral System, 1848–9], Budapest, 1963.

7 For statistical data see: Róbert Horváth, *A magyar választások a statisztika tükrében* [Hungarian Elections in the Mirror of Statistical Data] in *Állam és igazgatás* [State and Administration], 1953, Nos. 7–8; Alajos Kovács, *A magyar választójogi reformok számszerű hatása* [The Statistical Effects of the Electoral Reforms], Budapest, 1925; Miklós Ruszkai, *Az 1945 előtti magyar választások statisztikája* [Hungarian Election Statistics before 1945], in *Történeti-Statisztikai Közlemények* [Historical and Statistical Reports], 1959, Nos. 1–2.

8 Dr Ferenc Harrer, *A parlamenti választói jog terjedelme a nagyobb európai államokban* [The Scope of the Parliamentary Franchise In Major European Countries], Budapest, no date and 1896–1910; *Képviselőházi Napló* [Protocols of the Lower House of Parliament], Vol. 32, session of 16 January 1901, speech by Lajos Holló.

9 Imre Szivák, *Országgyűlési képviselőválasztások és curiai bíráskodás codexe* [Parliamentary Elections and the Code of Court Legal Proceedings], Budapest, 1901.

10 *Vázsonyi Vilmos beszédei és írásai* [Collected Speeches and Writings of Vilmos Vázsonyi.], Vol. 2, pp. 111, 155, 160 and 236, Budapest, 1927; and Dr Dezső Rakonitz and Pál Szende, Junior, *Az új választójogi törvény (1918:XVII.tc.)* [The New Election Law (17 of 1918)] and commentary, Budapest, 1918.

11 *1892–1896 Képviselőházi Napló* [1892–1896 Protocol of the Lower House of Parliament], Vol. 33, pp. 350–2.

12 József Kristóffy, *Magyarország kálváriája* [The Calvary of Hungary], Budapest, 1910, p. 229; and *Magyarország története 1890–1918* [The History of Hungary 1890–1918], editor-in-chief: Péter Hanák, Budapest, 1978, Vol. 1, p. 414.

13 András Gerő, *Az elsöprő kisebbség. Népképviselet a Monarchia Magyarországán* [The Decisive Minority: Political Representation In Hungary Under the Dual Monarchy], Budapest, 1988.

14 József Kun, *A parlamenti házszabályok* [House Rules], Budapest, 1902; Rezső Mantuano, *A magyar törvényhozás* [Legislation in Hungary], Budapest, 1900.

15 Ferenc Pölöskei, *Tisza István*, Budapest, 1990; Gábor Vermes, *Tisza István*, Budapest, 1994.

16 Csizmadia-Kovács-Asztalos, *Magyar állam– és jogtörténet* [The History Of The Hungarian State and Law], Budapest, 1976, pp. 489–96.

17 *Deák Ferenc beszédei* [The Speeches of Ferenc Deák], compiled by Manó Kónyi, Budapest, 1902, Vol. 6, pp. 383–416.

18 György Gábor Józsa, *Ferenc József zászlói alatt (1848–1914)* [Under The Flag of Franz Josef (1848–1914)], Budapest, 1990, pp. 128–31.

19 *A magyar polgári pártok programjai (1867–1918)* [The Programmes of Hungary's Bourgeois Parties (1867–1918)], collected and edited by: Gyula Mérei, Budapest, 1971; and Péter Hanák, *Magyarország a Monarchiában. Tanulmányok* [Hungary Under the Monarchy: Studies], Budapest, 1975.

10 Liberals, Anti-Semites and Jews at the Birth of Modern Hungary

The spring of 1848 promised the advent in Hungary of 'liberty, equality, and fraternity'. The gradual construction characteristic of the two decades of the Reform Period and the relentless struggle for the country's bourgeois transformation – parallel with changes elsewhere in Europe – brought their own results. The revolt of 15 March and the will of the parliamentary assembly in Pozsony (Bratislava) gave the impression that nothing could stand in the way of the notion of equality before the law.

The lineaments of freedom, however, began to show cracks from the outset. On 19 and 20 March, anti-Semitic rioting broke out in Pozsony, sparked by the granting of full civil rights to Jews in the town. Anti-Semitic demonstrations were not restricted to Pozsony, however. In Szombathely on 4 April, in Székesfehérvár and Pécs on 5 April and in Budapest on 19 April, Jewish communities were faced with the spectre of the pogrom. In this disturbing atmosphere the Budapest People's Assembly adopted the following resolutions: (1) payment of rents should be waived for a quarter, since there had been little opportunity for many to earn a living during the month of the uprising; (2) the situation of the workers should be improved; (3) Jews should be driven out of the country; and (4) Jews should not be allowed to become members of the national guard. The homogeneity and extent of these demands hardly justify great confidence in the popularity at the time of the notions of 'liberty, equality, and fraternity'.

Not without reason did Petőfi write, in the wake of the disturbances which followed the events of 15 March:

The harmony which has so far prevailed without exception in the capital is beginning to fall apart. German burghers, I denounce you before the nation and future generations for being the cause of its disintegration! May both pass judgement upon you. It was they who first declared that they would not take Jews into the ranks of the national guard, and so it

was they who first flung mud onto the virgin pure flag of 15 March! . . .
Or do not the words still hold true, did you not cry out with us: liberty,
equality, fraternity?[1]

The anti-Semitism which by Easter Monday (23 April) had degenerated into
a pogrom in Pozsony stimulated the most prominent liberals to take open
action. Not only Mór Jókai, Antal Csengery, József Bajza and Zsigmond
Kemény, but also Mihály Vörösmarty, who was considered the nation's poet
laureate, took a stand against the anti-Jewish provocations. In an article
published in May under the title 'The Jewish Question' Vörösmarty wrote:

> There can be no more bitter mockery of the proclaimed equality and
> fraternity than the hatred and rage which have raised their fists against the
> Jewish people throughout the world, though perhaps most savagely in our
> country. After the first few heady days of freedom, in which the noblest
> pearls of human emotion bubbled to the surface, the dregs have been
> stirred, by whose counterfeit claims the shining ideal of a civil society
> could so easily be plunged into darkness. After freedom had bravely stood
> up for its inalienable rights, lawlessness could not remain silent, wildly
> demanding the waiving of rents and the division of land, and many
> violated the peaceful process of petitioning by setting out, in the name of
> equality, to batter and plunder, above all others the Jews.[2]

The liberal intelligentsia responded to this anti-Semitism with unanimous
and unqualified rejection. On the other hand, liberal politicians and the
liberal parliament – to quote Vörösmarty – took action with an 'irresolute
hand'.

Kossuth himself called for the postponement of equality before the law
for Jews, saying 'let them be patient a little longer in the interests of the
homeland and the freedom of the people'.[3] He justified his standpoint by
saying that, although what had occurred was distressing, the manifest prejudice was a reality against which 'even the gods struggle in vain'. Behind
this position probably lay the conviction that for the sake of the current
interest reconciliation between the various social groups, a sacrifice should
be made – even if a question mark should thereby be put against the whole
process.

Naturally, not everyone shared Kossuth's views on the need for an important sacrifice of principle in the interests of real political advance. Samu
Bónis – reacting to his words – said in parliament that 'it is impossible to
take the same view as those who have regard for such violence; legislation
may not be dictated by sordid street demonstrations, but by justice and
principle alone. The heroes of disruption must be punished: they must not be
honoured to the extent that for their sake the notion of justice is neglected'.[4]

The voice of the liberal and democratic intelligentsia was raised to no avail, even in political circles, and the advocates of postponement prevailed. Only on 28 July 1849 did the parliament adopt the law governing the emancipation of the Jews, along with the law on nationality – scarcely two weeks before its already inevitable defeat.

Their aim of emancipation emboldened both by the outbursts of anti-Semitism and by the unprincipled policy of delay, Hungarian Jews reacted to the twofold challenge of 1848 in a twofold manner. The anti-Semitic atmosphere of the spring gave rise to bitterness and disillusion. Under the direction of Ede Horn, Adolf Dux and others, an office was established which set out to encourage Jewish emigration to the free, equality-embracing United States. This reaction soon faded, however, and with a significant number of Jews who had been pushed out of the national guard enrolled in the Hungarian army, the emigration office was transformed into a recruiting office.

The liberal objective of equality before the law and its anti-Semitic denial, impulses towards both assimilation and dissimilation: this was the dilemma at the birth of modern Hungary.

The liberal proposal: assimilation

For Hungarian liberals, the question of Jewish emancipation was not a new one: the Lower House had already raised it in the 1839–40 parliament with a view to granting them parity with other social groups outside the nobility. The bill failed in the face of resistance from the Upper House, but not without some gains being made. Law XXIX of 1840 – On Jews – allowed Jews to settle freely, except in mining towns, and Ferdinand V's decree of 27 July 1846 abolished the special tax levied on Jews, jocularly known as the 'tolerance tax'.

What principles guided the liberals, determining the proposed elements of assimilation? Valuable evidence is provided by the speech given in the Upper House by Baron József Eötvös in 1840, published later in the form of a treatise.[5] The Baron's reasoning, giving full expression to the Hungarian liberalism of the time, takes as its point of departure the view that:

> The time has come when the legislature should also extend its caring hand to this unfortunate section of the populace – this situation, in which the embourgeoisement of the people is called for, is new testimony to our progress, and shining proof of the process by which our Houses of Parliament are advancing towards freedom. In the firm conviction that a free constitution can only be built on the foundations of equal justice for all sections of the populace and equal respect for the rights of all, and that the future of the Hungarian people depends upon a commitment to justice

on the part of this House, I may perhaps make so bold as to say: the time
has come in which a better future shall announce itself for Hungarian
Jews.

Alongside the values of freedom and equality before the law, a new value
emerged – that of rational self-interest – in combination with which they
were unstoppable. Eötvös believed that the granting of equality before the
law to Hungarian Jews would ultimately strengthen the position of the
Hungarian people, constituting as they did a minority in the country:

> As an objection the argument is advanced that [the Jews] have until now
> shown no inclination towards assimilation, that is to say that in a country
> in which they have always been regarded as aliens they do not consider
> themselves true citizens; that with the nation from which they have
> received only contempt they have not become united; and that they have
> not shown much enthusiasm for the constitution of which they have
> known only the burdens. Reflecting upon this, I do not know whether I
> should admire those who raise these causes for complaint or pity those
> against whom they are brought. For can we be surprised if the
> downtrodden are not patriotic? . . . The German provinces of France,
> which in the course of a century have become French, and Great Britain
> where so many different peoples have come together as a single great
> nation, may be brought forward as evidence here and, all theoretical
> arguments to the contrary, clearly show that the most diverse peoples can
> unite into one great whole whenever and wherever the same rights
> homogenize disparate groups on the basis of similar interests, and that in
> Holland, France, England and the North American confederation, nobody
> accuses the emancipated Jews of a lack of patriotism. No one will be able
> to accuse them of this in our country either, as soon as their emancipation
> renders them full and free members of our nation, granting them the
> homeland without which no patriotism is possible.

But what would be the status of these new members of the nation? To
what extent could they be regarded as Hungarian? Eötvös addressed this
question with a view to the overwhelming emphasis placed by the opponents
of emancipation on the perceived negative characteristics of the Jewish
people, largely related to the commercial activities traditionally feared and
despised in agrarian societies. Eötvös argued – somewhat after Rousseau –
that any offensive behavioural traits exhibited by Jews were linked to their
oppression, and would thus disappear along with it. On the question of
commerce, he declared:

> I dare say that the Jews' orientation towards commerce is rather a conse-
> quence of their persecution. Having been forced to take this direction they
> attained perfection in it. I would venture to assert that after new avenues

have been opened to the Jews through the granting of civil rights this purely commercial inclination will diminish.

The question of what kind of citizen the emancipated Jew should be was not laid to rest, however, and was given ever new dimensions up to promulgation of the Law of 1849.

The demand for Hungarianization was manifest in two areas. Clearly the mass of new immigrants hampered efforts in this direction, since their assimilation could only prolong the process and perhaps even render it impossible, particularly if a great wave of immigration should take place within a short period of time. Thus a demand for a tightening of the law arose. Another demand was made which powerfully expressed the essence of Hungarian liberalism at that time: namely that the Jews, in the interest of their acceptance into Hungarian society, should make changes in their religious practices, the perceived behavioural traits which were associated with them, and in the rules or standards which set Jews apart from the rest of society.

Acceptance of the Jews – tacit or otherwise – was thus linked to certain conditions, which were related, in turn, to the main point of interest in the emancipation of the Jews: the strengthening of the Hungarian nation. To put it another way, the close interweaving of liberal values with perceived national interests resulted in anti-liberal measures, at least in their effects.

This peculiar state of affairs acquired clear expression in the formulation of the symbolically important emancipation law adopted on 28 July 1849. The bill introduced by Bertalan Szemere states:

(1) On the grounds that no distinction shall be made with regard to the rights and obligations binding on citizens of Hungary on the basis of religious differences, insofar as they were born within the borders of the state of Hungary or have legally settled here, those following the Jewish faith shall enjoy all political and civil rights pertaining to the citizens of any other religious faith.

(2) Conditions for legal settlement in Hungary shall be defined by the government, in a temporary decree.

(3) Marriages between followers of the Christian and Jewish faiths, with regard to their civil consequences, shall be declared valid. Such marriages shall be contracted before the civil authorities, and their procedure shall temporarily be determined by a decree.

(4) At the same time the interior minister shall be charged with the following:

   (a) Citizens of the Jewish faith shall call an assembly made up of their clergy and representatives to consider reforms to their ecclesiastical apparatus in concordance with the present age.

(b) The carrying into effect of this law shall include the obligation to implement a directive to guide, by way of suitable regulations, those of the Jewish faith to the practice of manual skills and agriculture.[6]

Careful examination of the text of this law leads to a twofold conclusion. The granting of civil equality before the law can only be complete if it covers religious issues: the emancipation of the Jews entailed not only the political and civil equality of individuals, but also intermarriage and so conversion to other religions. The second and fourth points, on the other hand – which do not contain preconditions but accessory considerations – lead in another direction. The demand for the regulation of legal settlement in the country in fact affected immigration policy, and could be valid only if the Hungarian government were sovereign, that is, able to decide for itself whom to admit into the country and whom not. This decision-making power, however, would cease to be available should the Hungarian state become part of a larger empire. This point is worth noting because in 1867 it acquired great significance. From our point of view, however, the declaration of religious reform – or rather, the resolution aimed at reshaping Jewish social structure – is more important, entailing as it did that the liberal state, which professed political and civil equality before the law, must in some way interfere in the free choices of its emancipated citizens. (This paradox would be repeated, of course, in the twentieth century, by no means affecting only Jews: we need only think of the restrictions on higher education, the administrative constraints enforced through chambers of commerce, and even the labour-camp system.) If the state steers a particular group of its supposedly free citizens along a predetermined course, then in what sense is it still liberal, violating as it does the principle of equality before the law? The 1849 law was not only illiberal, it was, in fact, impracticable if the state wished to maintain respect for the principles in the name of which it was brought forward.

The requirement of religious reform was not unequivocally illiberal, however, because the law called for its promotion rather than for its imposition. If the representatives of the Jews wanted religious reform, then so be it. What the law formulated, actually, was the executive power's expectation that such reform should take place.

If we wish to interpret the aims both of those wishing to expand or to harmonize civil rights, and of those who wanted to restrict them, we cannot remain content with the supposition that the Hungarian liberals were politicians struggling within the confines of well-defined prejudices.[7] The demands made of the Jews – whether they arose as preconditions or as auxiliary elements – point to one of the most important and defining elements of Hungarian liberalism at that time, which concerned above all not the Jews but the situation of the Hungarian people: nation-building.

We can take as our starting point the fact that the main objective of Jewish emancipation was the strengthening of the Hungarian nation and the Hungarian ethnic group. This was entirely understandable in a country with a heterogeneous population. The fundamental mission of Hungarian liberalism was to create, through the granting of equal rights to all, a nation in the civil sense of the word. The creation of a nation was inextricable from liberalism: at the same time, it was the pursuit of this very aim, this chipping away at the feudal concept of nationhood, that was gradually pushing into the foreground, and perhaps bringing to boiling point, the question of national status, with the attendant risk that the nationalities which constituted the numerical majority might seek to emulate it in relation to themselves. The task of creating a modern nation threatened to burden the Habsburg-Hungarian relationship with conflicts more numerous than ever before, since the danger of Germanization already threatened not only feudal privileges, but the entire extended concept of nationhood.

Aside from the creation of a concept of nationhood in the cultural sense (language and grammar reform, the development of a national literature and academia, etc.), the political concept of nationhood also gradually developed, based on liberal codes of law which granted no collective rights to the various nationalities making up the country, but instead focused on individual rights in the belief that they contained sufficient cohesive power to counterbalance collective tendencies.

In this context, the Hungarian consciousness of the liberals could not have been built on a culturally integrative – as opposed to assimilative – view of society. Rather, the contrary was the case: the aim was to homogenize the Hungarian people, or rather those groups who wished to be part of the Hungarian nation. This non-integrative liberal concept of nationhood which sought homogenization – quite logically – could not tolerate the notion of a Hungarian people with a diverse culture, and did everything it could to make identifiable, both concretely and culturally, all that was Hungarian or which it considered to be Hungarian. In these circumstances, the Jews, lacking a national identity, proved to be an ideal subject for assimilation. (It should be added here that Vienna, in its efforts at Germanization, had recognized this far sooner – we need only think of the decree ordering Jews to assume German family names.) Yet, however favourable the Jews' lack of national consciousness was, equally unfavourable was the strength of the Jewish religion. The reason for this is quite simple: the Jewish faith does not confine itself merely to questions of belief or to the formulation of principles and standards, but embodies a system of rules governing a whole lifestyle, from eating habits to married life. The historically evolved conception of the Hungarian nation as a homogeneous, and non-integrative, culture was therefore not acceptable to Jews. Thus, the aim of assimilating this divergent cultural type – whether concretely or largely in its cultural consciousness – was questionable from the outset.

Within this framework, it was by no means without reason that Hungarian liberalism expected not only political and linguistic, but also cultural identification from the Jews, and this aim was manifest even at the legislative level. Furthermore, it is symbolic that in 1849 both the emancipation law, which also aimed at cultural assimilation, and the law on Hungary's nationalities, which only partially undertook the ethnic integration of the Hungarian state, were adopted on the same day.[8] It is understandable that it was Kossuth who emerged, after 1849, from the ranks of the Hungarian liberals to adopt an unconditional standpoint consistently favouring equality before the law, and who in 1851 committed to paper his draft for a new constitution which envisaged an integrated society based upon cultural autonomy, at the state executive level.[9]

Although liberal Hungarian politics even following the Compromise of 1867 did not change its concept of homogeneity, Jewish assimilation was not the subject of legislation. The law passed in December 1867 consists of only two paragraphs. The first states that 'the country's Israelite residents shall henceforth be entitled to exercise all the civil and political rights enjoyed by Christian residents.' The second decrees that 'all laws, customs or decrees to the contrary are hereby abolished'.[10] No mention is made of immigration, religious reform or state direction of occupations. Their absence was not due to a liberal change of mind: a variety of causes played a part. The Hungarian parliament – because of the very essence of the Compromise – could not rule on immigration, nor could it prohibit or restrict the movement of capital or labour within the Empire.[11] In regard to the state's attempt to reorganize the occupational structure, however, it is probable that the legislators of 1867 could discern quite clearly that they would be enacting an impossibility, or more precisely, a measure which could only be carried into effect in an entirely illiberal manner. In regard to religious reform, the Minister of Education took the initiative, but this was not a matter that could easily be legislated.

The lack of legislation on religious matters meant that the main vehicle of Jewish culture was excluded from the emancipation process. The 1867 law does not refer even indirectly to the Jewish religion, and no guidelines were laid down for civil marriages until the mid-1890s. All this meant that emancipation or assimilation could only take place on the basis of voluntary cultural homogenization. The proposal of Hungarian liberalism in both 1849 and 1867 – despite differences in the texts of the laws – was the same: become a Hungarian, and you can become a citizen too. For the sake of this Hungarianness, renounce your own cultural standards and customs to the fullest extent possible. If you do all this, we will not only accommodate you, we will even be able to accept you.

A significant number of Jews accepted this offer.[12] Not only did they commit themselves politically to the Hungarian nation and embrace the Hungarian language, they also adapted themselves to Hungarian customs and values. The Jewish citizen also wanted to be a Hungarian citizen, and the attainment of the status of honorary Hungarian was for them less an uncomfortable constraint than a desirable goal. Their choice was made easier by the fact that the process of emancipation increasingly called into question the regulations of religious traditionalism. The liberal offer took the standpoint that Jews should seek emancipation not merely in the modernization of their cultural identity, but in its renunciation. If their co-religionists at various stages of the process came under attack, they responded with vigorous declarations of a Hungarianness which was not confined to use of the language and loyalty to the Hungarian homeland; it meant nothing less than the assumption of this culture as their own.

Hungarian liberalism's own fear of the Germanizing power of Habsburg rule, and of the predominance of other nationalities, was the main motivation behind its insistence on a homogeneous culture and national identity. The drive to assimilation was so strong that many Jews appeared willing to gradually abandon their own cultural identity in order to become Hungarian citizens. They believed that they could, nevertheless, remain Jews symbolically.

The anti-Semitic proposal: dissimilation

At the birth of modern Hungary in the spring of 1848, the desire for political emancipation and assimilation appeared alongside an anti-Semitism the avowed aim of which was to exclude Jews from the enjoyment of full civil rights.

From the mid-1870s, an anti-Semitism elevated to the rank of a political ideology made its appearance in Hungary.[13] It organized as a political party and even managed to gain seats in the Hungarian parliament. Its most infamous deed, which elicited an international reaction, was the Tiszaeszlár trial for ritual murder, which began in 1882. The judgement of the Royal Supreme Court on 10 May 1884 finally acquitted the Jews charged with the ritual murder of a young Hungarian girl. In my view, however, this ritual murder case, which was rooted in medieval anti-Judaism, is not crucial, since the breed of anti-Semitism which operated as a modern political ideology attained the form in which it was able to clamour for dissimilation precisely through its modernism and through its confrontation with contemporary emancipation. For this reason it is worth taking a look at some of this modern anti-Semitism's ideas.[14]

The modern incarnation of anti-Semitism was troubled principally by the successes of assimilation, though its thorough aversion to the social and material regroupings caused by capitalization and emancipation was also very important. It took its point of departure from the proposition that the Jews were not suitable for assimilation because of ingrained racial characteristics. In this conception, the Hungarian people figures as an ethnic category precluding the absorption of any group not 'originally' belonging to it. The Jews – invading the body of the nation through emancipation – are parasitic (in the anti-Semitic jargon, practicing 'money market liberalism'), and debilitate the nation (here they based their reasoning on the Röhling Talmud, which was later proved to be a forgery). Spurred on by radical German anti-Semitism (such as the Marr-Dühring brand), they claimed that the racial qualities of the Jews – 'greed', 'duplicity', 'lack of patriotism' – were irreconcilably opposed to the essential characteristics of the Hungarian nation: 'chivalry', 'openness' and 'an honest personality'. The Jews grew rich through the pursuit of unproductive forms of business, such as trade and finance: it was rare indeed to find a Jewish brakeman or guard. A favourite simile used to portray the relationship between the Jewish and the Hungarian peoples was that of 'thieving wasps plundering pollen from the flowers in contrast to productive bees'. Liberalism would present an opportunity for 'the wasps' – the Jews – to prevail, and so, following this logic, liberal politics favoured only the Jews. But even the opportunities of liberalism were not enough for the Jews, and they resorted to other methods driven by their most destructive impulses. The morally pure Hungarians 'were encouraged to take on such habits as rum drinking, cigar smoking and other kinds of extravagance by the Jews'. By means of the economic power they had acquired, they had corruptly seized control of the judiciary, public administration, parliament and the government.

A further accusation, as if such influence would not have sufficed, was that they were trying to seduce the whole of society to their dishonest ways. Liberal freedom of the press was largely to blame for making this possible. For the most part, if a newspaper or journal was not Jewish it was at least hand-in-glove with them. 'The Jewish press exercises a tyranny over public opinion, the crushing of which is the duty and right of every honest patriot', they wrote. (A thoroughly Hungarian – and therefore decent – tone, comparable to that of the *12 Pamphlets*, was indeed rare.)

Despite their alienness, offensiveness and subversive inclinations, the Jews were able to prevail because they worked night and day to create a political organization which was able, by means of its hierarchical structure and cohesion, to magnify their efforts tenfold. (The operation of this organization was conceived along the lines of the autonomous Jewish communities of Russia, the Kagal.)

On this basis, quite apart from their continuing failure to address the assimilation process actually in progress, the assimilation of the Jews could only be a sham, whose only aim would be to disguise the infiltration of alien elements. This argument worked well in regard to Jewish usage of the Hungarian language. Although it was true that an increasing number of Jews spoke Hungarian, it was considered by some a direct consequence of this that a corruption of the language had set in, the language of the town increasingly diverging from that of rural areas.

The simple fact was that the Jews had not and, indeed, could not become Hungarian. They were by nature parasites and their assimilation was merely a mask for the purpose of allowing them to worm their way even further into the body of the host: for all their seeming acceptance of Hungarian ways and the Hungarian state, they were in fact building up their own positions of power. At the same time, their religion and culture could never tolerate the thoroughgoing compromises that would be necessary for genuine assimilation, even to a mild degree – they were segregationists to the core. Their affinities lay solely with their co-religionists around the world, and for this reason they were irredeemably cosmopolitan, and so entirely incapable of patriotism towards Hungary.

What could be done to stop the spread of this contagion?

The proponents of modern political anti-Semitism offered several prescriptions which might be simultaniously utilized. Among their proposals, measures aimed at restricting or stripping away civil rights occupied pride of place: above all they demanded the revocation of emancipation. Immigration had to be obstructed and, at the same time, the emigration of Jews was to be encouraged. Laws also had to be introduced to render the 'cross-breeding of races' impossible. Both a *numerus clausus* (legislating the number of Jews admitted to university, for example) and a *numerus nullus* (legislating the admission of *no* Jews) might play a complementary role in this. The anti-Jewish laws on moneychanging and usury were considered beneficial in this connection, and the withdrawal of migration rights promised benefits which were not to be frowned upon either. Christian social campaigns might supplement legislative initiatives – for example, the 'Don't buy from the Jews' drive – and of vital importance was the creation of a patriotic press.

The result of this racially oriented, anti-assimilationist brand of domestic anti-Semitism was Jewish emigration and a diminution of Jewish influence in Hungary. Hungarian anti-Semitism raised the question of what the subsequent fate of these outcast Jews should be. Győző Istóczy, at the 24 June 1878 session of the Hungarian parliament, stated that the medieval solution to the Jewish question – mass executions – was not really practicable, for which reason he called upon the government to do everything in its power to assist in the creation of a Jewish state in Palestine, to which Jews could be deported. In fact, the Hungarian anti-Semites were the first in the world to demand a Jewish nation-state: their oft-repeated claim that their racial characteristics made the Jews incapable of living within the confines of a state had apparently been forgotten.

Cultural homogeneity was espoused by anti-Semites and liberals alike, with the crucial difference that the latter considered it acquirable. They shared the rejection of integration and the call for homogenization, only differing in regard to the substance of homogeneity: while the former pursued the homogeneity of individual ethnic groups through dissimilation, the latter pursued the homogeneity of the whole through assimilation. Both basic positions – although not devoid of internal inconsistencies – represented exceptionally powerful ideological frameworks; one might even say that they constituted a polar field in the Hungarian consciousness.

Anyone alluding to the cultural difference of the Jews might easily fall prey to the charge of anti-Semitism; anyone acknowledging it became the target of anti-Semitism himself. Any Jew disavowing or effectively renouncing all ties with his co-religionists fulfilled the requirements of the Hungarian liberals as regards cultural homogeneity at the cost of his cultural and religious inheritance, and, in many cases, lying both to himself and others. Stefan Zweig captured the controversial and strongly ambivalent character of the issue in a piece written about Tivadar (Theodor) Herzl who had himself trodden the path of assimilation, first with the Hungarians, then with the Germans (or 'Austrians', as Zweig referred to them), before he was eighteen years of age (as had his elder contemporary, Max Nordau). As a Jew with direct experience of fascism, he looked back to the world of the 1890s in the light of the Dreyfus case, a phenomenon which affected Jews throughout the Habsburg empire:

Theodor Herzl, this sincere, open, and proud man suffered from his Jewish destiny even as a student, and what is more, tragically bore it in enforced ignorance as to where this destiny might lead him; and yet the prophet's instinct for presentiment dwelt within him. Sensing that he had been born to lead, a role for which not only his imposing bearing but also his far-reaching mind and knowledge of the world qualified him, he fashioned a fantastic plan to solve the problem of the Jews once and for all, uniting Jews and Christians through mass, voluntary baptisms. He pictured everything in his mind, envisioning the Jews of Austria, in their thousands and tens of thousands, with himself at the fore, marching robustly and imposingly into the Stephanskirche, where they would symbolically melt into the greater community, and be rid of the curse of statelessness. He discovered soon enough, however, how fantastic this scheme was. In response he wrapped himself up in his work, and forgot about the age-old problem which he had once considered it his life's work to solve. Now, however, in the face of Dreyfus's degradation, the thought flashed before him once again like a bolt of lightning: under present circumstances the destiny of his people was to suffer eternal contempt. If segregation was inevitable, then let it be complete! If our destiny can only be to endure more and more humiliation, then let us face up to it with dignity. If we must otherwise suffer from statelessness, then let us create for ourselves a separate homeland! Thus inspired he published his tract entitled *The Jewish State*, in which he made it clear that for the Jewish people all thoughts of assimilation and tolerance were but vain deception. The only solution would be to build a state of their own in the ancient lands of Palestine. When this short but keenly worded proclamation was let loose upon the world, I was still a secondary school student, but I remember well even today the stupefaction and outrage of bourgeois Jewish circles in Vienna. 'What has got into this otherwise so clever, witty and cultured writer?', they cried in protest. 'What kind of foolishness is he scribbling? What would we do in Palestine? Our language is German, not Hebrew; our home is in beautiful Austria; and aren't we well off under honest Franz Joseph? We grow stronger quite honourably, we continue to consolidate our position. We are emancipated citizens, native residents of our beloved Vienna. And don't we live in a progressive age which seems likely to resolve all religious prejudices within a matter of decades? Why does this man, who speaks as a Jew and in the supposed interest of Jews, endanger us all by handing over arguments to our worst enemies; why is he trying to pull us apart, when every day we bind ourselves more intimately to the world of the Germans?'

Initially Herzl must have thought that his intentions had been completely misunderstood; in Vienna, where for years he had been so popular, he was now forsaken and ridiculed. Before long, however, he received such a thunderous response, such an ecstatic reply, that he was more startled than anyone: what a movement had he launched, what forces – far surpassing his own – had he unleashed with that slim pamphlet! The first wave did not come from the growing ranks of well-to-do, bourgeois Jews, but from the vast eastern masses in obscure Galicia, and from the Polish and Russian ghettos. Herzl had not even dreamed that his words could kindle the smouldering embers of freedom which, beneath the ashes of alienation, had kept warm the thousand-year-old messianic dream of a return to the Promised Land, as foretold in the holy scriptures. Yet it was this hope that gave some kind of meaning to the existence of millions driven into serfdom and exile. Whenever a prophet, even a false one, had over the course of the two thousand years of the *Golus* [Exile] touched this particular chord, the soul of the people had vibrated in harmony with it, though never as strongly as now. In the space of a couple of dozen pages a single man had, almost by accident, moulded into one the scattered, divided masses.

This initial period, while the notion still existed only in vague, dream-like form, was to be the happiest of Herzl's short life. As soon as he set about realizing his dream, he inevitably ran directly into the full weight of the differences which divided the Jews united only by ethnic origin and the situation it had historically placed them in: orthodox Jews, secular Jews, liberal, socialist, and capitalist Jews all gesticulating at each other in a motley confusion of tongues, and not one of them willing to submit to a unified, authoritative principle.[15]

The unspeakable disparity: integration

There can be no disputing that the overwhelming majority of Hungarian Jews during the last century moved towards assimilation, and this can be attributed to the Hungarian liberals' desire not only to grant the Jews equal rights, but to accommodate them as well. The Hungarian liberals – because of Habsburg rule which threatened Germanization, and the only gradually diminishing preponderance of other nationalities – demanded the Hungarianization of the Jews with the utmost vigour. And not only was linguistic Hungarianization and loyalty to the Hungarian state and the Hungarian people expected of the Jews, but also as far as possible complete cultural identification. In contrast, the anti-Semites rejected such cultural merging, maintaining its impossibility and necessary artificiality, thus calling into question the very notion of emancipation.

As a consequence of all this – to simplify – two ideological frameworks emerged. The first demanded that Jews be granted equality because they were Hungarian. The other took the position that, on the contrary, the Jews should have their rights restricted or even removed precisely because they were not Hungarian and could never become such. This is how it was, how it always had been and how it always would be.

The ideological space which grew up around these two poles came to occupy the entire scope of popular thinking. As a result, a number of representatives of the Hungarian Jews took it upon themselves to prove, with exaggerated enthusiasm, that their cultural assimilation was complete and that therefore their Hungarianness was beyond question – a tendency which persists to this day. Such a reaction was not altogether surprising, since the assertion of any Jewish cultural relic might constitute a challenge to the homogenizing efforts of the Hungarian liberals and provide grist to the anti-Semitic mill. In this way – on the conscious level – it was more or less impossible for Jews to attach themselves to Hungary, while both retaining and modernizing their own cultural identity. (Consciousness of this cultural identity might reveal itself in the more secular aspects of religion – for instance, in the fact that they celebrated their religious festivals in a form acceptable to Hungarians – but also in secularized standards separate from religion, or, to be more precise, in the open popularization of these norms). Assimilation could be achieved only gradually, in tandem with the gradual disappearance of various aspects of cultural difference. Neither can it be said that the only solution was dissimilation. What can be asserted with confidence is that genuine integration is impossible when those wishing to integrate cannot find a willing partner. The likely outcome of this is an overemphasis on assimilation, or a tendency to ever greater dissimilation. (Anti-Semitism does not derive its strength from the validity of its claims, but rather from its aggressive penetration of popular consciousness.)

Another consequence was that this state of affairs threatened the objectivity of interpretation of writers, both Jewish and non-Jewish, who dealt with the history and destiny of the Jews in Hungary. Commentators were themselves liable to fall into this ideological trap, becoming the prisoners of their subject matter. This was particularly the case in regard to the problem of integration. No one denied, either directly or indirectly, that the Jews represented a living culture, and that certain religious or secular standards played an important role in their lives. But because scholarly approaches fell into only two categories – homogeneous acceptance and homogeneous rejection – integration could not be consciously formulated as the subject of historical research. (Ample proof of the existence of this seemingly merely methodological, yet profoundly substantial, dilemma lies in the fact that outstanding Jewish scientific and artistic figures were always referred to as Jews rather than as Hungarians.)

In light of the preceding arguments, I believe there is a pressing need, in the interests of objectivity, to rethink the history of the Hungarian Jews and, if necessary, to bring to the surface aspects of Hungarian history that have not been discussed openly before.

Of course, such rethinking could not be merely a question of subjective determination, knowledge and experience. There is a far more vital preliminary condition. Just as the Hungarian national consciousness in the first half of the nineteenth century became capable of regeneration through liberalism, so today it must demonstrate this ability anew, and accept – in some ways building on the legacy of Kossuth – that the Hungarian nation is both a concept and a reality which can be interpreted not only in terms of homogeneity but also cultural integration. Just as, at one time, changes in the Hungarian national consciousness were able to create concrete opportunities for the self-determination of Hungarian Jews, so today no other scenario is possible. Only a transformation of such magnitude could put an end to an ideological dichotomy which has already exhausted its resources.

(1991)

Notes

1 Pages from the diaries of Sándor Petőfi, *Petőfi Sándor összes művei* [Complete Works of Sándor Petőfi], Budapest, 1955, pp. 445–6.

2 'The Jewish Question', in *Vörösmarty Mihály összes művei* [Complete Works of Mihály Vörösmarty], Vol. 16, Budapest, 1977, p. 80.

3 János Beér (ed.), *Az 1848/49. évi népképviseleti országgyűlés* [The Parliament of People's Representatives of 1848–9], Budapest, 1954, pp. 476–7.

4 Lajos Venetiáner, *A magyar zsidóság története* [History of the Hungarian Jews], Budapest, 1922, p. 169. (In the writing of this chapter I also made use of the 1986 edition with an introduction by Tamás Raj.)

5 The speech on the emancipation of the Jews was delivered on 31 March 1840. The Eötvös study dealing with emancipation was published in *Budapesti Szemle*, Vol. 2 (1840), pp. 110–56. Hereafter I shall quote from the version given in: *Eötvös József Művei: Arcképek és programok* [Works of József Eötvös: Portraits and Programmes], foreword and commentary by István Fenyő, Budapest, 1975, pp. 351–5.

6 Venetiáner, pp. 202–3.

7 Of course this can also play a part, just as much as attitudes which we might characterize as a mixture of ignorance and prejudice, in the behaviour of the most eminent. So, for example, Vörösmarty writes in the abovementioned article:

> I should mention one more aspect. In the matter of the Christian and Jewish religions there is a meeting of East and West: the eternal rigidity of the East and the West's perpetually rejuvenating and serpentine nature do not allow us to doubt that progress and victory shall go to the latter. The rigidity of the East, with all its delights and familial licence, cannot survive in places where the more universal and thus more humane freedoms of the West establish themselves, even only partially. Whether through its faith or hypocrisy the Christian West demands or pretends to a strict family life, despite all its debaucheries, and thereby has a great advantage over the East which delights in familial licentiousness, as a result of instilling in the hearts of parents the sacred duty of raising their children. Thus a more energetic, hardworking, educated and humane race is brought up, which besides inheriting similar principles and frailties and similar obligations, will always have an advantage over the races of Eastern upbringing. Is it possible for the adherents of Eastern religions to unite with a race of this kind without modification? Unquestionably it is not. The Eastern religious ceremonies and customs must be mitigated and either openly or clandestinely modified in order for this unification to take place. In this way, those Israelites who have voluntarily renounced the outward features of their religion and its non-essential or defective regulations and principles have been able to join with the Christian community. (p. 295.)

When Vörösmarty puts forward 'delight in familial licentiousness' as one of the main characteristics of Jewish orthodoxy, he is clearly thinking of polygamy in Islam. This, of course, is immeasurably distant from the Jewish religion, and demands of the Jews something which Christianity had in fact adopted from them, not to mention the fact that the orthodox view recognizes a fair number of obligatory regulations related to matrimony which do not always make possible the enjoyment of even one wife. Naturally, it is more than a question of Vörösmarty's ignorance, since if such a massive error could actually be published then presumably we are facing a lack not merely of knowledge peculiar to the writer, but which was commonplace and, as the above example demonstrates, this general ignorance may also have contributed towards the demand for religious reform.

8 Even this law was an enormous step forward for some Hungarian liberals when compared to the position they took in the spring of 1848, since – in order to avoid the conflicts which threatened to split the Batthyány government – they did not then wish to see the counties subject to popular representation. The law of 1849, among other things, accepted free language usage in county assemblies, although at the parliamentary level it continued to deny the use of the languages of the various nationalities. (See András Gerő, 'Hungary's Policy on National Minorities, 1848–9', *Társadalmi Szemle*, 6 [1987], pp. 63–73; and Chapter 6 of the present work.)

9 Lajos Kossuth, 'Proposal concerning the future political structure of Hungary, with regard to the solution of the national minorities problem', in *Szemelvények az abszolutizmuskori és dualizmuskori magyar történeti forrásokból* [Extracts from Hungarian Historical Sources from the Periods of Absolutism and Dualism], Budapest, 1974, pp. 14–33. Kossuth's views espousing integration quite strongly set him apart from the vast majority of Hungarian liberals, and his opinion – particularly as regards cultural autonomy – influenced subsequent Austrian social democracy.

10 *Magyar Törvénytár. 1836–1868. évi törvényczikkek* [Hungarian Statute Book. Laws of 1836–68], Budapest, 1896, Act. XVII of 1867.

11 However, the scale of immigration from Galicia had also decreased. See Alajos Kovács, *A zsidóság térfoglalása Magyarországon* [The Settlement of the Jews in Hungary], 1922. In the period following 1869 on the other hand, the number of Jews emigrating usually exceeded the number of immigrants. See Walter Pietsch, 'Immigration of the Jews from Galicia', in *Valóság*, 11/1988.

12 I would like to refer only to the most recent examples of the significant body of literature dealing with assimilation. On the religious aspect: Gyula Zeke, 'After the split. . .', in *Hét évtized a hazai zsidóság életéből. I. rész* [Seven Decades in the Lives of the Hungarian Jews, Part I], Budapest, 1990, pp. 145–61. The same source also provides statistical supplements on the assimilation process, pp. 185-97. Furthermore: Viktor Karády, 'Jewish identity and assimilation in Hungary', in *Mozgó Világ*, 8/1988. Idem., 'Principal Factors in the Emancipation and Modernization of the Jews in the History of Hungarian Society', in *A zsidókérdésről* [The Jewish Question], Budapest, 1989. Idem., 'Unequal Hungarianization', in *Századvég*, 2/1990. Also William O. McCagg Jr., *A History of Habsburg Jews 1670–1918*, Indiana University Press, 1989, pp. 123–39. And on East European interconnections, idem., *The Jewish Question in East and Central Europe*, Budapest, 1985.

13 See Judit Kubinszky, *Politikai antiszemitizmus Magyarországon (1875–1890)*

[Political Anti-Semitism in Hungary (1875-90)], Budapest, 1976. György Szabad, 'The assault on civil equality and its failure', *Társadalmi Szemle*, 8–9/1982.

14 A reconstruction of the various views is provided by Zoltán Barotányi. For the interpretation of this anti-Semitic reasoning, both Kubinszky's book and György Szabad's study were of invaluable assistance to me. I also made use of: *Istóczy Győző országgyűlési beszédei, indítványai és törvényjavaslatai* [The Parliamentary Speeches, Motions and Bills of Győző Istóczy], Budapest, 1904.

15 Stefan Zweig, *A tegnap világa* [The World of Yesterday], Budapest, 1981, pp. 101–3.

Part Three

National consciousness and the making of cults

11 The Millennium Monument

The year was 1881. The Budapest General Assembly submitted a proposal to the National Assembly to build a monument to celebrate the millennium of the conquest of Hungary. The monument was to record the events of a thousand years, appropriately commemorating the settlement of Hungary and the history of the Hungarian people. But the proposal represented a great deal more. Eight years earlier the capital, formed from the three cities of Buda, Óbuda, and Pest, had been engaged in an effort to become the true centre of the country. A great many of the city's inhabitants still spoke German, but the drive to assimilate to the Hungarian language and ways was well under way, providing all the more impetus for the development of a bourgeois culture. This period witnessed an unprecedented drive towards modernization and the development of national consciousness – the main objectives of Budapest in its golden age.

That same year, the first centralized telephone network in the capital – the third anywhere in the world – was established, and the Hungarian News Agency was founded to ensure a modern network for the exchange of information. It was a period of consolidation and progress; of flourishing literary circles, theatres, coffee houses and taverns flooded with patrons; the time of a stable currency and a boom in industry, trade, and credit; an era when the governing party was able to obtain a majority in the national elections, and when opposition parties spoke out but presented no particular threat; a period when the press was free. But however carefree Hungary seemed – and the regular conditions of life were relatively stable – it would be a mistake to overlook the significant political problems which remained unsolved.

With the Austro-Hungarian Compromise of 1867, the Habsburg Empire had assumed its final form which, although established within a constitutional framework, still embodied a good many absolutist principles. The Compromise accorded Hungary independence in domestic affairs and the right to maintain its territorial integrity, including areas with mixed nationalities. However, all this was achieved at great cost to the nation's ultimate independence. The ministries of foreign affairs, defence, and finance came under the empire's joint authority – a source of long-term harm to national self-esteem.

The political balance of power promoted acceptance of the status quo, but could do little to enforce the emotional identification of the people. Separate nationalities had no guaranteed collective rights under the Dual Monarchy, and in spite of the barrage of patriotic slogans, the arrangement far from pacified the national feelings of the majority of Hungarians, promoting as it did modernization without genuine national independence. Although everything appeared to be running smoothly, many were actually waiting for the opportunity to change things in their favour. The threat of conflicts between nationalists and nationalities only served to intensify the social tensions concomitant with modernization. However secure Franz Joseph, Austrian Emperor and Hungarian King, might have felt his position to be, his rule over the empire was clouded with uncertainty.

In these circumstances, the Millennial celebration was not just an occasion for revelry: it was an historic opportunity for the Hungarian government to construct an integrated national and historical ideology depicting the *de facto* imperfect state as *de jure* a whole, inspiring a sense of continuity, of permanent and unshakeable stability, while at the same time presenting the status quo as inevitable. But when would this opportunity be realized?

A great deal of controversy surrounded the issue of when the Magyars actually settled the territory of present-day Hungary. The Hungarian government solicited the help of the Academy of Sciences in 1882 to determine the exact year of the Magyar Conquest. Scholars widely disagreed over the matter, and after failing to reach a final consensus, reported: 'All that can be stated with any certainty from the data we have examined is that the territory of modern Hungary was not settled by the Magyars before 888 AD and that the occupation of the country was complete by 900 AD, by which time the existence of the Hungarian nation was certainly a fact.' The Academy had designated a 12-year time span during which the Magyars may have settled the country, and it was left to the government to decide when the Millennium should be commemorated. After considerable deliberation, a statute was issued in 1892 setting the Millennium for 1895. Initially disregarding the capital's proposal, the government set about planning a large representative exhibition, later opting for a more extended project comprising a whole series of public construction works. Since time for implementing the plans was running out, the simplest recourse was inevitably to issue a statute in 1893, postponing the Millennium until 1896.

Meanwhile, plans were beginning to take shape for the Millennial celebration. Among the various ideas, plans to establish a Millennium Monument were gaining ground. In February 1894, a parliamentary document was drafted with prime-ministerial approval outlining the plans in greater detail. Several points of view were revealed in the debate of the parliamentary committee established to look into the matter.

The problem of where to locate the monument emerged as a key issue. One proposal suggested locating the statue of Árpád, founder of the nation, on Gellért Hill where the Citadel is today – a suggestion not without historical and political implications. The Citadel was built after the allied Austrian and Russian forces had crushed the Hungarian Revolution in 1849 a revolution which had threatened Habsburg rule by proclaiming Hungary an independent state. The building of the Citadel had been ordered by General Haynau, the hated Lieutenant-Governor of Hungary, who had been invested with full authority by the young Franz Joseph. Completed in 1854, the Citadel was militarily obsolete, although it had not been intended to provide effective military defence. The Citadel's cannon were directed against Pest, site of the March Revolution of 1848, in order to intimidate the city's inhabitants. The building came to symbolize oppression and was somewhat ironically referred to as the 'Bastille of Gellért Hill'. When the Compromise was instituted between the crown and the nation in 1867, a suggestion was made to demolish the obsolete fortress, which was a disturbing reminder of Habsburg absolutism and quite out of keeping with the tenuous political accord. The proposal to place the statue of Árpád, the leader of the conquering Hungarian tribes, where the Citadel then stood had a clear political intent. The idea had surely been inspired by Count Széchenyi, who had earlier suggested building a pantheon on the hill where there was only a humble astronomical observatory. Instead of representing Hungarian subjugation, as the Citadel had, the statue would symbolize independence and glory.

The memorial on the hill was never built. Although the government weighed the merits of the proposal, anticipated high costs compelled it to table plans to demolish the Citadel and construct another monument. A far less colourful solution was chosen: the Citadel was symbolically dismantled in 1897, with the part above the entrance destroyed and some of the walls breached. The fortress stayed where it was, although much of its original charm had gone.

Another suggestion was a triumphal arch should be built at the end of Andrássy út (Avenue), a proposal which also won favour with the prime minister: instead of being built on the site of the 'Bastille', the arch would be located at the end of Budapest's 'Champs Élysées'! Once known as 'Sugár út' (Radial Avenue) and subsequently named after Count Gyula Andrássy, the first prime minister after the Compromise, Andrássy út in many ways represented Budapest's claim to the status of a major metropolitan centre. The imposing residences which line the street to this day were modelled on the famous Parisian boulevard, construction of which had been largely completed in the 1850s and 1860s. A triumphal arch was all that was needed in order to make the resemblance complete. Plans for the Paris Arc de Triomphe had been drawn up during the reign of Napoleon, taking their final form in 1836. The Hungarian arch was intended to symbolize '*grandeur et gloire*' in the same manner as its French counterpart; Andrássy út also represented the growing power of the middle class. It was also the site of the first underground railway on the continent (the second in Europe), completed in time for the 1896 Millennial, and still in operation today. The importance attached to historical continuity is further exhibited in the fact that the first plans for the street had been suggested in 1841 by Lajos Kossuth. Although the street was not situated where he had originally proposed, it nevertheless reflected an amalgam of national and middle-class interests.

At the end of Andrássy út, where the monument was to be built, had originally stood the Gloriette, a terraced fountain designed by the architect Miklós Ybl, which drew its waters from an artesian spring. Drilling for the fountain had been done by the engineer Vilmos Zsigmond in the 1860s and 1870s, yielding water at a temperature of 74 °C from a depth of 971 metres. This excellent spring also supplied water to the Széchenyi Baths in the City Park, opened in 1913. The Gloriette was relocated in 1898 to today's Széchenyi Hill. The place where the artesian fountain once stood is now marked on the square by a metal plaque.

Now that the plans and location of the monument had been decided upon, the search began for a designer and for the financial resources to cover expenses. The sculptor György Zala and the architect Albert Schickedanz were commissioned to draw up the plans. At that time, 1894, the 36-year-old Zala was still considered a relatively young artist. He had only been living in Budapest for 10 years, having studied in Vienna and Munich, as was then fashionable. His first major commission had been the Honvéd (Defence) Memorial on Dísz tér in the Castle District in 1893, which was dedicated to the memory of the Hungarian troops who had fought in the 1849 War of Independence and recaptured Buda from the Austrians. Unassuming and devoted to a subject of concern to the whole nation, this statue proved to be just the right letter of recommendation to the committee.

Schickedanz was 48 years old when he received his commission. That he was a teacher at the Budapest School of Applied Arts clearly indicated that he was a conservative artist, inclined to work in classical forms. He had already collaborated with Zala – designing the base of the Honvéd Memorial – and had considerable experience in building monuments. He had been charged with designing the statue of Lajos Batthyány, first Prime Minister of Hungary, whose execution had been commanded by Haynau in 1849. He had also designed, in 1882, the base of the statue of Ferenc Deák in today's Roosevelt Square. Two artists had been chosen who could be relied upon to create a monument which would appeal to the aesthetic sensibilities and notions of the committee, and who were experienced in expressing national values in concrete form.

Opposition to the monument centred on the fact that the envisaged group of statues would have a long-term impact on the cityscape; it would constitute not only the biggest, but also the costliest, of all the monuments built to date. Whomever was awarded the commission would not only be assured of a place in history, their professional future would also be secure. As the officially commissioned artists began work on the design, other sculptors and architects lobbied for an open competition to decide who would be honoured with the distinction of designing the monument. Designs for the monument having been finished quickly, the architectural branch of the Hungarian Engineering and Architectural Association convened a 52 member plenum in 1894. They objected to the Zala-Schickedanz plans primarily on aesthetic grounds. They felt that the monument would be out of place at the end of Andrássy út and furthermore, that it would be an eyesore and a public nuisance. Emphasizing the responsibility of the present to future generations, their conclusions threw more weight behind the demands for an open competition. Among the leaders of those opposed to the plans was Frigyes Schulek whose restoration of the Coronation Church, or Mátyás Templom, had made him a household name. (Not long after voicing his objections to the proposed monument, however, he participated in the city improvements projected for the Millennial celebration, drawing up the plans for the Fishermen's Bastion.)

The Prime Minister's opinion remained unswayed and Zala won the commission. A parliamentary committee was set up to examine the plans and proposed several changes. The City Park at the end of Andrássy út was still regarded as the best site for the monument. The demands for an open competition had been brushed aside on the grounds that the existing plans were sound and, more spuriously, that time was running out. Furthermore, the gate to the National Exhibition – one of the main attractions of the Millennial celebration – had been established where the monument was planned to be erected. Since the square could only accommodate one structure at a time, only after the exhibition had been taken down could the construction of the monument begin, a straightforward consideration which had apparently occurred to no one before Zala signed the contract in spring 1895. The contract stipulated that only the clay models for the statues would have to be ready by 1896, and that architectural work could begin later in the same year. The final completion date was set another five years after that. Some 800,000 forints had been earmarked for the project, an astronomical sum in those days and the largest amount of money which had ever been invested in a single work of art in Hungary. Indeed, the government spared no expense on this project. (To put this in perspective, the underground railway, one of the engineering wonders of the contemporary world, had cost 3.7 million forints.) How could the signatories of the contract have known that it would not be five but 35 years before the work would be finished, and that by the time the last bills were paid, neither the forint nor the korona which succeeded it would still be the official currency in Hungary?

By now, the artists were hard at work implementing their plans. Zala reserved one of the storerooms at Nyugati (Western) Railway Station, since it offered ample space for constructing the massive statues. The design, which only assumed its final form in 1929, was resolved rather ingeniously, envisaging an eclectic colonnade built in a double semicircle, 85 metres wide and 25 deep. The structure, facing the city, was planned to create the sense of an open triumphal arch. The base of the main group of statues stands a little forward at the centre of the colonnade, with Árpád, chieftain of the Magyar tribes and forebear of Hungarian kings, taking the foremost position. He is flanked by the equestrian statues of the other six tribal leaders. A 36-metre column emerges from the base capped by the bronze statue of the Archangel Gabriel, twice life-size, resting on a solid globe. In each hand he bears an important symbol: in one, the holy crown of the Hungarian kings, and in the other, an apostolic cross. In the distance, symbolic groups of bronze statues span the top of the colonnade. War is symbolized by the chariot galloping to the left of the semi-circle, flanked by statues symbolizing Work and Prosperity. On the right half of the semi-circle are the majestic chariot of Peace and the paired statues of Knowledge and Glory. Between the columns are the statues of leading figures from Hungarian history sculpted in the revivalist style; beneath them are reliefs depicting scenes from the relevant periods of Hungarian history.

The symbols used in the monument – War, Peace, Work, Prosperity, Knowledge, and Glory – are somewhat clichéd and might have been included in the national monument of any country. They were included, however, because of their specific associations in Hungary. The symbol of the Archangel Gabriel has a direct bearing on the nation's history. In addition to symbolizing victory, the holy crown and the raised apostolic cross represent the triumph of Hungarian nationhood as inseparable from Christianity. The choice of Gabriel is also apt since, according to legend, the archangel appeared to the first Hungarian king in a dream, charging him to convert his people to Christianity.

Which statesmen were to be represented in the monument, and the grounds on which they were to be selected, clearly manifest contemporary attitudes towards Hungarian history. There were 14 places to be filled and in what follows we shall present the history of each of the statues and reliefs, how they were originally conceived and erected at various times, and how some eventually came to be replaced by others.

Saint István (King Stephen) (997–1038), the Hungarian prince who converted the people to Christianity and, by accepting his crown from the Pope in 1001, had elevated Hungary to the status of kingdom and established it as a state in accordance with contemporary European norms, is represented in the first statue. Second is the statue of King Saint László (1077–95). In the relief below the statue, his slaying of a Cumanian abductor is depicted. The choice of the theme, in addition to its presentation, reveals the creators' intention to give expression to the Hungarian national character. The enemy attacking the country was evil – to the point of abducting defenceless women – until the forceful intervention of the Hungarian king: this was intended to represent the notion of lawful and valiant self-defence, thereby justifying an increase in Hungary's power.

In another relief, King Könyves Kálmán or Kálmán le Beauclerc (1095–1116) is shown annexing Croatia and Dalmatia, thereby establishing the nation's territorial claims. The next scene emphasizes Hungary's inseparability from Europe: the participation of King András II in medieval Europe's largest collective enterprise, the Crusades, symbolizing the active defence of the Christian faith and Christian devotion. The next relief depicts the Mongol Invasion of 1241–2, which dealt a devastating blow to the country. King Béla IV (1235–70) is shown rebuilding the medieval Hungarian state from the ruins of the invasion, embodying the ideal of unceasing, heroic activity and the spirit of reconstruction.

The subsequent statue-relief pair, one of the most unusual elements of the monument, represents Charles Robert (1308–42), the first Angevin king, who contributed greatly to the organization of the economic and political structure of the Hungarian state. In the face of internal dissension and incursions by powers such as the Habsburgs, Charles Robert successfully defended the nation. The relief below the statue depicts an unrelated scene: the battle of Mohács (Marchfeld) on 26 August 1278, where the Hungarian king, László IV (the Cuman, 1270–90), hastened to the assistance of Rudolf Habsburg. The allies proceeded to defeat the Czech King Ottocar, who had encroached upon their territory (and subsequently died in battle). Rudolf had this victory to thank for the acquisition of the Austrian princedom, later invaluable to the Habsburg dynasty. The content of the relief is striking not only because it is at variance with the statue above it, but because of its political message. Charles Robert was of incomparably greater historical significance as a ruler than László IV, and his presence in the monument suggests he was included out of respect for this, while the relief is meant to convey the debt owed to the Hungarian people by the Habsburgs for their position of power in Austria. No less noteworthy is the fact that, when the monument was constructed, a Habsburg ruled Hungary, which constituted one half of the Empire. The reference to the Battle of Mohács was also meant to show that acceptance of a common fate provided the sole guarantee of protection against the Slavs and other would-be conquerors. Interdependence, loyalty, and national pride were ideological factors which had figured prominently in the 1867 Compromise. Depiction of the Battle of Mohács – otherwise so incongruent with the rest of the monument – was an especially good choice for demonstrating the historical viability of Hungarian nationalism within the empire.

Chronologically, however, Habsburg domination was still a long way off: the next three statues depict figures representing periods of national greatness preceding Habsburg rule. The reign of Lajos I the Great (1342–82) saw the greatest expansion of territory in the nation's history. The relief focuses on the King's entry into Naples in 1348, where he was received by Johanna its ruler. (Lajos was later forced to relinquish possession of Naples, though he did receive financial compensation.) The next statue represents the only commoner in the monument, János Hunyadi (1407?–56), who despite being only the governor of Hungary held the actual power. The event recorded on the relief is one of global importance. In 1456, at Belgrade, Hunyadi's forces halted the Turkish onslaught, ensuring not only the security of Hungary, but that of all Europe. The relief shows a scene in which a Turkish soldier, who had attempted to hoist a Turkish banner on a parapet of the besieged fortress, is seized by a Hungarian soldier, the two of them plummeting together to their deaths. The inclusion of the Battle of Belgrade in the monument was meant to demonstrate that Hungary had not only defended its own territorial integrity, but had heroically defended Europe and European civilization. The final figure in this series is the great Renaissance ruler, Mátyás Hunyadi (Matthias Corvinus), who ruled (1458–90) after his father, the governor. Renowned for his humanist learning and enlightened court, Mátyás is depicted in the relief surrounded by scholars. By emphasizing Mátyás' role as a great patron of arts and sciences, the magnitude of the nation's cultural contribution was also expressed.

The statue and relief of Mátyás are followed by the representation of the Habsburg dynasty. The Habsburgs had ruled over Hungary continuously since the reign of Ferdinand I (1526–64), although Ferdinand himself was unable to defend the country from the Turks and, in fact, divided its forces in his struggle to maintain power. Once again, the relief is at variance with the statue. The scene depicted is the valiant and victorious battle at Eger Castle in 1552, when Hungarian soldiers successfully raised a Turkish siege. The battle is legendary for the role the women of Eger played in the struggle, taking up arms beside their menfolk. The inclusion of this relief under the statue of a Habsburg ruler expresses Hungarian resentment over the fact that Hungary had so often been left to defend itself.

The same contrast between relief and statue may be seen with regard to the statue of Károly III (1711–40). The relief beneath this statue depicts the decisive victory under Eugene of Savoy against Turkish forces at Zenta, in 1697, marking the end of 150 years of Turkish occupation. The ruler of Hungary at the time of this battle was, however, Leopold I (1657–1705), against whom the Hungarians had rebelled, first under Thököly's leadership and later under Ferenc Rákóczi II. Depiction of a king who had so flagrantly disregarded national rights and who had dealt with Hungary as though it were merely a subjugated province, incurred the risk of widespread popular resentment. If Rákóczi, who had fought so hard for national independence, was not to be included, there was no question that Leopold would be represented. Instead, Károly III – who, after the struggle for freedom led by Rákóczi, had brought the fighting to an end – was chosen. Károly III replaces Leopold as the ruler responsible for implementing the Austro-Hungarian agreement.

The inclusion of the statue of Maria Theresa (1740–80) reflects the view that if a ruler acted in accordance with Hungarian law, Hungarians would be quick to render assistance in time of need. The relief below the queen's statue depicts the vote in the Diet in 1741 to send her military support with the exclamation, *'Vitam et sanguinem!'* If Hungary had refused assistance at that crucial point in history, the Habsburg Empire would certainly have been destroyed, since Maria Theresa's right to the throne was not recognized abroad and the Prussians and Bavarians had launched an attack. Hungarian soldiers brought their campaign to a standstill, a fact which not only made possible the reoccupation of Austria and Bohemia, but also won diplomatic recognition of Maria Theresa's sovereignty. The relief refers to two historical events in which Hungary had proven itself a reliable buttress for the Empire: the aiding of the Habsburgs to power in the thirteenth century and the saving of the Empire from total collapse in the eighteenth century. The implication is that it would be only fitting if they were to receive help from a just ruler, in the event that their rights were violated; for this reason, the statue of Leopold II is also included. This is another example of the subordination of the artistic work to political considerations. Whereas Maria Theresa's historical prominence was indisputable, Leopold II had actually ruled for less than two years (1790–2). The sole reason for his inclusion in the monument was that it was under his rule that the Hungarian feudal constitution, which had been ignored by his predecessor – the son of Maria Theresa, Joseph II (1780–90) – was, at least formally, reinstituted. To avoid having to give an account of his actions to the Diet, Joseph II had not permitted himself to be crowned, sending the Holy Crown to Vienna. Leopold II's reign saw the restoration of the crown to Buda. This is the scene depicted on the relief, reflecting the restoration of relations between the Habsburgs and Hungary. To put it another way: provided that certain rules were adhered to, Hungarian-Habsburg relations would ensure the preservation of national interests. At the same time, the relief also indicates that the nation, in defence of its legal integrity, was capable of evoking honourable and successful resistance to Joseph II.

The last statue is that of Franz Joseph (1848–1916), the reigning monarch at the time of the monument's construction, depicted in full military dress. Everything concerning the Habsburgs in the monument, so far, had been presented in such a way as to depict his world as one in perfect harmony. The relief below it shows the crowning of Franz Joseph in 1867 by Prime Minister Gyula Andrássy and the head of the nation's Catholic Church. The graceful figure of Queen Elisabeth, much loved by the Hungarian people, is also present, along with Ferenc Deák, the leading figure behind the Austro-Hungarian Compromise. With the coronation of Franz Joseph the long-awaited peace between emperor and country had been established, and Hungary had at last settled into its role in the empire; a place it had duly accepted in the spirit of the Compromise which – as had been the firm inten-tion of its framers – would ensure the territorial integrity of the state, promote the development of the Hungarian nation, and provide a political forum for national sentiments and aspirations. Only through allegiance to both monarch and country – contemporaries believed – could true unity emerge.

It is true that in the eyes of contemporaries, this sense of harmony must have been disturbed somewhat by the figure of a monarch in full military garb. It served as a reminder that the supression of the 1848–9 revolution and the ensuing absolutist terror were embodied in the same person. Although those days might safely be regarded as over, the disconcerting thought remained that it was the monarch who was invested with the exclu-sive power to raise armed forces under the re-established constitution.

In short, given that this is not the best of all possible worlds, it was neces-sary to create a new view of history which immersed the present in the glories of the past, and provided an impression of unfailing continuity and fulfilment. In the Millennium Monument we find a unique fusion of national character and politics, interwoven with a unique history. It showed the Hungarian people as self-assured, courteous and heroic and capable of great undertakings both on their own account and for the sake of others. They were prepared to make sacrifices in defence of their rights, and were open to European culture. As long as the monarch was willing to respect their customs and laws, they would accord him their unbounded loyalty. Hungary's embracing of Christianity was not simply an expression of its becoming a European state, it also reflected a commitment to defend Christian values and to fight for them when necessary. The role the Hungarian state had assumed within the Habsburg Empire was not only regarded as an accepted possibility, it was the only possibility.

However great the initial surge of activity had been, construction work on the monument was slow, and extended so far beyond the deadline that it was overtaken by changes in government. Realizing that he would not be able to finish the statues on his own, Zala commissioned six other sculptors to help. He then set about the task of carving the Archangel Gabriel, which was ready by June 1897. The end of the year saw the establishment of the colonnade, and it finally seemed that work on the Millennium Monument would be completed on time.

Perhaps because of lingering hostility over the scrapping of the open competition, the Bureau of Engineers began to find fault with the construction. Insisting that the archangel would be swept from the 36-metre column by the first heavy storm, they consented to its erection only after an iron rod had been set into the column. This entailed the building of an entirely new column, which was finished by autumn 1901. Meanwhile, the bronze statue of Gabriel was sent to Paris for the 1900 World Exhibition where it received the Grand Prix. Though it was remarked by many that the elevation above the monument would put its fine details out of range of the naked eye, the statue has occupied this remote perch above Budapest since autumn 1910.

Although the colonnade and the archangel Gabriel were in position, the monument, in the absence of the long-awaited statues, was far from finished. The National Council of Fine Arts received the works in the order of their completion: first, the statue of Mátyás Hunyadi (by György Zala) cast in 1905, then those of Ferdinand I (Ede Margó), Béla IV (Miklós Köllő), Charles Robert (György Kiss), and Leopold II (Richárd Füredi). Work was then completed on the twin statues of Work and Prosperity, and those of Knowledge and Glory.

Statues finished by 1906 included those of King Könyves Kálmán (by Richárd Füredi), János Hunyadi (Ede Margó), and the Chariot of War (György Zala). Zala completed the statue of Franz Joseph and the symbolic figure of Peace by 1908. As the statues were erected, the colonnade slowly began to assume its final form. The year 1911 saw the casting of the statues of Saint László (by Ede Telcs), Saint István (by Károly Senyei), and Maria Theresa (by György Zala). The same year, five of the completed reliefs joined the monument which by this time was becoming the capital's newest landmark. To the existing statues were added, in 1912, the statues of András II (by Károly Senyei), Károly III (by Ede Telcs), and the equestrian statue of Árpád (by György Zala). In the course of 1914–15, four new reliefs were installed.

With five reliefs and the statues of one king and six leaders remaining, plans to complete the monument were interrupted by the First World War. Official propaganda was already stressing the themes of national greatness and glory; and as long as they were matched by victory in the field, they were effective. Later on, as the war dragged on and victories became fewer, ordinary Hungarians became increasingly conscious of what the nation's leaders had known from the outset: Hungary could only emerge from the war as a loser. Had the Monarchy – fighting on the German side – been victorious, it would have increased its territory, but Hungary would have remained as it was; apart from the *Csángó*, a Hungarian ethnic group living in Romania, all ethnic Hungarians were living within the country's borders. Furthermore, during the peaceful decades of the Dual Monarchy, the other nationalities had been effectively assimilated, and the 1910 census showed a Hungarian majority. The territorial expansion implied by a Habsburg victory, however, would have increased the proportion of Slav peoples, so jeopardizing the political hegemony of Hungarians within the country and also endangering the balance of power within the Dual Monarchy. On the other hand, defeat was likely to entail even worse consequences, bringing with it the threat of disintegration.

There were no national interests which could justify the loss of many thousands of Hungarian soldiers and civilians – Galicia and Italy were piled high with the corpses of Hungarians who had died far from their homeland. Meanwhile, the standard of living in the country had gravely deteriorated, the supply of goods and foodstuffs to the populace having been siphoned off for the war effort. When the Monarchy indeed lost the war, the minorities living within Hungary saw their chance to break free. The prediction made by the critics of the 1867 Compromise was fulfilled: Hungary, as part of the Habsburg Empire, was incapable of maintaining its territorial integrity, because it had failed to offer acceptable compromises to its minorities at the right time (see Chapter 6).

Defeat, combined with social tensions in Hungary during the post-war period, created a revolutionary climate. The revolution in October 1918 promised democratic rights and land reform. A republic was declared. It is perhaps understandable that the country, suddenly gaining its independence – although its borders had yet to be drawn – sought to define itself in marked contrast to the Habsburg Monarchy. Many Hungarians were convinced that this was the only way to recoup their losses.

Attempts were also made to reinterpret the nation's history, bringing into focus events – primarily those of 1848 – giving expression to anti-Habsburg sentiments. Indicative of the prevailing atmosphere was the fact that Joseph Habsburg, the king's representative, had proposed changing his last name to Alcsút, where he had an estate. Also characteristic of this period was the radical turn that events took in the social and political spheres as the proletariat assumed power in March 1919. While the problem of the nation's future officially became of secondary importance (if the world revolution were victorious, the issue of national boundaries would lose all relevance), the Habsburgs were now presented as agents of feudal-capitalist oppression. Statues of members of the Habsburg dynasty were duly removed from the monument, and the statue of Franz Joseph – directly associated with the regime that had lost the war – was smashed to pieces.

The revolution was short-lived and the victory of the counterrevolution saw the reinstatement of the monarchy, deriving its legitimacy from the legacy of the Dual Monarchy. This was necessary not only for reasons of internal legitimacy but from a foreign-policy standpoint. By 1920, external constraints imposed as a result of Hungary's defeat were more clearly defined in the Treaty of Trianon, forced upon it in the course of the Paris peace negotiations. Signing the peace had been a precondition of international recognition of the counterrevolutionary regime. Paradoxically, the government which owed its very existence to the signing of this treaty proceeded to direct its entire policy towards its revocation.

Under the terms of the agreement new borders were to be established. Hungary lost 191,735 square kilometres of territory from its original 282,870, and was left with less territory than was now being given to Romania alone. Eleven million people, from a population of 18 million, now found themselves citizens of neighbouring countries. Particularly difficult to accept was the fact that ethnic considerations had been ignored when the new borders were drawn up; moreover, no national plebiscite was called, as had been pledged by the victorious powers. Over three and a half million ethnic Hungarians were suddenly subject to foreign jurisdiction. War, revolutions, the severe economic terms of the peace agreement, and Hungarians relocating from other countries, exacerbated the situation. The country was plunged into a state of economic crisis. In addition, hundreds of thousands of families were mourning loved ones. The terms dictated by the Treaty of Trianon left the country in a defenceless and vulnerable position vis-à-vis its neighbours, whose territories had correspondingly increased. For every Hungarian soldier, there were five Czech, four Yugoslavian, and six Romanian soldiers.

The disintegration of historical Hungary left its people in a state of shock. The fact that so much had been lost on such inequitable terms outraged the nation's sense of justice. Hungarian national feeling would have found it difficult enough to accommodate the essentially inevitable disintegration of its historical borders, but the manner in which this came about proved intolerable. Neither bourgeois-democratic revolution nor proletarian class solidarity had been able to forestall the tragedy; the revolutions that had failed for a variety of reasons ultimately served only to reinforce adherence to conservative principles. The counterrevolutionary regime pointed to Trianon as the cause, rather than the result, of the nation's problems, blurring the distinction between manifestly different historical processes. The inability of other political forces to prevent the tragedy gave the government virtual *carte blanche* for a shift in ideology. The regime brought forth historical claims as an ideo-political counterbalance to the national tragedy, asserting that the loss of territory had been a direct consequence of national independence and that the Monarchy had proved the only enduring political framework. The liberal policies of the Austro-Hungarian Monarchy had led to the emergence of 'destructive' revolutionary forces. In this way, the Hungary of the Dual Monarchy was mythologized and an anti-liberal orientation emerged.

In the new political climate, the Habsburgs resumed their place of honour. Their statues were returned to their places, and that of Franz Joseph recast; though this time the king was no longer portrayed in full military regalia, but in his coronation robes. In this way, the regime hoped to emphasize its historical claims while rebutting the framers of the Treaty of Trianon. In the interest of avoiding re-establishment of the old regime, it had been decreed that no future Hungarian king could be descended from the Habsburg line, however. Paradoxically, a good many members of the Hungarian National Assembly wept while casting their vote for this measure in 1921. The coronation mantle thus became a political symbol of resistance and obstinate faith.

Although the statues of the Habsburgs were returned to the monument, the work as a whole was still unfinished. Schickedanz had died, and in 1921 György Zala sent a memorandum to Miklós Horthy, Regent of Hungary, requesting money to complete work on the monument. At this time, all the country's resources were tied up in post-war reconstruction; while the new regime would happily have appropriated the patriotic symbols embodied in the monument for its own purposes, the tight national budget would not allow it. Consequently, Zala and his monument had to wait.

At the beginning of this same year, a proposal had been made which, although apparently unconnected, would later have a direct impact on the Millennium Monument. The National Association of Hungarian War Veterans proposed that a large-scale memorial be raised to the heroism of Hungarians during the war. The suggestion won overwhelming support, and by late 1922 a movement was under way in support of it, with Minister of Education Count Klebelsberg giving final approval for the establishment of the monument. However, the decision was not implemented. It was not until 16 March 1924 that the National Council of Fine Arts announced a competition to choose the designer of the National Heroes' Memorial. Submissions were to remain anonymous until after the selection of the winning design. Competitors had only a short time to submit their applications before the 1 May deadline. The first prize was one million crowns, the second prize half that amount (to put this in perspective, taking into account the rampant inflation, the winner would have received the equivalent of three pounds sterling). In addition to the design, applications had to specify the future location of the work and its method of construction. Stiff rules, a short deadline, and an unattractive prize notwithstanding, the judge's committee received some 190 submissions.

Having received the permission and finance necessary for finishing the Millennium Monument, Zala was back to work by 1926, completing the remaining five reliefs that same year. By 1928, all the necessary conditions were in place for the memorial's completion. Zala worked furiously on the project, and the equestrian statues of the Magyar tribal leaders, Előd, Ond, Kond, and Tas were duly set up alongside that of Árpád.

Meanwhile, the idea was advanced by the Budapest City Council that, by way of protesting against the political consequences of the lost war, a memorial to those who had fallen in the war should be erected. Although many imaginative ideas were put forward, the final choice went to a simple slab to be placed at the base of the Árpád statue in the Millennium Monument. With the consent of Horthy, Prime Minister István Bethlen set the dedication day of the National Memorial for 26 May 1929, by which time, of course, the Millennium Monument would also have to be ready. Zala worked furiously on the equestrian statues of the chieftains Huba and Töhötöm (Tétény). All the statues were now in place; the effect was one of cold sobriety conveyed by a dreary eclecticism. Work on the memorial was also rushed. Owing to its massive proportions, the limestone block weighing 4.7 tonnes had to be transported to the square by special means. Six and a half metres long, 3 metres wide, and 1.3 metres high, the monument gave the impression of a coarsely worked tombstone. The monolith was surrounded by a stone parapet, inside which was a grassy area with a step leading up to it. The front was inscribed with the dates 1914–18, and the back with the words: 'Dedicated to the 1,000-year-old national borders.' In addition, the top was engraved with a cross in the shape of a sword-hilt.

It was finally decided that, instead of being dedicated to the unknown soldier, the memorial placed alongside the fierce warriors of the Magyar Conquest was to pay homage to heroes – not as an abstract representation of heroic valour, but in the context of a particular event, namely the First World War. The true heroes had fought to maintain the borders which had been in existence for 1,000 years, and to re-establish them once they had been lost. Ironically, the memorial was thus dedicated to the soldiers of a war in which they had lost everything they had been fighting for.

With the inclusion of the memorial in the Millennium Monument, its original message was to some extent modified. The original intention had been to convey a kind of complacent patriotism – to assert that Hungary had achieved its manifest destiny within the framework of the Dual Monarchy and that the assumption of this role marked the culmination, after one thousand years, of its historical development.

By the time the monument was finished, the Monarchy had collapsed and, along with it, the historical boundaries of Hungary. The conservative counter-revolutionary regime did not learn from these events that their former image of historical greatness had been illusory; instead, they single-mindedly sought to emphasize the injustice of Trianon and set as their unrealistic goal the restoration of the former boundaries. And while the original monument had been established to honour the present, by 1929 the monument had become the expression of the nation's future as envisaged by the regime.

By 1929 the monument had become an inseparable part of the capital and a national landmark. The site of the monument at the end of Andrássy út was named Heroes' Square in 1932, in line with the new conception which underlay it. During 1937–8 the square was paved with flagstones for the Eucharistic Congress. The trees, the flowers, and the fountains on either side were removed; the square lost much of its original charm and intimacy, becoming stern and imposing.

After thirty years of work of varying intensity, operations appeared to have reached a permanent standstill; however, this was not to be. Sixteen years later, individual statues and reliefs would once again be removed to make way for new ones.

In 1945 the nation lost another world war. The regime's political aims had drawn Hungary into an alliance with Nazi Germany, which also sought to revoke the Treaty of Versailles (of which Trianon was a part). Hungary initially benefited from the alliance, reclaiming annexed territories: the former Northern Hungary and Ruthenia from Czechoslovakia in 1938 and 1939, a section of Transylvania from Romania in 1940, and its southern territories from Yugoslavia in 1941. At the same time, the alliance with Germany entailed greater military involvement; Hungarian troops were soon at war with the Soviet Union, and war had been declared against the United States and Great Britain. By this time, government policy had ceased to serve the national interest, and was becoming increasingly fascist.

With the arrival of the Soviet troops, a new leadership was established in which all anti-fascist forces were represented, including the formerly banned Communist Party. The new political order rallied under the banner of democracy, and new democratic principles emerged. The political forces which had swept the country into war were as abhorrent to the new regime as their outmoded political slogans, and the new government sought to proclaim new ideals. To safeguard the nation's future, Hungary had to be kept democratic and independent, and in peaceful coexistence with its neighbours. The notion of an independent, democratic and popular state was at variance with the symbolism inherent in the Millennium Monument, and political forces once again sought to impose new values upon it.

The Habsburg statues – two of which had suffered extensive damage during the war – were removed again, in 1945, and exchanged for historical figures more in keeping with the theme of national independence. Ferdinand I was replaced by István Bocskai, who had led a successful uprising against the Habsburg dynasty at the beginning of the seventeenth century and was subsequently chosen by the estates as ruling prince (1605–6). The statue of Bocskai (by Barnabás Holló) was moved from what is today known as Kodály körönd – a residential roundabout encircling a park – to its new location at the end of Andrássy út. All the reliefs depicting scenes from the history of the Habsburg dynasty were also removed. The relief under Bocskai's statue (by László Martin) depicted his soldiers fighting imperial mercenaries.

Károly III's statue was replaced by that of Gábor Bethlen, Prince of Transylvania (1613–29) who, in the face of the disintegrating Hungarian war effort against the Turks and the Habsburg emperor, sought to perpetuate the national culture and statehood, attempting to reunify Hungary by building a strong Transylvania. While waging successful struggles against the Habsburgs, he had made an ill-fated alliance with the Czech estates who were quickly beaten by the emperor. The relief (by István Szabó), depicting the scene from Bethlen's colourful saga in which he enters into agreement with the Czechs, constituted a goodwill gesture towards the Czech people on the part of the new government: such an act had political implications in 1945, when Hungarians were being forcibly relocated from Czechoslovakia. Despite the new political order in Czechoslovakia, the principle of collective retribution was exercised against Hungarian nationals. Bethlen's statue was also moved from Kodály körönd to the Millennium Monument.

The statue of Maria Theresa was replaced by that of Imre Thököly, renowned for his role as leader of an anti-Habsburg movement during the 1670s and 1680s. The relief (by Jenő Graetner) depicts a scene from his short period of success: the battle of Szikszó fought on 3 November 1679. Bocskai's *Hajdu* footsoldiers and Thököly's *Kuruc* troops, both represented in the monument, symbolize military success in the struggle for national independence. Despite the catastrophic defeat in the Second World War, the monument served to reinforce the belief that the nation had at least been capable of military success when genuine national interests were at stake.

The statue of Leopold II was replaced by that of Ferenc Rákóczi II, Prince of Transylvania (1704–11). The leader of the largest Hungarian anti-Habsburg movement prior to the nineteenth century waged enormously successful struggles in the period between 1703 and 1711. Without the support of the peasants, who had high hopes of victory, the success of the movement would have been inconceivable. The relief depicts Rákóczi's return from Poland to the welcome of the serf army in 1703 under Tamás Esze, who had risen from peasant origins to assume command of the Hungarian insurgents.

Franz Joseph's statue was replaced by that of Lajos Kossuth. Known to Hungarians as 'Father Kossuth', the leader of the 1848–9 War of Independence has indeed become a part of Hungarian national mythology. His name is equated with national independence, not only because he proposed at the National Assembly in 1849 that the Habsburgs be dethroned, but also because he remained committed to Hungarian independence until his death in exile. The peasantry also held him in great esteem because they associated the abolition of serfdom with his name. The relief, indeed, shows him summoning the peasants of the Great Plain to arms. (The statues of Rákóczi and Kossuth are both the work of Zsigmond Kisfaludy-Stróbl.) The prominence of the peasantry in the representation of these two leading historical figures reflects the prevailing view that they constituted one of the mainstays of democratic Hungary and were largely responsible for its national glory.

The monument continued to undergo changes in form and meaning. The National Heroes' Memorial was removed in accordance with the new anti-revisionist policy. Furthermore, a relief depicting territorial expansion – originally below King Könyves Kálmán's statue, portraying the annexation of Croatia and Dalmatia – was removed, to be replaced by a relief depicting his prohibition of the burning of witches. Undoubtedly, the scene was intended to show his enlightened notions, but it omitted to mention that the king had not prohibited the burning of all witches, only the *strigas*: witches who had the power to take the form of animals were to be spared. In the interest of establishing friendly relations with Czechoslovakia, the relief beneath Charles Robert's statue depicting the Habsburg-Hungarian alliance against the Czechs at the 1278 Battle of Mohács was also marked for removal – perhaps for financial reasons, though, only the inscription below the relief was eliminated.

While upholding the medieval values of *grandeur et gloire* imbued with Christianity, the monument's emphasis shifted to national independence, and in the upward-spiralling history of the nation, an ever greater role was ascribed to ordinary people. Greater importance was also attached to the political order prevailing in Hungary, in contrast to the state of its borders. In this manner, the political system that came to power after 1945 stated its goal of building an independent and democratic new Hungary, while preserving the genuinely valuable parts of its tradition.

With the advance of Stalinism, the values embodied in the monument in 1945 received only formal recognition. During this period, the concept of independence became an empty slogan, while a similar fate befell democracy. Historical continuity was sought in other traditions. The regime ascribed particular importance to peasant uprisings and other forms of class struggle; in fact, to anything which could be reformulated along revolutionary lines. This period was also characterized by anti-religious sentiment which took institutionalized, as well as ideological, form. The regime stood in direct opposition to the symbolism of monarchy and of Hungary's Christian allegiance to Europe which were liberally represented in the monument.

They would gladly have wiped the monument, with its archangel and kings, from the face of the earth; they were unable to do so for two reasons. First, it had already appropriated many of the figures represented in the monument for its own purposes; second, the regime, which regarded itself as the agent of the reforms begun in 1945, could not do away with a monument that they had had a share in transforming. No attempt was made to build a new Heroes' Memorial, either. While the removal of the first memorial was viewed as entirely in line with post-war reform, the leadership did not erect a new one in its place because they regarded the Hungarian people as culpable for having stood by Hitler to the end of the war. To have built a memorial to the Unknown Soldier on the square would have meant honouring the Hungarian army, which had fought on the side of the fascists. Nevertheless, during the summer of 1956, in the political climate following the death of Stalin, the National Heroes' Memorial by Béla Gebhardt was returned to the site of the monument, this time inscribed to the memory of those who had given their lives for the freedom of the Hungarian people. With this event the moulding of the monument to the ideological standpoint imposed after 1945 essentially came to an end.

The Millennium Monument has retained its present shape since 1956, and the earlier process of transformation appears to have ceased. The monument was intended to condense the whole of Hungarian history into a single, complex symbol. The different forms this symbol has taken have faithfully mirrored all the historical and political changes which have taken place in the course of its lifetime.

(1987)

Bibliography

No entire work has yet been devoted to the history of the Millenium Monument. For the most comprehensive treatment of this period (until 1929) see Endre Liber: *Budapest szobrai és emléktáblái* [Statues and Memorial Plaques in Budapest], Budapest, 1934. From the point of view of art history the most useful works are Károly Lyka's *Szobrászatunk a századfordulón 1869–1914* [Hungarian Sculpture at the Turn of the Century: 1869–1914] and a study by Eszter Gábor entitled *Az Ezredévi Emlék . . .* [The Millenium Monument . . .] published in *Művészettörténeti Értesítő* [Art History Journal], 1983/4, pp. 202–17. Other writings at least partly concerned with the Millenium Monument – of which there is a very large number – draw heavily on the above works. Post-1945 developments – although their treatment is far from complete – are described under the relevant headings in the *Budapest Lexikon*, Budapest, 1973, and the *Budapest Enciklopédia*, Budapest, 1970. *Budapest építészettörténete, városképei és műemlékei* [A History of the Architecture, Landscape and Monuments of Budapest] by Béla Boross, Alajos Sódor, and Mihály Zádor, Budapest, 1959, covers Heroes' Square as a whole, including the Museum of Fine Arts which is also located there. *A Szépművészeti*

Múzeum (1906–56) [The Museum of Fine Arts: 1906–56], by Gábor Ö. Pogány and Béla Bacher, Budapest, 1956, and *Budapest Múzeumai* [The Museums of Budapest], edited by József Korek, Budapest, 1969, as their titles suggest deal primarily with the Museum of Fine Arts.

Az Ezredév [The Millenium], edited by László Tarr, Budapest, 1979, mentions, among other things, the Millenium celebrations; the bibliography gives a detailed account of publications on the Millenium and other writings on the spirit of the Millennium celebrations. The Appendix of Volume 2 of *Századok* [Centuries], Budapest, 1988, contains a statement by the Hungarian Academy of Sciences on the date of the Conquest of the Hungarian Homeland. A prime ministerial submission concerning the Millenium Monument may be found on page 363, Point 585, in Volume 17 of the Protocols of the 1892–7 parliamentary session. On related details from the history of Budapest the excellent *Hogyan épült Budapest?* [How was Budapest built?] by László Siklóssy, Budapest, 1931, should be consulted. On the Trianon Peace Treaty see *Igazságot Magyarországnak* [Justice for Hungary], Budapest, 1928, and *Magyarország küzdelmes évei* [Hard Times for Hungary], Budapest, 1923, and *Európa válaszúton: Háború vagy Béke* [Europe at the Crossroads: War or Peace] by László Buday, Budapest (year of publication not known). On the logic of the argument see also Gyula Szekfű: *Három nemzedék* [Three Generations]. On financial conditions and the value of the crown (Hungary's currency at the time) detailed information may be found in Volume 8 of *Magyarország története* [The History of Hungary], Budapest, 1976, pp. 495–6.

The speech given by Bethlen at the opening of the Millenium Monument was reported in the daily press on Tuesday, 28 May, having been delayed by a bank holiday. The press also gave a detailed account of the speech delivered by Mayor Sipőcz and the celebrations as a whole. An article entitled 'Miért vagyok olyan csúnya? Budapesti szobrok nyilatkozata megszületésük szomorú és jellemző körülményeiről' ['Why am I so ugly? The statues of Budapest on the sad and characteristic circumstances of their coming into being'] by Imre Keszi, *Szabad Nép* [Free Nation], 11 January 1948, is also worth mentioning.

For an overview I found particularly useful the study of press reports relating to the key moments in the history of the Millenium Monument. Finally, my special thanks go to György Rajna, who was kind enough to provide me with a great deal of information on the construction of the Monument from his own papers.

The best study on the subject to have appeared in recent years is *A Milleniumi Emlékmű mint kultuszhely* [The Millenium Monument as a Place of Worship] by Katalin Sinkó, *Medvetánc*, 1987/2, pp. 29–50.

12 A Hungarian Cult:
Queen Elisabeth of Bavaria

It is a rare phenomenon in Hungarian history that a member of the Habsburg Dynasty should have not only an official but a national cult, but Queen Elisabeth of Bavaria, despite fluctuations in popularity over the years, has managed both. She is commemorated by a statue in Budapest, various public areas and one of the most imposing bridges over the Danube have been named after her; in contrast, her husband's name does not survive – even on the map – and his bronze statue was swept away long ago by the tides of successive political regimes and public opinion.

There is more to the cult of Queen Elisabeth than her personality and biography. Why did the Hungarian people choose her, rather than anyone else, as the object of their adoration? Our story will concern the Hungarian people and the attitudes that shaped the cult, rather than its object.

Franz Joseph I formally ascended to the Hungarian throne in 1867, but his effective rule began much earlier. Still vivid in the nation's consciousness was 1849, and the oppression and humiliation of the 'long 1850s' that followed. The executions and absolutist rule which characterized this period were as much his initiative as the legality and period of consolidation that followed 1867. Even in the latter period the King endeavoured to keep afloat the symbols of the dark 1850s. He had a predisposition to use the colours of the Austrian flag – black and yellow – and the *Gotterhalte* (Austrian national anthem), and placed great emphasis on the cult of the Imperial Army that had taken up arms against the Hungarian people so ruthlessly. The coronation in no way marked a change of sentiment: he continued to regard Heinrich Hentzi, the Imperial Commander who fell during the siege of Buda, as a 'Modern Leonidas'. Hentzi's memorial – which was designed by Wilhelm Strenger and used to stand in Szent György tér (Saint George's Square) in the Buda Castle – and his commemoration were particularly close to the King's heart.

The political regime which came to power after the Compromise of 1867, though legitimate, was not devoid of ambivalence, both emotional and in regard to its identity; the Hungarian people had to reconcile their notion of legality and their historical dislike of Austrian rule with all the consequences of such an ambivalent psychological condition. What is more, the King's personality did not help to resolve this ambivalence. Franz Joseph I was a man of average intellect combined with an extraordinary sense of duty, discipline and ambition, a rigid personality devoid of humour or charm, and cursed with poor conversational skills. His personal deficiencies were compounded for Hungarians by memories of an unpleasant past and the fact that they would have to put up with him until the day he died.

Was there any possibility of resolving this situation? And if so, by what means?

Ever since the awakening of their national consciousness during the Reform Period, the Hungarian people had subconsciously sought a patron in the Habsburg dynasty as some form of alliance with it seemed ever more inevitable. The 'Hungarianization' of at least one member of the dynasty emerged as a psycho-political necessity, despite the fact that in crisis situations such aspirations always turned out to be illusory. This was the only way in which an emerging national feeling could be reconciled with the reality of foreign rule, not to mention with incorporation in a foreign empire. In the Reform Period, the object of a similar cult had been Joseph Palatine (or József Nádor as he was known in Hungary) who acted his role with aplomb. (His statue – by Johann Halbig – stands in Budapest to this day.) It must be said that the Palatine was lucky to have died in 1847, before the outbreak of the 1848–9 conflict between the Hungarian nation and the Habsburg Dynasty, and so escape having to reveal his true sympathies. His son István could not cope with a similar role and in the autumn of 1848 fled from Hungary. In 1847, even Franz Joseph had been the object of a national wish to see him as a 'good Hungarian'. He gave rise to unanimous acclaim when, upon the orders of Ferdinand V, he presided over István's inauguration as Lord Lieutenant of Pest County – and as Palatine – *in Hungarian*. It soon transpired, however, that the image of a Hungarian-Habsburg king was no more than an illusion: nothing in Franz Joseph's reign thereafter justified revision of this view.

From the mid-1860s, however, Elisabeth of Bavaria gradually came to take on the psychological role which, with the death of Joseph Palatine, had been left vacant.

In order to appreciate this psychological need fully, the traditional loyalty of the peasantry to the sovereign on the basis of the belief that he was their chief patron and protector against the nobility must be understood. The events of 1848–9, the Compromise and the combination of national with social grievances did great damage to this naive faith but did not altogether remove the yearning for a father figure.

9   Franz Joseph, King of Hungary, 1898

In the popular consciousness Lajos Kossuth came to replace the King as the father with a strict but fair hand. This was not altered by the fact that, after 1849, Governor Kossuth had no effective political influence over the lives of the peasantry; he continued to be known as 'our Father Kossuth' until the end of his long life, and even afterwards. It is a fair assumption that this yearning for a father figure would have faded had Hungary's history taken a more democratic turn – in other words, if the events of 1848–9 had come to a successful conclusion. If Kossuth's political programme had been implemented, there would have been no need for a Kossuth myth to comfort the nation in its abjection. That Hungary took a very different course can partly be blamed upon Franz Joseph I.

At the same time, faith in the King continued to a limited extent, partly as a matter of tradition and partly in view of the fact that the sovereign legitimately enjoyed considerable powers. Legitimacy was an important consideration, given that the Hungarian intelligentsia who had controlled the consciousness of the masses had founded its entire political programme upon legitimacy and the rule of law (they even called the events of 1848–9 a war of self-defence). In light of this, the sovereign could not be banished from the national consciousness merely because of any personal deficiencies he might have or because he constituted a foreign power.

It is a commonly recognized phenomenon in mass psychology that in societies where the top of the social and political hierarchy is beyond the reach of the ordinary citizen, the latter seeks somehow to bridge the gap. In Hungary the masses projected certain habits, views and attitudes of their own onto the figure of the sovereign and then onto Kossuth, who was generally accepted as leader of the nation. The perception of a resemblance – however illusory – between the common people and their leader has a reassuring effect, indicating that the latter is as human as we are; in turn, we must somehow resemble our superior, and on this basis have good reason to consider ourselves higher up the social ladder than we really are. In this way the masses can approach what otherwise would be entirely inaccessible to them. This phenomenon is also exploited by authoritarian regimes: an otherwise comprehensively repressed society is furnished with self-esteem with no risk of a rebellion.

With this in mind we should find it easier to disentangle the complex threads of social and political psychology which underlay the acceptance and rejection of Franz Joseph and, subsequently, the cult of Elisabeth of Bavaria.

Franz Joseph's personality and political image were out of step with the world view of the Hungarian peasantry, among whom the Kossuth myth flourished. Although the image created for him by official propaganda resembled that of Matthias Corvinus, Hungary's renaissance king, famous for his sense of justice and concern for the lower classes, there is no indication that a Franz Joseph cult ever got off the ground. Nevertheless, József Kristóffy argued in 1905:

After the lesson of 1849 this nation will never rise against your Royal Highness or your successors . . . The Hungarian peasant cannot be incited [to fight against the King] because in his eyes the King is the supreme 'overseer' of whose assistance he stands in great need: the King is there to keep an eye on state officials and to protect [the peasant] against their depredations should it prove necessary.

Kristóffy's appeal to the people's faith in the King notwithstanding, by the time it was written, Franz Joseph was no longer perceived as the nation's all-powerful protector. Nevertheless, the desire for a Habsburg ruler possessing Hungarian national feeling and a Hungarian temperament remained.

If the object of this desire was not Franz Joseph, who was it to be? The lucky person was Prince Rudolf, whose image was transformed into that of a folk hero. Lajos Kiss, the renowned ethnographer, includes the following Rudolf legend in his Hódmezővásárhely collection:

I was an eight year old schoolboy when Rudolf died. Coming from a poor family I heard many legends about him both at home and elsewhere, about his death, life, disappearance and wanderings. Of the more typical stories I recall the following:

As soon as the news of Rudolf's death spread throughout the country, rumour had it that his father had killed him because of [Rudolf's] great love for the Hungarian people – Rudolf was every inch a true Hungarian. When he wished to amuse himself he would order a gypsy to play Hungarian music for him on the violin. His favourite songs were: 'I Had a Mother Once' and 'Lajos Kossuth's Message Reads' [a popular song among Hungarian revolutionaries in their fight against the Austrians (!)]. He could also see through his father's ministers.

One day Rudolf led a very fat horse out of the stable and when his father asked why, he answered:

'This is how fat your ministers are.'

Then a horse which was all skin and bones was dragged before them.

'And this is your poor nation.'

Finally, a blind horse was led out.

'And this is you, father, because you have no eyes for the nation's misery and for the fact that the great ones are parasites on your people.'

These are the kinds of things that made his father angry with him.

The Rudolf legends are ample evidence that the Hungarian people sought elsewhere what they could not find in the sovereign.

It is, of course, not true that the King had his son murdered: we know that in 1889 Rudolf committed suicide. But it was common knowledge that he and his father did not get along: Franz Joseph's insensitivity and rigid adherence to the law of matrimony (Rudolf wanted a divorce) did not help to resolve their conflicts. The Hungarian people's dislike of Franz Joseph naturally led them to an affinity for Rudolf, regardless of his personal merits. It is significant that the news of Rudolf's death was not believed for a long time.

The following is another story from Hódmezővásárhely:

During the [First] World War Rudolf again became the subject of much talk. Even those who at first listened with suspicion later came to the conclusion that he was still alive. Some even claimed to know where he was:

'Of course, Rudolf has been wandering ever since his mother died, and he has been wandering in America. He did not tell his father how he was getting on or where he was, but as soon as the War broke out he telegraphed: "Do you need me?"

His father replied: "Since we have managed without you until now, no doubt we will get through this by our own efforts. But if you want to, you may come." '

In the nation's imagination, the good prince had either to die or go wandering – and all because of his father's malevolence. The King could not endure Rudolf's genuine Hungarian spirit, love of the Hungarian people and good heart. This was partly in praise of Rudolf and partly a criticism of Franz Joseph. Prince Rezső (as Rudolf's name was Hungarianized), the heir to the throne, and his father were considered polar opposites; from which comparison Franz Joseph came off very much second best.

But how can this be reconciled with the familiar-patriarchal Hungarian name, Ferenc Jóska, which was widely used in reference to Franz Joseph: surely this nickname indicates some degree of affection for him? The name Ferenc Jóska is partly of folk origin – it figures in the songs of regular soldiers in the Austro-Hungarian army, but in a particular context. The following lines come from the literary periodical *Magyar Szalon*, in 1892:

In Ferenc Jóska's courtyard there is a pond
A Hungarian Hussar fell into it on his horse
The horse's leg is being looked after by the Chief Vet
But the poor Hussar is not lamented by anyone.

When Ferenc Jóska mounts his horse
He remembers the times when he was a recruit
He wipes the tears from his eyes
But how much does a Hussar have to suffer?
He freezes in a riding school in the winter
And he gets soaking wet in the camp in the summer.

It would be difficult to discover a trace of warmth in these passages, even with the help of the most ingenious methods of textual analysis. The name is adapted to fit comfortably in a peasant's patriarchal world-view, but its bearer is associated with feelings of suffering and defencelessness, and a world in which a horse receives more care and attention than a human being who frequently risks his life for his King.

At the same time, other army songs – faithful to the spirit of the joint army – feature Franz Joseph as the King and Emperor. What could be the relationship between a Hungarian peasant boy and the Emperor, one might ask? While the name Ferenc Jóska is undoubtedly familiar it does not express the Hungarian people's willingness to accept its bearer. On the contrary, these songs express the incommensurable distance between the regular soldier and his supreme commander. The familiar-patriarchal name could only attempt to bridge this distance, it could not reduce it.

The nickname was much in use among the middle classes. It did not refer to the King himself, but designated a kind of jacket *de rigueur* for distinguished social occasions. Wearing the *ferencjóska* meant being presentable in 'good society'. This was a peculiar form of adjustment to the manners of the higher social classes: by wearing the frockcoat, or *ferencjóska*, a Hungarian gentleman set himself apart from his inferiors and claimed kinship with those above him. Such kinship was an illusion. In the Imperial Court the frockcoat would not have been considered presentable at all; in such elevated circles tails or festive Hussar dress were the norm. Still, the clothes one wears are one way of laying claim to a particular social status. Because the claimed status was, in this case, entirely imaginary it was sufficient that the name of the relevant garment had some connection, however tenuous, with the King. Most of those who proudly donned the *ferencjóska* could not expect much more: apart from the fact that they could not afford tails or festive hussar dress, they were never invited to social occasions where they would have been required. Through this turn of phrase the King is presented as a member of the petty bourgeoisie, someone who uses Jewish jargon, plays cards for small stakes and who reads the same newspapers as his fellows. No one seemed to care that this illusion had little in common with reality. On the contrary: even the highest political circles were not averse to circulating such obvious nonsense, for the simple reason that in this way the King at least emerged as a flesh and blood creature.

The petty bourgeoisie was the social stratum where, if anywhere, patriarchal feelings for the King could be found. For members of this class it was vital to keep well informed about everything concerning the sovereign, including his catarrh and anything else that which might point to similarities between the great lord and his faithful vassals.

In the magazine *Alkotmány* (Constitution), published on 3 June 1914, we find the following description:

230 Modern Hungarian Society in the Making

Yesterday the sovereign was in an excellent mood and in good health, defying the baneful influence of the weather; his doctors found his condition entirely satisfactory in the course of his evening check-up. Shortly after eight o'clock the King retired to bed and immediately fell asleep. He appeared so well that his personal physician did not deem it necessary to remain in the adjoining room overnight, as he was in the habit of doing in the initial stages of an illness, and went home as he had on a number of occasions in recent days. The King awoke with an irritation of the throat shortly after midnight; the irritated throat and a slight secretion of mucus continued to disturb his repose until morning. Despite this, the King rose at the usual hour, enjoyed a good breakfast and lunch and spent the rest of the day in his study dealing with important state matters. Naturally, his fitful night's sleep had left him less robust than in recent days, but this should represent no cause for concern: it is expected that the irritation in his throat will be but a temporary phenomenon, the royal physicians having concluded that the loosening of the catarrh and the retrogression of other symptoms are now fully under way. The following statement has been issued on the condition of His Royal Highness: Slight disturbance of night's repose – General condition satisfactory.

A similar report was issued every day of the year. The nation was left in no doubt concerning the condition of the King's catarrh, making it possible for everyone to share their concern for him and to discuss his condition at length. It appears to be a thrilling experience for some to discover that even the greatest and most powerful of men are vulnerable human beings. Béla Barabás, an independent member of parliament not devoid of petty bourgeois sentiments himself, counted it among the most touching memories of his life when the sovereign called Elisabeth of Bavaria 'my wife' in his presence. It meant that a wife was only a wife even in the Royal Family.

As we have seen, some social classes tended to mould the King in their own image: the peasantry rejected him and transformed his son into a folk hero, while the petty bourgeoisie found relief in making the King into the very model of a philistine.

The gentry was more ambivalent; for them, the King was the object of both total loyalty and total rejection. When a party of gentlemen had had a few too many one of them would always ask the gypsy violinist to play a bawdy song in the spirit of the following:

> Oh, the German is a crafty one
> Why does not the Devil eat
> His lungs and liver
> As well as his rib [a Hungarian slang term for 'wife'].

Nevertheless, another member of the party would almost certainly invite his fellows to drink to the King's health as soon as the song had finished, and everyone would join in shouting 'Long live the King!' The bourgeoisie seemed to have a double consciousness: one minute they would pose as the champions of Hungarian national resistance, and the next they would stick out their chests in the front row of a delegation welcoming their foreign overlord. For many, there appeared no contradiction in hanging the portraits of both Franz Joseph and Lajos Kossuth, next to each other. They declared their loyalty to the King of Hungary, but were unwilling to give up the 1848 spirit of resistance. When there was a political crisis, nothing was simpler than to utter the magic words – as was often done among parties of friends as described by Miklós Bánffy's portrait of the period entitled *Megszámláltattál* . . . (the title is a quotation from the Bible, literally: 'to have been measured and found too light') – 'The old executioner must be sacked from the Castle, and have done with it!' Too many words seldom result in action. But even this kind of patriotism both indicated and consolidated emotional rejection of the sovereign; those who set the tone had to find someone else onto whom what the King lacked could be projected.

The choice eventually fell upon Elisabeth of Bavaria, a royal figure with a history as the protector of the Hungarian people during the years of absolutism. Her role in bringing about the Compromise was also emphasized and much made of her supposed love for Hungary. Elisabeth already had her own political and psychological cult before Rudolf came to be blessed in the same manner. To a nation fundamentally oriented towards the past, it seemed quite obvious to return again and again to a notion that had already been widely circulated in newspaper articles and oral tradition and so to further heighten sympathy for Elisabeth. And Elisabeth was sensitive enough to seek to confirm such expectations by subtle signs of favour. After the Compromise she continued to appear grateful for Hungary's regard for her. Probably one of her most frequently quoted remarks was addressed to the writer Mór Jókai in 1873, words the Hungarian press ensured would go down in history: '[In Hungary] one feels eternally free.'

Those gazing through red-white-and-green spectacles and dreaming of a dynasty with Hungarian sympathies were entirely won over, discovering in this sentence infallible proof that Elisabeth adored Hungary, the Hungarian people and, unlike her husband the King, would not keep her sentiments a secret. Unfortunately, a letter written by the Queen to her mother from Gödöllő reveals a more prosaic reality: 'Here, far away from relatives and free from harassment, one is so free, whereas [in Vienna] one is surrounded by the whole Imperial Family. Here no one disturbs me, as if I were living in a village where I can come and go as I please.'

But the Hungarian people were not looking to understand Elisabeth; their sole desire was to integrate her in their own world-view. Indeed, as time

10   Queen Elisabeth of Bavaria, 1867

went on the Hungarian people professed to discover ever more similarities between their own plight and that of the Queen. Elisabeth was unable to break her alliance with her husband any more than the Hungarian nation could. At the same time, she, like the Hungarian people, would not simply abandon him. But Elisabeth's increasingly frequent travels without her husband and her separate agenda seemed to indicate that, again like the Hungarian people, she would leave him if she could. On top of everything else, Elisabeth was a beautiful woman, ever the potential object of tender feelings. National feeling combined loyalty, chivalry and admiration for Elisabeth and rejection of Franz Joseph. Elisabeth surrounded herself with Hungarian maids and minded not at all being known in Western Europe as the 'Hungarian woman'. But her true love was less the Hungarian people than her independence; less Hungarian soil, as such, than Gödöllő, where she could 'come and go as she pleased' and indulge her passion for horseriding.

Sándor Márki, the Queen's biographer, calculated that Elisabeth spent not much more than seven years in Hungary (114 days before 1867 and the remainder in the period between 1867 and her death in 1898). In the 44 years of her married life, the Queen was to be found six times as often outside Hungary as within it, though between 1868 and 1897 not a year went by without her visiting Hungary at least once. Perhaps more significant is the fact that all but 69 days of her time in Hungary were spent in Gödöllő – where the Hungarian people had made her the gift of a palace – and in Budapest, when duty beckoned. Márki wrote:

> She spent five weeks in Mehádia (1887) and four and a half weeks in Bártfa (1895); she once visited Zagreb and Fiume, but otherwise never entertained herself in Hungary [outside Gödöllő and Budapest], the natural beauty of which interested her so little that she travelled through Transylvania for the first time on a night express train (on 17 April 1887) and passed by the High Tatra Mountains in such bad weather (on 23 July 1895) that she could not see a thing. She never made the visit to Balatonfüred [a lake resort] which she had always planned, nor to Kovászna.

Elisabeth, an enthusiastic traveller, was little interested in Hungary.

In many stories, Elisabeth inspires sympathy because of her unfair treatment at the hands of her husband. Cecília Szekeres's 1987 collection includes the following anecdote told by an eighty year old peasant:

> And Franz Joseph was a great villain, you know. Jóska – as the old man called him – would sneak out every night while they were staying here to visit a peasant maid. He was such a greedy man. The Queen could not complain about this, though maybe she was glad he left her alone.

(Whatever credence might be given to this story, it nevertheless hints at the real relationship of the King and Queen.) Elisabeth emerged as role model for the Hungarian gentry, having done almost nothing to deserve the honour.

Two minor incidents illustrate the extent to which the Elisabeth cult had become a mass psychological phenomenon. In 1889, the Lower House was in turmoil over the new Defence Act. The opposition had organized a twenty thousand-strong demonstration against the proposal to make the rank of army officer dependant upon the possession of a language certificate in German. Many banners bore the inscription: 'Long live Lajos Kossuth!', while the masses shouted 'Long live the King!', at the same time demanding that the relevant passage of the act – included at the King's express wish – be withdrawn. The demonstration culminated in Franz Joseph tér (today: Roosevelt Square), in front of the Lloyd Building which housed the governing party's club. Mór Szatmári, an eyewitness, described the events as follows:

> The crowd turned to face the Royal Palace and thousands of hats were waved in the air. The King was hailed. Then the human river moved onto the Corso [a promenade by the river Danube], every flag was lowered towards the Royal Buda Palace and the words were taken up by everyone:
>   'Long live the King!'
>   I wonder whether Franz Joseph I was watching? I doubt it. But whether he was or not this was the climax of the whole demonstration as the protesting masses paid tribute to the Hungarian King. All eyes were fixed on the palace windows: will any of them open? Is there someone behind them?
>   Suddenly a murmur began to circulate in the crowd: a white female hand had been seen waving a white handkerchief from one of the windows. There was no doubt that both hand and handkerchief belonged to Queen Elisabeth. Hundreds confirmed aloud that they too had seen the white handkerchief. In fact, no one had seen anything. Patriotic fantasies and the crowd's auto-suggestion were at play. But the legend grew and so did the number of those who believed in it.

The myth – undisturbed by facts – continued to live and thrive.

In 1894, Kossuth died and his ashes were laid to rest on Hungarian soil. A crowd of a hundred thousand paid their last respects to Franz Joseph's great antagonist. The government was not officially represented at the funeral: the Prime Minister, Dezső Bánffy, claimed to have urgent matters to attend to. Ordinary Hungarians, naturally, sought to satisfy both sides of their split consciousnesses. They wished to find similarities between Kossuth's funeral and that of Deák 18 years before. At Deák's funeral, though the King had excused himself, Elisabeth paid her respects at the catafalque and Kossuth, then in exile, sent cypress boughs to the funeral of his former comrade and godfather of his eldest son, their conflicting views on the Compromise notwithstanding. The fact that the King and the government had chosen not to pay their respects, while the whole nation mourned their 'Father', might have had serious consequences had the story not got around that among the many thousands of wreathes lay one dispatched in secret by Queen Elisabeth, who – in defiance of her husband – positively admired Kossuth, the hero of the Hungarian Revolution and Freedom Fight, its once living symbol. Elisabeth's wreath served as clear proof that it was possible both to serve Franz Joseph and to feel an affinity with Kossuth, at least symbolically.

The fact is that Queen Elisabeth had not sent a wreath, nor had she waved a white handkerchief. But this is beside the point. The cult of Queen Elisabeth was needed to reconcile the deep-seated ambivalence inevitably brought into being by historical conditions and it must be said that she played her role – as the personification of qualities that she lacked quite as much as her husband, Franz Joseph – well.

Just as the peasant consciousness had framed Rudolf's suicide to its own liking, so the consciousness of the gentry presented the death of Elisabeth, suggesting she had been murdered. Two years after the queen's death, Gyula Gábel published a book in her honour, including the reminiscences of members of the Habsburg dynasty and outstanding Hungarian public figures which clearly reveal the extent of the mythology surrounding the Queen's person. Some of these stories could not be openly discussed before, not because it was forbidden, but because while Elisabeth was alive the facts of her life too obviously belied them.

The pearl of the writings dedicated to the national cult of Queen Elisabeth was a poem by Lajos Pósa entitled 'The Queen's Dream' ('*A királyné álma*'), of which the following is an extract:

> What was the dream, our good Queen,
> That you saw in your Crypt in Vienna?
> 'I dreamt I was back at home
> In my beautiful Hungary.'
>
> [. . .]
>
> I dreamt there was heavy rainfall:
> Not from the drizzly skies,
> But from the sad eyes
> Of my faithful Hungarian people.

In accordance with Habsburg custom, Elisabeth was buried in the Capiscan Crypt in Vienna. Later in the poem the tears of the sad Hungarian people grow into a sea which penetrates the Crypt, lifts up the coffin and carries it back to Hungary to rest, for which in the last line of the poem the poet asks the blessing of God.

After her death, Hungary became Elisabeth's undisputed homeland. And this homeland is grateful for the privilege: a number of posthumous memorials and statues were erected to Elisabeth. (The first, in Felsőmuzsa, dates back to 1899.) In 1932, the Elisabeth Memorial was finally completed, after many vicissitudes, from donations that started to come in soon after her murder. 'If her tomb must be in Vienna, she must at least have her statue in Budapest, the city that she so dearly loved,' wrote *Vasárnapi Újság* (The Sunday Newspaper) eight days after the assassination. (Today the statue – by György Zala – stands at the Buda end of the bridge over the Danube named after her.)

Elisabeth's undoubtedly attractive person became the object of a national cult largely because of the ambivalent relationship between Franz Joseph and the Hungarian people, which cherishes her memory and the faith it has invested in her to the present day.

(1992)

Bibliography

The first work in Hungarian historiography to be devoted entirely to the person of Queen Elisabeth of Bavaria was by Sándor Márki, *Erzsébet, Magyarország királynéja* [Elisabeth, Queen of Hungary], a memorial speech held at the Gala General Assembly of the Franz Joseph Royal Academy of Sciences on 19 November 1989 in Cluj (Kolozsvár).

Contemporary publications quoted in the text are:

Gyula Gábel (ed.), *Erzsébet. Megemlékezés Magyarország nagy királynéjáról* [In Memoriam Elisabeth, Queen of Hungary], Budapest, 1900. A new, more representative edition was published in 1906.

There are a number of local publications about Queen Elisabeth, but one often gets the impression that the authors were seeking to commemorate themselves more than anything else. See: Gyula Telléry (ed. and publisher), *A Szepesség gyásza, Emlékalbum Erzsébet királyné emlékére* [Szepesség in Mourning: Album Dedicated To The Memory of Queen Elisabeth], Budapest, 1899; and Dezső Arányi (ed.), *Emléklapok dicsőült Erzsébet királyné szobrának Bártfafürdőn 1903. évi augusztus 16–án történt leleplezése alkalmából* [Memorial Lists Commemorating The Unveiling of The Late Queen Elisabeth's Statue At Bártfafürdő on 16 August 1903], Bártfa, 1903.

In the period between the two world wars Elisabeth inspired a novel: Julianna Zsigray's *Erzsébet, magyar királyné* [Elisabeth, Queen of Hungary], 1937. Interest in Elisabeth never abated: on 5 December 1935 an auction was held of the books and relics of Queen Elisabeth. (The Auction Catalogue gives a detailed description of the items on sale: *Erzsébet királyné hagyatékában maradt díszművek műbecsű emlékkönyvek és egyéb műkincsek* [Queen Elisabeth's Legacy: Decorative Articles, Collectors Books and Works of Art], Budapest, 1935.)

On sculptures of Elisabeth see: *Erzsébet királyné emléke* [Queen Elisabeth's Memory], Report by Count Gyula Foster, President of the Executive Committee commissioned by the National Committee set up in connection with the memorial statue to Queen Elisabeth, Budapest, 1907. On the history and for a description of the statue erected in 1932, removed in 1953 and reinstalled in 1986, and other Elisabeth memorials in Budapest see: György Rajna, *Budapest köztéri szobrainak katalógusa* [Catalogue of Public Statues in Budapest], Budapest, 1989.

The most recent book on the murder of Queen Elisabeth is the work of Emil Niederhauser, *Merénylet Erzsébet királyné ellen* [Queen Elisabeth's Assassination], Budapest, 1985. In the 1986/3 issue of the cultural magazine *Valóság*, a study by John T. Salvendy analyses the personality of Elisabeth, among other figures, from the point of view of modern psychology. The many recent publications directly or indirectly concerned with Elisabeth indicate a continuing interest in the subject: András Gerő: *Ferenc József, a magyarok királya* [Franz Joseph, King of Hungary], Budapest, 1988; Éva Somogyi, *Ferenc József* [Franz Joseph], Budapest, 1989. A reprint of Egon Casar Corti's 1935 biography of Elisabeth (1989); and Brigitte Hamann's *Queen Elisabeth* in Hungarian translation [*Erzsébet királyné*], 1988. Finally, mention should be made of *Három nemzedék ereklyetárgyai a Magyar Nemzeti Múzeumban (1823–75)* [The Relics of Three Generations at the National Museum of Hungary, 1823–75], Budapest, 1988, a publication including relics of Queen Elisabeth among others.

The Grafenegy Exhibition and its documentation published in four volumes touched upon the cult of Elisabeth in Hungary but did not discuss it in detail: *Das Zeitalter Kaiser Franz Josephs 1848–80*, Vols. 1–2, 1984, and *1880–1916*, Vols. 1–2, 1987. A further exhibition at the Museum of History in Vienna was documented in: *Elisabeth von Österreich*, Vienna, 1987.

On the 150th Anniversary of Queen Elisabeth's birth, exhibitions were held in Szeged and Gödöllő. The Szeged exhibition was complemented by an Exhibition Guide, while in Gödöllő a fifty page publication was produced for the Anniversary: *Városi Helytörténeti Gyűjtemény kiállítása Erzsébet királyné születésének 150. Évfordulójára* [Local History Exhibition on the 150th Anniversary of Queen Elisabeth's Birth], Gödöllő, 1987. The 1987/10 issue of the magazine *Gödöllői Mindenes* contains modern ethnographic collections in a section entitled '*Emlékek a királynéról*' [Memories of the Queen]. A number of the quotations in the present work come from here. A large number of Queen Elisabeth relics featured in the exhibition of the National Museum of Hungary entitled '*Kiegyezés, 1867*' [The Compromise, 1867], organized by Katalin Körmöczi, who also wrote the guidebook.

In 1991, the Eisenstadt Museum of Culture in Austria devoted a modest exhibition to Elisabeth's memory, partly based on Hungarian materials and entitled 'Elisabeth, Queen of the Hungarian People'.

Other works cited in the present volume are: *Magyarország kálváriája. Az összeomlás útja. Politikai emlékek 1890–1926* [Hungary's Calvary: On the Road to Collapse, Political Memoirs, 1890–1926 – the memoirs of József Kristóffy], Budapest, 1927; and *Emlékirataim. 1850–1929* [Memoirs, 1850–1929], Arad, 1929. I also consulted various newspapers and journals, which I have indicated in the text. The collection of folk legends regarding Rudolf referred to is the work of Lajos Kiss, *Vásárhelyi Kistükör* [Vásárhely Mirror], Budapest, 1964. I have also made reference to the landmark work of Mór Szatmári, *Húsz év parlamenti viharai* [Twenty Years in Parliament], Budapest, 1928.

13 March the Fifteenth

The bloodless revolution that was started by young, radical Hungarian intellectuals in Pest (the flat side of today's Budapest) on 15 March 1848 set the political stage for getting Hungary out of the feudal rut. The programme they asserted had been gradually elaborated over the preceding two decades by reform-minded deputies of aristocratic origin, both in the Diet (assembly of estates) and in the press. These liberal noblemen demanded equality before the law, the compulsory abolition (with compensation) of peasants' dues and services, and sovereignty for Hungary, but they lacked the political strength to realize their aims. It was the wave of revolutions throughout Europe in 1848 and the popular fervour of the citizens of Pest on 15 March of that year that brought the long-awaited breakthrough which, on 11 April, resulted in promulgation of the laws embodying the evolution of a parliamentary political system. The Habsburg court at first seemed willing to accept this turn of events.

After this honeymoon period, however, Vienna sought to instigate civil war between the Hungarian and non-Hungarian sections of the population, sent Austrian troops to quell the uprising and, when these measures proved fruitless, appealed to the Tsar. As a bastion of conservatism and with a larger field army than any other European nation, Russia was quick to lend a hand. Overpowered by intervention from all sides, the Hungarian leaders had no other option but to surrender. In August 1849, the Hungarian revolution and war of independence were crushed.

Now that we have summed up the facts associated with 15 March 1848, it should be easy to understand why it has become the symbol of two sequences of historical events in the Hungarian mind: the age of reform that culminated in a revolution, and an heroic armed struggle, which involved the proclamation of national independence, waged for political and social freedom.

Back in 1848–9, the importance of those events was clear to all. In fact, certain episodes, personalities and symbols were immediately placed in the nation's spiritual pantheon. The Hungarian revolution contributed in no small measure to the formation of the Hungarian national consciousness – no wonder it became part of Hungarian mythology. The statesman who served as minister of finance in the revolutionary government and as Governor of Hungary in 1849, became 'Kossuth, our father' in Hungarian folklore; and when he entered the town of Debrecen, the gatekeeper wrote under 'occupation': 'the Moses of the Magyars'. The radical young intellectuals probably drew upon their studies of the French Revolution when they chose the cockade in the national colours of red, white and green as the symbol of their own revolution. (Members of 1956's voluntary army of national self-defence would use the same red, white and green colours to decorate their armbands.)

Contemporaries did not regard 15 March and its aftermath as a time for celebration however, nor did they have time to indulge themselves, engaged as they were in making history. Not that solemn words and deeds were entirely absent. A fine example of this was the occasion when radical intellectuals seized (without encountering any resistance) printing presses in order to issue a handbill carrying their twelve principal demands and another carrying Sándor Petőfi's revolutionary poem, 'Arise, Hungarians!'. Those present knew that they had witnessed the birth of a free press in Hungary. In the same solemn manner they set free one of the few (in fact, two!) political prisoners, Mihály Táncsics, a left-wing writer and politician. They were fully aware that there was more at stake than the freedom of one man: rather, the freedom of political persuasion itself.

Lajos Kossuth often spoke in a lofty style, and not just because he was a gifted orator and because Romanticism remained a strong influence at this period. When, in July 1848, his appeal for money and a large number of new recruits for the defence of the homeland was approved in the Diet by acclamation, he expressed the hope that, if its implementation were as enthusiastic as its approval, Hungary could not be destroyed even by 'the gates of hell'. Contemporaries, sensing and appreciating the solemnity of the biblical reference, overlooked the fact that gates rarely destroy anything.

The heady period between 15 March 1848 and 13 August 1849 (the date of surrender to the Russians at Világos) saw many memorable occasions suitable for later celebration. It was left to subsequent generations to decide whether this opportunity should be taken up.

The fifteenth of March only had one real rival: 14 April 1849, when the Hungarian Diet declared Hungary an independent state. (The Declaration of Independence was promulgated on 16 April.) Had the independent Hungarian state been able to survive, it would probably have traced its birth to that day, and celebration of 16 April would have been irresistible. The drafters of the declaration, principally Kossuth, were well aware of this. The adoption of the declaration was made a solemn ceremony – the deputies of the Diet approved it in the largest Calvinist cathedral in Debrecen, the town to which they had fled from the advancing Austrian troops, and the document was richly ornamented.

This rival to 15 March had a number of serious drawbacks, however. As an official state function it could not be considered a spontaneous act of popular history-making. More importantly, united as the members of the rump Diet seemed on this issue, there was no real consensus over the declaration. This may have been one of the reasons why it was silent on Hungary's future form of government (later defined as republican by Prime Minister Bertalan Szemere). The day the declaration was adopted was never as intimately associated with the concept of freedom to the extent that 15 March was.

Moreover, history did not allow Hungarian politicians to choose between the two days. Some 200,000 Russian and 160,000 Austrian troops converged on the country to restore Habsburg authority. The decision was left to the people.

An era of heavy-handed Habsburg absolutism followed, in which there could be no public reference to any such dangerous matters. Officially sanctioned terror came to be followed by a somewhat less repressive period, however, in which the Austrian bureaucracy and secret police managed the country's affairs, although no open expression of opposition to Habsburg rule was permitted. Even veiled protest could only be expressed indirectly at such apolitical occasions as the funeral in 1855 of the Hungarian poet Mihály Vörösmarty. Owing in part to a wind of change in European politics, Habsburg absolutism had lost some of its hauteur by the late 1850s, and nationalist protests became increasingly open. The fashion of wearing suits tailored in a traditional Hungarian style emerged, the centenary of the birth of Ferenc Kazinczy – the writer responsible for reforming the Hungarian language – was carefully observed, and performances of Ferenc Erkel's historical opera *László Hunyadi* were used to vent patriotic emotions.

Under repressive Habsburg absolutism both Hungarian national ideals and the notion of independence were officially rejected. Hungarians responded by seeking an institution that gave at least some degree of expression to their aspirations. They found one. But the first public commemoration of 15 March went down in the annals of Hungarian history as a tragic episode. It was in 1860 that some Hungarians, full of patriotic fervour, decided to go beyond the use of random occasions for the expression of nationalist protest.

On receiving the news that, after repeated attempts, the people of Tuscany and Modena had at last freed themselves from Habsburg rule and joined Piedmont under the Conte di Cavour, students in Pest decided to observe 15 March publicly. The Court in Vienna was clearly disconcerted; and while it did not dare to ban the demonstration, it used force to contain it. When a number of young demonstrators were about to march into a cemetery, army detachments at hand to maintain order opened fire. Several people were wounded and one of them, Géza Forinyák, later died. A large crowd, at least a quarter of the residents of Pest-Buda, joined his funeral cortège on 4 April.

The timing of this street demonstration showed that the Hungarian people had made up its mind regarding its national holiday. At a time when Hungary was under occupation by a foreign power, the ideals of both national progress and independence had come to be associated with this spontaneously chosen holiday. As the Hungarian government of the time was seen by most as representative of the alien oppressors, the holiday chosen by the people had to express opposition both to it and to the political status quo. That is why the rival 14 April, an event arranged from above, was pushed aside. That people were prepared even to risk their lives for it further enhanced the appeal of the new holiday of national freedom, independence for the political opposition – and independence for the man in the street, too. All subsequent governments were forced to recognize it at least to some degree.

It goes without saying that the neo-absolutist governments of the 1860s pretended they knew nothing of the birth of this popular holiday. Little changed even after 1867, when a compromise reached between the court in Vienna and some moderate Hungarian liberals restored limited autonomy to Hungary. Even if it had wanted to, however, the government of Austria-Hungary could not have given official status to 15 March, as King Franz Joseph would never have consented. The demands put forward on 15 March 1848 – the running of the country's affairs in accordance with a constitution approved by parliament, the assertion of national interests – remained in place, with few exceptions, after 1867. Several imperial prerogatives remained intact: foreign affairs, defence and their financing remained under joint Austrian-Hungarian control, and more and more landed estates were subject to entailment. In sum, the Hungarian authorities turned a deaf ear to the demands of 1848.

Although the Establishment disavowed it, 15 March and commitment to the ideals of 1848, in general, began to gain in popularity after 1867. Because Hungary proper was more or less a liberal country, society – but not the state – was allowed to make a more or less independent choice of a holiday and a cult to attach to it. In the final decades of the nineteenth century, the political opposition sought to utilize this (by now somewhat anachronistic) popular commitment to the ideals of 1848. It strove for the incorporation of 1848 in Hungarian popular mythology and to promote the cult of 15 March as far as it was able.

The tradition of 1848 was perpetuated in the various associations of veterans of the 1848–9 war of independence, in those of burghers and workers, and by those local authorities among whose constituencies the opposition was in a majority. Publishers of books and periodicals discovered that there was money to be made by satisfying popular interest in this topic. Statues of Kossuth were erected, financed by local government or public contributions, and their inaugurations were occasions on which tribute could be paid to the ideals of 1848. When, in 1882, the bronze statue of Sándor Petőfi (the work of the sculptors Miklós Izsó and Adolf Huszár) was erected on the bank of the Danube in the heart of Pest, Hungarians were presented with an ideal opportunity to commemorate 1848.

By contrast, the state remained inactive. The government was aware of this groundswell of popular feeling, but did not respond.

This paradoxical situation lasted until 1897, when Ferenc Kossuth (the son of Lajos Kossuth, who had died in exile in 1894; on resettling in Hungary, the younger Kossuth had become an opposition member of parliament) came forward with a recommendation to declare 15 March a national holiday. His proposal was timely because the fiftieth anniversary of 1848 was at hand.

The prime minister of the time, Count Dezső Bánffy, approved the idea of selecting a day for the commemoration of 1848. However, ignoring the choice of the people, he recommended a day that no one before him had considered a holiday, even if it did have some significance from a legal and constitutional point of view. He put forward 11 April, in commemoration of the laws consolidating the principles of the revolution. (Perhaps he chose 11 April because on that day in 1848, in Bratislava [Pozsony], the Archduke Franz Joseph was also present. Later, as King, speaking at the inauguration of the prime minister, Franz Joseph encouraged Bánffy to suppress the cult which had grown up around Lajos Kossuth.) Although the people had chosen 15 March, the parliament gave preference to 11 April as the official holiday. The decision was implemented in Law V of 1898.

The parliamentary majority was convinced that what they had done was the best possible solution. Hungarians now had the opportunity to commemorate 1848 with the blessing of the King. They cherished the hope that the memory of 15 March would gradually fade, in which hope they were to be disappointed. Their temporizing move backfired and further strengthened the unofficial holiday's popular appeal and oppositional character.

When in October 1918 a democratic revolution broke out in Hungary following the collapse of the Habsburg Empire, for a short while it seemed that 15 March would at last assume the position it deserved. The newly founded democratic republic, for which the political opposition had been fighting for so long, had a natural preference for this date as a symbolic representation of their ideals: equality before the law, independence, democracy and a compassionate social policy. That both society at large and the democratic government were in agreement regarding this holiday was shown by the manner in which 15 March was observed in 1919.

The short-lived democratic regime fell only six days later. The propaganda machine of the Soviet-type communist dictatorship that followed replaced national ideals with international ones, although it, too, was toppled before it had the chance to decide how it would commemorate the holiday of freedom and national independence.

How 15 March should be celebrated posed a difficult question for the authorities during the long rule of Regent Miklós Horthy. The conservative and authoritarian regime, which defined itself as counterrevolutionary, rejected anything that smacked of revolution, especially when it had a connection with the democratic revolution of 1918 – whose leaders had stressed their regime's continuity with the ideals of 1848 – and the communist episode of 1919. What is more, it went as far as ascribing the ills of Hungary to what it described as 'excessive freedom'. Everything seemed to militate against the celebration of 15 March. At the same time, the regime could not afford to pass up any opportunity allowing it to draw upon the heritage and principal symbols of 1848.

In 1920, Hungary – which had been on the losing side in the First World War – had to sign the treaty of Trianon, which gave to its neighbours two-thirds of its former territory and a third of the Hungarian population. As the Horthy regime sought the revision of that treaty, it badly needed an array of national ideals for the purpose of rallying popular support.

Although Hungary had ended up on the wrong side, it was by that time an independent country and some of the demands of 1848 were, consequently, no longer taboo. Hungary was still a monarchy, but – owing to international political considerations – the Habsburgs had had to forfeit the throne. In such circumstances, to pretend that 15 March did not exist would have been a grave mistake; the government knew that if it failed to exploit the potential inherent in the holiday of 15 March, the democratic and left-wing forces in opposition would do so instead.

It was several years however before the government was able to make up its mind. At last, the eightieth anniversary of the revolution offered the chance to celebrate without losing face. The dilemma was resolved by Minister of Culture Kunó Klebelsberg. He decided to 'nationalize' those parts of the 1848 ideology that suited the regime's requirements for an official holiday.

On 6 November 1927, a statue of Lajos Kossuth by János Horvay was unveiled in front of the parliament building. The idea had first been raised by the Budapest Metropolitan Council 24 years before. The mood of both Kossuth and his ministers of 1848 standing around him was represented as gloomy. On the back of the stone wall behind the statue there was a relief showing a man saying goodbye to his wife and child, an enthusiastic young man, a military drummer, an old man waving a flag, a man and his son as they set out for a battle, and a wounded soldier. The overall message of the

11 Celebration of the spirit of the nation (Béla Barabás addresses the crowds in front of the National Museum, 15 March 1906)

memorial was the militarization of the nation, rather than national freedom and independence. It conveyed the idea that the nation was ready to fight, despite oppression.

In the same month, the Upper House enacted Klebelsberg's bill (Law XXXI of 1927) in which 15 March was declared an official national holiday. (The same law annulled Law V of 1898 which declared 11 April a national holiday.) Law XXXII of 1927 spelled out Kossuth's undying virtues.

When selecting locations for this commemoration they opted, in addition to the obvious choice of Budapest's National Museum, for places that had little to do with 15 March, but were ideal for driving home the ideas of irredentism and militarism. That is why in subsequent years, 15 March was often observed in front of statues commemorating irredentism and before the National Memorial Stone of National Heroes in Budapest's Heroes' Square. (The inscription there reads: 'To regaining the thousand-year-old frontiers'.) The nationalization of 15 March marked the beginning of a process of expropriation. The further the authorities went in turning it into a vehicle for their own ends (for instance, as an occasion for admitting youths to the ranks of the *levente* [a paramilitary youth organization] or for the consecration of flags, etc.), the more popular the interpretation of the opposition, primarily the social democrats – to associate this holiday with freedom and the welfare of the people – became. The social democrats, whom the Horthy regime denounced as men without a homeland, cited the tradition established by the workers' associations under Austria-Hungary. The more democratically-minded among the burghers of Budapest also grew dissatisfied with the official commemorations and arranged their own, usually at the statue of Petőfi on the bank of the Danube. That is also where the most noteworthy 15 March opposition demonstration of the era took place, in 1942, when the speakers denounced fascism, hailed democracy and spoke of the genuine interests of the Hungarian nation.

In 1945, when the Red Army drove out the German army and occupied Hungary, one of the first measures of the new democratic government was to issue Prime Ministerial Decree No. 1390 of 1945 in which 15 March was declared a national holiday, although the war was still raging in some parts of the country. At the beginning, the political forces that accepted (or pretended to accept) parliamentary democracy staged joint memorials. The celebrations organized by the Hungarian Communist Party (MKP), however, indicated that the process of expropriating the ideals attached to this holiday was once again under way. The MKP posed as the heir – soon as the only heir – to the ideals of 1848. Accordingly, it selected personalities whom, after they had been provided with a suitable new identity, it could refer to as protocommunists. Sándor Petőfi, Mihály Táncsics and Lajos Kossuth were among those chosen, on the strength of their role in the Hungarian national mythology of 1848, for the job of legitimating Hungary's Soviet-type communism. By 1948, the centenary of the revolution, when the communists were in almost full possession of political power, the image of these personalities had been entirely remoulded. Among the other commemorative banners, the portrait of the all-powerful leader of the Communist Party, Mátyás Rákosi, was flanked by those of Petőfi and Kossuth.

By 1949, after they had eliminated all rival parties and forced the social democrats to join them, the communists, renamed the Hungarian Workers' Party (MDP), had gone further than any other political forces before them in expropriating the memory of 15 March. Hungary had by then been turned into a totalitarian state in which the respect for human rights was worse than under the Horthy regime.

The arrogance of the regime can be illustrated with a few examples. In 1951, with only five days to go until 15 March, the government issued a decree in which it was struck from the list of bank holidays. Although it remained the practice to celebrate 15 March, and schools were closed on that day, the trappings were changed. The national colours of red, white and green were amply complemented with red, the colour of the communists. The banners carried political slogans of the day and the portraits paraded included, in addition to Petőfi, Kossuth and Táncsics, those of Rákosi, Lenin and Stalin. As far as the presence of Stalin at the 15 March celebrations is concerned, it is enough to be aware of the following historical paradox, a visual realization of this theatre of the absurd. In 1849, it had been the intervention of the Russian tsar that struck the fatal blow to Hungary's drive for national independence. In the 1950s, the Stalinist oppressor, disguised as the Soviet ally, repeated the favour.

To match the dominant ideology of the 1950s, Horvay's gloomy statue of Kossuth in front of the parliament building had to be replaced, in September 1952, with an optimistic counterpart. Sculpted by Zsigmond Kisfaludy-Stróbl, András Kocsis and Lajos Ungvári, the monument – which is still there – comprises a five-metre-high figure of Governor Kossuth, flanked by a worker, a student and a peasant, all ready to attack the enemy. They are there to symbolize the strength of the alliance of workers and peasants as they work together with the intellectuals. As the years went by, it was noticed that the statue had begun to sink. When experts examined its foundations, it was revealed that the pedestal was hollow.

The revolution of 1956 (23 October–4 November) proved the futility of all attempts to misuse 15 March. Although the actual events did not take place in March, the ideals of 1848 played a key role in the ever stronger demand for destalinization and democratization, and in the uprising itself. Apart from the flag with a hole in place of the coat of arms, the revolutionaries used the symbols of 1848: the radical intellectuals' circle was named after Petőfi, the volunteers in the self-defence militia wore an armband in national colours, and the new coat of arms was that associated with Lajos

Kossuth. The holiday, always a grassroots institution of special significance to the opposition, retained its time-honoured features; during the 1950s it also survived because Hungary was not free. The politically oppressed people of an occupied country had no alternative but to hark back to ideals elaborated under similar conditions by previous generations.

The revolutionaries of 1956, of course, demanded that 15 March should again be an officially approved national holiday.

At first, the politicians installed in power by the mid-twentieth century Russian intervention seemed a little wiser than their counterparts of less than a century before. (By contrast, the authorities in the nineteenth century did not refer to 1848–9 as a counterrevolution.) In December 1956, the government issued a decree restoring 15 March to the status of national holiday, but only a few months later, again just five days before 15 March, the holiday was demoted to the rank of a working day for adults, although students did not have to go to school.

It became clear that the regime of János Kádár, the newly installed leader of the Communist Party, did not regard 15 March as a national holiday in the same way as his predecessor. The practice of expropriating the holiday was continued, but, although the colour red was ubiquitous, the portraits of the leaders were no longer displayed.

Year after year, 15 March was officially observed without genuine popular participation. Indifference set in, until members of the opposition organized alternative commemorations, especially in 1971 and 1972, when young demonstrators were dispersed by the police. In response to this development, government ideologists came up with a new way of remaking 15 March, in order to offset its oppositional character. So emerged the so-called 'revolutionary youth days', which survived to the middle of the 1980s. The fathers of this new device integrated into a single campaign of commemorations 15 March, 21 March – the day when the communists proclaimed their 'dictatorship of the proletariat' in 1919 – and 4 April, the day on which the Second World War ended for Hungary. The fathers of this scheme noted how close these days were to each other in the calendar; more importantly, they attempted to find a common denominator. It is as if the portraits of Lajos Kossuth, Béla Kun (leader of the short-lived communist regime in 1919) and, say, Marshal Malinovski (who was instrumental in occupying Hungary in 1944–5) were to be placed on the same banner. The 'revolutionary youth days' fared poorly, much as other similar communist devices had before and afterwards.

As the official celebrations were gradually losing popular appeal, from the early 1980s the democratic opposition began to stage counter-celebrations. These included a walk from the statue of Petőfi to the statue of the Polish-born hero of the 1848–9 Hungarian war of independence, General Jozef Bem. The purpose of the walk was to call attention to the continuity of 1848, 1956 and the events of the 1980s, when popular demands for democracy were becoming ever louder. Once again, it became clear that 15 March is the holiday of a national commitment to freedom which no government can exploit. Those who were there need only recall the number of uniformed (and plainclothes) police officers that the regime deemed necessary to keep order to measure its assessment of the potency of this date.

The status of 15 March changed in the late 1980s: the government restored it to the position of official national holiday in 1988. The decision – thirty-one years in the making – indicated a slackening of the dictatorship, and showed the government's readiness, finally, to face the fact that this day had been a holiday for Hungarians since 1860, regardless of the will of their overlords.

The final years of the decade witnessed something of a climax in the history of 15 March, as Hungarians sensed the imminence of freedom, national independence and democracy. Hundreds of thousands of people turned out for the celebration to listen to the words of people who, only two years before, had been harassed or even beaten up by the police. Banners carried demands for immediate change. The forces of law and order were still well-represented, but, as a bizarre twist of Hungarian history, policemen whose uniform caps were adorned by a red star, put cockades in national colours on their steely jackets. One was left to wonder which would have most influence should a disturbance arise. The popular 15 March commemorations went off without confrontation, indicating that an opportunity for a peaceful transition from dictatorship to democracy was at hand.

The manner in which 15 March was observed in 1990, a few days before the first free elections in forty years, revealed that the rival political forces disagreed on which of them should observe it, where and how. Later that same year, the freely elected multi-party parliament was faced with the problem of deciding what the principal national holiday of the democratic and independent Republic of Hungary (a 'people's democracy' no longer) should be. There were three possibilities: 15 March, 23 October (the day the revolution of 1956 broke out), and 20 August, associated with Saint István (King Stephen I), founder of the Hungarian state. When it came to a vote, 20 August was chosen (although some MPs did not vote with their party). The vote did not remove 15 March from the ranks of official national holidays, but it diminished its prestige. Once again, the powers that be chose not to take 15 March to their hearts.

Ever since it was spontaneously selected by Hungarians as their holiday, 15 March has suffered all the trials and tribulations a holiday could endure: persecution, denial, nationalization, expropriation and demotion. A string of governments did to it everything that a government could do to disappoint its people's ambitions. Nevertheless, 15 March has managed to retain its original mandate as the holiday of freedom and national independence for all Hungarians. As in 1848, it will remain nonconformist, rebellious and revolutionary.

(1992)

Bibliography

I have relied heavily on newspaper articles on the 15 March holiday, published throughout the period under consideration in this article, as they best indicate its prestige and the nature of the contemporary political context.

Interest in 1848–9 has been steady. Initiated by Martha Lampland and commissioned by the University of San Diego, Judit Bíró and Marcell Sebők have compiled a bibliography of publications on 1848–9 put out between 1849 and 1990. For the time being, it remains in typescript.

Regarding how 15 March was chosen as a holiday, see the introduction to György Szabad, *Forradalom és a kiegyezés válaszútján* (1860–61) [Between Revolution and Compromise (1867–1918)], Budapest, 1967; Szabad's book proves convincingly that the ideals of 1848–9 have had a long-lasting influence. On the demand that 14 April be selected as a national holiday, see the draft platform published on 14 April 1913 by the National Republican Party, in *A Magyar polgári pártok programjai* (1867–1918) [Programmes of the Hungarian Bourgeois Parties (1867–1918)], selected and edited by Gyula Mázi, Budapest, 1971, p. 289.

On the selection of the holiday under the Austro-Hungarian Monarchy, see Péter Hanák, '*1898 – a nemzeti és az állampatrióta értékrend frontális ütközése a Monarchiában*' [1898 – Confrontation Between National Ideals and Those of the State under the Monarchy], first published in *Medvetánc,* Nos. 2–3, 1984. On the ambiguities surrounding 15 March, see Mrs. Dezső Kosztolányi, *Dezső Kosztolányi,* Budapest, 1938.

On how 15 March was nationalized under the Horthy regime, see articles and parliamentary speeches by Kunó Klebelsberg. Regrettably, the ideological pattern of the Horthy regime as a whole has not yet been properly analysed. The relevant passages of the eighth volume of the *History of Hungary* (1976) are useless on this question. See, however, Miklós Szabó's collection of political essays: *Politikai kultúra Magyarországon 1896–1986* [Political Culture in Hungary, 1896–1986], Budapest, 1989. On how sculpture contributed to the making of cults in the Horthy era and in the 1950s, see György Rajna, *Budapest köztéri szobrainak katalógusa* [Catalogue of Statues in the Squares of Budapest], Budapest, 1989.

On the political atmosphere in 1948, the year of the centenary, and afterwards, see: *1848–49. Száz év a szabadságért* [1848–9: One Hundred Years in the Service of Freedom], Budapest, 1948. It includes papers by Sándor Haraszti, Mátyás Rákosi, Aladár Mód and Erzsébet Andics. On the role played by 1848 in the ideology of the era, see József Révai, *Válogatott történelmi írások I–II* [Selected historical writings], Budapest, 1966; and Márton Horváth, *Lobogónk, Petőfi* [Petőfi, Our Banner], Budapest, 1951. On legal regulations governing holidays in general after 1945, see the article by László Kovács Kikova and Kocsárd Székely in the 6 April 1988 issue of the daily *Magyar Nemzet.* How parliament chose between 15 March, 23 October and 20 August was amply covered by the Hungarian daily press.

Biographical index

Ady, Endre (1877–1919), poet, publicist. Studied law, then became a journalist with opposition newspapers. Published his first volume of poems in 1899. In 1901 sentenced to three months detention in a prison for political prisoners for anti-clerical writings. Liberal and freemason.

Albrecht, Ferenc József Károly, Archduke (1897–1956), Hungarian Royal Habsburg Archduke. Member of the Upper House. Fought in the First World War. Later proposed as candidate for the throne by legitimists. In 1943 nominated for governor by extremists. Emigrated to Argentina.

András II (1176–1235), King of Hungary (1205–35). Under pressure from the Pope launched a crusade. By distributing royal dominions he first tried to win the support of feudal lords, then, through a policy of liberalization, that of the burghers, the so-called 'royal servitors'.

Andrássy, Gyula, Count (1823–90), Hungarian Prime Minister (1867–71). In 1847 delegated to parliament. During the 1848–9 Revolution and Freedom Fight Lord Lieutenant, Commander of the National Guard, Adjutant to the Head of the Hungarian Army and Ambassador to Constantinople. During the period of repression was sentenced to death *in absentia*. As a supporter of Ferenc Deák urged compromise with Austria. As Prime Minister was also Minister of Defence. In 1871 became Foreign Minister of the Austro-Hungarian Monarchy and in this capacity supported Balkan expansion and an anti-Russian diplomatic policy.

Andrássy, József (1806–52), conservative politician. Delegate at the 1832–6 and 1832–40 Diets. Loyal to the dynasty. Member of Council of Governor-General and Privy Councillor.

Andrássy, Tivadar, Count (1857–1905), Gyula Andrássy's son. Liberal MP (1881–1905). Painter. Patron of Hungarian art and theatre. Between 1890 and 1896 Deputy Speaker of the Lower House.

Andreánszky, Gábor, Baron (1845–1909), MP, first of anti-Semitic (1884), then of moderate-liberal sentiments. Law graduate. In 1875 became member of the Upper House.

Apponyi, Albert, Count (1846–1933), Minister of Education (1906–10, 1917–18). MP, first in opposition; from 1899 in the governing party; and, from 1904, once again in opposition. Between 1901 and 1903 Speaker of the Lower House. Head of the Trianon Peace Treaty delegation. Chief delegate to the League of Nations.

Árpád (?–907?), chieftain of the Hungarian tribes which settled in the Carpathian Basin. Founder of the Árpád Dynasty in power until 1301.

Bach, Alexander (1813–93), Austrian politician. First displayed liberal, later conservative sentiments. Justice Minister, 1848. Minister of the Interior of the Habsburg Empire, 1849. Associated with the decade of absolutism and Germanization following the 1848–9 Revolution and Freedom Fight.

Bajza, József (1804–58), poet, publicist. Leading literary figure in the Reform Period in Hungary. Came from a middle ranking landowning family. Law graduate. Literary and theatre critic, newspaper editor and theatre director.

Balcescu, Nicolae (1819–52), Romanian politician and historian. Leader of the Havasföld Revolution in 1848. In the summer of 1849 signed the Romanian-Hungarian Draft Peace Treaty with Kossuth. Emigrated to France and later Italy.

Balogh, János (1796–1872), opposition reform politician. From 1832 delegate to the Lower Chamber. Later sub-prefect. Hungarian officer in the 1848–9 Revolution and Freedom Fight. During the years of repression was sentenced to death *in absentia*. From 1861, reinstated as MP.

Bánffy, Dezső, Baron (1843–1911), Prime Minister (1895–9). Governing-party MP. Lord Lieutenant. Between 1892 and 1895 Speaker of the Lower House. From 1904 opposition MP.

Bánffy, Miklós, Count (1874–1950), writer. Prime Minister (1921–2). Lord Lieutenant. Later governing-party MP. A leading literary figure in Transylvania. From 1939 supporter of the extreme right. In 1940 appointed Transylvanian representative to the Upper House.

Barabás, Béla (1855–1934), independent politician. Law student. As a student organized political demonstrations. Independent MP for Transylvanian districts. Lord Lieutenant. Coalition supporter. Minister of Religion and Public Education of the counter-revolutionary government formed in 1919 in Arad. Leader of the Hungarian minority in Romania. From 1926 Senator in the Bucharest parliament.

Barnutiu, Simion (1808–64), Romanian national minority politician. Teacher. Opponent of János Lemény. In 1848 opposed the Hungarian Revolution and Freedom Fight at the Romanian National Assembly. After 1849 studied law in Vienna and Padua. University lecturer.

Baross, Gábor (1875–1926), governing-party politician. Minister of Labour and Transport (1886–9). Law graduate. County official and later newspaper editor. In 1875 Liberal-Party MP. In 1833 State Secretary of Labour and Transport. The outstanding parliamentary economist in the sphere of feudal infrastructural development under the Dual Monarchy.

Bartha, Miklós (1848–1905), independent politician. Law graduate and junior clerk of the Royal Court. From 1873 opposition politician with conservative and anti-Semitic sentiments.

Batthyány, Lajos, Count (1806–49), President of the first independent Hungarian government (1848). Studied military affairs and law. Following a trip to Western Europe carried out economic reforms on his landed estates in Hungary. In the Reform Period, leader of the opposition in the Upper Chamber. In 1847 Chairman of the opposition party. Prime Minister during the 1848–9 Revolution and Freedom Fight, parliamentary representative. Committed to upholding the constitutional principle and compromise with the Habsburg Dynasty. On 6 October 1849 executed on charges of treason.

Beksics, Gusztáv (1847–1928), publicist, governing-party MP. Studied arts and law. Journalist and clerk at the Royal Court before 1874 election to parliament. 1894–6 advisor to the Prime Minister's Office. From 1909 editor of the *Budapest Journal*.

Béla IV (1206–70), King of Hungary (1235–70). Broke fundamentally with the policies of his father, András II, strengthened royal power and the royal landed estates. Lacking the support of the country's aristocracy in 1241 was defeated at Muhi by Mongol invaders and fled the country. Initiator of new policies on inheritance, urbanization and the establishment of a defence system. Entered into alliances against the Mongols.

Bem, Jozef (1794–1850), Polish army officer, Hungarian general. Graduated from an artillery school in Poland. Participated in the Polish Uprising, 1830–1, then emigrated. Fought in the revolutions in Galicia and Vienna, then rose to the position of commander-in-chief and lieutenant-general in the Transylvanian army. In the summer of 1849 his army was defeated by the Russians. Emigrated to Turkey. Became army commander in Syria.

Berzeviczy, Albert (1853–1936), governing-party politician. Minister of Culture (1903–5). MP in 1881 and again from 1910. Ministerial Advisor, then State Secretary. Deputy Speaker 1895–8, Speaker of the Lower House 1910–11. From 1927 member of the Upper House. From 1932 chairman of the Hungarian Pen Club. In 1936 chairman of the Hungarian National Academy of Science.

Bethlen, Gábor (1550–1629), Prince of Transylvania (1613–29). Son of a family from the lower nobility, participated in wars waged by the Transylvanian Principality against the Turks and the Romanians. Excellent soldier and diplomat, entered into alliance with the Turks against the Habsburgs. Elected Prince of Transylvania by the Kolozsvár parliament. After his election tried to become independent both of the Habsburgs and the Turks. Centralized the state administration, pursued a mercantilist economic policy and with a mercenary army consolidated Transylvania's independence. But one defeat against the Habsburgs followed another. In response to these defeats entered the Alliance of Protestant Powers in 1626.

Bethlen, István, Count (1874–1947), Prime Minister (1921–31). Law graduate and graduate of the Academy of Agriculture. MP from 1901, first with the governing party, later with an opposition agenda. In 1920 member of the Hungarian Trianon Peace Treaty delegation. As Prime Minister shared the vision of a conservative, so-called 'gentlemanly' Hungary, satisfying the political and economic interests of large landowners and capitalists. Major figure of the so-called counter-revolutionary period. Formed a new governing party. Achieved acceptance of Hungary by the League of Nations and arranged a loan for the consolidation of the Hungarian economy. Dissociated himself from the extreme right that came to replace him. In 1939 became life member of the Upper House. In the Second World War supported Anglo-Saxon orientation in politics. Died in a Soviet prison.

Bibó, István (1911–79), opposition politician, historian. Law graduate. Climbed to the top of the legislative hierarchy. In the meantime became private university lecturer. In 1945 Head of Directorate at the Ministry of the Interior. Member of the National Peasant Party. From 1946 lectured mainly on constitutional matters and public administration. In 1950 was removed from the university; became librarian. In 1956 became Minister in the Imre Nagy government. After the suppression of the 1956 Revolution arrested and sentenced to life imprisonment. Released 1963. Continued to work as librarian.

Bittó, István (1822–1903), Prime Minister (1872–4). Law graduate. MP in 1848. Emigrated in 1849. From 1861 MP in Deák's party. In 1869 Deputy Speaker, in 1872 Speaker of the Lower House. Justice Minister (1871–2). As Prime Minister supported coalition politics. Later became member of the Upper House.

Blaskovics, Ferenc (1864–?), priest and politician. Graduated in theology in Vienna. From 1887 taught Catholic theology. In 1892 President of the Association of Délvidék Agricultural Labourers. MP 1869–1901. In 1902 titular abbot, in 1904 canon, of Csanád.

Bocskai, István (1557–1606), Prince of Transylvania (1605–6). Son of a family from the lower nobility, page at the Viennese court, later leading figure of the anti-Turkish party in Transylvania. Became disappointed in Habsburg rule of Transylvania because of its oppressive nature. Escaped Habsburg imprisonment only with the help of *Hajdus* (Hungarian footsoldiers). Members of the lesser and greater nobility joined the Freedom Fight under him. His ultimate – unfulfilled – aim was to make Transylvania independent.

Bod, Péter (1712–69), priest, religious writer. Son of a Székely family from the lower nobility. Studied theology at the University of Leiden. In 1744 consecrated priest.

Bónis, Sámuel (1810–79), reform politician. Legal and technical studies. In the Reform Period parliamentary delegate, in 1848 elected representative. In 1849 Secretary of Justice. Government Commissioner during the freedom fight. Arrested during the period of repression, sentenced to death; sentence later commuted to imprisonment. Released in 1856. Between 1861–9 resumed his post as MP.

Borsiczky, Dénes (1806–53), reform politician. Lecturer at the Law Academy in Pozsony (Bratislava). In the Reform Period delegate in the Lower House.

Bródy, Sándor (1863–1924), writer. Did not complete high-school studies. Published first short stories at eighteen. Newspaper editor in Transylvania, then Budapest. His writings concern the life and mentality of the bourgeoisie.

Chorin, Ferenc (1879–1964), tycoon. Between 1928–42 Chairman of the National Association of Manufacturers. Prominent member of the economic elite under the Horthy regime. In 1944 allowed to emigrate when he turned his assets over to the Germans.

Csáky, Albin, Count (1841–1912), Minister of Religion and Education (1888–94). From 1865 governing-party MP, later Lord Lieutenant. In the Upper House main advocate of civil marriage and acceptance of the Jewish religion, a programme that he also promoted as Minister of Culture. In 1894 banned students from attending Kossuth's funeral. In 1900–6 and 1910–12 Speaker of the Upper House. Was among the first advocates of domestic tourism and travel.

Csanády, Sándor (1814–99), independent politician. From 1861 to his death elected

MP on ten occasions.

Csemegi, Károly (1826–99), criminal lawyer. During the 1849 Freedom Fight head of irregular troops, for which he was imprisoned and enrolled in the Austrian army against his will. From 1867 worked at the Justice Ministry, eventually in the capacity of State Secretary. Between 1879–93 President of the Supreme Court. Prepared laws for the modernization of legislative organizations. Liberalized the Penal Code.

Csengery, Antal (1822–80), reform politician. As a student worked as parliamentary correspondent, later as newspaper editor. During the Revolution and Freedom Fight advisor to the Minister of the Interior. Not a radical revolutionary and so avoided repression: worked as writer, lecturer and translator. As Deák's confidante played a part in the Compromise. From 1868 governing-party MP. Outstanding scientist.

Csernátony, Lajos (1823–1901), journalist. In 1848–9 Lajos Kossuth's personal secretary. Emigrated to France. In 1851 sentenced to death by Austria *in absentia*. After being expelled from Paris, settled first in Great Britain then in Italy. While in exile worked for various newspapers. In 1867 – the year of the Compromise – returned to Hungary and became a governing-party MP.

Damjanich, János (1804–49), Hungarian general. Imperial officer of Serb origin who joined the Hungarian Freedom Fight and conducted successful campaigns. During the period of repression was executed by General Haynau on 6 October 1849.

Dániel, Gábor (1824–1903), governing-party politician. Law graduate. Held office first at the Royal Court in Vienna, and later at the Chancellor's Office in Transylvania. In 1863 became MP. Between 1875–92 Lord Lieutenant. General Superintendent of the Unitarian Diocese.

Deák, Ferenc (1803–76), Justice Minister (1848–9). The principle proponent of the 1867 Compromise. Son of a family from the middle rank of the nobility. Law graduate. Delegate to the Diet at the early age of thirty; outstanding figure of the Reform generation. In 1848 elected representative. Brought negotiations with the Habsburgs to a successful conclusion; retired to his estate. Introduced a policy of passive resistance to Habsburg absolutist oppression. After 1867 would not take up office or accept a medal or rank from the Habsburgs. MP until his death.

Dragos, Jan (1810–49), Romanian national minority politician. Law graduate. Kossuth's confidante. Minority representative in the Hungarian parliament with pro-Hungarian sentiments. Assassinated by Romanian rebels.

Dux, Adolf (1822–81), Austrian journalist. Learned to speak Hungarian during law studies in Hungary. Correspondent of German newspapers. Translator of Hungarian poets and writers into German.

Elisabeth of Bavaria, Queen (1837–98), Elisabeth Amalia Eugenia Wittelsbach, the wife of Franz Joseph (1854–98). Princess of Bavaria. As wife of the King of Hungary spent much time in Gödöllő (Hungary), spoke good Hungarian and maintained relations with Hungarian aristocrats, politicians and artists. Had four children: Sophia (died young), Rudolf (committed suicide in 1889), Gisella and Maria Valeria. Assassinated by Luccheni, an Italian anarchist.

Előd (no dates), according to chronicle sources chieftain of one of the seven Hungarian tribes who settled in the Carpathian Basin.

Eötvös, József, Baron (1813–71), Minister of Religious Affairs and Education (1848) and Minister of Religion and Education (1867–71). Law graduate. Among the first nineteenth century realist novelists. During Reform Period member of the liberal opposition. Believed that Hungary could not afford to be independent from Austria. In support of this view emigrated Autumn 1848. From 1861 once again MP, supporter of the Compromise. As Minister of Culture introduced universal and mandatory education; legislated the religious emancipation of the Jews.

Eötvös, Károly 1842–1916), independent politician. Law graduate. In 1863 participated in a conspiracy against the Habsburgs and as a result was sentenced to imprisonment. Supported the Compromise. In 1872 governing-party MP and an effective orator in parliament. From 1877 professed opposition views. In 1883 won acquittal of Jews accused of ritual murder in politically motivated Tiszaeszlár court case.

Erkel, Ferenc (1810–93), composer (among other things of the Hungarian national anthem). As conductor of the National Theatre Orchestra composed operas on themes from Hungarian history featuring famous Hungarian historical figures (*Bánk Bán*), musically borrowing from so-called 'recruiting' music. As a music teacher participated in the establishment of the Hungarian Music Academy. Supreme Director of the National Opera which opened in 1884.

Esze, Tamás (1666–1708), *Kuruc* military leader. Ran his own salt trade network in violation of the Habsburg Emperor's monopoly on salt. Obtained the support of outcast wanderers, the so-called 'poor lads', and widened their struggle against salt officials into a more general movement against the Habsburg Court. In 1703 headed the delegation that invited Ferenc Rákóczi to be the leader of an uprising against the Habsburgs. Ennobled by Rákóczi, elected commander of the Hungarian insurgents for his military successes. Died in a battle between two Kurutz camps.

Falk, Miksa (1828–1909), publicist. Son of a merchant family. First published at fifteen. Published anti-Habsburg articles in opposition Hungarian newspapers, and anonymous pro-Viennese articles in official newspapers. Belonged to the circle of Széchenyi. Supported the Compromise. Between 1875–1905 governing-party MP.

Fejérváry, Géza, Count (1777–1857), Defence Minister (1884–1903) and Prime Minister (1905–6). Ennobled in connection with his military career. Confidant of Franz Joseph, Commander of the Royal Guard. On the collapse of the Hungarian governing party Franz Joseph made him head of the new government in violation of rules of parliament.

Felsőbüki Nagy, Pál (1777–1857), first a liberal, then a conservative politician. In the 1880s as delegate at the Diet spoke up for the peasantry and the development of the Hungarian economy and language. Excellent orator. In the early 1830s the Habsburg Court obtained his support for Austrian policies.

Ferdinand I (1503–64), King of Hungary (1526–64). Younger brother of Karl V, member of the Habsburg Dynasty. Became King of Hungary under a family agreement with the Yagello Dynasty following Hungary's defeat by the Turks at Mohács. In 1556 became Holy Roman Emperor. Entered into the Religious Peace of Augsburg for the sake of unity against the Turks. His failures in diplomacy and military affairs contributed to the Turkish occupation of Hungary's midlands.

Ferdinand V (1793–1875), King of Hungary (1835–48). Member of the Habsburg Dynasty. Feeble mental and physical constitution; merely a puppet on the throne. In December 1848 forced by the Camarilla to abdicate to Franz Joseph.

Forinyák, Géza (1840–60), law student. Lost his life at an opposition demonstration when the army fired into the crowd. His funeral grew into a huge anti-Habsburg demonstration.

Franz Joseph I (1830–1916), King of Hungary and Habsburg Emperor (1867–1916). Following the suppression of the Hungarian Freedom Fight first conducted a policy of dictatorship, later of absolutism and centralization. Under the threat of Prussian military and diplomatic hegemony came to support the idea of the Compromise. Under the Austro-Hungarian Dual Monarchy the country's economy was modernized along with the rest of the Empire but the Dual Monarchy proved politically inflexible. His foreign policy was oriented towards expansion in the Balkans and alliance with Germany and Italy in opposition to the Russian Empire. After his death and defeat in the First World War the Habsburg Empire fell apart.

Füredy, Richárd (1873–1932), sculptor. Representative of academic school. Made the sculpture of graveyard monuments into an art form.

Gábel, Gyula (1858–?), journalist and teacher. Invented a new method for teaching children how to read and write.

Ghyczy, Kálmán (1808–88), Finance Minister (1874–5). Law graduate. In 1843 delegate to the Diet, then Lord Lieutenant. In 1848 State Secretary of Justice and MP. In 1849 submitted to Habsburg rule. In 1861, then between 1875–79, Speaker of the Lower House. From 1885 Speaker of the Upper House.

Gömbös, Gyula (1886–1936), Defence Minister (1929–32), then Prime Minister (1932–6). Professional army officer. Was elected to parliament first on a small-holders' then on a governing-party ticket. Supporter of Miklós Horthy. In 1923 organized a racist party. As Prime Minister announced a National Working Schedule based on contemporary German and Italian models. Implemented extreme right-wing policies mainly with the support of army officers and the middle peasantry. Entered into agreement with Italy, Austria and Germany.

Halbig, Johann (1814–82), German sculptor. Created the sculpture of Palatine Antal József Nádor in Budapest.

Hatvani, Imre (?–1856), Headed an irregular troop during the 1848–9 Revolution and Freedom Fight. Law graduate. Fought in Transylvania, then emigrated to North America. In 1850 went to Transylvania *incognito* to organize an uprising against the Habsburgs but was captured and imprisoned. Died in prison.

Haynald, Lajos (1816–91), Archbishop of Kalocsa (from 1867), and Cardinal (from 1879). Consecrated priest in 1839. In 1846 and 1848 primatial secretary, then head of department. Refused to allow the announcement of the Declaration of Independence, as a consequence of which in June 1849 was removed from his post. In 1852 Bishop of Transylvania. Supported the union of Hungary with Transylvania. In 1863 condemned Habsburg absolutism and resigned. Worked at the Vatican. After his return to Hungary opposed the Civil Marriage Act but supported the emancipation of Judaism. Member of the Upper House. Amateur botanist.

Haynau, Julius (1786–1853), Austrian general. During the time of the Italian and Hungarian 1848–9 revolutions achieved many military victories. He was the so-called 'Hyena of Bresca'. Executed the Prime Minister of the first independent Hungarian government, Lajos Batthyány, and 13 Hungarian generals in 1849, among others.

Hegedűs, Sándor (1899–1906), Trade Minister (1899–1902). Studied law and economics; worked as a journalist. Related through marriage to the writer Mór Jókai. From 1875 until 1905 governing-party MP. Lutheran diocese general superintendent. From 1905 member of the Upper House.

Helfy, Ignác (1830–97), independent politician. In 1848–9 worked in Kossuth's office. In 1854 went to Italy where he became a newspaper editor and maintained close contacts with Hungarian emigrants. Opposed the Compromise. In 1870 returned to Hungary. Became an independent MP; later changed his views and came to support the Compromise.

Hentaller, Lajos (1852–1912), independent politician. Journalist, supporter of Lajos Kossuth. From 1881 independent MP.

Hentzi, Heinrich (1875–49), Austrian general. During the 1848–9 Revolution and Freedom Fight made an oath of allegiance to the Constitution but betrayed it later. The Home Defence Committee court-martialled and sentenced him to imprisonment. When Austrian troops occupied Buda, he was appointed commander. Ordered his artillery to fire on Pest, inhabited exclusively by civilians. Died in the taking of Buda by the Hungarian army. In 1852 the Habsburg Court erected a statue in his memory despite repeated protests. Until 1899 the statue remained in place. In 1918 the memorial, after having been transferred to a new location, was destroyed by the bourgeois democratic revolution.

Herczeg, Ferenc (1863–1954), writer. Son of a Délvidék German family. Studied law. Was sentenced to three months imprisonment for participation in a fatal duel. His novels were highly popular with the contemporary gentry. Journalist. From 1896 governing-party MP. Unconditionally devoted to István Tisza. From 1927 member of the Upper House. From 1829 Chairman of the Revisionist League.

Hermann, Ottó (1835–1914), natural scientist, independent politician. In 1863 participated in the Polish Uprising. Wrote articles in support of the Paris Commune. Worked as photographer, ethnologist and ethnographer. From 1879 independent MP. Carried on correspondence with Kossuth.

Herzl, Tivadar (Theodor) (1860–1904), Zionist born in Hungary. Journalist in Vienna. As the founder of Zionism was the first to propose the formation of a Jewish state in Palestine. Organized the 1897 Congress of Zionism in Basel.

Hieronymi Károly (1836–1911), Minister of the Interior (1892–5) and Trade Minister (1903–5 and 1910–11). Chief Engineer, then State Secretary of Transport. From 1882 General Director of Austro-Hungarian Railways. As Minister of the Interior played an important role in the elaboration of liberal laws on religion. As Trade Minister focused on the technological development of industry and transport.

Hock, János (1859–1936), President of the Revolutionary National Council (1918). Abandoned a career in the Catholic Church. In 1887 became governing-party MP. Later joined opposition parties. Excellent orator. Later became a supporter of Mihály Károlyi. Fear of a workers' dictatorship forced him to emigrate. Lived in the United States, Paris and Vienna and published a number of articles condemning the counterrevolutionary regime. Upon his return to Hungary was imprisoned for this.

Hodza, Milán (1878–1944), Czech politician. Member of the Hungarian (1905–18), and later of the Czech (1918–38), parliaments. Head of the Agrarian Party. Minister 1919–35, Prime Minister 1935–8. Emigrated to the USA 1939.

Holló, Barnabás (1865–1917), sculptor. Responsible for a number of statues of Kossuth.

Holló, Lajos (1859–1918), journalist. Law graduate. From 1887 independent MP; supported Gyula Justh. During the war quit the opposition.

Horánszky, Nándor (1818–1902), Trade Minister (1902). Law graduate. From 1872 independent, later governing-party MP. Upon the signing of the economic compromise quit the governing party. After a government reshuffle joined the liberal party.

Horn, Ede (1825–75), liberal politician. Studied to be a rabbi but later switched to economics. During the 1848–9 Freedom Fight Jewish army chaplain. Emigrated. In 1860 joined Garibaldi's forces. In 1869 returned to Hungary and worked as a journalist. Later became an MP and State Secretary of Trade.

Horthy, Miklós (1868–1957), conservative politician. Defence Minister of the counterrevolutionary government (1919). Regent of Hungary (1920–44). Aide-de-camp to Franz Joseph I (1909–14). Commander-in-Chief of the Navy. In 1919 Commander-in-Chief of the National Army of the Counterrevolution. As Regent prevented the King's return to the throne. Joined the Berlin-Rome Axis and entered the Second World War on the side of the Axis powers. In 1944 attempted to leave the war but failed; German troops occupied Hungary. In 1945 became Allied prisoner of war. After his release lived in Portugal until his death.

Horváth, Boldizsár (1822–98), Justice Minister (1867–71). In 1848 elected representative; nine times elected MP.

Horvay, János (1873–1944), sculptor. Studied in Vienna, then went on a long study trip abroad. Made a number of statues of Lajos Kossuth. Fashionable memorial sculptor.

Huba (no dates), according to chronicle sources chieftain of one of the seven Hungarian tribes who settled in the Carpathian Basin.

Hunyadi, János (around 1406–56), Governor (1446–52). Son of a Havaselve boyar. His military career culminated in service to the King. Became familiar with Turkish military tactics. Viceroy of Szörény and Lord Lieutenant of Temes, Transylvania. During his Balkan campaign his troops penetrated deep into the Turkish Empire. Came into confrontation with members of the Hungarian high nobility as well as the Holy Roman Emperor. Resigned from his post as Governor. In 1456 recruited a peasant crusader army which defeated Turkish invaders at Nándorfehérvár. Died of plague which broke out after the battle.

Hunyadi, Mátyás, or Matthias Corvinus (1443–90), King (1458–90). Son of János Hunyadi. Educated by humanists, spoke several languages. In 1457 was sentenced to confiscation of property and death, along with his brother, by rival families of the high nobility. Following his brother's execution was educated in Vienna, then Prague. In 1458 elected King under pressure of the lesser nobility which had supported his father. Created a strong centralized state.

Hurban, Josef (1817–88), Slovakian Evangelical priest and writer. In 1848 headed the Slovakian national minority movement.

Huszár, Adolf (1843–85), sculptor. Studied at the Academy of Vienna. After the Compromise one of the most fashionable sculptors in Hungary. His works represent the academic style.

Iancu, Avram (1824–74), leader of Romanian insurgents 1848–9. Conducted negotiations with both Balcescu and Kossuth. Known among Romanians as the 'King of the Highlands'. Went insane.

Illyés, Gyula (1902–83), poet and writer. Son of an artisan-peasant family. Student during the time of the 1918–19 revolutions. In 1920 emigrated to Austria, then to France. Lived in Paris until 1926, studied at the Sorbonne. Prominent representative of the so-called '*népi*' or popularist – as opposed to the urban or cosmopolitan – trend in literary and academic circles. Between the two world wars conducted talks with political leaders of the extreme right. After 1945 National-Peasant-Party MP. In 1948 retired from public life.

Irányi, Dániel (1822–92), independent politician. Studied philosophy and law; student leader. Played an important role in bringing about the events of the March 1848 Revolution involving the March Youth. In 1848–9 State Secretary at the Justice Ministry. Voluntary member of the Hungarian army, later government commissioner. Emigrated for fear of repression and maintained contact with fellow-emigrants: visited Bismarck as Kossuth's representative. From 1868 MP, member of the 1848 Party. In 1884 Chairman of the Independence Party.

Irinyi, József (1822–59), politician of the 1848 generation. Studied law. Later went on a study trip abroad and went into journalism. Leading figure of the revolutionary March Youth in 1848. MP. Later Hungary's Counsellor in Paris. Sentenced to death by Haynau but reprieved. Later worked as a literary translator.

Istóczy Győző (1842–1915), politician with anti-Semitic sentiments. Law graduate. In 1872 became an MP as a supporter of Deák. In 1875 became a member of the Liberal Party. Founder of the Anti-Semitic Party. Sued for writings inciting racial hatred.

István, Archduke (1817–67), Palatine (1847–8). From 1843 Czech civil governor. From 1847 Governor of Hungary and Lord Lieutenant. Elected Palatine by parliament. Presented the parliament's petition to the King and entrusted Count Lajos Batthyány with the forming of the first independent Hungarian government. Entrusted with command of Hungarian army by parliament, on which he fled to Vienna and resigned. Lived a quiet life in Germany and was reconciled with the Habsburg Court in 1858.

István, Saint (King Stephen) (967–1038), King of Hungary (997–1038). Creator of the Hungarian state. Having defeated pagan chieftains, made Christianity the state's official religion. Beatified in 1803.

Ivánka, Imre (1818–96), Hungarian army officer, MP in Tisza's party. Graduated from Military Academy. In 1848 Prime Ministerial Secretary of the National Guard, Commander of the National Guard. Was captured and released in 1850. First elected MP in 1861; from 1875 governing-party representative. From 1895 member of the Upper House. Freemason.

Izsó, Miklós (1831–75), sculptor. Member of the Freedom Fight; forced into hiding, first in Budapest, later in Vienna where he worked with a number of artists. Studied at the Munich Academy. Was one of the first sculptors to be inspired by folk art.

Jansky, Leopold (no dates), Austrian brigadier. In 1886 his speech at the Hentzi memorial caused riots lasting for several days and a domestic political crisis.

Jellacic, Josip Count (1801–59), Viceroy of Croatia. Military leader of the Croatian uprising in 1848. As commander of the southern army in 1849 fought to suppress the Hungarian Freedom Fight. Received a Maria Theresa medal. In 1854 was made a Count by Franz Joseph I.

Johanna, Queen of Naples (1326–82). Member of the Anjou Dynasty. Ordered the murder of her first husband, the younger brother of Hungarian King Lajos I. Lajos I fought a war with her. The Pope dethroned her. Strangled.

Jókai, Mór (1825–1904), novelist. Born into the gentry. Law graduate. Became a successful novelist in both the Romantic and folk genres. Supported the Hungarian Revolution and Freedom Fight to the end. Returned to Budapest in 1850 to continue writing novels. Newspaper editor and journalist; imprisoned for a month for one of his articles. MP 1865–96. In 1875 joined the governing party. After retirement from politics continued to be a prominent literary figure. For decades the most popular Hungarian writer.

Joseph II (1741–90), Hungarian King (1780–90). Son of Maria Theresa. Member of the Habsburg Dynasty. His enlightened absolutist regime strengthened the powers of the state, took the Catholic Church under state control, and reduced the power of the nobility. He was the so-called 'king with a hat' because he would not be crowned. Under pressure from the nobility – who were against his policy of Germanization and his economic policy – withdrew the majority of his reforms on his deathbed.

József, Antal János (1776–1847), Palatine (1795–1847). Austrian Archduke. Son of King Leopold II. The 'pro-Hungarian Habsburg', played a part in providing bail for Kossuth and Wesselényi among others.

Justh, Gyula (1850–1917), Independence-Party politician. Law graduate. Between 1884–1917 Independence-Party MP. In 1891 deputy chairman and in 1893 Chairman of the Independence Party. Between 1905–9 Speaker of the Lower House. Later supported bourgeois radicals, primarily Mihály Károlyi. In 1912 headed the campaign of obstruction against István Tisza.

Kabos, Gyula (1888–1941), actor. Fame came to him with the introduction of the talkies in the 1930s. His art was the embodiment of the timorous Hungarian petty bourgeois. In 1939 emigrated to the USA.

Kádár, János (1912–89), Communist politician. Minister of the Interior (1948–50). Studied as office equipment technician. From 1930 member of the Hungarian Communist Party. Arrested. In 1935 joined the Social Democratic Party. From 1941 member of the Communist Party leadership. In 1945 Deputy Police Chief of Budapest. MP 1945–8. Arrested in 1951; in 1954 paroled from life imprisonment. Once again became party leader. In 1956 became the head of the Revolutionary Party of Workers and Agricultural Labourers, destined to carry out reconstruction following the 1956 Revolution. Until 1988 supreme head of the Hungarian Socialist Party.

Karl III (1685–1740), King of Hungary (1711–40). King of Spain (1706–14) and as Karl VI also Holy Roman Emperor. Member of the Habsburg Dynasty. Distributed Hungarian areas reclaimed from the Turks among members of foreign nobility. Continued to try to drive out the Turks. Passed a law on the succession of the female line of the Habsburg Dynasty. Discriminated against protestants.

Karl IV (1887–1922), Hungary's last King (1916–22). Member of the Habsburg Dynasty. Made an attempt to quit the First World War by way of a series of separate peace agreements. Made promises of autonomy to the Empire's national minorities. In Hungary urged the introduction of universal suffrage. His promises could not prevent the outbreak of a democratic revolution in October 1918 which finally caused him to abdicate and refrain from interference with Hungarian affairs. Moved to Switzerland. In 1921 the Hungarian National Assembly declared the removal of the Habsburg Dynasty. 1922 made two attempts to regain the throne

Károly, Róbert (1288–1342), King of Hungary (1307–42). Member of the Anjou Dynasty. Ascended to the throne after prolonged internal fighting following the ending of the Árpád Dynasty. Having secured his place on the throne, immediately proceeded to deal with the provincial lords. Started to build a strong centralized regime by introducing domestic and financial reforms. The economic agreement he concluded with the Polish and Czech sovereigns amounted to an alliance against Vienna.

Károlyi, István, Count (1845–1907), independent politician. In 1866 adjutant in the Austro-Hungarian Legion. From 1887 MP, first with governing-party and later with independent-party sympathies.

Károlyi, Mihály, Count (1875–1955), Prime Minister (1918–19), and President of the Republic (1919). From 1901 member of the governing party, then from 1905 Independent-Party MP. In 1910 became an MP with an independent agenda. In 1912 joined Gyula Justh's Independent Party to become its Chairman the following year. Devoted to the idea of universal suffrage, condemned the war effort and advocated democratic reforms. Became the leader of the bourgeois-democratic revolution. Head of State and Government. The external and internal pressure that followed Hungary's defeat in the war forced him to resign in March 1919, thereby opening the way to the Council Republic. Emigrated in the summer of 1919 and settled in Paris after the counterrevolutionary regime confiscated all his property. In 1946 returned to Hungary. Between 1947–8 Hungary's Ambassador to Paris. Later emigrated again.

Kazinczy, Ferenc (1759–1831), writer, language reformer. Law graduate. Freemason from 1784. Held posts in county administration and education. In 1794 joined the Hungarian Jacobin movement; was sentenced to death, although the sentence was later commuted to detention. Released in 1801. Attended to his estate and launched a language-reform campaign, which was not devoid of political and social aspects.

Keglevich, István, Count (1840–1905), governing-party politician. After a military career, in 1865 became a conservative MP; in 1884 became a governing-party representative in the Lower House. One of the chief organizers of theatre life in Hungary. Died in a duel.

Kemény, Zsigmond, Baron (1814–75), writer and politician. Law graduate. Wrote pamphlets against the abuse of power by counties. Supported the politics of centralization. In 1848–9 MP, later Counsel to the Minister of the Interior. Shared peace-party views and was not attracted by the radicalism of the Hungarian Revolution; opposed the idea of independence for Hungary. Deported during the period of repression. Published two infamous anti-revolutionary pamphlets which managed to turn both fellow-Hungarians as well as the suspicious Habsburg court against him. Joined the camp of passive resistance. Supported the Compromise. Towards the end of his life went insane.

Kertész, K. Róbert (1876–1951), architect. Graduated from the Technical University. In 1922–34 State Secretary at the Ministry of Culture. Winner of a number of architectural competitions.

Khuen-Héderváry, Károly, Count (1849–1918), twice Prime Minister (1903 and 1910–12). From 1875 governing-party MP, later Lord Lieutenant. Between 1883–1903 Governor of Croatia. Headed the Hungarian government of 1903 for no longer than five months. Between terms was member of the Tisza government as minister in charge of looking after the King. During his second term as Prime Minister formed the National Labour Party.

Kisfaludy-Stróbl, Zsigmond (1884–1975), sculptor. Studied in Budapest and in Vienna. Was primarily known for his portraits. Creator of the Liberation Monument which was erected in 1974 in memory of the Soviet army and which became the symbol of the whole communist regime in Hungary.

Kiss, György (1852–1919), sculptor. Studied in Graz and Munich. Master of ornamental and realistic sculpture.

Kiss, Lajos (1881–1965), ethnologist. Initially studied to be an actor, but became first a museum usher, then a museum director. Collected articles of peasant culture.

Klapka, György (1820–92), Hungarian general. Member of the Viennese Guard. At the beginning of 1848 left his borderguard regiment; later Deputy Defence Minister. MP. After the capitulation of the main Hungarian army continued to defend the castle entrusted to his command for several months. During his years of exile organized and participated in campaigns, some against Austria. In 1866, in the course of the war between Austria and Germany set up the Klapka Legion. After 1867 became an MP.

Klebersberg, Kunó, Count (1875–1932), Minister of the Interior (1921–2) and Minister of Religion and Education (1922–31). Studied in Budapest, Berlin, Munich and Paris. Held several important posts in the administration: from 1914 State Secretary at the Ministry of Culture; in 1917 Deputy State Secretary without Portfolio at the Prime Minister's Office. Governing-party MP. A new educational infrastructure developed during his term as Minister of Culture. Educational reforms were sought to both bring about and to demonstrate Hungary's cultural supremacy in the face of the Trianon Peace Treaty.

Kocsis, András (1905–76), sculptor. Student of Kisfaludy-Stróbl. Distinguished himself primarily with monuments and memorial statues. Master of the monumental in size also.

Kodály, Zoltán (1882–1967), composer. In addition to graduating from the Music Academy, studied fine arts. In 1905 embarked on a series of folk-song collecting tours in Hungarian-speaking areas. In 1919, the period of the Council Republic, was appointed Deputy Director of the Music Academy. In 1920 had to pay for this appointment by enforced retirement. However, in 1921 returned to teach at the Academy. His most outstanding achievement related to children's choirs and musical education. The so-called 'Kodály method' of teaching music has received world-wide recognition. The teaching of folk music in schools was his personal achievement.

Kölcsey, Ferenc (1790–1838), poet. Law graduate, later went into business. County Recorder and county delegate at the first Session of the Reform Diet (1832–5). Translated Descartes, Kant and Holbach. Author of the lyrics of the Hungarian National Anthem.

Köllő, Miklós (1861–1900), sculptor. Studied in Munich and Budapest. Mostly sculpted ornamental statues for buildings. Worked in the realist style.

Komlós, Aladár (1892–1980), literary historian and writer.

Komócsy József (1836–94), poet. Began as a bootmaker's apprentice, but later rose to become an assistant, then a full-time teacher. Newspaper editor from 1868. Founder and chairman of an important literary society. Author of serene, light-hearted poems.

Kond (alternatively: Kund, Könd) (no dates), according to chronicle sources chieftain of one of the seven Hungarian tribes who settled in the Carpathian Basin.

Könyves, Kálmán, or the Beauclerc (1074–1116), King of Hungary (1095–1116). Member of the Árpád Dynasty. Conquered Croatia and Dalmatia. Caused his brother and his young son to be blinded. Named 'Könyves' (an adjective derived from *könyv*, meaning book) in recognition of his erudition.

Korizmics, László (1816–86), governing-party politician. As agrarian engineer worked at large and medium-sized estates. In 1848 State Secretary of Agriculture. Chairman of the highly influential Hungarian National Economic Society. Participated in the formation of the Land Credit Institute. From 1868 until his death governing-party MP.

Kosáry, Domokos (1913–), historian. Currently President of the Hungarian Academy of Sciences.

Kosciusko, Tadeus (1746–1817), Polish freedom fighter. First fought in the American Civil War on the side of Washington, later in the Polish Uprising. Taken captive by the Russian army. Died in France. His body was later buried by the Tsar alongside the tombs of the Polish kings.

Kossuth, Ferenc (1841–1914), Trade Minister (1906–10). Son of Lajos Kossuth. Grew up in exile. Conducted technical studies, then worked in Great Britain and Italy in the capacity of transport engineer. In 1894 accompanied his father's body back to Hungary for burial and settled down in Hungary for good. In 1895 chairman of the Independence Party and MP. Supported the Compromise. As Minister renewed the Tariffs and Trade Agreement with Austria.

Kossuth, Lajos (1802–94), Finance Minister (1848) and Governor-President (1849). Son of a middle-gentry family without landed estates. Law graduate. In 1832 became an MP representing absent members of the feudal aristocracy. His publications kept the public informed of the latest legislative developments. His newspaper was banned, and Kossuth himself was arrested and sentenced to four years in prison. After being released returned to newspaper editing and through his newspaper demanded bourgeois freedoms and constitutional independence. Took a stand for economic independence. Author of the Declaration of the Opposition, a document which became the programme of the Opposition Party. In 1847 delegate in parliament; played a decisive role in pushing through laws consolidating the achievements of the transformation brought about by the 1848 Revolution. Following the dissolution of government, president of the National Defence Committee (a post identical to that of head of government). While in exile drafted a constitution taking into account national minority interests; held a series of lectures throughout Europe and America; supported preparations for military action opposed to the Compromise. In 1889 lost his Hungarian citizenship, in protest against which a number of Hungarian towns and cities elected him an honorary citizen. Hungary's Prime Minister at the time, Kálmán Tisza, was brought down by the ensuing fracas. Died in Turin; buried in Budapest.

Kostic, Laza (1841–1910), Serb poet. Studied law in Vienna and Budapest. Teacher, notary and MP.

Kovács, Gyula (1875–?), opposition politician, MP. In 1912 fired a gunshot at Speaker of the House István Tisza in the Session Hall. Attempted suicide. Was acquitted by the jury. Resigned from Parliament.

Kristóffy, József (1857–1928), Minister of the Interior (1905–6). First Deputy County Recorder, later Lord Lieutenant. Minister of an unconstitutionally appointed government. His political strategy included a promise to introduce universal suffrage and secret ballots. Confidante of Franz Ferdinand. Governing-party MP 1911–13.

Krúdy, Gyula (1878–1933), writer. Correspondent for a large number of newspapers and magazines. His prose described primarily the bourgeoisie under the Dual Monarchy, sometimes in the style of Romanticism, sometimes in that of Impressionism.

Kubicza, Pál (1824–93), politician. In 1848 representative to the Diet, MP 1865–7. Lord Lieutenant 1867–90.

Kun, Béla (1886–1939), Commissar of Foreign Affairs and Defence (1919). From 1902 member of the Social-Democratic Party. During the First World War Russian prisoner of war. Joined the Bolsheviks; from 1918 head of the Hungarian section; took part in the formation of the Hungarian Communist Party. Arrested in early 1919; released from prison during the Council Republic. Emigrated after its fall. From 1920 lived in the Soviet Union. Participated in command of the Crimean operations of the Red Army. Between 1921–36 member of the Executive Committee of Comintern. In 1937 arrested and executed.

Lánczy, Leó (1852–90), tycoon. From 1881 Chief Executive Officer and later President of the Pest Hungarian Commercial Bank. From 1893 Chairman of the Chamber of Commerce and Industry. Between 1893–1901 governing-party MP. From 1905 member of the Upper House.

Láng, Lajos, Count (1849–1918), Trade Minister (1902–3). Liberal journalist. From 1878 MP; between 1896–8 Deputy Speaker of the Lower House. University lecturer in statistics. Founder and leader of the Hungarian Economic Society.

László, Saint (1040–95), King of Hungary (1077–95). His legislation was directed towards strengthening feudal private property. Strengthened the Church and assisted the development of religious culture. In the conflict between the Pope and the Holy Roman Emperor first supported the Pope, then the Emperor. Conquered Croatia. Declared a Saint in 1129.

László IV, or László the Kun (1262–90), King of Hungary (1272–90). Ascended to the throne as a child and was unable to establish independent rule over feuding feudal warlords. As a result sought the help of the Kuns and the Mongols. Murdered by assassin hired by members of the feudal oligarchy.

Lechner, Jenő (1878–1962), architect. Studied in Budapest, later became a lecturer at the Technical University. His works were completed in the style of the Renaissance and Classicism. Restored buildings, conducted research in the history of architecture.

Lemény, János (1780–1861), Greek Catholic Bishop in Romania. Graduated in Nagyvárad (Oradea). Became a Bishop in 1832. Charismatic figure of the pro-Hungarian wing of the Romanian-nationalist movement. In May 1848 tried to appease the Hungarian Revolution and Romanians. During the period of repression sentenced to 20 years of detention, but pardoned; removed from his bishopric.

Leopold (Lipot) I (1640–1705), King of Hungary (1675–1705). Member of the Habsburg Dynasty. Educated for priesthood by Jesuits. Made peace with the Turks at the cost of recognizing all Ottoman conquests in Hungary. A group of Hungarian feudal warlords conspired against him. The conspiracy was bloodily suppressed in 1671. After this ruled with an iron hand. Persecuted Protestants. Pushed the Turks back from large areas. When it came to distributing landed estates he favoured foreigners; in response another revolt broke out against him, this time supported by the lesser nobility. The Spanish War of Succession that broke out in 1701 weakened his empire's standing abroad.

Leopold (Lipot) II (1747–92), King of Hungary (1790–92). Member of the Habsburg Dynasty. Enlightened-absolutist monarch. Caused the feudal constitution to be restored, thereby reducing the resistance of the Hungarian nobility to Habsburg rule. Entered into alliance with the Prussian King in order to participate in the intervention in the French Revolution.

List, Friedrich (1789–1864), German economist. Put forward a theory of nationally oriented economics in opposition to traditional bourgeois economic theory. The economic policy he advocated – based on the national economy and a system of protective tarrifs – had a profound effect on Lajos Kossuth.

Lukács, György (1885–1971), philosopher, aesthetician. In 1918 became a member of the Hungarian Communist Party. Cultural politician during the time of the Council Republic. Emigrated to Vienna; between 1930–45 lived in the Soviet Union. Until 1949 private lecturer in Marxist aesthetics and philosophy at Budapest University. Between 1949–56 pushed into the background by Hungary's communist leadership. In 1956 deported to Romania as a member of the circle of Imre Nagy. Returned to Hungary six months later.

Madách, Imre (1823–64), poet and writer. Studied liberal arts and law. Deputy County Recorder, then County Commissioner 1846–9. In 1848 resigned on health grounds. Supporter of centralist politics. Sentenced to one year's imprisonment for hiding Kossuth's personal secretary. In 1861 Appeals Court Judge and MP.

Madarász, József (1814–1915), opposition politician. Law graduate. While a student attended sessions of the Reform Age parliament. Held radical-leftist views during the 1848 Revolution and publicized these views in newspapers of which he was the editor. During the period of repression sentenced to detention, released only in 1856. MP in 1861 and from 1865 to his death.

Mailáth, György (1818–83), Lord Chief Justice. In the Reform Period parliamentary representative, Sub-Prefect, county administrative official and Lord Lieutenant. In 1847–8 a leader of the Conservative Party. Retired when the Revolution broke out. In the age of absolutism played a part in the arch-conservative trend seeking compromise with the Habsburg court. Lord Chief Treasurer, later President of the Council of the Governor-General. In 1861 member of the Imperial Council. From 1865 High Chancellor. From 1867 Speaker of the Upper House. From 1882 President of the Supreme Court. Murdered by robbers.

Margó, Ede (1872–1946), sculptor. Studied in Paris. Came under the influence of Rodin. Worked in the realist style.

Maria Theresa (1717–80), Queen of Hungary (1740–80). Member of the Habsburg Dynasty. Upon her ascent to the throne the Austrian War of Succession broke out in which she obtained the support of the Hungarian feudal nobility. A strongly centralized political regime was combined with reforms and modernization (including bringing education within the competence of the state). Changed the legal status of serfs; reduced the Hungarian economy to a service provider for Austria.

Márki, Sándor (1853–1925), historian and writer. High-school teacher and later university lecturer. His general interests included peasant uprisings and revolutionary movements.

Matlekovics, Sándor (1842–1925), MP. Member of the board of the Hungarian Academy of Sciences. In 1880 State Secretary. His area of expertise was the national economy.

Mikszáth, Kálmán (1847–1910), writer. Born into the lesser nobility. Studied law, worked as a journalist. Specialized in political sketches. Worked for liberal newspapers. His novels enjoyed great popularity in his time.

Mocsáry, Lajos (1826–1916), independent politician. During the time of the Revolution and Freedom Fight was receiving therapy abroad. In 1861 member of the party demanding the reinstitution of the laws of 1848 (the so-called April Laws), an opponent of the Compromise. Sub-prefect, and between 1867–69 delegate at the Diet. Played an important role in the foundation of the Independent Party. Supporter of the idea of 'personal union' with Austria. Opposed expansion into the Balkans. Supported a moderate national-minority policy. Later maintained close ties with bourgeois radicals.

Murgu, Eftimie (1805–70), politician of the Romanian national minority. Solicitor. University lecturer. In 1848 national-minority representative with pro-Hungarian sentiments. In the period of repression was sentenced to imprisonment. From 1861 served his second term as political representative.

Nagy, Lajos (1326–82), King of Hungary (1342–82). Son of the Anjou King Charles Robert. Waged wars against Naples and Lithuania and in the Balkans. Passed laws on the rights of the Hungarian nobility and on inheritance procedures. In 1370 succeeded to the Polish throne. Initiator of the culture of chivalry in Hungary.

Nagyatádi, Szabó István (1863–1924), Minister of Agriculture (1918, 1919, 1920–1 and 1922–4), Minister of the National Economy (1919), Minister of Public Catering (1919–20) and Minister Without Political Portfolio in charge of Smallholders' Affairs (1920–1). Chairman of the party of affluent smallholders and peasant landowners. From 1908 MP, from 1920 member of the National Assembly. In 1918–19 Chairman of the National Smallholders' Party. In the course of negotiations with the Liberal Block became a member of the Christian Block. Introduced land reforms in 1920.

Németh, Albert (1820–87), independent politician. Political representative in 1848. Elected to parliament six times, begining in 1861.

Neuman, Armin (1845–1909), lawyer. Governing-party MP 1887–1903. University professor. Founder of the Horticultural College of the Israelite Agricultural and Handicrafts Association.

Nicholas I (1796–1855), Russian Tsar. Supressed the Polish Uprising 1830–1; in 1848 offered his assistance to the Habsburgs in the suppression of the Hungarian Uprising. In 1853 launched the Crimean War, in which Austria remained neutral despite his expectations.

Nordau, Max (1849–1929), German writer born in Pest. Settled in Paris. A leading figure in the Zionist movement.

Nyári, Pál (1806–71), liberal politician from the nobility. County Recorder; in 1848 delegate in the Diet. During the 1848 Revolution a radical, later turned pacifist. Condemned the Declaration of Independence. In the period of repression sentenced to detention in a castle from which he was released in 1856. From 1861 Sub-Prefect, later MP. Committed suicide.

Ond (no dates), according to chronicle sources chieftain of one of the seven Hungarian tribes who settled in the Carpathian Basin.

Orczy, Béla, Baron (1822–1917), Minister with Responsibility for the King (1879–90). Defence Minister (1882 and 1884), Minister of Public Services and Transport (1886) and Minister of the Interior (1887–9). Graduated in liberal arts and later in law. In 1848 a member of the National Guard, later adjutant in the Hungarian army. MP 1865–8 and a supporter of Deák. In 1868 Head of Department at the Austro-Hungarian Ministry of Defence. From 1895 Lord Chief Justice.

Orosz, József (1790–1851), publicist. Law graduate. Solicitor, Appeals Court Judge, and later delegate in the Diet. In the Reform Period co-editor with Kossuth of the Parliamentary Reports. Disapproved of reform endeavours. During the 1848 Revolution held a post in the Ministry of Foreign Affairs. Emigrated only to live in poverty. Committed suicide.

Ottokar II (1253–78), Czech King. Fought the Habsburgs for Czech independence – in which he was assisted by the Hungarian people – but was defeated; Ottokar himself fell in the battle of Morvameze.

Palóczy, László (1783–1861), liberal reform politician. At sessions of the Reform Age Parliament spoke up for religious tolerance. Was the first to propose that parliamentary protocols be recorded in Hungarian. Second Sub-Prefect. In 1848 Father of the Lower House, Chairman of the Court of Grace. During the period of repression sentenced to death. The sentence was later commuted to imprisonment. In 1861 delegate in the Diet and Father of the House.

Paskievich, Ivan Fedorovich, Count (1772–1856), Russian field-marshal. In 1849 as Commander-in-Chief of the Russian Army assisted in the suppression of the Hungarian Freedom Fight. Between 1806 and 1854 participated in every Russian military campaign.

Pataki, Bernát (no dates), parliamentary correspondent of *Pester Lloyd* in the period of the Dual Monarchy.

Pavlovic, Ljubomir (1850–1901), Serb national minority representative. Solicitor.

Péchy, Tamás (1828–97), Minister of Public Services and Transport (1875–80). 1848–9 major general in the Hungarian army. From 1867 sub-prefect, and later MP. Speaker of the Lower House 1881–92.

Perczel, Dezső (1848–1913), Minister of the Interior (1895–9). From 1877 Sub-Prefect, and later governing-party MP. Twice Speaker of the Lower House: 1899–1901 and 1903–5. As Minister was among the enforcers of religious laws aiming at the separation of church and state. As Speaker of the House devoted his efforts to curb obstructionism in parliament. In 1910 founder of the National Workers' Party.

Perczel, Mór (1811–99), Hungarian general. In 1830 as a cadet organized a campaign in support of the Polish Uprising for which he was imprisoned. From 1843 MP with radical sentiments. During the Freedom Fight created an irregular unit. As corps commander in the Hungarian army emigrated in fear of repression. Sentenced to death *in absentia*. His conflict with Kossuth and hurt pride prompted him to support the Compromise of 1867.

Petőfi, Sándor (1823–49), poet of Slovak origin. Started to write poems and act at an early age. Made copies of the Parliamentary Reports and translated novels. Lived in poverty. Published his first volume of poems in 1844. In 1846 founding member of the so-called 'Society of Ten'. Leader of the March Youth in 1848. The lyrics of the hymn of the 1848 Revolution – 'National Song' – were from his poem. His radicalism prevented his election as a delegate to the Diet. Captain in the Hungarian army, and later adjutant to General Bem. Left the army after a confrontation with the army high command. First led a quiet life, then joined Bem's troops once again. Disappeared in the battle of Segesvár. His 700 poems have been translated into some 50 languages.

Podmaniczky, Frigyes, Baron (1824–1907), governing-party politician. Deputy Clerk, and later member of the Upper House. Hussar Captain in the Freedom Fight. As part of the subsequent repression was reduced to being a common soldier. Active in literature. Between 1873–1905 as Chairman of the Budapest Public Services Commission worked towards the modernization and development of Budapest. MP 1861–1906. From 1889 Chairman of the governing party.

Polonyi, Géza (1848–1920), Justice Minister (1906–7). Law graduate. From 1881 Pro-Independence-Party MP. As a leader of the opposition mediated between the sovereign and parliament during the time of the constitutional crisis. In 1918–20 Chairman of the Budapest Public Services Commission. Deported under the Council Republic.

Pósa, Lajos (1850–1914), poet, lecturer, journalist. Edited a children's magazine. Wrote poems in the style of folk songs.

Pulszky, Ágoston (1846–1901), philosopher of law, sociologist. Son of Ferenc Pulszky. From 1871 governing-party, later moderate-opposition MP. University lecturer. State Secretary of Religion and Public Education 1894–5.

Pulszky, Ferenc (1814–97), politician, supported Kossuth and later Deák. Law graduate. Participated in the work of the Reform Age Diet in the capacity of jurist. Travelled around Europe. Delegate in the Diet, reform opposition publicist. In 1848 State Secretary of Finance, later a diplomat in Great Britain. Remained in exile until 1866. After returning to Hungary supported Deák, later became an independent MP of the 1867 generation. Organized fine art and archeological collections.

Pulszky, Károly (1853–99), art historian. Son of Ferenc Pulszky. Director of fine art collections. As Director of the National Gallery enriched the gallery's collections. In 1884 Liberal Party MP. Having come under political attack committed suicide.

Rajacic, Josif (1785–1861), Serb patriarch. In 1848 headed anti-Hungarian Serb-nationalist movements. The Habsburg Court rewarded him with the title of Patriarch.

Rákóczi, Ferenc II (1676–1735), Prince of Hungary (1704–11). Came from an aristocratic Transylvanian family. The Viennese court entrusted his education to Czech Jesuits. Was the first to receive the hereditary title of Lord Lieutenant. In 1697 was invited to head the Hegyalja peasant uprising. In 1700 accused of conspiring against the Habsburgs, imprisoned. After making his escape fled to Poland. In 1703 accepted an invitation to join the insurgents; the anti-Habsburg Freedom Fight dominated by the lesser nobility and the peasantry soon broke out. As Prince of Transylvania was committed to centralized government, a regular army and mercantilism. Failed to break the political isolation of upsurgent Transylvania. Although in 1707 he dethroned the Habsburgs he was in the end overpowered by the Habsburg army. In 1711 emigrated. Died in Turkey.

Rákosi, Mátyás (1892–1971), Prime Minister (1952–3), Deputy Prime Minister (1949–52). Commissar during the Council Republic. During the years of emigration Secretary of the Executive Committee of Comintern. In 1925 arrested in Hungary and imprisoned; released in an exchange deal with the Soviet Union (in return for 1848–9 Hungarian army banners) in 1940. General Secretary of the Communist Party (1945–56). Enjoyed a personality cult in Hungary similar to the one of Stalin in the Soviet Union. In July 1956 removed from his post; in 1962 expelled from the Party by communists. Lived in the Soviet Union until his death.

Révai, József (1898–1959), Minister of Public Education (1949–53). In 1918 founding member of the Hungarian Communist Party. Member of a leading Budapest organization of the Council Republic. Emigrated to Vienna where he worked as a correspondent for communist newspapers. Was arrested during illegal visit to Hungary. After release went to the Soviet Union where he worked for Comintern. During the Second World War made radio broadcasts in Hungarian and was engaged in the ideological re-training of Hungarian prisoners of war. In 1944 became a member of the Hungarian National Assembly; one of the three members of the National High Council. From 1945 chief editor of the Communist Party's newspaper. MP (1945–53) and member of the two most important seats of power: the Central Committee and the Politburo. Deputy Chairman of the Presidential Council after Stalin's death in 1953. After the 1956 Revolution once again emerged as a Communist Party leader.

Rosenberg, Gyula (1856–?), MP in 1892.

Rudolf (1858–89), Heir to the Hungarian throne, son of Franz Joseph I and Elisabeth of Bavaria. Committed suicide in Mayerling under mysterious circumstances.

Saguna, Andrei (1809–73), Romanian politician. In 1847 Greek Orthodox Metropolitan in Transylvania. Carried out the separation of the Romanian Church from the Serbian Church.

Savoyai, Jenő, Prince (1663–1736), Austrian army officer of French origin. Statesman. Fought successful wars against the Turks. From 1697 commander of Austrian troops in Hungary. In 1718 liberated Hungary completely from Turkish occupation. Became Governor of Belgium.

Schickedanz, Albert (1846–1915), architect. Studied in Austria. Worked in the Eclectic style.

Schulek, Frigyes (1841–1919), architect. Studied in Austria. Teacher of drawing. Became the architect of the Architectural Monument Committee and a university lecturer. Was mainly engaged in the restoration of medieval monuments. Worked in the Eclectic style.

Schwarzenberg, Felix, Prince (1800–52), Austrian Prime Minister. In 1849 announced the March Constitution which deprived Hungary of its independence. Gave General Haynau a free hand to implement bloody and merciless repression. His main political ambition was the creation of a unified Austrian Empire.

Sennyei, Pál, Baron (1824–88), conservative politician. Secretary to the council of the Governor-General, then to the Chancellor's Office. Delegate to the Diet. In 1860–5 Deputy Chairman, and in 1865–7 Chairman of the Council of the Governor-General. MP (1865–7 and 1872–81); Speaker of the Upper House (1884–8). From 1884 Lord Chief Justice.

Senyei, Károly (1854–1919), sculptor. Studied in Budapest, Vienna and Munich. Distinguished himself in the production of 'genre' and decorative statues for buildings.

Simonyi, Ernő (1821–82), pro-independence politician. Member of the National Guard, leader of a guerilla troop during the Freedom Fight. Emigrated. Studied chemistry and natural sciences in Paris. Came under the influence of Marx in Great Britain. In 1868 returned to Hungary; became an Independence-Party MP.

Singer, Zsigmond (1850–1913), journalist. Graduated in law in Austria. From 1867 Budapest correspondent of *Neue Freie Presse*; from 1906 chief editor of *Pester Lloyd*. In 1912 became member of the Upper House.

Sobieski, Jan III (1624–96), King of Poland (1674–96). In 1683 participated in the defeat of Turkish troops laying siege to Vienna; became known as a saviour and hero of Christianity.

Stratimirovic, Djordje (1823–1908), leader of Serb insurgents in 1848–9. Important adversary of Kossuth. Became President of the Serb National Assembly. From 1849 colonel in the Austrian army, and diplomat. In 1865–8 and 1869–72 national-minority representative. Consul General to Palermo.

Supljikac, Stefan (1790–1848), Serb national-minority politician. Served in the Austrian and the French armies. In 1842 colonel in the Austrian army. Elected Voivode by the Serb National Assembly in Spring 1848. Died unexpectedly on the very day of his inauguration – is thought to have been poisoned.

Szapáry, Gyula, Count (1832–1905), Prime Minister (1890–2); Minister of the

Interior (1873–5); Finance Minister (1878–87); Minister of Public Services and Transport (1880); Minister of Agriculture, Industry and Trade (1889); and Minister of Agriculture (1890–2). Nine times elected governing-party MP. Resigned from his post as Prime Minister during controversy over draft laws on religious policy. Quit the governing party. Speaker of the Upper House.

Szapáry, Pál, Count (1873–1917), conservative politician. In 1905 appointed Governor of Fiume. Resigned in 1906 when the opposition came to power.

Szatmári, Mór (1856–1931), journalist. Law graduate. Worked for pro-independence newspapers. From 1904 editor of *Budapest,* a popular newspaper. Pro-Independence-Party MP (1902–10).

Széchenyi, István, Count (1791–1860), Minister of Transport and Public Services (1848). After travel in Western Europe, introduced horse breeding to Hungary, founded the Academy of Sciences and organized the National Casino. Wrote books on economic policy in Hungary and the prospects for national transformation. Through his books emerged as a prominent politician in the reform movement. Initiated modernization and bourgeois development on a wide scale. Was opposed to Hungary's independence from the Habsburg Dynasty, constitutionally, politically or economically. As a delegate in the Upper House in 1847 opposed holders of more radical views, primarily Lajos Kossuth. By the end of 1848 suffered a nervous breakdown and was hospitalized in an Austrian lunatic asylum. At the end of the 1850s wrote a number of speeches and pamphlets on the subject of absolutism. Committed suicide.

Szekfű, Gyula (1883–1955), historian. Between the two world wars was a leading figure in historiography, and chief historical ideologist of the so-called 'counter-revolutionary period'. Ambassador to Moscow after the Second World War. MP from 1953.

Széll, Kálmán (1843–1915), Prime Minister (1899–1903) and Finance Minister (1875–8). Was related to Ferenc Deák through marriage. Became an MP in 1869; governing-party representative until 1911. Founded a bank and a model farm on his estate.

Szemere, Bertalan (1812–69), Prime Minister (1849) and Minister of the Interior (1848). As a student attended the sessions of Reform Age parliament, travelled in Europe and took up county politics. Opposition leader in parliament. In 1848 became a member of the National Defence Committee. Became Prime Minister after the Habsburgs had been dethroned. Emigrated in fear of repression. Was sentenced to death *in absentia.* In the 1850s made contact with Marx. Supported the Compromise with Austria. Returned to Hungary in a state of mental illness.

Szemere, Miklós (1856–1919), politician and writer. Studied in Vienna, Geneva and Oxford. Secretary of Embassy in Paris, St. Petersburg and Rome. MP from 1901. Contributed to the introduction of horseracing to Hungary.

Szentiványi, Károly (1865–1947), religious writer. In 1889 entered the priesthood. From 1905 director of the Hungarian Catholic Society. Papal Prelate.

Szilágyi, Dezső (1865–1901), Justice Minister (1889–95). Law graduate. Appointed to high juridical posts. University lecturer. In 1871 and 1875 governing-party MP. From 1877 opposition, and from 1889 once again governing-party, politician. Speaker of the Lower House (1895–8). His Act on Legal Procedures became law under his successor. Legislation on the separation of church and state was adopted during his term as Minister.

Szlávy, József (1818–1900), Prime Minister (1827–74); Minister of Agriculture, Industry and Trade (1870–2); Finance Minister (1873–4). Mining engineer. In 1848 government commissioner in charge of iron and steel supplies for the army. Imprisoned for two years during the repression. Became Lord Lieutenant and from 1867 governing-party MP.

Szontágh, Jenő (1873–?), politician. Lord Lieutenant. Member of the Upper House.

Szontágh, Pál (1820–1904), opposition and later governing-party politician. Leader of the county opposition in the Reform Age. After the Freedom Fight was sentenced to two years imprisonment. Became MP in 1865. Deputy Speaker of the Lower House (1879 and 1881–7).

Táncsics, Mihály (1799–1884), opposition politician. Serf, artisan, graduate of the Teacher Training College. Studied law. Worked as an instructor, wrote course books and published on linguistics. Wrote works of propaganda thinly disguised as novels, promoting the ideal of bourgeois transformation. Wrote pamphlets envisioning a classless communist society. Imprisoned 1847. His release from jail was one of the first acts of the 1848 Revolution. Delegate in the Diet; his radicalism caused conflict with the leaders of the Reform movement. During the repression was sentenced to death *in absentia*. Pardoned in 1857; in 1860 arrested again and sentenced to 15 years. Released seven years later. MP (1869–72). Member and president of the General Workers Union.

Tas (no dates), according to chronicle sources chieftain of one of the seven Hungarian tribes who settled in the Carpathian Basin.

Telcs, Ede (1872–1948), sculptor. Studied in Vienna. Early career as 'genre' portraitist.

Teleki, László, Count (1811–61), studied in Pest and Berlin. Opposition leader of the Upper House at the 1843–4 session of the Reform parliament. In 1848 representative of Pest County, later envoy of the Hungarian government to Paris. In the spring of 1859 (with Kossuth and Klapka) formed the Hungarian National Directorate. In 1860 arrested in Prussia and extradited to Austria. In 1861 invited to be a member of the Upper House, and later elected MP. Leader of radicals in parliament during negotiations with the Habsburgs. Committed suicide.

Thököly, Imre, Count (1657–1705), Governor of Upper Hungary and Transylvania (1690). In 1678 headed the Freedom Fight against the Habsburgs. His marriage to the widow of Ferenc Rákóczi I – a feudal Prince of Transylvania earlier executed by the Habsburgs – helped to finance military action; entered into an alliance with the Turks. From 1683 suffered repeated defeat; the Turks themselves attacked him from the rear. Exiled to Asia Minor in 1699.

Tibád, Antal (1843–1902), governing-party politician. Law graduate. In 1872 became a judge. MP (1873–1902). As State Secretary at the Ministry of Internal Affairs supported liberal religious laws. Quit the governing party.

Tisza, István, Count (1861–1918), twice Prime Minister (1903–5 and 1913–17). Son of Kálmán Tisza. Studied law and economics in Budapest, Berlin and Heidelberg. From 1886 governing-party MP. In 1897 inherited the title of Count from his uncle. Bank chairman. Supporter of the Compromise. After his first term as Prime Minister amended the House rules in order to curb obstructionism. In retirement 1906–10. In 1910 founded a new party which soon became the governing party. In 1912 as Speaker of the Lower House was shot at by an opposition MP. In his second term of office as Prime Minister opposed joining the First World War but consented to the dispatch of an ultimatum to Serbia. After his resignation went to the front as a hussar commander. Murdered by soldiers when the bourgeois revolution broke out.

Tisza, Kálmán (1830–1902), Prime Minister (1875–90); Minister of the Interior (1875–87). Nephew of Count László Teleki. Held office at the Ministry of Culture under the Hungarian government of 1848. Emigrated for eighteen months in the face of repression. From 1859–60 in the front rank of Hungarian politics; protector of Hungarian constitutionality. Deputy Speaker of the Lower House (1861). From 1865 opposition-party leader. Criticized the Compromise from a radical point of view. In 1868 announced a programme in which he called for the further strengthening of Hungary's sovereignty. In 1875 gave up his political principles and formed a party based on acceptance of existing public law. This party governed for 30 years. His office as Prime Minister was marked by – among other things – the economic consolidation of Dual Monarchy, an expansionist policy in the Balkans and the modernization of state administration.

Tisza, Lajos, Count (1832–98), Minister of Public Services and Transport (1871–3); Minister Responsible for the King (1892–4). Younger brother of Kálmán Tisza. In 1861 MP, first on the side of the opposition, later with the governing party. Lord Lieutenant (1867). Deputy chairman of the Budapest Council of Public Services. Received the title of Count in 1883.

Töhötöm (also: Téteny, Tuhutum) (no dates), according to chronicle sources chieftain of one of the seven Hungarian tribes who settled in the Carpathian Basin.

Trefort, Ágoston (1817–88), Minister of Religion and Public Education (1872–88); Minister of Agriculture, Industry and Trade (1876–8). Studied law. Opposition politician in the Reform Age, delegate in the Diet. In 1848 State Secretary of Agriculture, Industry and Trade. Emigrated in fear of repression. Later retired to his estate. Supported the Compromise. As Minister of Culture focused on the modernization of public education.

Ugron, Gábor (1847–1911), son of a Székely noble family. In 1870 fought in Garibaldi's Legion. In Paris at the time of the Commune. In 1872 became an opposition MP; later one of the founders of the Pro-Independence Party. Organized troops against the Russians during the Russian/Turkish War (1877). From 1878 pro-independence MP.

Ugron, Gábor (1880–1960), Minister of the Interior (1917–18). Son of Gábor Ugron. Studied law in Leipzig, Geneva and Budapest. Chief administrative officer of county, and later Lord Lieutenant, in Transylvania. From 1915 opposition MP. In 1918 Royal Commissioner in Transylvania. During the bourgeois-democratic revolution organized the Székely National Council. From 1920 leader of the National Bourgeois Party. From 1926 member of the governing party.

Urbanovszky, Ernő (1826–?), governing-party politician. Elected MP nine times (1865–92).

Valero, Antal (no dates), silk manufacturer. Came from a Viennese family of Spanish origin. Took over management of silk factory in Pest (1814). Founded a bank and a milling company, commissioned the construction of factory buildings.

President of the Chamber of Commerce and Industry (1850). Returned to Vienna where he engaged in wholesale trade.

Varga, Jenő (1879–1964), communist politician and Marxist economist. High-school teacher (1907). Member of the left-wing Social-Democratic Party; publicist for Hungarian and German newspapers with similar orientations. During the bourgeois-democratic revolution State Secretary to Mihály Károlyi. Appointed university lecturer. Commissar of Finance and chairman of the National Economic Commitee under the Council Republic. Emigrated; lived in the Soviet Union until his death. Member of the Soviet Union's Communist Party and member of the Exeutive Committee of Comintern.

Vastagh, György (1868–1926), sculptor. Studied in Munich. Master of animal statues and later of decorative scuplture.

Vázsonyi, Vilmos (1868–1926), Justice Minister (in 1917 and 1918). Law graduate. Founded the Democratic Circle (1894). From 1901 Democratic-Party MP. Obtained nationwide fame for court cases involving corruption and trade unions. Drafted an electoral law. Emigrated because of the revolution. Organized the Democratic Block (1924).

Verhovay, Gyula (1849–1906), opposition politician, journalist. Law graduate. Worked for opposition newspapers. From 1878 Pro-Independence-Party MP. Quit the party to pursue an anti-Semitic line in politics (1880). Anti-Semitic-party MP (1884–7).

Vörösmarty, Mihály (1800–85), poet and playwright. Law graduate. Wrote lyric and epic poems. Editor of literary magazines. Wrote a book on Hungarian grammar. Author of the 'second national anthem' of Hungary, the *Szózat* (Appeal). In 1848 elected political representative. Went into hiding. Pardoned 1850. Translator of Shakespeare.

Wahrmann, Mór (1832–92), wholesaler, governing-party politician. Student of liberal arts. President of the Chamber of Commerce and Industry. From 1869 to his death governing-party MP. President of the Israelite Religious Community in Pest (1883–92).

Wekerle, Sándor (1848–1921), three-time Prime Minister (1892–5, 1906–10 and 1917–18); Finance Minister (1889–95 and 1917–18); Minister of the Interior (1918). Law graduate. From 1870 held office at the Finance Ministry. Modernized the taxation system of the Dual Monarchy. The first Prime Minister of Hungary who was not a nobleman. Balanced the state budget and passed religious laws allowing the separation of church and state. Represented the interests of financial circles. MP (1887–96, 1906–10, 1917–18 and 1920–1).

Wenczel, Gusztáv (1812–91), law graduate. Lectured at Pest University and later at the Theresianum in Vienna. From 1889 member of the Upper House. Foremost Hungarian authority on European legal history.

Wesselényi, Miklós, Count (1796–1850), reform politician from the aristocracy. Leader of the opposition in Transylvania (1835); prominent figure in sessions of the Reform Era Diet. Charged with treason; pardoned because of poor eyesight. Lord Lieutenant in Transylvania (1843–8). Emigrated to Austria in fear of the possible consequences of the 1848 Revolution.

Windischgrätz, Alfred, Prince (1787–1862), Austrian army officer. As Czech Military Governor (1840–8) suppressed the Prague Uprising (1848).

Commander-in-chief of the Austrian army which suppressed the Hungarian Revolution of the same year. Occupied Pest-Buda. In the spring of 1849 was removed from his post following a number of military defeats.

Ybl, Miklós (1814–91), architect. Studied in Vienna, Munich and Italy. Built palaces in the Roman, Renaissance and neo-Renaissance styles. His public buildings are a prominent feature of modern Budapest. His most important creation is the National Opera House.

Zala, György (1858–1937), sculptor. Studied in Budapest, Vienna and Munich. Created a number of memorial statues. Favoured the Baroque style.

Zrínyi, Miklós, Count (1508–66), Governor of Croatia (1542–56). Distinguished himself in campaigns against the Turks. Died defending a Hungarian castle besieged by the Turkish army.

Zsigmondy, Vilmos (1821–88), mining engineer. Mining engineer for the Austrian State Railways (1846). In 1848 transformed the production of mines owned by the State Railways to suit the needs of the Freedom Fight. Sentenced to imprisonment during the repression. Lived in Pest from 1860; primarily engaged in finding wells. From 1875 to the end of his life governing-party MP.

Zsolt, Béla (1895–1949), publicist. A journalist in Transylvania; correspondent for liberal and radical newspapers in Budapest. Subject to forced labour during the Second World War. Deported by the Germans in 1944 but managed to escape to Switzerland. On his return home in 1945 became editor of a national, bourgeois-radical newspaper.

Zweig, Stefan (1881–1942), writer. German literary figure and publicist of Viennese origin. In 1933 emigrated from Germany. Committed suicide.